HISTORICAL DICTIONARIES OF SPORTS

Jon Woronoff, Series Editor

Competitive Swimming, by John Lohn, 2010.
Basketball, by John Grasso, 2011.
Golf, by Bill Mallon and Randon Jerris, 2011.
Figure Skating, by James R. Hines, 2011.

Historical Dictionary of Figure Skating

James R. Hines

The Scarecrow Press, Inc.
Lanham • Toronto • Plymouth, UK
2011

Published by Scarecrow Press, Inc.
A wholly owned subsidiary of The Rowman & Littlefield Publishing Group, Inc.
4501 Forbes Boulevard, Suite 200, Lanham, Maryland 20706
http://www.scarecrowpress.com

Estover Road, Plymouth PL6 7PY, United Kingdom

British Library Cataloguing in Publication Information Available

Library of Congress Cataloging-in-Publication Data

Hines, James R. (James Robert), 1937–
Historical dictionary of figure skating / James R. Hines.
p. cm. — (Historical dictionaries of sports)
Includes bibliographical references.
ISBN 978-0-8108-6859-5 (cloth : alk. paper) — ISBN 978-0-8108-7085-7 (ebook)
1. Figure skating—Dictionaries. I. Title.
GV850.4.H563 2011
796.91'203—dc22 2010048185

∞™ The paper used in this publication meets the minimum requirements of American National Standard for Information Sciences—Permanence of Paper for Printed Library Materials, ANSI/NISO Z39.48-1992. Printed in the United States of America.

Dedicated to
Benjamin T. Wright,
my colleague, friend, and mentor,
who has continually encouraged
my figure skating research.

Contents

Editor's Foreword

In every sport there is an element of art, but in none is this so striking and visible as in figure skating and actually now more than ever since the compulsory figures and compulsory dances have been eliminated. Executing the actual figures and jumps requires an incredible amount of skill, self-control, and strength, and skating to music may appear more agreeable but certainly not simpler. Thus, anyone engaged in the basic competitive categories of men's and ladies' singles, pairs, ice dancing, and synchronized skating must have an extraordinary set of talents. This sporting side explains why figure skating has become increasingly prominent in the Winter Olympics and among other competitive events, but it is the more artistic side which is making it an uncommonly popular form of show business, with competitive skaters retiring not into oblivion or entering a coaching career as in most other sports but rather appearing with various shows that tour winter and summer performing before large and appreciative audiences.

This *Historical Dictionary of Figure Skating* covers the field both as a sport and an art with a multitude of entries in the dictionary section on the top skaters over the years. Indeed every skater who has won a gold medal in any of the eight major championships is included, as well as other prominent people and governing bodies. There are entries on the leading countries that produce skaters as well as entries on the basic disciplines and assorted jumps, spins, and spirals. Figure skating did not appear out of nowhere but evolved from rather simple forms in the Netherlands and England as early as the late Middle Ages, and this long development is traced in one chronology, while another presents the sport's defining moments. The history is plotted out more substantially in the introduction. And to follow events, it is helpful to have the handy list of acronyms and abbreviations. While these sections will be extremely interesting for general and specialist readers, it is the extensive appendixes which will absorb the real skating buffs most with lists of medalists, members of the World Figure Skating Hall of Fame, and key information on the International Skating Union.

This volume was written by James R. Hines, professor emeritus of music at Christopher Newport University. He is a musicologist and an active member of related societies. But here it is his avocation which assumes the spotlight, namely as a historian of figure skating. He has written the definitive history of the sport, *Figure Skating: A History*, a second book, *The English Style: Figure Skating's Oldest Tradition*, as well as articles for various publications including the *Journal of Olympic History*. On top of all this, Dr. Hines is an elector for the World Figure Skating Hall of Fame. This latest publication, a historical dictionary which presents the information in a handy, easy-to-use format will certainly be added to the collections of those truly interested in the sport and art of figure skating.

Jon Woronoff
Series Editor

Preface

Figure skating, one of the most popular Winter Olympic sports, lacked a comprehensive dictionary of skating and skaters. Although information on individual skaters, results of international competitions, and information on the sport itself appear in a variety of sources, many of them are not readily available, even in large libraries, making it difficult for interested persons to find answers to relatively basic questions about the sport and its participants. The *Historical Dictionary of Figure Skating* fills this void. It includes entries on hundreds of skaters, past and present, but also on skating countries, governing bodies, skating disciplines, technical elements, skating styles, and many other subjects. For those seeking additional information, a comprehensive, topical bibliography lists sources, some readily available and others that can be retrieved through interlibrary loan. Coupled with my previous history of the sport, *Figure Skating: A History*, interested persons, skaters, commentators, coaches, officials, skating fans, and librarians now have at their disposal complementary sources that can provide answers to many questions and direct them to additional sources for further study.

The dictionary entries include all of the champions from the most important international figure skating competitions, specifically the World Championships, the European Championships, the Four Continents Championships, the North American Championships, the Olympic Winter Games, the Grand Prix Finals, and the World Junior Championships. Other skaters whose careers have made a significant impact on the sport, positively or negatively, are included, persons such as Janet Lynn, one of the most artistic skaters of the 1970s, and Tonya Harding, whose misdeeds influenced the popularity of the sport during the 1990s. Important persons, skaters and nonskaters, from the early history of the sport, presidents of the International Skating Union (ISU), influential judges and referees, and major writers are also included. Twenty-one countries are included, specifically all of those that have fielded skaters who won world or Olympic titles. Skating elements, such as jumps and spins, and all disciplines, including the newer ones such as theater on ice, are described. Through extensive cross-referencing, information on people not represented by separate entries but who are mentioned in those entries becomes available.

Appendixes include lists of current members of the ISU and major office-holders throughout its history. Another appendix identifies all members of the World Figure Skating Hall of Fame. The remaining appendixes name all medalists through the 2010 skating season for each of the eight international championships named earlier. The bibliography is preceded by an explanatory introduction to make it as useful as possible.

The spelling of proper names presents a challenge, primarily a result of variant spellings which occur in official documents. In the case of Russian and other Slavic languages, this often results from transliteration of the Cyrillic alphabet. An effort has been made to maintain consistency while employing logical spellings or those most frequently found. For medal winners in ISU championships before 1992, the spellings are those printed in *Results: Figure Skating Championships, 1968–1991*. It provides complete results for competitors within the indicated dates but also lists of earlier medalists from the World Championships, the European Championships, and the World Junior Championships.

Dates for skaters are often difficult to obtain, especially death dates, which occur many years after their competitive careers or other involvement with the sport. ISU and federation records often but not always include birth dates. Some lists of skaters that include birth dates have been compiled, but none are complete. For dates needed, I have contacted respective federations and requested any information included in their records. Some dates, however, were not known at the time of the printing of this publication.

Skating seasons usually begin in October and end in March, always spanning two calendar years. Grand Prix events are held during the fall; the World Championships, the Olympics, and most other events are held in the new year. For consistency and to avoid confusion, all events in each skating season are referenced to the new year. Thus, the Grand Prix Finals, held in early December 2009, are considered as events in the 2010 skating season.

Although it is acknowledged that today females are most often referred to as women, in the sport of figure skating, from the 18th century to the present, the term "ladies" has been employed for young novice skaters through the oldest adult skaters. It was a subject of discussion at an ISU Congress, the result of which was confirmation that in figure skating there are only men and ladies. In an attempt to be historically accurate and correct, the term "ladies" has been used extensively throughout this book.

Figure skating, like all sports, evolves rapidly. This book, including its appendixes, is complete through the 2010 skating season. The photos are of all Olympic champions who have won multiple titles.

ACKNOWLEDGMENTS

I want to acknowledge those people who have contributed to the success of this book. Special appreciation goes to Benjamin T. Wright, to whom this book is dedicated. Since beginning my figure skating research and writing 14 years ago, Ben has become my mentor, colleague, and friend. He has read the entire manuscript for this book, as he did for my two previous books, and made many excellent suggestions. His knowledge of the sport, a result of his involvement, nationally and internationally, for more than 70 years, his training as a historian, and his own comprehensive books and numerous articles have served as my models in an attempt to continue the high level of scholarship he established many years ago. I also want to acknowledge the late Dennis Bird who was the historian for the National Skating Association of the United Kingdom. His personal files on individual skaters, of which I have copies, have been invaluable. Other persons who have answered various questions are listed here in alphabetical order. They include Vicki Binder, Karen Cover, Judy Edmunds, Joyce Hisey, Lennart Månsson, David Raith, and Huub Snoep. Appreciation is expressed to the World Figure Skating Museum and Hall of Fame in Colorado Springs, which has generously furnished the pictures included in this book, and Paul Harvath, who furnished the cover picture. Finally, I want to thank Jon Woronoff of Scarecrow Press, the series editor, who offered me the opportunity to write this volume, and Kellie Hagan, the production editor, who readily aceded to my many requests. They provided much guidance, responded promptly to my questions, and made numerous useful suggestions.

Acronyms and Abbreviations

Country Abbreviations for ISU Members

Prior to 1998, the country abbreviations used by the International Skating Union (ISU) were based on its official language, English since 1948. At its 1998 congress, the ISU adopted the country abbreviations used by the International Olympic Committee (IOC), which are based on one of its official languages, French. The former ISU designations are indicated where different because they occur in pre-1998 sources, but to avoid confusion, in this book the IOC designations are employed throughout.

Country	IOC	ISU
Andorra	AND	
Argentina	ARG	
Armenia	ARM	
Australia	AUS	
Austria	AUT	
Azerbaijan	AZE	
Belarus	BLS	BLR
Belgium	BEL	
Bosnia Herzegovina	BIH	
Brazil	BRA	
Bulgaria	BUL	
Canada	CAN	
China	CHN	
Chinese Taipei	TPE	
Croatia	CRO	
Czech Republic (Czechoslovakia)	CZE	CSR
Denmark	DEN	
Estonia	EST	
Finland	FIN	
France	FRA	
Georgia	GEO	

Germany	GER	
Federal Republic of Germany	FRG	
Democratic Republic of Germany	GDR	
Great Britain	GBR	GRB
Greece	GRE	
Hong Kong	HKG	
Hungary	HUN	
Iceland	ISL	
India	IND	
Ireland	IRL	
Israel	ISR	
Italy	ITA	
Japan	JPN	
Kazakhstan	KAZ	
Democratic People's Republic of Korea	PRK	DPK
Republic of Korea	KOR	ROK
Latvia	LAT	
Lithuania	LTU	LIT
Luxembourg	LUX	
Mexico	MEX	
Monaco	MON	
Mongolia	MGL	
Netherlands	NED	
New Zealand	NZL	
Norway	NOR	
Poland	POL	
Portugal	POR	
Puerto Rico	PUR	
Romania	ROM	RUM
Russia	RUS	
Scotland*	SCO	
Serbia and Montenegro	SCG	
Singapore	SIN	
Slovakia	SVK	
Slovenia	SLO	
South Africa	RSA	SAF
Soviet Union	URS	
Soviet Union (1992 only)	CIS	EUN
Spain	ESP	SPN
Sweden	SWE	

Switzerland	SUI	SWI
Thailand	THA	
Turkey	TUR	
Ukraine	UKR	
United States	USA	
Uzbekistan	UZB	
Yugoslavia	YUG	

*Scotland is not a member of the ISU; however, the Junior Grand Prix Finals in Figure Skating were held there in 2001.

Other Abbreviations

ABC	American Broadcasting Corporation
ASC	American Skating Congress
CBE	Commander of the Order of the British Empire
CFSA	Canadian Figure Skating Association
IJS	International Judging System
IOC	International Olympic Committee
IPSA	International Professional Skaters Association
ISU	International Skating Union
ISUofA	International Skating Union of America
MBE	Master of the British Empire
MGM	Metro-Goldwyn-Mayer
NBC	National Broadcasting Corporation
NISA	National Ice Skating Association of the United Kingdom
NSA	National Skating Association
OBE	Officer of the British Empire
PSGA	Professional Skaters Guild of America
SCofB	Skating Club of Boston
USFSA	United States Figure Skating Association
USOC	United States Olympic Committee
WSF	World Skating Federation

Chronology

Figure Skating

c. 1220 The *Prose Edda* provides our first written sources for northern myths which include mentions of skating.

13th century The Dutch revolutionized skating by sharpening steel blades.

1396 Lydwina of Schiedam, Netherlands, fell to the ice while skating. Her injuries led to a life of suffering. St. Lydwina is the patron saint of figure skating.

1572 The Dutch used skates as a tool of warfare against Spanish troops at Amsterdam during the Dutch revolt against the Spanish. Traversing the frozen sea wearing clogs with spikes, the Spanish soldiers were attacked by Dutch musketeers on bladed skates, moving with the mobility the skates provided, who routed and massacred the Spanish attackers.

1652 The Stuarts after the infamous Rump Parliament fled to Holland during the Cromwellian era where they learned how to skate and to do the Dutch roll.

1660 The birth of figure skating occurred in England after the Restoration.

1713 British officers stationed in Nova Scotia following its seizure from the French probably skated there. It is presumed to be the first skating on bladed skates in the New World.

1738 Benjamin West, an important painter and America's first well-known skater, was born in Philadelphia. While working in England in the 1760s, he was called the best skater then on the ice.

1744 The world's first skating club was founded in Edinburgh, Scotland.

1772 Robert Jones published in London the first book on skating, *A Treatise on Skating*.

1813 Jean Garcin published the first book on skating in France, *Le vrai patineur* (The True Skater).

1830 The London Skating Club was formed. It continues today as the Royal Skating Club and is the oldest skating club in existence.

1833 The first known skating club in the New World was formed at St. John, New Brunswick.

1849 The Philadelphia Skating Club was founded. In 1861, it became the Philadelphia Skating Club and Humane Society. The club, which is still active today, was an original member of the United States Figure Skating Association, established in 1921.

c. 1860 Jackson Haines is believed to have invented the sit spin.

1863 Edward F. Gill published *The Skater's Manual*, the first North American book on skating.

1864 Jackson Haines, later to be called "America's Skating King," departed for Europe.

1867 Der Wiener Eislaufverein (Vienna Skating Club) was formed. It still exists today.

1869 H. E. Vandervell and T. Maxwell Witham in their book, *Figure Skating*, became the first to refer to the sport as "figure skating."

1876 The first artificial ice rink opened in Chelsea, London, England.

1879 Madison Square Garden became the first large artificial rink in the United States. The National Skating Association was formed. It is today called the National Ice Skating Association of the United Kingdom.

1881 *Spuren auf dem Eise* (Tracings on the Ice), the most extensive book on figure skating yet published, was written by three members of the Vienna Skating Club. A second and expanded edition was published in 1892.

1882 The first major international competition, the Great International Skating Tournament, was held in Vienna sponsored by the Vienna Skating Club. Axel Paulsen did a special figure jump that now bears his name.

1890 A major international competition was held on the occasion of the 25th anniversary of the skating club in St. Petersburg, Russia.

1891 The first European Championship was held at Hamburg. The winner was Oskar Uhlig of Germany.

1892 Internationale Eislauf-Verein (International Skating Union (ISU) was formed in Scheveningen, Netherlands. Willem Mulier of Netherlands was elected the first chairman (president).

1893 The results of the European Championship held in Berlin were annulled by the ISU because of a scoring controversy over the application of conflicting rules.

1895 The ISU adopted formal rules for figure skating. Viktor Balk of Sweden became the second president of the ISU and served for 25 years.

1896 The first World Championship was held at St. Petersburg, Russia. It was for men only. Gilbert Fuchs of Germany won the title. The first championship in English style skating, the Challenge Shield for combined skating, was held. The winning team included A. E. Crawley, J. Le Fleming, R. Readhead, and G. R. Wood.

1902 Madge Syers of Great Britain entered the World Championship held in London, viewed as an all-male event, and placed second to Ulrich Salchow. The European Championship scheduled for Amsterdam was canceled for lack of ice. It was canceled again in 1903 for the same reason.

1905 The first Canadian national championships were held. The winners were Ormond B. Haycock, Anne L. Ewan, and in pairs, Katherine and Ormond Haycock.

1906 The first World Championship for ladies, called simply a Championship of the ISU, was held in Davos, Switzerland. Madge Syers of Great Britain became the first lady world champion.

1908 The first Olympic Games to include figure skating were held at London. The winners were Madge Syers of Great Britain in the ladies' competition, Ulrich Salchow of Sweden in the men's competition, Anna Hübler and Heinrich Burger of Germany in the pairs' competition, and Nikolai Panin of Russia in the special figures' competition. The first World Championship for pairs, called simply a Championship of the ISU, was held in St. Petersburg, Russia. The champions were Anna Hübler and Heinrich Burger of Germany. Irving Brokaw of the United States became the first North American to compete in an Olympic figure skating competition. He placed sixth. Special figures were contested at the Olympic Games for the only time in world or Olympic competition. The winner was Nikolai Panin of Russia.

1910 Charlotte Oelschlagel of Germany, figure skating's first major theatrical star, began appearing in ice ballets in Berlin. In 1914 she moved to the United States to perform at New York's Hippodrome.

1911 Ulrich Salchow of Sweden became the first and only man to earn 10 world titles. They were not consecutive.

1913 The Figure Skating Department of the Amateur Skating Association of Canada was established, separating figure skating from speed skating. The name Canadian Figure Skating Association was adopted in 1939 and then changed to Skate Canada in 2000. The first Connaught Cup competition in fours between Canada and the United States was held in Ottawa, Ontario. It was the first competition held in North America in which the international style was employed.

1914 The first of what are now designated as the United States Championships were held in New Haven, Connecticut. The winners were Theresa Weld in the ladies' competition, Norman Scott in the men's competition, Jeanne Chevalier and Norman Scott in the pairs' competition, and Theresa Weld and Nathaniel Niles in the waltz competition.

1915–1922 The European and World Championships for seven years and the Olympic Winter Games of 1916 were not held because of World War I.

1916 Charlotte Oelschlagel appeared in a six-part serial, *The Frozen Warning*, the first motion picture to include figure skating.

1920 The first postwar Olympic Games were held at Antwerp, Belgium. They included figure skating events and for the first time ice hockey. The winners were Magda Mauroy-Julin of Sweden in the ladies' competition, Gillis Grafström of Sweden in the men's competition, and Ludowika Eilers and Walter Jakobsson of Finland in the pairs' competition. Theresa Weld of the United States became the first North American to win an Olympic medal. She won the bronze medal in the ladies' competition.

1921 The United States Figure Skating Association (USFSA) was founded.

1923 The first North American Championships were held at Ottawa, Ontario. The singles champions were Theresa Weld Blanchard and Sherwin Badger both of the United States, and the pair winners were Dorothy Jenkins and Gordon McLennan of Canada. The first issue of *Skating* magazine was published by the USFSA. It is still being published today.

1924 Beatrix Loughran of the United States became the first North American to win a medal at the World Championships. It was bronze. The ladies and pairs ISU Championships were upgraded to World Championships.

1925 Austrian men Wilhelm Böckl, Fritz Kachler, and Otto Preissecker swept the medals at the World Championships in Vienna. Austrian men did so again in 1927 and 1928. Ulrich Salchow of Sweden became the third president of the ISU and served for 12 years.

1927 Sonja Henie of Norway won the first of 10 consecutive world titles in a controversial decision, defeating five-time champion Herma Szabo of Austria.

1928 Gillis Grafström of Sweden won his third Olympic title. Only Grafström and Sonja Henie of Norway have won three Olympic titles in singles skating.

1930 Ladies and pairs competitions were held at the European Championships for the first time. The World Championships were held in New York City, the first time outside of Europe.

1932 The Olympic Winter Games were held at Lake Placid, New York, the first time in North America and outside Europe. The first Open Professional Championships organized by the National Skating Association (Great Britain) were held.

1933 Competitions to encourage the invention of new ice dances were sponsored by the Westminster Skating Club and the *Skating Times*.

1935 The ISU set limitations on the number of entrants from a country that could compete in each discipline, specifically four for singles and three for pairs. The numbers were further reduced in 1959 to two in each discipline with that number raised to three for any discipline in which the country had an entry that placed in the top 12 the previous year. Further adjustments have since been made, most recently at the Congress in 2010.

1936 Karl Schäfer of Austria became the first and only man to win seven consecutive world titles. Ulrich Salchow of Sweden holds 10, but they are not consecutive. Cecilia Colledge became the first woman to complete a double jump in competition, a double Salchow at the European Championships. The Ice Follies, the first large touring skating show, made its debut in Tulsa, Oklahoma. Sonja Henie of Norway won her third Olympic title. Only Henie and Gillis Grafström of Sweden have won three Olympic titles.

1937 Twentieth Century Fox released *One in a Million*, the first of nine films featuring Sonja Henie. Gerrit W. A. van Laer of the Netherlands became the fourth president of the ISU and served for eight years.

c. 1938 Pat Low of Scotland identified and published lists of all possible jumps and indicated those currently being done. The list is included in T. D. Richardson's *Modern Figure Skating*, 1938 edition.

1939 Ice dancing became a national-level competition in Great Britain. Daphne B. Wallis and Reginald J. Wilkie were the first champions.

1940–1946 Seven years of the European and World Championships and the Olympic Winter Games of 1940 and 1944 were not held because of World War II.

1941 Ice Capades made its first tour of 25 cities in the United States.

1945 Herbert J. Clarke of Great Britain became the fifth president of the ISU and served for eight years. Holiday on Ice made its first tour in the United States.

1947 Barbara Ann Scott of Canada became the first North American to win a world title. The ISU established a permanent headquarters in Switzerland and adopted English as the official language of the union.

1948 Barbara Ann Scott of Canada and Dick Button of the United States won titles at the last European Championships in which non-Europeans could compete. Barbara Ann Scott of Canada and Dick Button of the United States claimed the first Olympic titles won by North American skaters. Dick Button completed the first double Axel Paulsen jump in competition at the Olympic Winter Games.

1949 Frank Zamboni perfected his ice resurfacing machine, replacing a crew of five men previously required to resurface the ice at his rink, Paramount Iceland, in the city of Paramount in Los Angeles County.

1952 Ice dancing became a world discipline. Jean Westwood and Lawrence Demmy of Great Britain were the first champions. Dick Button completed the first triple jump done in competition, a loop, at the Olympic Winter Games in Oslo, Norway. He is the only man since World War II to hold two Olympic titles.

1953 James Koch of Switzerland became the sixth president of the ISU and served for 14 years. Tenley Albright of the United States became the first American lady to win a world title. She also became in 1956 the first American lady to win an Olympic title.

1956 Carol Heiss of the United States won the first of five consecutive ladies world titles. Other than Sonja Henie of Norway, who won 10, only Herma Szabo of Austria in the 1920s had done so. Michelle Kwan of the United States holds five, beginning in 1996, but they are not consecutive.

1959 The first comprehensive history of figure skating, Nigel Brown's *Ice Skating: A History*, was published.

1960 The Squaw Valley Olympic Winter Games were the first to have the figure skating events televised throughout.

1961 Sabena Airlines flight 548 crashed near the Brussels, Belgium, airport killing the entire U.S. World team en route to Prague, Czechoslovakia. The ISU's Judges Handbook for compulsory figures appeared. Handbooks for all other disciplines followed: free skating, 1965; pair skating, 1966; ice dancing, 1974; and synchronized skating, 1994.

1962 Donald Jackson of Canada landed the first triple Lutz jump done in competition at the World Championships in Prague, Czechoslovakia. Eva Romanová and Pavel Roman of Czechoslovakia, a young sister and brother, became the first non-British ice dancers to win a world title. It was their first of four. Otto and Maria Jelinek of Canada returned to Prague, the city from which they had escaped with their parents in 1948, to compete. They won the pair title.

1964 The Protopopovs won the Soviet Union's first Olympic title at the Olympic Winter Games in Innsbruck, Austria. The short program was introduced into pairs competition at the European and World Championships but not at the Olympic Winter Games until 1968.

1966 Peggy Fleming became the first skater from the United States to win a world title in any discipline after the 1961 plane crash.

1967 All events at the World Championships other than the compulsory figures and dances were held outside for the last time. Ernst Labin of Austria became the seventh president of the ISU. He served just six weeks before his untimely death. Jacques Favart of France, the vice president for figure skating, assumed the presidency and subsequently served for 13 years. The 75th anniversary of the ISU was celebrated. Neither a 25th nor a 50th anniversary celebration could be held because they occurred during war years, 1917 and 1942. In connection with the 1967 celebration, the ISU published *75 Years of European and World Championships in Figure Skating, Results in Figure Skating*. Sonia Bianchetti of Italy became the first woman officeholder in the ISU.

1969 Irina Rodnina of the Soviet Union won the first of 10 world pair titles with her first partner, Alexei Ulanov. They won three more. She then won six with her second partner, Alexandr Zaitsez.

1971 The last North American Championships were held at Peterborough, Ontario.

1973 The short program was introduced into singles competition at the World Championships but not at the European Championships until 1974.

1976 Ice dancing became an Olympic discipline. Liudmila Pakhomova and Alexandr Gorshkov were the first champions. The World Figure Skating Hall of Fame was established.

1977 The ISU banned all Soviet judges for the entire 1978 season. Minoru Sano won Japan's first world medal. It was bronze.

1978 Vern Taylor of Canada completed the first triple Axel Paulsen jump done in competition at the World Championships in Ottawa, Ontario. The World Junior Figure Skating Championships were established. The first winners were Jill Sawyer of the United States, Dennis Coi of Canada, in pairs Barbara Underhill and Paul Martini of Canada, and in ice dancing Tatiana Durasova and Sergei Ponomarenko of the Soviet Union. Junior championships had been held for the two previous years as a test and in preparation for the first World Junior Figure Skating Championships.

1979 A history of the National Skating Association in England, *Our Skating Heritage*, was written by Dennis Bird on the occasion of its 100th anniversary.

1980 A rule was adopted requiring that all competitions be held in a completely covered and enclosed rink. The rule was extended to include practice rinks in 1984. Olaf Poulsen of Norway became the ninth president of the ISU and served for 14 years.

1981 The Jacques Favart Trophy was established in memory of the ISU's seventh president. It is awarded to outstanding skaters in either figure skating or speed skating in recognition of their contributions to the sport. The first recipient was pair skater Irina Rodnina of the Soviet Union.

1983 The ISU adopted a rule prohibiting the repetition of triple jumps except once and only then when done in combination or sequence. It is commonly referred to as the "Zayak Rule," named for 1982 World Champion Elaine Zayak of the United States who had included six triple jumps, four toe loop jumps, and two Salchows in her program. Most ladies at that time were doing no more than two triple jumps.

1984 Ice dancers Jayne Torvill and Christopher Dean of Great Britain earned 19 perfect 6.0s at the Olympic Games and 29 at the World Championships.

1985 The Georg Häsler Medal was established in memory of the general secretary for his outstanding service and dedication to the ISU for 29 years. Up to four awards can be made annually, two to speed or figure skaters and two to administrators in recognition to their contributions to the sports. The first two were awarded to administrators, Willi Zipperlen of Switzerland who was active in the International Skating Club Davos for many years and Zoltán Balázs of Hungary who had served his national federation for many years.

1986 Debra Thomas of the United States became the first and only black world champion.

1988 Katarina Witt became the only lady since World War II to win two Olympic titles. They were consecutive. Kurt Browning of Canada landed the first quadruple jump, a quadruple toe loop, in competition at the World Championships. The World Junior Figure Skating Championships were held in Brisbane, Queensland, the first time any ISU championship was held in Australia.

1989 Midori Ito of Japan became the first lady to land a triple Axel Paulsen jump in competition at the World Championships in Paris, France. She became Japan's first world champion in any discipline.

1990 Compulsory figures were skated for the last time at the World Championships in Halifax, Nova Scotia.

1991 American ladies Kristi Yamaguchi, Tonya Harding, and Nancy Kerrigan swept the medals at the World Championships in Munich, Germany.

1992 Following the breakup of the Soviet Union, members of the former Soviet Bloc entered skaters in international competitions through newly formed federations, but for one year a unified team representing primarily Russia and Ukraine entered their skaters under the designation Commonwealth of Independent States (CIS). The ISU celebrated its 100th anniversary. Three books were published on the occasion, including Benjamin T. Wright's *Skating Around the World, 1892–1992: The One Hundredth Anniversary History of the International Skating Union; Results: Figure Skating Championships, 1968–1991;* and *The ISU Office Holders through the Years and the ISU Congresses, 1892–1990*, all published by the ISU.

1994 Nancy Kerrigan was attacked at the U.S. Championships in Detroit, Michigan. Many former champions were reinstated and competed at the Olympic Winter Games. They included Katarina Witt, Brian Boitano, Viktor Petrenko, Gordeeva and Grinkov, and Torvill and Dean. Only Gordeeva and Grinkov won additional gold medals. Torvill and Dean won bronze medals. Witt placed seventh, Boitano sixth, and Petrenko fourth. The Olympic Winter Games were held just two years after the previous games because the International Olympic Committee decided to alternate the summer and winter games in a two-year rotation. Ottavio Cinquanta of Italy became the 10th president of the ISU and remains in that position today. *Skating in the Olympic Games*, which includes the complete results of both figure skating and speed skating through the 1994 games, was published by the ISU. It was "Dedicated to the International Olympic Committee on the Occasion of Its 100th Anniversary."

1995 Lu Chen of China became the ladies world champion. It was that country's first world title.

1996 The Grand Prix Series was begun. Winners at the first Grand Prix Finals were Michelle Kwan of the United States, Alexei Urmanov of Russia, Evgenia Shishkova and Vadim Naumov of Russia in pairs, and Oksana Grishchuk and Evgeny Platov of Russia in ice dancing. *Skating in America: The 75th Anniversary History of the United States Figure Skating Association* by Benjamin T. Wright was published on that occasion.

1997 Tara Lipinski of the United States became the youngest ever ladies world champion at age 14 years, 9 months, 12 days.

1998 Tara Lipinski of the United States became the youngest ever ladies Olympic champion at age 15 years, 8 months, 10 days.

1999 The Four Continents Championships were first held. The winners were Tatiana Malinina of Uzbekistan, Takeshi Honda of Japan, Xue Shen and Hongbo Zhao of China in pairs, and Shae-Lynn Bourne and Victor Kraatz of Canada in ice dancing.

2000 Synchronized skating became a world discipline in Minneapolis, Minnesota. The winning team was Team Surprise of Sweden.

2001 The last competition in English style skating was held.

2002 The judging scandal in the pairs competition at the Salt Lake City Games resulted in the awarding of duplicate gold medals to Jamie Salé and David Pelletier of Canada.

2003 The formation of the World Skating Federation was announced at the World Championships in Washington, D.C.

2004 The International Judging System, also known as the "Code of Points," was adopted by the ISU.

2006 The first throw triple Axel Paulsen jump was completed by Rena Inoue and John Baldwin at the United States Championships.

2009 Yu Na Kim of Korea became the ladies gold medalist at the World Championships in Los Angeles, California. She was the bronze medalist in 2008, becoming the first medalist of any color in any discipline from that country.

2010 The World Figure Skating Championships were held for the 100th time in Torino, Italy.

Figure Skating's Defining Moments

The following 15 pivotal points in the history of figure skating include ones of historical importance and others that have had lasting effects on the sport, changes that have influenced what skaters do on the ice and what the sport's many fans see at competitions and skating shows.

1. Invention of the bladed skate (before the 14th century): Prior to the invention of the bladed skate, sometime before the 14th century and probably in Holland, skates were made from leg bones of large animals and strapped to skaters' shoes. They were not sharpened. Poles like those used in skiing were employed to push the skater along. With the invention of the bladed skate, the poles could be discarded as the skater pushed off from one skate and glided on the other. When this was done from one skate to the other, the sport's first figure, the "Dutch roll," resulted. Skating's most basic elements, stroking and gliding, had been discovered.
2. Robert Jones's *Art of Skating*, our earliest book on figure skating (1772): Robert Jones, a lieutenant in the British Royal Artillery and a devoted skater, wrote the first book on skating, describing basic technique and figures then being skated. Five advanced figures are included with sketches showing skaters doing three of them. The book appeared in several later editions with minor changes made by unnamed persons. Jones was sentenced to death but then exiled for sodomy in the year of his book's publication. From that date, 1772, we can trace the development of the sport of figure skating.
3. Jean Garcin places equal importance on skating backward (1813): Robert Jones, author of the first book on skating, saw no need to skate backward. He called it "whimsical," although he noted that some skaters were experimenting with it. One of his figures, a heart-shaped design, actually required it. Jean Garcin, a member of the skating fraternity in France known as the Gilets Rouge (red waistcoats), emphasized artistry over athleticism, relating skating to ballet. Most important, however, in his book, *Le vrai patineur* (The True Skater), Garcin gives skating backward equal importance to skating forward, a necessity for the rapidly increasing body of figures being skated in the 19th century.
4. The words figure and skating get connected (1869): Figure skating is an English language term. The sport is called patinage artistique in France and Eiskunstlauf in German, for example. England can be considered the birthplace of the sport, beginning after the Restoration in the 17th century, but the term "figure skating" was not employed for 200 years. It was first used by George Anderson specifically for advanced figures, those done on one foot, in his book, *The Art of Skating*, published under the pen name Cyclos in 1852. Seventeen years later,

in 1869, Henry Eugene Vandervell and T. Maxwell Witham employed the term for the title of their book, *A System of Figure Skating*, thus referring to the sport itself as figure skating.

5. The National Skating Association (NSA) is founded in England (1879): Skating is regulated in each member country of the International Skating Union by a national federation which adopts policies and rules relative to competitions and establishes test structures to rank skaters and to determine what competitions they can enter and at what level. This had become necessary after the mid-19th century because skating clubs, which existed in many countries, often sponsored competitions without clearly defined rules and with minimally qualified judges. The NSA in Great Britain was organized in 1879 specifically to regulate speed skating but within a year the figure skaters had joined. It is the oldest national federation.
6. The International Skating Union (ISU) is founded (1892): By the 1870s, competitions for both speed and figure skating were being held within clubs, between clubs, regionally, nationally, and sometimes across national boundaries. During the 1880s, a few international competitions were held, the first being the Great International Skating Tournament sponsored by the Vienna Skating Club in 1882. Another held in St. Petersburg, Russia, in 1890, sponsored by the Neva Skating Association, was the first known to have included a competitor from across the Atlantic. Louis Rubinstein of Canada won one of three gold medals awarded. A minor controversy resulted from differences in skating styles. It demonstrated clearly that international oversight was needed, although that incident did not have a direct influence on the founding of the ISU in 1892. The ISU regulates both speed and figure skating. Initial emphasis was placed on speed skating with the first official World Championship held in 1893. The regulation of figure skating followed relatively quickly. It was necessary first to establish a schedule of compulsory figures to be skated and to adopt a specific skating style, that being the international style. The first World Championship in figure skating was held at St. Petersburg, Russia, for men only in 1896. The ISU is the oldest governing body for a winter sport. Only the rowing federation, formed also in 1892, is older, for a summer sport.
7. Skating's first modern ice dance, the Three Step Waltz (1894): Dancing on skates can be documented back to the 1860s, but it was different from what is today associated with ice dancing, specifically speed and flow across the ice. Early ice dancers took to the ice dances similar to those done on a dance floor, often in a relatively confined space

and with both skates on the ice most of the time. In 1894, Monsieur Richard, the skating instructor at the Palais de Glace in Paris, reportedly first skated the "Three Step Waltz," which was done around the perimeter of an ice rink. It became a craze throughout Europe, and within a few years, most of the older ice dances had disappeared as skaters from beginners to those more advanced were waltzing on ice.

8. Madge Syers becomes the first woman to enter world competition (1902): The World Championship in 1902 was held in London. Competitive figure skating had long been viewed as a sport specifically for men, although there was no rule against women competing. Madge Syers of Great Britain, a former English style champion, entered the competition and placed second behind the reigning champion, Ulrich Salchow. As a result and in response, the ISU established a championship for ladies, and in 1906, Syers became the first ISU ladies' champion. At the Olympic Games in 1908, the first to include figure skating events, Syers became the Olympic ladies' champion as well.
9. Jumping becomes an important part of free skating (1930s): Figure skating's most difficult jump, the Axel Paulsen, dates back to 1882 when Paulsen did it as his special figure at the Great International Skating Tournament in Vienna, but jumping did not become a major part of the sport or an expected element in free skating programs until the years between the two World Wars. In the 19th century, jumping was sometimes referred to as "ugly." It was viewed as a practical necessity to leap over impediments often found on frozen ponds. Adding jumps to free skating programs began in the 1920s, and by the mid-1930s, all of the jumps done today had been described and had become a part of free skating programs. All except the Axel Paulsen jump were being doubled. In the post–World War II era, further development in jumping consisted of adding revolutions to the prewar jumps, which had become basic elements in free skating.
10. Birth of major skating shows (1936–1943): Professional figure skaters had been appearing in shows, at fairs, in hotels, and at any place a sheet of ice could be set up since the beginning of the 20th century both in North America and in Europe, when in the years just before entrance into World War II, three large touring shows were created in the United States: the Ice Follies in 1936, the Hollywood Ice Review in 1937, and Ice Capades in 1941. A fourth, Holiday on Ice, first toured in 1943. These and other lavish shows continued after the war, touring in North America, Europe, and throughout the world for many years. They took spectacular skating to large audiences, contributing to the development of the sport's first major fan base.

11. ABC's Wide World of Sports launches coverage of the World Championships (1962): Twenty-five years after the birth of the major skating shows, ABC launched its Wide World of Sports programs in 1962. Among the events covered that year was the World Figure Skating Championships held in Prague, Czechoslovakia, and it was a particularly exciting competition. Coming one year after the plane crash in Belgium which killed the entire 1961 U.S. world team, American domination of singles skating ended. Sjoukje Dijkstra of Netherlands won the first of three consecutive world titles; Donald Jackson of Canada completed the first triple Lutz jump done in competition to win the men's competition; pair skaters Maria and Otto Jelinek of Canada returned to their native country which they had left at the time of the communist takeover in 1948 and won the title; and Eva Romanová and Pavel Roman of Czechoslovakia, a young teenage ice dancing couple, won their first of four titles decisively in an upset, the first non-British couple to win a world title in ice dancing since the discipline had become a title event in 1952. Dick Button did the commentary, and he continued with ABC for more than four decades, educating the skating public about athletic and artistic aspects of the sport and clearly contributing to its popularity.
12. Competitions move indoors (1968): The development of artificial ice beginning in the 1870s provided the opportunity for skating competitions to be held indoors. Although some early competitions were held indoors, including the World Championships in 1902 and the Olympic skating events in 1908, competing on natural ice and coping with adverse conditions such as rain, high winds, and bitterly cold temperatures remained a problem but also an accepted tradition for many years. In 1967, on the occasion of the 75th anniversary of the ISU and the centenary celebration of the Vienna Skating Club, all events at the World Championships, which were held in Vienna, except for the compulsory figures were held outdoors for the last time. As so often had happened in the past, the weather conditions were poor. The ISU at its congress that year passed a rule requiring that the European and World Championships and the Olympic Winter Games be held in covered ice rinks. Other championships were not yet affected. The rinks did not have to be enclosed, but 12 years later, in 1980, enclosed rinks became a requirement, and beginning in 1984, practice rinks had to be indoors as well.
13. Compulsory figures are removed from international competition (1990): Skating became figure skating in the mid-19th century, a reflection of skaters' fascination with the tracings they left on the ice.

The figure eight and a similar three-lobed figure became basic to good skating at all levels of difficulty, and it was these figures that eventually became the most important part of competitions. The ISU adopted a regimen of compulsory figures that counted 60 percent of the score in singles skating. In the post–World War II era, the number of figures skated and their relative value was reduced several times as free skating, which originally counted 40 percent, gained in popularity and importance. In 1990, the ISU abolished the compulsory figures completely, a decision that most skaters and coaches supported, but still today, one hears discussions about the ramifications of what the sport gave up—training for edge control, good carriage, and form—and thus how it has affected the artistic quality of free skating.

14. Nancy Kerrigan is attacked at the United States Championships (6 January 1994): Figure skating reached the apex of its popularity about 1998. From 1994 through 1998, the public could not get enough skating on television. There were sometimes choices as to which televised skating program one would watch. This sudden and accelerated popularity resulted from the attack on Nancy Kerrigan as she exited the ice following a practice session at the United States Championships in 1994. The perpetrator but not the actual attacker was the husband of Tonya Harding, a skater who was Kerrigan's primary challenger. Sensationalized media coverage was continuous as the investigation proceeded. It was an Olympic year, and because the investigation was not complete, both ladies were allowed to compete in Hamer, Norway, at the Olympic Winter Games. They shared the same practice ice, adding to the drama. The viewership for the ladies short programs set all-time records as figure skating attracted a large but not lasting group of new fans. For the short term, however, skaters, professional shows and competitions, and the sport's governing bodies enjoyed a financial windfall that could not last. Four years later, the bubble burst. Most of the newly established shows and professional and pro-am competitions from that period disappeared quickly as television ratings dropped. Skaters enjoyed fewer professional opportunities, and the sport's governing bodies suffered from less lucrative television contracts.
15. Controversy results in a new judging system (2004): The pairs competition at the 2002 Olympic Winter Games in Salt Lake City ended in controversy resulting from apparent bloc judging. The "swing judge," Marie-Reine Le Gougne of France, stated after the free skating event that she had been "pressured" by her federation to favor the Russians, Elena Berezhnaya and Anton Sikharulidze, over the Canadians, Jamie Salé and David Pelletier. Extensive media coverage followed, and a

protest was filed by the Canadian Federation. Ultimately, duplicate gold medals were awarded to the Canadians. Ottavio Cinquanta, president of the ISU, began pushing immediately to replace the long-standing 6.0 and placement judging system with a point-earning system in which each skating element would have an established value and would be judged in competition on its quality relative to the given value. After two years of testing, the International Judging System was adopted at the ISU Congress in 2004. It was a sweeping change for the sport because it affected all figure skating disciplines including synchronized skating.

Introduction

Figure skating is the most popular televised sport at the quadrennial Olympic Winter Games and the oldest of the winter sports, having first been contested at the games of the fourth Olympiad in London in 1908. The first official Winter Games were held 16 years later in Chamonix, France.

What makes figure skating so popular? No other sport creates such a perfect balance between athleticism and artistry. Competitive figure skating is done in costume, is choreographed, and interprets the music. Strength and stamina are necessary to accomplish the big jumps, to lift one's partner, and to complete a four-minute or longer program chock-full of difficult elements, only after years of training on the ice coupled with weight training and other exercises. Christine Brennan, a respected sports writer, noted perceptively that "figure skating does a grand job of hiding its athleticism under layers of disguise." It must look effortless. Brennan then quoted ice dancer Elizabeth Punsalan, who said that "if we were huffing and puffing and sweating, you'd see how athletic it was."[1] This defines figure skating today, which is much different from its early history. The sport has evolved continually over a long period of time and has seen many changes, from the skating of basic figures in the 19th century to the complex free skating programs of today.

Skating is defined as "the act, art, or sport of gliding on skates." Figure skating is defined as "skating characterized by the performance of various jumps, spins, and dance movements and formerly by the tracing of prescribed figures."[2] These definitions beg an important question that historians must ponder: Is figure skating a sport or an art? Historically, the answer is neither clear nor simple, primarily because it has evolved and changed over time. For the past century, figure skating has purportedly been a balanced blend of sport and art. Without both elements being present, could skaters be successful at any level, beginner or advanced, amateur or professional, in competition or in shows? This balance represents the uniqueness of what we call figure skating.

Skating had a long history before the term "figure" was connected to it.[3] Myths from Scandinavia and other northern countries tell of leg bones from large animals being strapped to shoes to facilitate traversing frozen surfaces during cold winter months, an aid in hunting and a necessity for survival. The bones were not sharpened. Poles, like those used in skiing, were employed to propel skaters across the ice. Skates in the ancient world served as a tool, a practical innovation probably employed for thousands of years. But skating must have become a recreational activity as well, especially among young people. By the 12th century, William Fitz Stephen in his description of life in London tells of people sliding on the ice, with those "more skilled" tying bones to their feet and pushing themselves along with poles while being "borne along swift as a bird in flight." Skating became a recreational activity but also a combative one with young men on skates. Fitz Stephen reported that "Youth is an age greedy of renown, yearning for victory, and exercises itself in mimic battles that it may bear itself more boldly in true combats."[4] Those young men were competing on skates.

By the 14th century, presumably first in Holland, bone was replaced by a steel blade that was sharpened to form an edge that could cut into the ice. This allowed skaters to push off from the edge of the blade and to discard the poles previously used to push themselves along. The sport's first figure, the Dutch roll, followed. By leaning from side to side, skaters could traverse great distances rapidly. Enamored with this ability, the Dutch eventually became leaders in the sport of speed skating. For the further developments in figure skating, we must cross the English Channel.

During the decade of the Cromwellian era, members of the British royal family sought refuge in Holland where they learned how to skate and how to do the Dutch roll. Following the Restoration in 1660, reports of skating in London abound. The populace was still skating on bone skates, as they had done for centuries, but others, including the future James II, skated on bladed skates. Expanding on the Dutch roll, they invented new figures as skating's popularity grew throughout the British Isles during the ensuing century, especially among the aristocracy and the clergy. In 1744, the first skating club was formed in Edinburgh, Scotland, and in 1772, the first book on skating, Robert Jones's *A Treatise on Skating* was published in London. Jones provides detailed descriptions of the figures then being skated and the proper technique required. He includes pictures showing correct body positions. From that date, a clear history of figure skating can be chronicled.

Skating's second book, *Le vrai patineur* (The True Skater) by Jean Garcin, was published in Paris in 1813. It was subtitled *How to Skate with Grace*. In France, emphasis was placed primarily on artistry, which in addition to the body positions employed and the figures skated is evident in the clothing skaters wore. At the forefront was the Gilets Rouge, an elite group of skaters whose credo was artistic sophistication.[5] Skating reflected the French love of ballet, and Garcin dedicated his book to Geneviève Gosselin, the premier dancer at the Academy of Music in Paris.

George Anderson's *The Art of Skating*, published under the pseudonym Cyclos, appeared in Glasgow, Scotland, in 1852. After covering skating technique thoroughly, Anderson began his fifth chapter stating: "I now come to those figures which require such proficiency on the part of the skater as will enable him to dwell for some space on one foot."[6] He entitled the chapter "Figure Skating." Here the words figure and skating are connected for the first time with the term clearly reserved for people who have developed their skating skills to a high level. Anderson's book appeared in a second edition 16 years later, 1868, published under his own name. He then provided further clarification: "The term 'figure skating' is more frequently applied to those figures which are done on one foot and which may therefore be supposed to be the most difficult."[7] Many people were skating recreationally, but presumably only those more advanced, the elite skaters of their day, could be called figure skaters. Just a year later, however, Henry Eugene Vandervell, a member of the London Skating Club, collaborating with a younger colleague, T. Maxwell Witham, published the first edition of a monumental book, *A System of Figure Skating*. Since 1869, the term "figure skating" has represented the sport or art from the moment a beginner steps on the ice through the development of the elite skater capable of the most advanced figures.

Vandervell has been called the "Father of English Figure Skating," a title that has validity on several levels. Anderson had preferred but did not require the rigid body carriage associated with the developing English style of skating. Vandervell demanded it. He was the first person to propose proficiency tests, believing they "would create just emulation" as skaters strove to perfect more difficult figures, but strong opposition from members of the London Skating Club thwarted their adoption for a decade.[8] Tests, they believed, would be something akin to competition. Speed skaters, they noted, had races, and that led to gambling, a thought that horrified club members. Skating for them was a sophisticated recreational activity, primarily for the upper classes. Test structures were not implemented until the founding of the National Skating Association (NSA) 10 years later, in 1879. The NSA's stated purpose was "to promote, ascertain, and reward speed in skating," but the following year, the figure skaters joined. Vandervell was named the first chair of the Ice Figure Committee, a position he held until his death in 1908. Test structures became the first order of business and were established within months. By the 1890s, just over a decade later, competitions in English style skating were being held. Figure skating, formerly a recreational activity, had become a sport in England.

Figure skating competitions were by that time being held with increasing frequency in other places in Europe and North America at the club, regional, and national levels. The first important international competition, the Great

International Skating Tournament, sponsored by the Vienna Skating Club, was held in 1882. There, Axel Paulsen of Norway did, as his special figure, the jump that today bears his name. In 1890, the St. Petersburg, Russia, Skating Club on the occasion of its 25th anniversary held an international competition at which Louis Rubenstein of Canada won one of three gold medals awarded. Controversy followed not related to the capability of judges or any dishonesty but rather as a result of differences in skating styles. At that time, there were three distinct styles of skating: the English style, the American style, and the international style.[9] Reliable judging was not possible when skaters in individual events were skating in different styles. A universal set of standards adopted by an international governing body was needed.

In July 1892, 16 delegates from six countries—Austria, Germany, Great Britain, Hungary, the Netherlands, and Sweden—attended a three-day conference in Scheveningen, Netherlands, to form an international organization to regulate skating. Letters of interest were sent from Norway, Russia, and the United States. The resulting Internationale Eislauf-Verein (International Skating Union [ISU]) was established to govern the sports of speed skating and figure skating.[10] It was a pioneering sports organization, the first international governing body for a winter sport. Initial emphasis was placed on speed skating, and in 1893, the first World Championship under the auspices of the ISU took place at Amsterdam. In 1895, a committee was appointed to recommend rules for figure skating, and in 1896, the first World Championship for figure skating, for men only, was held at St. Petersburg, Russia. Four skaters from three countries competed. Gilbert Fuchs of Germany became figure skating's first world champion.

Since the 17th century figure skating had remained primarily a recreational activity enjoyed by amateurs when and where weather conditions provided ice on which to skate. By the mid-19th century, the best of those amateurs were experimenting with increasingly difficult figures, and by the 1880s they were competing in a growing number of competitions. While figure skating has always been and will always be a recreational activity enjoyed by many people, with the growing number of skating clubs, the establishment of national federations, and the formation of the ISU in 1892, figure skating became a sport in which elite competitors could climb through the ranks and vie to be the best in the world.

Figure skating is viewed today by some skeptics and critics as a "ladies sport," but is it? During the 19th century women sought opportunities to skate, and from as early as Jones's book of 1772, authors have addressed it, sometimes in a negative way. Jones "saw no reason why the ladies are to be excluded," arguing that "to object to it as not being hitherto practised is the effect of prejudice and confined ideas."[11] Some later writers, however, considered it unfeminine. The "fairer sex," they feared, might injure themselves by falling, and they noted that the long dresses of the 19th century were not conducive to sporting activities. Acknowledging that "the girls of England have been taking to skating in considerable numbers," Vandervell and Witham in the "Ladies' Chapter" commented chauvinistically that "should we find you wearing a dress rather short, we would smilingly approve," but "at the sacrifice of supposed elegance," they insisted on the "absence of the tremendously high heels at present in vogue."[12] In spite of such comments, concerns, and objections, women persevered. Their numbers grew, and by the 1870s they were being granted membership in skating clubs. They took the NSA's proficiency tests, and they wanted to compete. But the entrance of Madge Syers of Great Britain into the World Championship of 1902, held in London, shocked the skating world. The possibility of a woman entering what was viewed as an all-male competition had not been considered, but there was no rule against women competing. Syers placed second behind the reigning champion, Ulrich Salchow. Recognizing the need to provide competitive opportunities for women, at its congress in 1904 the ISU established a competition for them, and in 1906, Syers became the first lady world champion.[13] She repeated the following year.

Combined skating, usually teams of four skaters, was practiced originally by all men, but eventually women began to participate. Madge Syers was a member of the winning team at the Challenge Shield in 1899. On the other hand, hand in hand skating, which became tremendously popular in England by the 1890s, was done specifically by a man and a woman. Women had broken the gender barrier. From an activity specifically for men early in the century to one in which women participated equally, the environment had gradually changed. By the eve of World War I, figure skating had evolved from a purely recreational activity almost exclusively for men from the upper classes to one in which international level competitive skating had become the goal of serious and talented practitioners, both men and women.

Today more women compete than men, but women do not dominate the sport at the championship level. More young girls than boys enter beginning classes, a statistic reflected by a larger number of entrants in ladies' events through all competitive levels. But the disciplines of pair skating and ice dancing require an equal number of men and women. On the other hand, figure skating's newest discipline, synchronized skating, although not specifically designated as a women's sport, is almost exclusively practiced by females.

During its early history, skating was limited to countries where weather patterns provided natural ice on which skaters could practice their sport. With the ability to efficiently make artificial ice, it became a year-round activity, one that could be practiced anywhere. This development occurred at approximately the same time the ISU was formed and annual competitions were established, although most competitions continued to be held outdoors on natural ice. The European Championship was first held in 1891; the ISU was formed in 1892; and the first World Championship was held in 1896. By World War I, 20 European and 19 World Championships had been held. The competitors represented just nine countries, all of which had long skating traditions: three Scandinavian countries, Finland, Norway, and Sweden; Russia; the Germanic countries, Austria and Germany; France; Great Britain; and Hungary. Significant expansion occurred during the years between WWI and WWII when an additional 12 countries participated in international competitions, including the North American countries, Canada and the United States, and the first Asian country, Japan.

Various countries and their skaters have dominated competitive figure skating at different times throughout its history, often in specific disciplines. England is the birthplace of figure skating, but by the last quarter of the 19th century, skaters from several other European countries, particularly Austria, France Germany, Russia, and the Scandinavian countries, were participating actively in the sport. Most successful in the early championships were the Swedes who won 12 of 19 world titles prior to World War I, primarily a result of Ulrich Salchow's success in winning 10 of them. Salchow also won the men's title at the Olympic Games in 1908. Another Swede, the incomparable Gillis Grafström, won three world and a record-setting three Olympic titles in the postwar period, but after Grafström's retirement, Swedish skaters won no additional world or Olympic titles in any discipline until 2000 when Team Surprise, the most successful synchronized skating team, won its first of five world titles.

Gilbert Fuchs of Germany became the first world champion in 1896. He won a second world title in 1906. Germany also claimed the first world pair title in 1908. The unbeatable Anna Hübler and Heinrich Burger won twice and became the first Olympic pair champions as well. In the 1930s, Germany fielded another outstanding pair, Maxi Herber and Ernst Baier. In 1936, they won the Olympic title and the first of four consecutive world titles.

Madge Syers of Great Britain became the first lady world champion in 1906. She repeated in 1907 and then won the first Olympic ladies' title in 1908. The British husband-and-wife pair Phyllis and James Johnson placed behind Hübler and Burger three times but proceeded to become world pair champions twice, in 1909 and 1912. The Johnsons wrote a valuable article on pair skating, published in Irving Brokaw's *Art of Skating*, which provides our best description of pair skating then in its infancy.[14] British skaters came to the fore again in the late 1930s. Cecilia Colledge and Megan Taylor won a combined three world ladies' titles beginning in 1937, and Graham Sharp won the men's title in 1939. After World War II, Jeannette Altwegg won the world ladies' title in 1951 and the Olympic title in 1952. A brother and sister, Jennifer and John Nicks, won the world pair title in 1953. With the advent of ice dancing as a world discipline in 1952, English skaters excelled, winning every title through 1960. Since 1960, two British couples have each won four consecutive world dance titles, Diane Towler and Bernard Ford, 1966–1969, and arguably the most popular ice dancers of all time, Jayne Torvill and Christopher Dean, 1981–1984, who also won the Olympic dance title in 1984. Two British men have reached the top of the medal stand in Olympic competition, John Curry in 1976, considered by some to be the most artistic male skater in the history of the sport, and Robin Cousins in 1980. Curry won all three major international competitions in 1976, the European and World Championships and the Olympics.

For many years, Austrian skaters were among the most dominant in competitive figure skating, continuing a tradition of excellence and innovation that dates back to Jackson Haines's periods of residence in Vienna first in 1865 and again in 1870, the establishment of the Wiener Eislauf Verein (Vienna Skating Club) in 1867, and the development of the Viennese (international) style of skating, which was subsequently adopted by the ISU.

Two Austrian men, Gustav Hügel and Fritz Kachler, claimed a combined five world titles before World War I. After the war, three men claimed 12 of 15 world titles. Kachler added one to his two prewar titles in 1922; Willy Böckl followed Kachler with four; and the period closed with the remarkable Karl Schäfer who won seven consecutive world titles in addition to Olympic titles in 1932 and 1936. Austria's finest and only post–World War I world ladies' champion, Herma Szabo, won five consecutive titles as well as the 1924 Olympic ladies' title before being bested in 1927 by Sonja Henie of Norway. It would be remiss not to mention two outstanding Austrian ladies who were among eight skaters from various countries who placed second behind Henie during her 10-year reign. Fritzi Burger in 1929 and 1932 and Hilde Holovsky in 1931, a talented youngster who some thought had the talent to defeat Henie. Unfortunately, she died at age 15. Three Austrian pairs won a total of five titles during the 1920s. Austria's combined record of 22 world titles between the wars is especially significant when one realizes that during the more than 50 years since World War II, Austria has compiled a total of just six. Pair skaters Elisabeth Schwarz and Kurt Oppelt won in 1956; Emmerich Danzer won three men's titles, 1966–1968; and Trixi Schuba, a master of compulsory figures, won twice, 1971 and 1972.

The post–World War II period has been called the "golden age of American skating." Three men won 12 of 14 world and all four Olympic titles through 1960. Dick Button, one of the best known names in figure skating, began his string of five world and two Olympic titles in 1948. He was followed by the Jenkins brothers, Hayes and David, who won seven world titles plus two Olympic titles. Between 1953 and 1960, two ladies, Tenley Albright and Carol Heiss, won seven of eight world titles and both Olympic titles. These champions had all retired by February 15, 1961, the darkest day for American skating. On their way to the World Championships, scheduled for Prague, Czechoslovakia, a young, relatively inexperienced but talented American team expecting to carry on their country's winning tradition was aboard a Sabena Airways flight that crashed while attempting a landing at Brussels, Belgium. There were no survivors.

Although American success after the war had been in singles skating, a brother-and-sister pair, Karol and Peter Kennedy won the world pair title in 1950, the first of only two American pairs to win world titles. Beginning in 1954, Canadians dominated pair skating, winning every world pairs' title—less one—through 1962. Frances Dafoe and Norris Bowden won twice, 1954 and 1955, but slipped to second behind Schwarz and Oppelt in 1956. Canada's most successful pair, Barbara Wagner and Robert Paul, won four consecutive world titles beginning in 1957 and the Olympic title in 1960. Following the plane crash in 1961, Maria and Otto Jelinek won the world pairs' title in 1962, but it would be 22 years before another Canadian pair would win again.

During the 1960s, a new powerhouse in figure skating appeared with its first success in pair skating. The Soviet Union and since its breakup in 1992 Russia have won more world and Olympic titles than any other country.[15] In an upset at the Olympic Games in 1964, Liudmila Belousova and Oleg Protopopov won their first Olympic pair title. Four world titles and a second Olympic title followed. Although Russian skaters had competed in all disciplines during the early years of international competition, prior to World War I, and won the title in special figures at the 1908 Olympics, Russian membership in the ISU ceased following the Bolshevik Revolution in 1917, and as a result, no Russians competed in international competitions for 40 years. The Soviet Union joined the ISU in 1948, but another decade passed before Soviet skaters cautiously but methodically entered world competition, sending three men and two pairs, including Belousova and Protopopov, usually referred to as the Protopopovs, to the championships in 1958.[16] Four years later in 1962, the Protopopovs ascended to the second tier of the medal stand behind Marika Kilius and Hans-Jürgen Bäumler of the Federal Republic of Germany and claimed the first Soviet World medals. The Protopopovs had placed second behind Kilius and Bäumler four times at the European and World Championships when, in what has been called "the story" of the 1964 Olympics, they upset the reigning champions. Enterprising merchants had been so sure of the outcome that souvenirs proclaiming the Germans as champions had gone on sale before the event was skated. But a month later at the World Championships, Kilius and Bäumler, in their final international competition, defeated the Protopopovs for a fifth time.

The Protopopovs were followed by the most successful pair skater in the history of the discipline. With two different partners, Irina Rodnina won 10 consecutive world titles, tying the records set by Ulrich Salchow and Sonja Henie. She also won three Olympic pairs titles, tying the records set by Gillis Grafström and Sonja Henie. The Soviet pair skating dynasty thus established has continued. Only six non-Soviet or Russian pairs won world titles during the 36 years from 1965 through 2000, and Soviet pairs won every Olympic title through 2006. Their record of 12 consecutive Olympic titles was broken in 2010 by the Chinese pair Xue Shen and Hongbo Zhao.

The Soviets also excelled in ice dancing, first appearing at the World Championships in 1966. Four years later, Liudmila Pakhomova and Alexandr Gorshkov won their first of six world dance titles, a record not yet duplicated. From 1970 through the end of the century, Soviet and Russian ice dancers won 26 of 31 world titles. When ice dancing became an Olympic discipline in 1976, Pakhomova and Gorshkov won the title. Soviet and Russian ice dancers won seven of eight Olympic titles when the Canadians Tessa Virtue and Scott Moir won in 2010.[17]

Although their success in singles skating does not equal that achieved in pairs and ice dancing, Soviet and Russian men have accumulated a total of 11 world and four Olympic titles. Seven of the world titles are consecutive, 1998–2004, won by Alexei Yagudin and his younger rival Evgeny Plushenko. The four Olympic titles are likewise consecutive: Alexei Urmanov in 1994, Ilia Kulik in 1998, Yagudin in 2002, and Plushenko in 2006. In 1999 Maria Butyrskaya became the first Russian lady to become a world ladies' champion. Irina Slutskaya, a major rival of the American Michelle Kwan, won the world ladies' title twice, 2002 and 2005. No Russian lady has yet won an Olympic title.

The United States lost its best skaters in the 1961 plane crash, but five years later, Peggy Fleming, one of America's most artistic skaters, won the first of three consecutive world ladies titles and in 1968 the Olympic title as well. Tim Wood followed with two world titles in 1969 and 1970. Five other men have since won world titles, Charlie Tickner in 1978, Scott Hamilton from 1980 to 1984, Brian Boitano in 1986 and 1988, Todd Eldredge in 1996, and Evan Lysacek in 2009. Hamilton, Boitano, and Lysacek have won Olympic titles as well.

The ladies were even more successful. During the period from 1976 through 2006, the United States fielded 10 lady champions who accumulated 16 of the 31 world titles awarded. They include some of America's most popular skaters, Dorothy Hamill, Kristi Yamaguchi, and Michelle Kwan, as well as Linda Fratianne, Elaine Zayak, Rosalyn Sumners, Debi Thomas, Jill Trenary, Tara Lipinski, and Kimmy Meissner. Hamill, Yamaguchi, and Lipinski also won Olympic titles as did Sarah Hughes.

Challenging U.S. dominance since 1989 and continuing to the present, Asian skaters, Japanese and Chinese, and most recently a talented South Korean, have stepped to the fore. By century's end, three ladies, Midori Ito and Yuka Sato of Japan and Lu Chen of China, had won world titles, but already in the 21st century, four have won titles, Japan's Shizuka Arakawa, Miki Ando, and Mao Asada and Korea's phenom, Yu Na Kim. Arakawa also won Japan's first Olympic title in 2006. China's strength has been primarily in pair skating. World titles have been won by Xue Shen and Hongbo Zhao in 2002, 2003, and 2007 and by Qing Pang and Jian Tong in 2006 and 2010. Shen and Zhao also won China's first Olympic figure skating title in 2010.

Figure skaters at the international level have a limited number of competitions annually in which to compete. The Grand Prix Series, during the fall, includes six competitions held essentially for six consecutive weeks. They serve as qualifying events for the Grand Prix Finals typically held in December. Skaters can compete in up to three of the qualifying events, but scores from only two, designated in advance, count toward entrance into the finals where the top six point winners in each discipline—ladies, men, pairs, and ice dancing—compete. The Grand Prix Series was begun in the 1996 season, although most of the qualifying competitions already existed as ISU sanctioned events, some for many years. The series is particularly valuable for major skating countries such as Canada, Japan, Russia, and the United States which have more good skaters than can be accommodated at the small number of other major international championships. It also provides skaters with opportunities to try out new programs and to be judged on them in front of large audiences early in the competitive season. Fifty-three percent of the medalists at the Grand Prix Finals have gone on to become medalists at the following World Championships. A Junior Grand Prix Series was implemented in the 1999 season which currently includes seven qualifying competitions and the Junior Grand Prix Finals.

Most countries, including the United States, hold their national championships in January following the fall Grand Prix Series. Entries into the upcoming international championships are typically selected from national medal winners. Other than in Olympic years, these include two competitions, first the European Championships for skaters from that continent and the Four Continents Championships for all others. The Four Continents Championships, implemented in 1999, provide competitive opportunities for non-Europeans who since 1948 have not been allowed to enter the European Championships. For many years, the biennial North American Championships, a competition between Canada and the United States, served as a parallel competition to the European Championships, but they were last held in 1971. At that time Asians, Australians, and Africans did not have skaters capable of winning medals at the international level. North American skaters with well-established international success were left without a competition parallel to the European Championships, although Skate Canada and Skate America, events on the Grand Prix Series today, were begun as ISU sanctioned international competitions in 1973 and 1981 respectively.[18]

The World Championships, typically held in March, provide the culminating and premier event of each skating season. They have been held every year since 1896, except for seven years each during World Wars I and II and in 1961, the year of the plane crash. In 2010, Torino, Italy, served as the site of the 100th holding of the World Championships.[19] Becoming a world champion is the goal of every skater. This pinnacle of success has been reached by 47 ladies, 45 men, 44 pairs, and 26 ice dancing couples.

The Olympic Winter Games precede the World Championships. Because they are quadrennial, they seem to hold an aura of importance above that of the World Championships, and to most skaters, they represent the ultimate achievement. Figure skating is the original winter Olympic sport, having first been contested at the London Games in 1908. The games, originally scheduled for Rome, Italy, were moved to London in an eleventh-hour decision where the local skating community easily convinced the British Olympic Committee to include figure skating events. Competitions for ladies, men, pairs, and special figures were held on indoor ice at the Prince's Skating Club. Skating was not included at the Stockholm, Sweden, games in 1912, but when Olympic competition was reinstated after the war, at Antwerp, Belgium, in 1920, figure skating was again included and ice hockey was added. The first separate Olympic Winter Games were held in Chamonix, France, in 1924 with other sports including speed skating.[20] Figure skating, the oldest and the most popular winter Olympic sport, has been included in 23 holdings of the games.

Competitions in figure skating for both singles and pairs include two programs, a short or technical program including eight required elements and a long program or free skate without specific required elements but with prescribed limitations. The short program for singles skaters includes three spins, three jumps, and two step sequences. For the ladies a spiral sequence is done in place of one of the step sequences. Short programs for pair skaters also include eight required elements, specifically two spins, one side by side, the other a pair spin; two jumps, one side by side, the other a throw jump;

two lifts, one of them a twist lift; a death spiral; and a footwork sequence. Ice dancers skate three events, prescribed compulsory dances, an original dance, and a free dance, but at the 2010 congress, the ISU eliminated compulsory dances from competition beginning in 2011.

Compulsory dances like compulsory figures for singles skaters, which have not been required since 1990, reflect figure skating's emphasis in the early days on set patterns skated by all competitors with judges evaluating them on assigned figures or dances employing clearly understood criteria. The first European Championship in 1891 included only compulsory figures. Free skating was added the following year, its value being 40 percent of the total score. That 60:40 ratio remained in effect until the short program was added in 1973. Likewise, when ice dancing became a world discipline in 1952, compulsory dances counted 60 percent, the free dance 40 percent. In 1967, the original dance, a design created by the competitors, was added, taking the place of one of the compulsory dances. Other changes followed, further reducing the number of compulsory dances skated while increasing the values of the original dance and the free dance.

Many things contributed to the reduction and eventual elimination of compulsory figures and dances but perhaps none more than television. Compulsories, which are not exciting for television audiences, were usually not broadcast. The viewers saw only the free skating and as a result did not always understand the outcomes. No better example occurred than in the early 1970s when Trixi Schuba of Austria, an outstanding skater of compulsory figures but not a strong free skater won two world ladies' titles and an Olympic gold medal. Her chief rivals were Karen Magnussen of Canada and Janet Lynn of the United States, both of whom were strong free skaters but who always placed well below Schuba in the compulsory figures. The value of the compulsory figures was lowered when the short program was implemented at the World Championships in 1973, one year after Schuba retired.[21] Seventeen years later, in 1990, the ISU discontinued compulsory figures completely, thus ending a tradition in figure skating since time immemorial.

Figure skating is a subjectively judged sport. For the compulsory events with all competitors doing the same figures or dances, clearly defined criteria, and well-trained judges, correct results can be expected, and analysis of results over many years confirm consistency and accuracy. Free skating is more subjective, but again, analysis of judges' scores and the results show the same consistency and accuracy. However, there have been examples of dishonest judging, which can, unfortunately, exist in any subjectively judged sport and is probably unavoidable. The role of the ISU is to assure competitors that they will be judged competently and fairly, and the union has consistently striven to do so. Judging handbooks have been written for each discipline, judging seminars are held regularly, and rigorous test judging is required at every level. It takes many years and much experience to become a championship judge. Those few who reach that status are well trained and competent, but that does not guarantee honesty.

Dishonesty in judging creates a difficult problem. Controversies appear throughout the history of the sport, but the ISU has dealt effectively with them, creating rules to assure that problems will not resurface in the future. An early example occurred at the World Championships held at Oslo, Norway, in 1927. In the ladies' events, five judges were on the panel, three from Norway and one each from Germany and Austria. By a split of three to two, the five-time and reigning world champion, Herma Szabo of Austria was defeated by the 14-year-old Sonja Henie of Norway. The three Norwegian judges placed Henie first in both the compulsory figures and the free skating. The German and Austrian judges did likewise for Szabo. In response, the ISU adopted a rule limiting to one the number of judges on a panel from any country. A particularly disturbing controversy resulted from Austrian officials who for several years manipulated outcomes in favor of their skaters by signaling their judge to give specific marks. The scheme became known as the "calculation office." In response, the ISU suspended two Austrian officials for life, one of them being the chair of the figure skating technical committee. Serious judging problems surfaced frequently during the Cold War era when bloc judging became prevalent, especially among the Eastern bloc countries. Many judges were suspended during the 1960s and 1970s, and in 1977, the ISU took the unprecedented step of banning all Soviet judges for the entire 1978 season.

Bloc judging was at the root of figure skating's most recent judging scandal, which occurred a quarter century later, in 2002, in the pairs competition at the Salt Lake City Olympic Winter Games. The short program provided no surprises. Elena Berezhnaya and Anton Sikharulidze of Russia placed first with Jamie Salé and David Pelletier of Canada second. In the free skating, by a five to four split of the judges, the Russians defeated the Canadians. Both pairs skated well, although Sikharludize stepped out in the side-by-side double Axel Paulsen jumps. Judges from East European countries placed the Russians first, whereas most from Western countries placed the Canadians first. The swing judge, who was from France, stated later that day that she had been "pressured" by the French federation to favor the Russians, presumably in exchange for a similar advantage for the French ice dancers, Marina Anissina and Gwendal Peizerat. The egregious conduct of the French judge, Marie-Reine Le Gougne, to which she readily admitted, elicited an instantaneous outcry from the media and a challenge filed by the Canadian Federation. A result of the uproar was the awarding of duplicate gold medals to the

Canadians, in effect declaring a tie. Precedence for the awarding of duplicate medals existed in other sports, but no such precedent existed in figure skating.

As in the case of previous controversies, it was prudent for the ISU to reexamine judging and the judging system. Because referees and judges cannot speak publicly, Ottavio Cinquanta, president of the ISU, became the official spokesman. He began promoting immediately a major change in figure skating's judging system, specifically the replacement of the 6.0 mark and ordinal placement system with a point-earning system in which numerical values would be assigned to each skating element based on its degree of difficulty. The age-old ordinal placement system, however, was unique to figure skating and deeply entrenched. It was a tradition understood and appreciated by all in the field—skaters, judges, and officials—and perhaps of more importance, by the sport's many fans. Clearly, such a radical change would be a hard sell to those constituents.

At the 2002 congress, two major judging changes were discussed, one of them being the point-earning system promoted by Cinquanta, the other the employment of a large panel of judges with scores from a prescribed number of them, selected randomly, counting and with the judges who assigned the scores being anonymous. This random selecting of judges was tested for the first time at Skate America the following October. Scores of nine judges, selected from a panel of 14, were posted, but no one knew which judges assigned them. The ordinal placement system was retained. Few criticisms stemmed from the random selection of judges, but having them remain anonymous caused an uproar in the skating community, especially among fans. At the World Championships held in Washington, D.C., in March 2003, a grassroots movement, "Skate Fair," protested the anonymity of judges scores by wearing pins and placing posters in multiple languages throughout the arena. In addition, a group of well-known former skaters and officials selected that occasion to announce the formation of an organization called the World Skating Federation, which they proposed would take over figure skating from the ISU.

The ISU Council at its March 2003 meeting voted to test the point-earning system at the Grand Prix events during the fall and to retain the randomly selected judging panel with anonymity, thus ignoring the primary criticism of the system tested in the 2003 season. Ultimately, the International Judging System (IJS) was approved and adopted at the 2004 congress. The anonymity of judges was retained although Alexander Lakernik, chair of the ISU figure skating technical committee and one of the developers of the system, noted that "anonymity is not an essential part of the system." It is, he said, "a separate principle either accepted or not."[22] The IJS is now employed for all ISU competitions. Although it is not a requirement at the national level, most major skating countries have adopted it.

Like gymnastics in the Olympic Summer Games, figure skating in the Olympic Winter Games is the most popular sport for television audiences. Figure skating is a spectator's sport that can appeal to men and women of all ages. Its popularity dates back to amateur shows called carnivals beginning in the 19th century and to lavish professional shows in the mid-20th century. With the advent of competitive skating and its inclusion as an Olympic sport, champions and high-ranking competitors at major competitions eventually had the opportunity to skate professionally and become stars in the large touring shows. Sonja Henie anchored the Hollywood Ice Review beginning in 1937, but she was also featured in nine successful films released by Twentieth Century Fox, taking figure skating to an even larger audience and further bolstering its popularity.

After the war, events began to be televised, and in 1962, ABC's Wide World of Sports began broadcasting the World Championships. Audiences enthusiastically watched rising stars such as Peggy Fleming and the Protopopovs in the 1960s, John Curry, Pakhomova and Gorshkov, and Dorothy Hamill in the 1970s, and Scott Hamilton and Torvill and Dean in the 1980s, some of the most artistic and popular skaters in the history of the sport, all of whom were world and Olympic champions. An increasingly large audience which had previously known little about the sport became fans who watched their favorite skaters progress through their eligible careers and then become professional skaters, anchoring major shows.

For athletes in all sports, becoming an Olympian is the ultimate goal, and it is in this light that we must try to understand the Kerrigan-Harding debacle of 1994. What would lead an athlete to criminal activity? At the United States Championships three years earlier in 1991, Tonya Harding landed a triple Axel Paulsen jump, the first by an American lady, defeating Kristi Yamaguchi and Nancy Kerrigan and collecting her only U.S. title.[23] At the World Championships in Munich, the American women—Yamaguchi, Harding, and Kerrigan—swept the medals, the only time that has happened in ladies competition.[24] In 1992, Harding faltered at the National Championships, placing third behind Yamaguchi and Kerrigan but still earning a place on both the world and Olympic teams. She placed fourth and sixth respectively. Yamaguchi had already retired when Harding skated poorly at the 1993 National Championships and slipped to fourth behind Kerrigan, Lisa Ervin, and Tonia Kwiatkowski, thus not earning a place on the world team.

Harding, although an inconsistent competitor, remained a viable candidate for another world medal and possibly an Olympic medal. American fans were anticipating an exciting continuation of the rivalry between their two skaters who offered greatly contrasting styles, Harding's athleticism and Kerrigan's elegance. By 1994, Kerrigan had become America's latest "ice princess." Her femininity, popularity, and competitive success weighed on Harding as she entered the new season. Determined not to be excluded again, she became involved in a sinister plot, one intended to ensure her position on the world and Olympic teams. At the National Championships, following a practice session, a man approached Kerrigan, who had just exited the ice, and struck her just above the landing knee with a metal baton, doing serious but not permanent damage. Initial speculation included the possibility that it was the work of a deranged fan, but attention soon turned to Harding, a skater with much raw talent but an inconsistent and faltering record.

The attack was a scheme devised by Harding's husband Jeff Gillooly and three of his friends including Shane Stant, the actual attacker. Gillooly implicated Harding. She was not incarcerated but ultimately performed 400 hours of public service, paid fines totaling $160,000, and was placed on probation. Most devastating was the end of her eligible skating career. After the games, the United States Figure Skating Association banned Harding for life and stripped her of the 1994 national title, which she had won in Kerrigan's absence.

The Lillehammer Games were held before the investigation was completed. Although mounting evidence cast a shadow over Harding's innocence, she had not yet been found guilty of criminal wrong doing, and the United States Olympic Committee allowed her to compete. The media attention was overwhelming. Kerrigan and Harding shared the same practice ice, adding to the drama. In the short program, Kerrigan skated brilliantly and won; Harding placed a dismal 10th. In the free skating, Kerrigan placed second, Harding seventh. Kerrigan won the Olympic silver medal behind Oksana Baiul of Ukraine. Harding placed eighth. Neither Kerrigan nor Harding proceeded to the World Championships.

Figure skating, already a popular sport, was thrust into the limelight at the games owing to the Kerrigan-Harding incident, and for the next several years it enjoyed unprecedented popularity. The public could not get enough figure skating. Virtually every competition was broadcast; new professional and pro-am competitions were created; and numerous shows were presented. Eligible skaters were turning professional immediately after winning titles to tap into the many opportunities available. But such heightened popularity could not be sustained, and by century's end, television ratings had declined substantially. Except for major competitions, most televised events disappeared. The bubble had burst. "For us and for everybody, the sport just got saturated," remarked Rob Correa, a senior vice president for CBS sports.[25]

Figure skaters and their fans have had to adjust to these dramatic changes as they entered the 21st century. The decreasing number of competitions being broadcast and the fewer live shows being presented have reduced the opportunity to see skating. Most of the skaters, eligible and ineligible, who were so popular during the late 1990s have retired or are appearing much less frequently. Among those skating at the turn of the century were some of the most artistic, including Michelle Kwan and Alexei Yagudin. More recent skaters have found it difficult to reach that level of artistry and popularity, possibly because they have had fewer opportunities to perform. The most popular touring shows, Stars on Ice and Champions on Ice, continued but experienced gradually dwindling audiences. Champions on Ice, dating back to 1969, was continually infused with new world and Olympic champions, but the show ceased in 2008 with the retirement of Tom Collins, its owner and producer.

The new judging system adopted in 2004 remains a mystery to many fans, partially a result of the high numerical values of the scores, which are hard to remember or understand. Fans found it easier to relate to the perfect 6.0, which represented skating perfection and served as every skater's goal. One is reminded of Tai Babilonia's statement after she and Randy Gardner had just won their world pair title in 1979. The single 6.0 awarded seemed almost more important as is reflected in her comment: "Our first 6.0. That was my dream."[26] But skating is changing, and it has new stars. Fans cannot be anything other than proud when a young skater like Yu Na Kim of Korea becomes a small country's first world champion and does so as an artist, skating musically and within the new judging system.

It is appropriate to end this introduction with an attempt to address and perhaps answer the opening question. Is figure skating a sport or an art? Any sport is an art in the sense of the dictionary definition, "a skill acquired by experience," but most modern skaters and writers use the term "art" in the sense of artistry, and that definition includes the requirement of "showing imaginative skill in execution." This takes figure skating out of the realm of being simply athletic. Several early books, British and American, are entitled *The Art of Skating*, with the emphasis placed specifically on technique. The French call the sport "patinage artistique" (artistic skating) and as early as Garcin's book of 1813, the emphasis was clearly placed on artistry like that associated with ballet. Thus, the question of art or sport is one that has been addressed indirectly for at least 200 years. George Meagher, the first important Canadian writer on the sport, entitled his book of 1913 *A Guide to Artistic Skating*. It too deals primarily with skating technique but with concern about appearance, especially arm position. Its title reflects changing ideas and serves as a precursor of skating in the post–World War I era, a period of increasing emphasis on artistry and interpretation of the music.

Throughout the 19th century skating was tied to the three basic styles, but with the formation of the ISU, the adoption of the international style, and a growing emphasis on free skating, the question of art or artistry became increasingly relevant. To do compulsory figures perfectly was an art, but when skaters began connecting multiple figures with dance steps to create free skating programs, set them to music, and attempted to interpret the music, they were skating artistically. Free skating and short programs were judged with separate scores which counted equally, one for technique, the other for artistry. Under the IJS, the component scores, included specifically to judge artistry, represent just 29 percent of the score.[27] We have to some degree returned to the 19th-century emphasis in which the art of completing individual elements perfectly, that is, athletic aspects hold the larger numerical value. Although the ratio has changed, skating remains a balance of sport and art—technique and artistry—and that defines its uniqueness.

Finally, it is noteworthy that when one thinks about great skaters of the past, they are invariably those remembered for their artistry. Prior to World War II, they include Gillis Grafström and Sonja Henie; after the war, Dick Button and Tenley Albright. In the latter 1960s, following the plane crash, a new artistry became prevalent. Among the most revered skaters from that era are Peggy Fleming and the Protopopovs. In the 1970s, Janet Lynn, John Curry, and ice dancers Pakhomova and Gorshkov carried on that tradition. In the 1980s, Scott Hamilton, Katarina Witt, and pair skaters Gordeeva and Grinkov come to mind; and in the 1990s, it was Lu Chen, the ever popular Michelle Kwan, and ice dancers Usova and Zhulin. Entering the 21st century, naming those who will be most remembered is more difficult, possibly because we are too close to them historically but also owing to less television coverage and the fact that fewer skaters become repeat champions or win multiple consecutive titles. The current emphasis on designing programs with technically difficult elements for the purpose of gaining points under the IJS makes choreography more difficult to design and skating with the music, rather than during the music, more difficult to accomplish. One sees today an increasing number of falls, which are disruptive to the choreography and intended artistry in the programs. Even in ice dancing and synchronized skating, falls are more prevalent than in the past. Technically difficult programs, when skated well, are exciting, but the probability of getting through them without falls has diminished significantly from the past.

NOTES

1. Christine Brennan, *Inside Edge* (New York: Scribner, 1996), 17.
2. *Merriam Webster's Collegiate Dictionary*, 10th ed. (Springfield, Mass.: Merriam-Webster, 1993).

3. The term "figure skating" is unique to the English language.

4. William Fitz Stephen, *Norman London* (New York: Ithica Press, 1990), 58–59.

5. The name Gilets Rouge (red vests) reflects the clothing worn: neatly fitting waistcoats, tight fitting leotards, and hats, either mortarboards or berets. For a color picture see James Hines, *Figure Skating: A History* (Champaign: University of Illinois Press, 2005), 64.

6. Cyclos, *The Art of Skating; with Plain Directions for the Acquirement of the Most Difficult and Elegant Moves* (Glasgow: Thomas Murray & Son, 1852), 49.

7. George Anderson, *The Art of Skating: Containing Many Figures Never Previously Described* (London: Horace Cox, 1868), 40.

8. H. E. Vandervell and T. Maxwell Witham, *A System of Figure Skating, Being the Theory and Practice of the Art as Developed in England, with a Glance at Its Origin and History* (London: Macmillan and Co., 1869), 31.

9. The international style, which evolved in Vienna after Jackson Haines's two stays there, was originally called the Viennese style.

10. The Internationale Eislauf-Verein became the ISU in 1946 when English replaced German as the official language of the union. To avoid confusion, ISU is used exclusively in this book.

11. Robert Jones, *A Treatise on Skating* (London: np. 1772), xi.

12. Vandervell and Witham, 231–32.

13. The competitions for ladies and for pairs beginning in 1906 and 1908, respectively, were called "championships of the ISU." The term "world" was not attached to them until 1924 when the titles were renamed "Lady World Champion," and "World Pair Champions." The term "World Champion" was reserved for men as it still is today.

14. Irving Brokaw, *The Art of Skating* (New York: Charles Schribner's, 1910), 122–29. Note: Brokaw published four books between 1910 and 1926 all under the same title, *The Art of Skating*. The Johnsons' article is printed only in the 1910 book.

15. Through 2010, the Soviet Union and Russia have 24 Olympic and 72 world titles. The United States is second with 14 Olympic and 51 world titles.

16. The Soviets began sending skaters to the European Championships two years earlier, in 1956.

17. The British ice dancers Jayne Torvill and Christopher Dean won in 1984.

18. Skate America started in 1981 as a natural progression following the Flaming Leaves Competition, which was held for just one year in 1979 as a test competition for the 1980 Olympic Winter Games.

19. Although this was the 100th holding of the World Championships, only the men have competed 100 times. For the ladies who first competed in 1906 it was the 90th time. For the pairs who first competed in 1908, it was the 88th. For the synchronized skating teams, which first competed in 2000, it was the 11th. The synchronized championship in 2010 was held in Colorado Springs, Colorado.

20. The Chamonix Games were part of the eighth Olympiad held in Paris that year, but two years later, the International Olympic Committee officially designated them as the first Olympic Winter Games.

21. The short program was added at the European Championships one year later, 1974, and at the Olympic Winter Games in 1976.

22. Lois Elfman, "To the Point: The Skating World Tries Out a New Judging System," *International Figure Skating* 10 (March–April 2004): 44.

23. Each skater has one national ladies title, Harding in 1991, Yamaguchi in 1992, and Kerrigan in 1993.

24. There have been sweeps of the medals in the other disciplines: in the men's competitions, three times by the Austrians and three times by the Americans; in the pairs, twice by the Soviets; and in ice dancing, three times by the British and twice by the Russians.

25. Mark A. Lund, with Lois Elfman and Rebecca Patrick, *Frozen Assets: The New Order of Figure Skating* (Worcester, Mass: Ashton International Media, Inc., 2002), 116.

26. Quoted from the videocasette *Magic Memories on Ice*. New York: CBS/FOX Video Sports, 1990.

27. Program component scores are awarded for skating skills, transitions/linking footwork and movement, performance/execution, composition/choreography, and interpretation. In the compulsory dance an additional component, timing, is included.

ABBOTT, JEREMY (1985–) (USA). Jeremy Abbott became the **United States** junior champion in 2005. He did not compete in 2006. As a senior he placed fourth for two years before winning the national title in 2009 and 2010. He was the bronze medalist at the **Four Continents Championships** in 2007, but two further efforts resulted in fifth-place finishes. He qualified for and won the **Grand Prix Finals** in 2009. Sent to the **World Championships** three times, beginning in 2008, he placed 11th twice before placing fifth in 2010. Abbott's one Olympic effort in 2010 resulted in a ninth-place finish.

ADULT SKATING. Adult skating is one of the newest and fastest growing areas of competitive figure skating. The first Adult Championships in the **United States** were held in 1995. The first international competition, the Mountain Cup International, was held in Vilard de Lans, **France**, in 1999. Events are held for former skaters as well as for those who take up skating as adults and progress to a competitive level.

AGOSTO, BENJAMIN. *See* BELBIN, TANITH AND AGOSTO, BENJAMIN.

AHRENS, JANETTE (1923–) (USA). Janette Ahrens competed in three disciplines: **pair skating**, **fours**, and singles. She won her first two senior medals, both silver, with her pairs partner Robert Uppgren at the **United States** Championships in 1942 and 1943. Uppgren then retired, but Ahrens continued with a new partner, Arthur Preusch, and in 1944 won a third consecutive silver medal. In the uniquely North American discipline of fours skating, Ahrens, Mary Louise Premer, Robert Uppgren, and Lyman Wakefield Jr., known as the "St. Paul Four," were the national champions in 1940 and 1941, and in 1941 became the first four in the history of the discipline to defeat the Canadians at the **North American Championships**. As a singles skater, Ahrens placed second behind **Gretchen Merrill** three times at the United States Championships, 1945–1947. At the North American Championships, she won a bronze medal in 1946 and a silver medal in 1947. When the **World Championships** were resumed in 1947, Ahrens entered and placed sixth. Upon turning professional, she taught skating.

ALBRIGHT, TENLEY EMMA (1935–) (USA). Tenley Albright was the first woman from the **United States** to win either a world or Olympic title. In 1946, Albright contracted a mild case of nonparalytic poliomyelitis. Skating provided much needed physical therapy. Under the guidance of her coaches **Willie Frick** and later **Maribel Vinson**, Albright won the novice title at age 13 and the junior title at age 14. Four months before winning her first senior national title in 1952, she won the silver medal at the **Olympic Winter Games** in Oslo, **Norway**. Her career totals include five national titles, 1952–1956, consecutive North American titles in 1953 and 1955, world titles in 1953 and 1955, and the Olympic title at Cortina, **Italy**, in 1956. While competing, Albright completed a premed program at Radcliffe College and proceeded to Harvard Medical School. For many years she was a practicing surgeon in Boston. She continued to support her sport, primarily in the area of sports medicine, and served as secretary of the United States Olympic Committee. Albright was elected to the **World Figure Skating Hall of Fame** in 1976.

ALLEN, SCOTT ETHAN (1946–) (USA). Scott Allen began competing at the senior level one year after the **plane crash** in 1961 which took the lives of the entire **United States** world team. He was the national champion in 1964 and 1966. Competing at the **World Championships** for seven consecutive years, 1962–1968, he garnered only one medal, silver in 1965. A year earlier, he won the bronze medal at the Innsbruck **Olympic Winter Games**.

ALLINGHAM, MILDRED. *See* RICHARDSON, THOMAS DOW.

ALTWEGG, JEANNETTE ELEANOR (1930–) (GBR). Jeannette Altwegg of **Great Britain** was an all-round athlete. In 1946, she placed second at Wimbledon in the junior finals in tennis and that same year became the British junior champion in figure skating. Afterward, she devoted her effort totally to figure skating, becoming one of the sport's finest practitioners of **compulsory figures**. Her competitive record includes four national titles. Placements of fourth at the **European Championships** and fifth at the **World Championships** in 1947 and 1948 were preludes to successive bronze, silver, and gold medals at those competitions. Her two Olympic bids resulted in as many medals, bronze in 1948 and gold in 1952. Retiring from skating rather than turning professional, Altwegg undertook humanitarian work at the Petalozzi Village in Trogan, **Switzerland**. She was elected to the **World**

Figure Skating Hall of Fame in 1993. On the recommendation of Winston Churchill, she was awarded the highest honor given to a figure skater in England, Commander of the Order of the British Empire (CBE).

AMERICAN SKATERS GUILD. *See* PROFESSIONAL SKATERS ASSOCIATION.

AMERICAN STYLE. Prior to the establishment of the **International Skating Union** (ISU) in 1892, there were three prevalent styles of skating: **English style**, American style, and **international style**. The ISU adopted the international style. The American style disappeared completely by World War I; the English style continued into the 21st century. The English and international styles can be described by the body position employed for their figures. A generally rigid body style was employed by the British in combined skating, the favored discipline in the English style. A more relaxed body style, associated with the international style included greater use of the arms. It was employed by the Viennese and others on the continent where there was strong interest in dancing on ice and various artistic figures. The American style tended to be an amalgamation of the two. The Americans enjoyed combined skating and they danced on ice but special figures, which fascinated them, were not tied to specific body positions. **Special figures**, especially difficult open one-foot designs such as letters and numbers were an important aspect of their skating, and those body positions were not part of that discipline. **Grapevines**, a uniquely North American innovation, required the skater to keep both feet on the ice throughout the duration of the figure.

ANDERSON, BONNIE. *See* DORE, DAVID M.

ANDERSON, GEORGE. George Anderson, the second major British writer on figure skating, was the president of the Glasgow, Scotland, skating club for many years. Anderson's valuable book *The Art of Skating*, dating from 1852, was published under the pen name Cyclos. Nearly half of the book is devoted to the state of skating in mid-century **England** and Scotland and its place in that society. A second edition was published under Anderson's own name and appeared in 1868 without the historical section.

ANDO, MIKI (1987–) (JPN). Miki Ando, the Japanese junior ladies' champion in 2003, became the ladies world junior champion in 2004. She won national titles as a senior for two consecutive years, 2004–2005. Competing at the **Four Continents Championships** just once, in 2008 she claimed the bronze medal. Two trips to the **Grand Prix Finals**, in 2007 and 2009, resulted in fifth- and sixth-place finishes. Ando competed at five **World Championships**, winning the title on her third try in 2007. She also won a bronze medal in 2009. In two Olympic efforts, she placed 15th in 2006 and fifth in 2010. Ando is the only lady who has landed a quadruple jump in competition, a **Salchow jump** at the Junior Grand Prix Finals in 2002. *See also* JAPAN.

ANISSINA, MARINA (1975–) (URS/FRA). Marina Anissina was twice the world junior ice dancing champion from **Russia** with **Ilia Averbukh** before moving to **France** and partnering with Gwendal Peizerat (1972–). Anissina and Peizerat's medal count at the **European Championships** includes bronze medals in 1998, silver medals in 1999 and 2001, and gold medals in 2000 and 2002. At the **World Championships** the count includes silver medals in 1998, 1999, and 2001 and gold medals in 2000. They won gold medals also at the **Grand Prix Finals** in 2000. Their Olympic results include bronze medals in 1998 and gold medals in 2002. Anissina and Peizerat are the only ice dancers from France who have won an Olympic title. They retired from eligible skating after the Salt Lake City **Olympic Winter Games**.

ARAKAWA, SHIZUKA (1981–) (JPN). In 2006 Shizuka Arakawa became the first Japanese figure skater to win an Olympic gold medal, defeating **Sasha Cohen** of the **United States** and **Irina Slutskaya** of **Russia**. It was her only Olympic effort. Two years earlier, in 2004, she won the world title by defeating Cohen and **Michelle Kwan** of the United States. It was her only world medal. Both titles were upsets in which Arakawa skated clean programs. In Grand Prix events, she won the gold medal at NHK Trophy in 2005 and the silver medal at the **Grand Prix Finals** that season. Arakawa won the Japanese junior title for three consecutive years but never the senior title. She is remembered for her artistry but could also complete triple-triple combination jumps. Her signature move was a layback **Ina Bauer**. Arakawa turned professional after the 2006 Olympics. She has since appeared in shows and worked as a television commentator. Arakawa undertook university studies while competing and graduated in 2004, the year of her world title.

ARMITAGE, PAUL. *See SKATING* MAGAZINE; UNITED STATES OF AMERICA.

ARTIFICIAL ICE. Other than the developments of the bladed skate in the 14th century and the fastening of boots permanently to the skates in the 19th century, nothing has had a greater effect on figure skating than the development of artificial ice. It allowed indoor year-round skating anywhere in the world. No longer was it necessary to cancel competitive events for lack of ice. The 1902 **World Championship** in London was the first to be held on artificial ice. That same year the **European Championship** scheduled for Amsterdam was canceled for lack of ice. Artificial ice allows skaters to include elements in their programs that would be difficult, sometimes impossible, to do on less-perfect outdoor ice while defying elements such as wind, rain, and snow. The World Championships in 1967 at Vienna were the last at which all events other than the **compulsory figures** were held outside. A rule was adopted later that year requiring covered but not enclosed rinks. Enclosed indoor venues were not a requirement for all events until 1980 and for practice sessions until 1984. The **Olympic Winter Games** were last held outdoors in 1956 at Cortina, Italy, and last held in a covered but not enclosed rink at Squaw Valley, California, in 1960.

Early attempts at making artificial ice occurred in the 1870s in **England** and the **United States**. The first rink of importance was constructed in 1876 by John Gamgee in Chelsea on the north bank of the Thames River in London. It was small, measuring 24 by 40 feet. By the end of the century, many major cities throughout Europe and North America boasted rinks with artificial ice.

ASADA, MAO (1990–) (JPN). Mao Asada became the Japanese ladies junior champion in 2005. As a senior, she won a silver medal in 2006 and then claimed national titles through 2010. She won titles at the **Grand Prix Finals** in 2009, the **Four Continents Championships** in 2008, and the **World Championships** in 2008 and 2010. Her one Olympic bid, in 2010, resulted in a silver medal behind **Yu Na Kim** of **Korea**. During the six years from 2005 through 2010, Asada entered 23 competitions, national and international, and medaled in 22 of them, collecting one bronze, seven silver, and 14 gold medals. She is one of a relatively small number of ladies who has landed a triple **Axel Paulsen jump** in competition. *See also* JAPAN.

ATWOOD, DONNA (1923–2010) (USA). Donna Atwood was the national pair champion with **Eugene Turner** in 1941 and was the junior ladies' champion as well. Following cancellation of the **World Championships** for the second time owing to World War II, she turned professional and joined **Ice Capades**, partnering first with Jimmy Lawrence and then for nearly two decades with Bobby Specht, the 1942 U.S. men's champion. Atwood and Specht anchored many of the company's musical numbers including *Anthony and Cleopatra*, *Snow White*, *The Student Prince*, *Cinderella*, and *An American in Paris*. She remained with the company until it was sold to Metromedia in 1963. In 1949, Atwood married the president of Ice Capades, **John Harris**.

AUSTRALIA. Figure skating in Australia is regulated by the National Ice Skating Association of Australia, which was founded in 1931. It includes seven geographically separate associations, the oldest of which is the Victorian Ice Skating Association, founded in 1911. Others include the New South Wales Ice Skating Association, the Ice Skating Association of Queensland, the South Australian Ice Skating Association, the Western Ice Skating Association, the Australian Capital Territory Ice Skating Association, and the Tasmanian Ice Skating Association. Australian skaters first competed at the **World Championships** in 1947. Participation was sporadic for another 25 years. They have competed every year since 1972 but have not yet produced medal winners. World Championships have not been held in Australia, although the **World Junior Figure Skating Championships** have twice been held in Brisbane.

AUSTRIA. Austria was one of six countries represented in Scheveningen, **Netherlands**, in 1892 at the inaugural congress of the **International Skating Union** (ISU). The others were **Great Britain**, **Germany**, **Hungary**, **Sweden**, and Netherlands. Austria has a long tradition in figure skating, especially in Vienna, and is home to one of the world's oldest and most active skating clubs. The Wiener Eislaufverein (**Vienna Skating Club**) was formed in 1867. **Jackson Haines**, who lived there twice for short periods, was instrumental in the establishment of the club and the development of the Viennese style. One of the most important 19th-century books on figure skating, *Spuren auf dem Eise* (Tracings on the Ice), was written by three members of the club. At the first **World Championship** in 1896, **Gustav Hügel** of Austria won the silver medal and then became a three-time world champion. Austrian men dominated the sport during the years between World War I and II. **Fritz Kachler**, **Willy Böckl**, and **Karl Schäfer** collectively won 14 of 18 world titles. For the ladies, **Herma Szabo** won five consecutive titles, 1922–1926. During the 10-year reign of **Norway**'s unbeatable **Sonja Henie**, beginning in 1927, four talented Austrian ladies, **Fritzi Burger**, **Melitta Brunner**, **Hilde Holovsky**, and **Liselotte Landbeck**, claimed 11 of the 20 bronze and silver medals awarded. Burger was twice an Olympic silver medalist as well. Austrian pair skaters claimed 20 medals. Gold medals were won by **Helene Engelmann** and Alfred Berger in 1922 and 1924, Herma Szabo and **Ludwig Wrede** in 1925 and 1927, and **Lily Scholz and Otto Kaiser** in 1929. Since World War II, Austria has produced fewer elite skaters but some have been outstanding, including World and Olympic champion **Beatrix Schuba**, who is remembered especially for her **compulsory figures**, three-time World champion **Emmerich Danzer**, World and Olympic champion **Manfred Schnelldorfer**, and World and Olympic pair champions **Elisabeth Schwarz and**

Kurt Oppelt. Vienna has been the site for 11 World Championships, sometimes for just one discipline. Innsbruck has twice hosted the **Olympic Winter Games**, 1964 and 1976. *See also* BIETAK, WILHELM; BOHATSCH, MAX; EIGEL, HANNA; ENGELMANN, EDUARD, JR.; HEITZER, REGINA; HERZ, ERNST; HORNUNG, ILSE; KASPAR, FELIX; KRISTOFICS-BINDER, CLAUDIA; KUTSCHERA, HANS; LABIN, ERNST; PAPEZ, IDI AND ZWACK, KARL; PAUSIN, ILSE AND ERICH; PAWLIK, EVA; PUTZINGER, EMMY; RADA, EDI; REICHMANN, GISELA; SCHOLDAN, EDI; SCHWARZ, WOLFGANG; SEIBT, HELMUT; STENUF, HEDY; WALTER, HANNA; WENDL, INGRID; WREDE, LUDWIG.

AVERBUKH, ILIA. *See* LOBACHEVA, IRINA AND AVERBUKH, ILIA.

AXEL PAULSEN JUMP. The **Axel Paulsen** jump, typically called the Axel jump, was first performed as a **special figure** at the **Great International Skating Tournament** held by the **Vienna Skating Club** in 1882. Axel Paulsen of **Norway** placed third. **Charlotte Oelschlagel**, a popular show skater following World War I, is reportedly the first lady to complete the jump. **Dick Button** of the **United States** doubled the jump in 1948 at the **Olympic Winter Games**. Vern Taylor of **Canada** added an additional revolution at the 1978 **World Championships**, landing the first triple Axel. **Midori Ito** of **Japan** became the first lady to complete a triple Axel in competition at the World Championships in 1989.

The Axel Paulsen jump has a takeoff from a forward outside **edge** with a landing on a backward outside edge on the opposite foot after one and one-half revolutions. Variations include the one-foot Axel and the inside Axel. The one-foot Axel has the same takeoff as the regular Axel, but the landing is on an inside backward edge on the takeoff foot. It was first done by **Cecilia Colledge** of **Great Britain**. The inside Axel has a takeoff from a forward inside edge with a landing on the same foot on a back outside edge as in a regular Axel. It was first done by **Willy Böckl** of **Austria** and was sometimes called the Böckl jump. A variation popular prior to the double Axel becoming commonplace, one rarely seen today, is the delayed Axel, the exemplar of whom was **Felix Kaspar** of Austria. It is identical to the regular Axel, but there is an appearance that the rotation stops momentarily while the skater is in the air. *See also* JUMPS.

B

BABILONIA, TAI REINA (1959–) AND GARDNER, RANDY (1957–) (USA). Tai Babilonia and Randy Gardner were paired together by **Mabel Fairbanks** in 1967. Neither of them ever had another partner. By the 1971 season, their probable success internationally was foreseen, and they began training with coach **John Nicks**. At their first **United States** Championships as juniors in 1973, they placed first. As seniors, their record includes second place twice, 1974 and 1975, followed by five consecutive titles from 1976 to 1980. At the **World Championships** beginning in 1974, they placed 10th twice, fifth once, and third twice before winning the title in 1979. At the **Olympic Winter Games** in 1976 they were fifth. Disappointment for them and their American fans came at the Lake Placid Winter Games of 1980. The previous year they had won the world title when **Irina Rodnina** and Alexandr Zaitsev, the six-time and reigning world champions, did not compete owing to the birth of Rodnina's child. Babilonia and Gardner's fans wondered whether the talented pair could defeat figure skating's most successful pair, but an earlier injury suffered by Gardner recurred at a practice session. They had to withdraw, and that marked the end of their eligible career. As professionals, Babilonia and Gardner toured with **Ice Capades** for four years and with **Champions on Ice** for two years. They skated in many shows, entered professional competitions, and became the **World Professional Champions** in 1985.

BACK FLIP. The back flip is a backward somersault popular in show skating. From a backward one-foot takeoff with a toe pick assist, the skater rotates upward and over landing on both feet. It had been done by show skaters since the 1930s when, at the **World Championships** in 1976, Terry Kubicka (1956–) of the **United States** included one in his **free skating** program. At its next congress, the **International Skating Union** banned back flips from competition as being dangerous and having no aesthetic value. More recently it has been associated with several popular professional skaters, especially **Scott Hamilton**, **Kurt Browning**, and **Surya Bonaly**. Bonaly lands the back flip on one foot, the only skater to do so.

BACON, FRANK. *See* BROWNE, GEORGE HENRY.

BADGER, SHERWIN CAMPBELL (1900–1972) (USA). Sherwin Badger was the junior men's champion at the **International Skating Union of America** championships in 1918. Competing also in pairs, he won silver medals with Clara Frothingham that year and then with Edith Ratch two years later. In 1920 he entered the senior men's competitions, and by 1924 had won five consecutive gold medals, which beginning in 1922 were in competitions of the newly established **United States Figure Skating Association** (USFSA). Badger returned to **pair skating** in 1928, and with **Beatrix Loughran** won three consecutive national titles, 1931–1933. Loughran and Badger competed at three **World Championships**, placing fifth in 1928 and winning bronze medals in 1930 and 1932. At the **Olympic Winter Games**, they placed fourth in 1928 and won silver medals in 1932. Badger was twice the president of USFSA, 1930–1932 and 1934–1935, and is the only president who has been a national champion at the same time. He was also a world judge. *See also* UNITED STATES.

BAESS, SABINE (1961–) AND THIERBACH, TASSILO (1956–) (GDR). From 1965 until the fall of the iron curtain, Soviet skaters dominated **pair skating**. They were defeated just three times in world competition, once each by skaters from the **United States**, **Canada**, and the **German Democratic Republic**. Sabine Baess and Tassilo Thierbach first entered the **European Championships** in 1977 and the **World Championships** in 1978. They competed every year through 1984 missing only the European Championships in 1981. Their first medals were bronze at the European and World Championships in 1979. They won gold medals at both championships in 1982 defeating the Soviets. Their Olympic results were fifth in 1980 and fourth in 1984.

BAIER, ERNST (1905–2001) (GER). Ernst Baier began his career as a singles skater, first appearing at the **European Championships** in 1929 and placing seventh. A year later he placed fifth, and three silver medals followed. In four appearances at the **World Championships**, 1931–1934, he collected two bronze and two silver medals. His two Olympic efforts resulted in fifth place in 1932 and a silver medal in 1936. Although he was a strong singles skater, Baier never received a gold medal. Those were the years in which **Karl Schäfer** of **Austria** won eight consecutive European titles, seven consecutive world titles, and Olympic titles in 1932 and 1936. It was in pairs with his only partner, Maxi Herber (1920–2006), who later became his wife, that Baier excelled. Herber was fifteen years younger than Baier. She too competed in singles, three times at the European Championships beginning in 1935, placing as high as fourth, and once at the World Championships, 1934, placing seventh. In Herber and Baier's first outing as a pair, the World Championships of 1934, they won the bronze medals. Owing to an injury, they did not compete in 1935, but returning in 1936, they won gold medals and were unbeatable for the remainder of the prewar period, claiming four consecutive world titles plus Olympic gold in 1936. Herber and Baier pushed the envelope of **pair skating** both athletically and artistically. They were elected to the **World Figure Skating Hall of Fame** in 1979. *See also* GERMANY.

BAINBRIDGE, WALTER H., JR. *See* WARING, LOIS AND BAINBRIDGE, WALTER H., JR.

BAIUL, OKSANA (1977–) (UKR). Oksana Baiul, a petite and artistic 15 year old, first appeared at the **European Championships** in 1993 and claimed the silver medal behind **Surya Bonaly** of **France**. Eight weeks later at the **World Championships,** Baiul defeated the more experienced Bonaly and won the gold medal. The 1994 Olympic year began like the previous one with Baiul claiming the silver medal behind Bonaly at the European Championships. At the **Olympic Winter Games**, Baiul won the gold medal. Retiring immediately, she closed one of the shortest competitive careers in the history of figure skating. It was just 13 months from her first European appearance to her Olympic title. Moving to the **United States** she entered professional competitions and toured with **Champions on Ice**. *See also* UKRAINE.

BAKER, RONALD S. *See* HOGG, GLADYS MARGARET.

BAKUSHEVA, NINA (1934–) AND ZHUK, STANISLAV (1935–1998) (URS). Skaters from the **Soviet Union** appeared on the international stage in 1956 for the first time since the Russian revolution. Three men and two pairs competed at the **European Championships**. Most successful were the pair skaters Lidia Guerassimova and Turii Kissele who placed eighth in their only international competition, but it marked the beginning of what was to become Soviet domination in **pair skating** a decade later. In 1957, Nina Bakusheva and Stanislav Zhuk placed sixth in their first European effort. They then married and won the Soviet Union's first international medals, silver for three years, 1958–1960, at the European Championships. Three attempts at the **World Championships** resulted in a best placement of fifth in 1960, after which they retired. The Zhuks did not compete at the **Olympic Games**.

BALÁZS, ZOLTÁN. *See* HUNGARY.

BALCK, VIKTOR G. (1844–1928) (SWE). Viktor G. Balck was **Sweden**'s representative at the meeting in 1892 called by the Dutch association for the purpose of discussing international competitions in skating. It resulted in the formation of the **International Skating Union** (ISU). Willem J. H. Mulier was elected and served as president until a **controversy** over the application of the scoring rules at the 1893 **European Championships** led to his resignation in 1895, before the end of his term. Balck succeeded Mulier and served for 30 years, 1895–1925. He was a prominent sportsman and has been called the "Father of the **Nordic Games**." During his tenure as president, strong ties existed between the ISU and the Nordic organization. Several times, **World Championship** events were held simultaneously with the Nordic Games. Balck was also a charter member of the International Olympic Committee (IOC) in 1894.

BALDWIN, JOHN, JR. *See* INOUE, RENA AND BALDWIN, JOHN, JR.

BALLET ON ICE. *See* THEATER ON ICE.

BANGS, CHAUNCEY. *See* McDOUGALL, MARION AND BANGS, CHAUNCEY.

BARAN, RIA (1922–1986), AND FALK, PAUL (1921–) (FRG). German skaters reappeared internationally in 1951 for the first time since World War II. Ria Baran and Paul Falk were one of three pairs entered in the **European Championships** that year. Their eligible career had been curtailed by the war. In 1940, as teenagers, they placed fourth at the German Championships. When national competitions were reinstated in 1947, Baran and Falk became the champions. They won the 1951 European Championships decisively and proceeded to the **World Championships** where they defeated the reigning champions **Karol and Peter Kennedy** of the **United States**. Marriage followed, and the couple remains known today in the skating world as "the Falks." As husband and wife in 1952, they won their second European and world titles and added Olympic gold to their laurels. After turning professional, the Falks skated in shows on both sides of the Atlantic Ocean. Paul continued his involvement as a prominent coach in **Germany**. The Falks were also world pair champions in roller skating. They were elected to the **World Figure Skating Hall of Fame** in 1993.

BARBER, KAREN. *See* DEWHIRST, JOAN AND SLATER, JOHN E.

BARCELLONA, GRAZIA. *See* ITALY.

BARNA, PETR (1966–) (CZE). Petr Barna did not compete internationally as a junior. First appearing at the **European Championships** at age 16 in 1983, he placed 18th. Throughout his 10-year career, Barna continually improved in the rankings while maintaining a relatively consistent balance between the **compulsory figures** and **free skating**. Although he never medaled at the **World Championships**, his best result being fourth in 1991, during his last four competitive years, 1989–1992, he medaled every year at the European Championships, one bronze, two silver, and one gold. His European title in 1992 was significant because he defeated **Viktor Petrenko,** keeping Petrenko from winning all three major international titles that year. Barna competed twice at the **Olympic Winter Games**, placing 13th in 1988 and claiming the bronze medal in 1992. *See also* CZECHOSLOVAKIA.

BATTLE OF THE BRIANS. One of the great rivalries in modern figure skating developed and climaxed at the Calgary **Olympic Winter Games** in 1988. **Brian Boitano** of the **United States** won the world title in 1986. **Brian Orser** of **Canada** won it in 1987. A preview of the Olympic showdown had occurred in the same venue, the Saddledome, four months earlier at **Skate Canada** when the two skaters debuted their Olympic long programs, both of which featured military motifs. Orser defeated Boitano by a narrow margin. Media hype for the Calgary games was augmented by the fact that Orser was not only the reigning world champion but was also competing in his own country. The pressure to become the first Canadian man to win an Olympic gold medal was daunting. The Battle of the Brians proved to be one of the greatest head-to-head matchups in the history of figure skating. Boitano placed second in the **compulsory figures**; Orser was third. Orser won the **short program**; Boitano was second. It was a virtual dead heat entering the **free skating**. Boitano skated a perfect program; Orser presented a fine program but with two minor flaws. He stepped out of a triple flip jump and doubled the planned triple Axel jump. By a five-to-four vote of the judges, Boitano won the Olympic title.

BATTLE OF THE CARMENS. The Calgary **Olympic Winter Games** will long be remembered for the **Battle of the Brians**, but there was another media-fed battle known as the Battle of the Carmens. The reigning world ladies' champion, **Katarina Witt** of the **German Democratic Republic**, and the 1996 world ladies' champion, **Debi Thomas** of the **United States**, had both selected music from Bizet's opera *Carmen* for their **free skating**. Witt won the short program, but Thomas won the **compulsory figures** and was the leader entering the free skating. Witt presented a dramatic portrayal of the seductive Carmen and received high marks, including seven 5.9s. Thomas skated last and was not at her best. She bobbled her opening combination jump and fell on a later jump. In addition, her nonliteral interpretation of Carmen lacked the dramatic impact of Witt's portrayal. Witt won the gold medal, Thomas the bronze medal behind **Elizabeth Manley** of **Canada**.

BAUER, INA (1941–) (FRG). Ina Bauer was a national champion for three years, 1957–1959. She competed internationally from 1956 to 1960 continually improving in the rankings. From 13th at the **European Championships** and 20th at the **World Championships** in 1956 she rose to fourth in both competitions in 1959. She withdrew after the **compulsory figures** at the European Championships in 1960 and did not compete at the World Championships. She never competed in the Olympics. Bauer is remembered for the dramatic free-skating move she invented that today bears her name, a variation of the **spread eagle** figure in which the two feet trace parallel lines. One leg is deeply bent at the knee while tracing a flat or a shallow forward outside edge. The body is bent backward so the other leg is on a parallel line tracing a backward inside edge. Known today as the "Ina Bauer," it is employed in many free-skating programs. As a professional, Bauer toured with the **Ice Follies**. *See also* GERMANY.

BAUGNIET, PIERRE. *See* LANNOY, MICHELINE, AND BAUGNIET, PIERRE.

BÄUMLER, HANS-JÜRGEN. *See* KILIUS, MARIKA.

BEATTY, HENRY M. "HANK" (1900–1972) (USA). Hank Beatty served figure skating continuously for 27 years beginning in 1940 as a member of the **United States Figure Skating Association** (USFSA) executive committee. From 1946 through 1949 he was the association's president. He served as a world judge and referee with assignments as referee or assistant referee at eight **World Championships**, three **North American Championships**, and the **Olympic Winter Games** in 1964. **Walter Powell**, a member of the **International Skating Union** (ISU) Council, was aboard the Sabena Airlines flight that crashed in 1961, killing the entire U.S. world team. At the ISU Congress four months later, Beatty was elected to succeed Powell, and he served effectively until his retirement in 1967.

BELBIN, TANITH (1984–) AND AGOSTO, BENJAMIN (1982–) (USA). Tanith Belbin, originally from **Canada**, and Benjamin Agosto competed in **ice dancing**. They began skating together as juniors in 1999 and won the **United States** junior title in 2000, the junior Grand Prix title in 2001, and the world junior title in 2002. As seniors, they placed second at the United States Championships for three years before winning the title for five consecutive years, 2004–2008. Competing at the **Four Continents Championships** for six years, 2002–2007, they claimed three silver and three gold medals. They placed second at the **Grand Prix Finals** in 2008. At seven consecutive **World Championships**, 2003–2009, their medal count is two bronze and two silver. They competed at the **Olympic Winter Games** in 2006 and won the silver medals. In 2010, they placed fourth.

BELGIUM. Belgium has a long history in figure skating with skating clubs dating back to 1910. The **Olympic Games** of 1920, the second to include figure skating, were held in Antwerp two years after World War I and two years before the European and **World Championships** resumed. The only Belgians to compete in 1920 were the pair of Georgette Herbos and Georges Wagemans. They placed sixth. Robert van Zeebroeck, the first Belgian to compete at the World Championships placed seventh in 1926. Surprisingly, he reappeared 12 years later, in 1938, and placed ninth. Zeebroeck is one of just three Belgian skaters, two men and one lady, who competed during the years between the world wars. Yvonne de Ligne-Geurts, whose best result in five championships was sixth in 1932, competed that year against a talented list of skaters including **Sonja Henie**, **Fritzi Burger**, **Constance Samuel**, **Maribel Vinson**, and **Vivi-Anne Hultén**. After the war, Belgium produced its most successful skaters, the pair of **Micheline Lannoy and Pierre Baugniet** who became world, European, and Olympic champions in 1948. No Belgian skater has since won any of those titles. Administratively, Marcel Nicaise held important positions in the **International Skating Union** for 10 years, 1949–1959, including vice president for figure skating for four years. He was elected as an honorary member in 1959.

BELITA. *See* JEPSON-TURNER, GLADYS LYNNE.

BELOUSOVA, LIUDMILA (1935–) AND PROTOPOPOV, OLEG (1932–) (URS). Liudmila Belousova and Oleg Protopopov, already in their 20s, began skating together in 1955. After their marriage, Liudmila continued competing using her maiden name, but the couple is usually referred to as the Protopopovs. During 15 years of competitive skating, they won the **Soviet Union**'s first world and Olympic titles in any discipline, and they changed dramatically the direction of **pair skating**, making it much more balletic. In their first year of international competition, in 1958, they placed 10th at the **European Championships** and 13th at the **World Championships**. In 1959 they advanced to fourth at the European Championships but were not sent to the World Championships. Their placements in 1960 were fourth and eighth at those competitions and ninth at the **Olympic Winter Games**. They did not compete internationally in 1961. The European Championships were held in West Berlin without Soviet participation, and the World Championships were canceled owing to the **plane crash** in **Belgium**. The years 1962 through 1964 were ones of anticipation as the Protopopovs claimed six silver medals behind **Maria and Otto Jelinek** of **Canada** and **Marika Kilius and Hans-Jürgen Bäumler** of the **Federal Republic of Germany**, but at the Innsbruck Winter Games in 1964, the Protopopovs upset Kilius and Bäumler to win the **Soviet Union**'s first Olympic title. During the next Olympic cycle, 1965–1968, the Protopopovs could not be defeated as they claimed nine gold medals in world, European, and Olympic competition. Returning for one final year in 1969, they medaled at both the European and World Championships, but that year the Soviet's most successful pair skater, **Irina Rodnina**, with her first partner **Alexei Ulanov**, claimed the first of her 11 European and 10 world titles. Then in their mid-30s, the Protopopovs began a long career as show skaters, and were still making cameo appearances as recently as 2008. In 1979, the Protopopovs defected from the Soviet Union and were granted political asylum in **Switzerland**. They were elected to the **World Figure Skating Hall of Fame** in 1978.

BEREZHNAYA, ELENA (1977–) AND SIKHARULIDZE, ANTON (1976–) (RUS). Pair skaters Elena Berezhnaya and Anton Sikharulidze are among the best known names in figure skating, a result of the judging **controversy** at the 2002 **Olympic Winter Games** in Salt Lake City. It was the third major hurdle that Berezhnaya had to overcome in her 10-year international skating career. She skated for three years, 1993–1995, representing Latvia with partner Oleg Slachov. At two European and three **World Championships**, their best placement was fifth. They were eighth at the 1994 **Olympic Winter Games**. In January 1996, while practicing side-by-side camel **spins**, they drifted too close together, and Slachov's skate sliced Berezhnaya's head penetrating her skull. Emergency surgery was necessary, and she was in the hospital for a month. Moving back to St. Petersburg, she began skating with Sikharulidze under the watchful eye of **Tamara Moskvina**, **Russia**'s most successful pairs coach. Berezhnaya missed only the 1996 season. Returning to competition in 1997, Berezhnaya and Sikharulidze won bronze medals at the European Championships and placed ninth at the World Championships. A year later in 1998, they won those competitions plus the **Grand Prix Finals**. They also collected silver medals at the Olympic Winter Games. In 1999 they placed second at the Grand Prix Finals, withdrew from the European Championships after the short program owing to illness, and won a second world title.

Berezhnaya's second hurdle came in 2000 when the pair was not allowed to defend their world title. During the preceding European Championships, Berezhnaya inadvertently took a medication for bronchitis that contained an illegal stimulant causing a positive reading of her doping test and led to the mandatory revocation of the European title. In 2001, Berezhnaya and Sikharulidze reclaimed the European title but placed second behind **Jamie Salé and David Pelletier** of **Canada** at the World Championships. The stage was set for an exciting contest between two outstanding pairs at the Salt Lake City Olympic Winter Games in 2002, but it resulted in the third hurdle. After the short program, Berezhnaya and Sikharulidze were indisputably in first place followed by Salé and Pelletier. In the free skating, by a five-to-four split of the judges, the Russians defeated the Canadians. Both pairs skated well, although Sikharulidze stepped out on the side-by-side double **Axel Paulsen jumps**, an obvious mistake. Salé and Pelletier skated a completely clean program. Not atypically, judges from eastern European countries placed the Russians first, while those from western countries placed the Canadians first. Following the event, the swing judge, who was from **France**, stated that she had been "pressured" by the French Federation to favor the Russians. As a result of media pressure and a protest filed by the Canadian Federation, the **International Skating Union** (ISU) subsequently recommended to the International Olympic Committee (IOC) that duplicate gold medals be awarded to Salé and Pelletier. Neither Berezhnaya and Sikharulidze nor Salé and Pelletier competed at the following World Championships. Both pairs turned professional and have experienced successful professional careers. As a result of the Salt Lake City controversy, the ISU adopted a totally new judging system based on a point-earning system aimed at preventing judging dishonesty.

BERGER, ALFRED. *See* ENGELMANN, HELENE.

BERNHARDT, ALF. *See* INTERNATIONAL SKATING UNION.

BESSON, FANNY. *See* GUHEL, CHRISTIANE AND JEAN PAUL.

BESTEMIANOVA, NATALIA (1960–) AND BUKIN, ANDREI (1957–) (URS). For three years Natalia Bestemianova and Andrei Bukin were silver medalists behind the great British ice dancers **Jayne Torvill and Christopher Dean**, but when the champions retired, Bestemianova and Bukin assumed that role. Like their predecessors, they were unbeatable for an entire Olympic cycle. Bestemianova and Bukin had first appeared at the **World Championships** in 1979 and placed 10th. In 1980 they competed at the **European Championships** and placed fifth. A year later in 1981, they competed at both championships placing fourth at the European and third at the World Championships. Silver and gold medals followed at every subsequent competition. Bestemianova and Bukin competed at three **Olympic Winter Games** placing eighth and second before winning gold medals in 1988. Their free dance programs tended to be unconventional and avant garde, but they were equally strong in the more conservative **compulsory dances**. Bestemianova and Bukin were dramatic in the sense of Torvill and Dean but in a less suave, more energetic vein. Upon turning professional, they skated in shows including **Champions on Ice** and **Holiday on Ice**.

BEWERSDORFF, UWE. *See* MAGER, MANUELA AND BEWERSDORFF, UWE.

BEZIC, SANDRA (1956–) (CAN). Sandra Bezic was a five-time national champion in pairs, 1970–1974, with her brother Val. They competed each of those years at the **World Championships** with a best placement of fifth in 1974. Bezic soon embarked on a career as a choreographer and has since worked with many elite skaters. Among her early successes was **Brian Boitano**'s free-skating program at the Calgary **Winter Olympic Games** in 1988. Another was **Kurt Browning**'s free-skating program at the Lillehammer Olympics in 1994, which remains one of figure skating's most memorable. She served as choreographer for Stars on Ice, which provided the opportunity of creating programs for the many former Olympic champions associated with that company. Bezic is also a respected television analyst.

BEZIC, VAL. *See* BEZIC, SANDRA.

BIANCHETTI, SONIA (1934–) (ITA). Sonia Bianchetti was one of many skaters whose career was affected by World War II. She took up skating in 1940 but was forced to quit following the bombing of Milan a year later. Starting again at age 14 and showing much interest, she was sent to London in 1952 to study with **Arnold Gerschwiler**, but in 1955 she gave up performing. It was as an official that Bianchetti was to become respected and appreciated. She became an international judge in 1964, served for four years, and in 1968 became a championship referee. She officiated at the **European Championships** every year through 1992 except for 1990, a total of 24; at the **World Championships** every year through 1991, a total of 24; and at every holding of the **Olympic Winter Games** through 1988, a total of six.

Bianchetti was elected in 1967 to the **International Skating Union**'s (ISU) figure skating technical committee, becoming its chair in 1973. She served until 1988 when she became the first woman to be elected to the ISU council, serving for four years. In each role, Bianchetti developed a reputation as an active participant. Under her leadership, an annual system of seminars for judges and referees was initiated in 1973, many of which she conducted. In 1978, she developed and conducted annual examinations for the appointment and promotion of judges. She was instrumental in the updating of the judges' handbooks for **compulsory figures**, singles, and pair skating. Bianchetti believed that compulsory figures should be discontinued as a part of competitive figure skating. She fought diligently and successfully for their elimination in 1990.

Since the judging controversy in the pairs competition at the Salt Lake City **Olympic Winter Games** in 2002 and the subsequent adoption of the **International Judging System**, Bianchetti has argued continually against the new system and remains one of its most outspoken critics.

BIELLMANN, DENISE (1962–) (SUI). Denise Biellmann is one of just three Swiss skaters who have become world champions, the others being **Hans Gerschwiler** in 1947 and **Stéphane Lambiel** in 2005 and 2006. Biellmann's relatively brief international career resulted in three medals, bronze at the **European Championships** in 1979, and gold at the the European and **World Championships** in 1981. In her one Olympic bid in 1980, she placed fourth. Biellmann's forte was **free skating**, particularly the more athletic aspects of it. Her programs included outstanding jumps and fast spins. The difficult spin she popularized, which now bears her name, is included in many free-skating programs. She reached back over her shoulder, grabbed the blade of her free foot, and raised it over her head, a move that requires much strength and extreme flexibility. Biellmann followed her eligible career with a long professional career in show skating including tours with **Holiday on Ice**. *See also* SWITZERLAND.

BIELLMANN SPIN. *See* BIELLMANN, DENISE.

BIETAK, WILHELM "WILLY" (1947–) (AUT). Willy Bietak, a pair skater, competed nationally and internationally with three partners over a period of nine years, 1963–1971. His best placements came in 1964 with Gerlinde Schönbauer: ninth at the **European Championships**, 10th at the **World Championships**, and 12th at the **Olympic Winter Games**. His greater success came as a manager and producer of many skating shows, including **Ice Capades** and **Holiday on Ice**. He created his own production company and has been involved in many television productions. In recognition of his management and production of skating shows, he was elected to the **World Figure Skating Hall of Fame** in 2009.

BIRD, DENNIS (1930–2005). Dennis Bird was a leading historian and writer on figure skating, serving for many years as archivist and historian for the **National Ice Skating Association of the United Kingdom** (NISA). His book, *Our Skating Heritage*, commemorates the 100th anniversary of the NISA. Earlier in his writing career, which dates from the late 1940s, he wrote under the nom de plume John Noel. Bird wrote numerous articles for *Skating World*, ***Skating*** magazine, *The Times*, and other publications.

BLACK ICE. *See* SYNCHRONIZED SKATING.

BLAIR, ELIZABETH. *See* NORTH AMERICAN CHAMPIONSHIPS.

BLANCHARD, THERESA WELD (1893–1978) (USA). Theresa Weld Blanchard can be called the “grande dame” of American figure skating. Known as “Tee” Blanchard to her numerous skating friends, she collected 32 medals in her career, was a voice of encouragement to several generations of skaters, and was of assistance to many coaches. She was a founding editor of ***Skating*** magazine in 1923 and continued as its editor for 40 years. Prior to the creation of the **United States Figure Skating Association** (USFSA) in 1921, the **International Skating Union of America** (ISUofA), a group of five regional skating organizations formed in 1907, held four competitions, one before and three after World War I. Theresa Weld was the lady champion at three of them, two before she was married in 1920, after which she competed under her married name. Blanchard become the first USFSA lady champion in 1922 and repeated twice. She competed also in pairs with Nathaniel Niles (1886–1932), winning titles at three ISUofA competitions and accumulating six more after the founding of USFSA. Blanchard was the lady champion at the first **North American Championships** in 1923 and two years later the pair champion with Niles. She entered no world competitions in singles but competed at three consecutive **Olympic Winter Games**, winning the bronze medal in 1920, the first Olympic medal won by a North American figure skater. She placed fourth in 1924 and 10th in 1928. At the games and with Niles, she placed fourth, sixth, and ninth in pairs. *See also* UNITED STATES.

BLAUER, JOHN G. *See* HOGG, GLADYS MARGARET.

BLUMBERG, JUDY (1957–) AND SEIBERT, MICHAEL (1960–) (USA). Ice dancers Judy Blumberg and Michael Seibert won bronze medals in 1979 and silver medals in 1980 before becoming **United States** champions four times, 1981–1985. At the **World Championships** after a sixth-place finish in 1980, they placed fourth twice and then won three consecutive bronze medals, 1983–1985. Competing at the **Olympic Winter Games** twice, their best result was fourth place in 1984. Seibert and a previous partner, Kelly Morris, had been national junior champions in 1977. Blumberg and Seibert skated in several **Champions on Ice** tours during the early 1980s.

BOBEK, NICOLE (1977–) (USA). Nicole Bobek was a talented skater who did not live up to her potential. In her first competition as a novice in 1989, at age 11, she placed a promising second. A year later she placed fourth at the junior level. As a senior, annual improvement was demonstrated beginning in 1991 with placements of eighth, seventh, fifth, and third before winning the national title in 1995. Other titles include the Vienna Cup and the U.S. Olympic Festival, both in 1991. Her one Olympic bid in 1998 resulted in a 17th-place finish. Bobeck changed coaches at least 11 times and worked with many of the best, including **Richard Callaghan**, **Frank Carroll**, **Carlo Fassi**, and Mary and Evy Scotvold. Bobek is most remembered for her signature move, a **spiral** with the free leg extended very high, which was clearly an influence on skaters such as **Michelle Kwan** and **Sasha Cohen**. *See also* UNITED STATES.

BOBRIN, IGOR (1953–) (URS). Igor Bobrin was first sent to the **World Championships** in 1976 where he placed sixth. He did not appear at international competitions in 1977 but from 1978 through 1982 he competed at every European and World Championship as well as the **Olympic Winter Games** in 1980. His first medal at the **European Championships** was gold in 1981. A month later he won the bronze medal at the World Championships. During his final year of competing, 1982, placements were third and seventh at the European and World Championships and sixth at the Olympic Games. *See also* RUSSIA.

BÖCKL, WILHELM "WILLY" (1896–1975) (AUT). Willy Böckl appeared on the international scene in 1913, skating in both the European and **World Championships**. By the end of the next season, the last before the war, he had earned one silver and three bronze medals. When competition resumed in 1922, he won six European titles, which were continuous except for 1924 when he did not compete. At the World Championships, following a bronze medal in 1922 and silver medals in 1923 and 1924, he became a four-time champion, 1925–1928. At the **Olympic Games** he was the silver medalist behind **Gillis Grafström** in 1924 and 1928. Böckl's free skating was especially strong, and at the Chamonix Games in 1924, he defeated Grafström in that part of the competition. Böckl invented the inside **Axel Paulsen jump**, which he called the Böckl jump. Following his eligible career, he moved to New York City where he taught a generation of American skaters. As a writer, he left detailed descriptions of **compulsory figures** and **free skating** in his book *Willy Böckl on Figure Skating*. Böckl was elected to the **World Figure Skating Hall of Fame** in 1977. *See also* AUSTRIA.

BODEL, CARMEL WATERBURY (1928–) AND EDWARD (1926–) (USA). Although American ice dancers have not yet won a world or Olympic title, the **United States** has continually fielded strong couples who have won bronze and silver medals. Carmel Waterbury and Edward Bodel won their first national medals, bronze, in 1946, one year after World War II. Three years later and now married, they again won bronze medals. Competing annually through 1956, they became three-time national champions, 1951, 1954, and 1955. Internationally, the Bodels won titles at the **North American Championships** in 1951 and 1955. Beginning with the first **World Championship** in **ice dancing**, held in 1952, they competed for six consecutive years with a best placement of third in 1954.

BOFROST CUP. *See* GRAND PRIX SERIES.

BOHATSCH, MAX (AUT). Max Bohatsch was the Austrian national champion twice, 1901 and 1904. He competed at three **World Championships**, winning the bronze medal in 1903, and silver medals behind **Ulrich Salchow** in 1905 and 1907. Competing at two **European Championships**, he won the silver medal in 1904, again behind Salchow, and the gold medal in 1905, a year in which Salchow did not compete. Bohatsch may be the inventor of a revised version of an important ice dance. **Irving Brokaw** describes in his book *The Art of Skating* (1910) a slightly simplified version of the ten-step which he calls the Bohatsch march. *See also* AUSTRIA.

BOITANO, BRIAN ANTHONY (1963–) (USA). Brian Boitano, the national junior champion in 1978, won the bronze medal at the **World Junior Figure Skating Championships** held for the first time that same year. As a senior, he competed for five years at the national championships before placing high enough to be named to a world team. His first efforts in 1983 and 1984 produced no medals, but for the next four years, he was the national champion and a medalist at the **World Championships** each year, winning the title in 1986 and 1988. At the Calgary Games in 1988, the media-inspired "**Battle of the Brians**," a head-to-head battle with **Brian Orser** of **Canada**, drew tremendous interest. Boitano won the Olympic gold medal. Included in his program at Calgary was a jump associated with Boitano that has taken his name. The "Tano Lutz" is a triple **Lutz jump** in which one arm is extended upward above the head making the jump much more difficult. Turning professional, Boitano had a long and successful career competing in professional competitions and appearing in many shows. He was a longtime member of the **Champions on Ice** cast. Boitano was elected to the **World Figure Skating Hall of Fame** in 1996. *See also* UNITED STATES.

BONALY, SURYA (1973–) (FRA). Surya Bonaly was born in Nice, **France**, of African parents and was adopted as an infant by Caucasian parents. She is the most successful black skater in the history of the sport. At age 16 she became the French national champion for the first of nine consecutive years, and beginning in 1991 she was the European champion for five years as well. During her most successful competitive years, 1989–1994, there were wins at many major competitions, including all of the **Grand Prix** events: Trophée Lalique in 1989 and 1990, **Skate Canada** in 1991, Nations Cup in 1992, NHK Trophy in 1992 and 1993, and **Skate America** in 1994. Although she won the world junior ladies title in 1991, the coveted world title always eluded her. She won silver medals behind **Oksana Baiul** in 1993, **Yuka Sato** in 1994, and **Lu Chen** in 1995. Bonaly competed at three **Olympic Winter Games** but failed to medal. Her best placement was fourth in 1994. As a professional, Bonaly had a long career, entering and winning professional competitions and skating in many shows including **Champions on Ice**. Bonaly is remembered especially for her signature **back flip** landed on one foot.

BOURNE, SHAE-LYNN (1976–) AND KRAATZ, VICTOR (1971–) (CAN). Shae-Lynn Bourne and Victor Kraatz were five-time Canadian **ice dancing** champions. They appeared on the international scene in 1993 and placed 14th at the **World Championships**. A year later they advanced to sixth after placing a respectable 10th at the Lillehammer **Olympic Winter Games**. They advanced to fourth at the World Championships in 1995 and followed with four consecutive bronze medals, 1996–1999. At the Nagano Olympics in 1998 they placed fourth. After not competing in 2000, they returned in 2001 and placed fourth at the World Championships. Their third Olympic effort in 2002 at Salt Lake City saw a repeat of their fourth-place finish in Nagano. At the World Championships that year they won the silver medals. A year later in 2003, they won the world title, the first North American ice dancers to do so. At the **Four Continents Championships**, three efforts resulted in gold medals in 1999, 2001, and 2003. At the **Grand Prix Finals**, they won gold medals in 1997 and 2002. After retirement from eligible skating, both skaters became coaches in **Canada**.

BOWDEN, ROBERT NORRIS. *See* DAFOE, FRANCES AND BOWDEN, ROBERT NORRIS.

BRASSEUR, ISABELLE (1970–) AND EISLER, LLOYD (1963–) (CAN). Pair skaters Isabelle Brasseur and Lloyd Eisler won their national title in 1989, slipped to third in 1990, reclaimed the title in 1991, and held it for their remaining three years of eligible skating. It had been nine years since a non-Russian pair had won a world title when in 1993 Brasseur and Eisler, twice silver and once bronze medalists, skated brilliantly, won both programs, and stood atop the medal platform. In 1994, an Olympic year, the medals were silver at the **World Championships** and bronze at the games. They turned professional following the 1994 season and embarked on successful careers including **Champions on Ice** tours. *See also* CANADA.

BROADMOOR SKATING CLUB. *See* TUTT, WILLIAM THAYER.

BROKAW, ISAAC IRVING (1869–1939) (USA). Irving Brokaw, the Champion of America in 1906, never competed at the **World Championships** but represented the **United States** at the London **Olympic Games** in 1908 and placed sixth. In 1910, he completed the first of four books all bearing the same title, *The Art of Skating*. He sought the expertise of leading skaters for several chapters of the first book, including **Georg Sanders** of **Russia** for **special figures**, **Phyllis and James Johnson** of **England** for **pair skating**, and **Gilbert Fuchs** of **Germany** for an essay entitled *Theory of Skating*.

BROWN, TIMOTHY TUTTLE (1938–) (USA). Tim Brown was the youngest of three American men born in successive years who, during the second half on the 1950s, continued the tradition begun by **Dick Button** and **Hayes Jenkins**, a period known as the "golden age" of American skating. The other two men were **David Jenkins** (1936) and **Ronald Robertson** (1937). Brown was the national junior champion in 1954. As a senior, he placed fourth twice before winning a succession of national silver medals behind David Jenkins from 1957 through 1960. Competing at the **World Championships** three times, he collected silver medals in 1957 and 1958 and a bronze medal in 1959. In his one Olympic effort in 1960, he placed fifth. Brown competed also in **ice dancing** with Susan Sebo, and in 1958 they won bronze medals at the **United States** Championships.

BROWNE, GEORGE HENRY (1857–1931) (USA). George H. Browne, a Harvard graduate and headmaster of the Browne and Nichols School in Cambridge, Massachusetts, was an original member of the **Cambridge Skat-**

ing Club founded in 1898. He spent the winter of 1902–1903 on a sabbatical in **St. Moritz** where he was converted to the **international style** of skating. After returning to Boston, he arranged for a demonstration of the style at the Cambridge Skating Club with **Irving Brokaw**, Karl Zenger, and Frank Bacon as featured skaters. Browne, an important writer on figure skating, described the strict **English style** and the more relaxed **American style** in two earlier books, a time when he was less familiar with the evolving international style, but his later books, especially *The New Skating: International Style* dating from 1910, show his total conversion. Browne served as the first secretary of the **United States Figure Skating Association**.

BROWNING, KURT (1966–) (CAN). Kurt Browning was **Canada**'s novice champion in 1983 and junior champion in 1985. His senior record includes three silver and four gold medals. Internationally, four world titles between 1989 and 1993 were interrupted by a silver medal in 1992, a year in which he suffered from a severe back injury that had a particularly negative effect on his Olympic bid. He placed sixth. The Winter Games were moved ahead two years after the 1992 games, influencing Browning's decision to remain eligible with the hope of winning a medal in 1994, but again it proved illusive. He placed fifth. Browning is remembered for outstanding interpretive programs. His free skating performance in winning his fourth world title in 1993 is the most memorable. Choreographed by **Sandra Bezic** and set to music from the film *Casablanca*, Browning, wearing a white dinner jacket, portrayed Rick Blaine, as Humphrey Bogart had done 52 years earlier. Since retiring from competitive skating, the ever popular Browning has appeared in made-for-television films and toured with **Stars on Ice**. He was elected to the **World Figure Skating Hall of Fame** in 2008.

BRUNET, ANDRÉE (1901–1993) AND PIERRE (1902–1991) (FRA). Pair skaters Andrée Brunet, nee Andrée Joly, and Pierre Brunet were the first skaters from **France** to win gold medals in world, European, or Olympic competitions. Their first outing, the 1924 **Olympic Winter Games**, resulted in bronze medals. At the **World Championships** the following year, 1925, they placed second behind **Herma Szabo** and **Ludwig Wrede** of **Austria** in one of the closest contests in **pair skating** history. Thereafter, they won every competition entered, accumulating one European title in 1932, four world titles in even numbered years, 1926, 1928, 1930, and 1932, and two Olympic titles, 1928 and 1932. They were married in 1927 and since then have been known in the skating world as the Brunets. Retiring from eligible skating after the 1932 season, they moved to New York where they became highly respected and successful coaches. Among their many students was the 1960

Olympic gold medalist **Carol Heiss**. The Brunets were honored with election to the **World Figure Skating Hall of Fame** with the initial class in 1976.

BRUNNER, MELITTA (1907–2003) (AUT). Melitta Brunner consistently placed second at the Austrian national championships from 1926 through 1930. For the last three of those years, she placed fifth, third, and fifth at the **World Championships**. Her greater success came as a pair skater with **Ludwig Wrede** for three years, 1928–1930. Their results were silver, bronze, and gold medals at the Austrian Championships and bronze followed by two silver medals at the World Championships. *See also* AUSTRIA.

BRYN, ALEXIA AND YNGAR. *See* NORWAY.

BUCK, ANGELIKA (1950–) AND ERICH (1949–) (GDR). Ice dancers Angelika and Erich Buck competed internationally for eight years. They were contemporaries of the Soviet ice dancers **Liudmila Pakhomova and Alexandr Gorshkov**. The Bucks first entered the **European Championships** in 1966, placing 13th, and the **World Championships** in 1967, placing 10th. Showing steady improvement for the next two years, they placed sixth and fourth at the European Championships and eighth and fifth at the World Championships. During the four years from 1970 through 1973, they medaled at every competition, accumulating one bronze, six silver, and one gold medal at the 1972 European Championships. Their bronze and silver medals were always behind the Soviets, Pakhomova and Gorshkov, except at the 1972 European Championships where they defeated the Soviets by a narrow margin. *See also* GERMANY.

BUCK, ERICH. *See* BUCK, ANGELIKA AND ERICH.

BUKIN, ANDREI. *See* BESTEMIANOVA, NATALIA AND BUKIN, ANDREI.

BULGARIA. The Bulgarian Skating Federation, which regulates figure skating and ice hockey, was founded in 1949. It joined the **International Skating Union** (ISU) in 1979. The first figure skater to enter an ISU competition, the **European Championships** in 1979, was Margarita Dimitrova. Skaters have since appeared in all disciplines, although not until 1999 in pairs. The greatest success has been in **ice dancing**. **Albena Denkova and Maxim Staviski** accumulated one bronze and two silver medals at the European Championships. At the **World Championships**, their medals include bronze in 2003, silver in 2004, and gold in 2006 and 2007. Judges from Bulgaria have officiated at ISU competitions since 1986.

BURGER, FRITZI (1910–1999) (AUT). Fritzi Burger, the national champion from 1928 through 1931, was perhaps the best of several outstanding Austrian ladies who competed contemporaneously with **Sonja Henie** of **Norway**, the 10-time world champion and three-time Olympic champion who was never defeated between 1927 and 1936. In 1930, Burger's first year on the international stage, she won the ladies' title at the European Championships. It was the first year a ladies competition was held and one in which Henie did not compete. In nine other European, world, and Olympic competitions, Burger accumulated six silver and three bronze medals, all in competitions won by Henie. Bronze medals at the **World Championships** came in 1928 behind Henie and **Maribel Vinson** of the **United States** and in 1931 behind Henie and **Hilde Holovsky** of **Austria**. Her bronze medal at the **European Championships** came behind Henie and **Cecilia Colledge** of **Great Britain**. Burger competed in the **Olympic Winter Games** of 1928 and 1932, winning silver medals behind Henie each time. *See also* BELGIUM; CANADA.

BURGER, HEINRICH (1881–1942) (GER). Heinrich Burger competed once at the **European Championships** and three times at the **World Championships**, collecting one bronze and three silver medals. Greater success was achieved as a pair skater with Anna Hübler (1895–1976). They had only three outings, the World Championships in 1908 and 1910 and the **Olympic Games** in 1908, all of which they won. Contemporary accounts recognize them for their strength and speed, noting that they always skated in perfect time with the music. *See also* GERMANY.

BURKA, PETRA (1946–) (CAN). Petra Burka was the Canadian junior champion in 1961 and the senior champion from 1964 through 1966. Five consecutive appearances at the **World Championships**, 1962–1966, resulted in bronze medals in 1964 and 1966 and a gold medal in 1965. The gold medal was the result of defeating soundly **Regina Heitzer** of **Austria**, the only time she did so in five world and Olympic meetings. As a professional, Burka toured with **Holiday on Ice**. *See also* CANADA.

BURROWS, MURIEL. *See* JENKINS, DOROTHY AND McLENNAN, A. GORDON.

BUSCH, GUNDI (1935–) (FRG). It was five years after World War II when German skaters first returned to international competition. Two men, four women, and three pairs competed in 1951. Most successful of the ladies was Gundi Busch who placed sixth at the **European Championships** and 10th at the **World Championships**. She competed for just four years, winning silver medals at both competitions in 1953 and gold medals at both competitions in 1954. At her one Olympic effort in 1952, she placed eighth. Turning professional, Busch moved to the **United States** and toured with the **Hollywood Ice Review**. *See also* GERMANY.

BUSHKOV, ANDREI. *See* ELTSOVA, MARINA AND BUSHKOV, ANDREI.

BUTTLE, JEFFREY (1982–) (CAN). Jeffrey Buttle was the Canadian national champion for three years, 2005–2007. Five appearances at the **Four Continents Championships** resulted in a fourth-place finish, two silver medals, and gold medals in 2002 and 2004. From an equal number of appearances at the **World Championships**, he won two medals, silver in 2005 and gold in 2008. In his one Olympic effort in 2006 he was the bronze medalist. Trips to the **Grand Prix Finals** in 2005 and 2006 resulted in silver medals. Buttle ended his competitive career in 2008. *See also* CANADA.

BUTTON, RICHARD TOTEN "DICK" (1929–) (USA). Dick Button's competitive career as a senior skater began in 1946 at the **United States** Championships. It was the first time the senior men's event had been held since 1943, although the other disciplines had continued uninterrupted through the war years. Having won the novice title in 1944 and the junior title in 1945, Button completed an unprecedented three-year sweep through the ranks of men's skating by winning the senior title in 1946. It was the first of seven consecutive national titles, tying the record set by Roger Turner, 1928–1934, a record not since duplicated by skaters in any discipline. Button won all three North American titles from 1947 through 1951. The **World Championships** resumed in 1947, and in a close decision with the judges split three to two, Button placed second to the more senior **Hans Gerschwiler** of **Switzerland**. A year later, in 1948, Button soundly defeated Gerschwiler at all three competitions, the **European Championships**, the **Olympic Winter Games**, and the World Championships. Button represented what came to be known as the "American School," a more athletic style than that of Gerschwiler, who had competed before the war, and the other Europeans. At the Olympics in 1948, Button became the first skater to complete a double **Axel Paulsen jump** in competition. He won the **free skating** from all nine judges and **compulsory figures** from all but one. Button was unbeatable through the remainder of his career of four more years. He won unanimously every international competition entered and on just two occasions did an individual judge not place him first in both compulsory figures and free skating. Button had other important firsts. He was the first to do a "triple double," a combination of three double jumps, and the first to do a triple jump, specifically a triple **loop**. He is also credited with inventing the flying camel spin, sometimes referred to as the "Button camel." Throughout his competitive career, Button was coached by the legendary **Gustave Lussi**.

After retiring from eligible skating, Button enjoyed a short career as a show skater with **Ice Capades** and **Holiday on Ice**, but it is in other roles that he has had the greatest influence. Perhaps no name is better known in figure skating, a result of his visibility for more than 40 years as a commentator for ABC. Through that forum, he had the opportunity to champion the sport more than any other person. His tenure with ABC began in 1962, exactly 10 years after his career as a competitive skater ended, providing him with a historical perspective possible only from watching the sport evolve for more than a half century. Button established professional competitions as early as 1973. First was the **World Professional Figure Skating Championships**, an invitational competition usually referred to as the "World Pros." The **World Challenge of Champions**, a one-event competition with exhibitions following, was added in 1985. Both competitions continued almost through the 1990s when the companies were sold and eventually disbanded. These two invitational competitions were the most important and longest running. Button was inducted into the **World Figure Skating Hall of Fame** with the first class in 1976. *See also* CANADA.

BUTYRSKAYA, MARIA VIKTOROVNA (1972–) (RUS). Maria Butyrskaya, a six-time Russian national ladies' champion, competed internationally for a decade beginning in 1993. Her first medals, which were bronze, came in 1996 at both the **European** and **World Championships**. In 1997 her placements were fourth and fifth, but from 1998 through 2002, she won three gold and two silver medals at the European Championships and from 1998 through 2000, one gold and two bronze medals at the World Championships. By winning the gold medal in 1999, Butyrskaya became **Russia**'s first lady world champion. Her two Olympic efforts resulted in a fourth-place finish in 1998 and a sixth-place finish in 2002. Butyrskaya has since skated in various shows, including tours with both **Champions on Ice** and **Stars on Ice**.

CALLAGHAN, RICHARD (USA). Richard Callaghan as a competitive skater was coached by Donald Laws. His best placement was fifth at the **United States** Championships in 1965. Turning professional a year later, he toured for five seasons with **Ice Capades** and **Holiday on Ice** before turning to coaching. Callaghan was the coach of **Todd Eldredge** throughout his entire career and led him to a world title in 1996. He coached **Tara Lipinski** during the time she won her world and Olympic titles. Among other elite skaters who have been his students are **Nicole Bobek**, **Angela Nikodinov**, **Shizuka Arakawa**, **Kimmie Meissner**, and **Jennifer Kirk**.

CALLAWAY, BETTY DAPHNE (1928–) (GBR). Betty Roberts (Callaway) was an ice dancer in the days before it became an international discipline, which may have, in addition to economics and the war, influenced her to turn professional in 1944 at age 16 to skate in shows. While skating in a show, Roberts met E. Roy Callaway, whom she married in 1948. Both of the Callaways had been taught skating by **Gladys Hogg**. Betty Callaway became the coach of two world champion **ice dancing** couples, **Krisztina Regöczy and András Sallay**, world champions and Olympic silver medalists in 1980, and **Jayne Torvill and Christopher Dean**, world champions from 1981 through 1984 and Olympic champions in 1984. She also taught Prince Charles to skate. Her country honored Callaway through the awarding of Master of the British Empire (MBE) in 1984.

CALLAWAY, E. ROY. *See* CALLAWAY, BETTY DAPHNE.

CALMAT, ALAIN (1940–) (FRA). Alain Calmat had one of the longest careers in postwar skating, competing internationally for twelve years without missing a European, world, or Olympic championship. Methodical and consistent development is demonstrated by his three Olympic placements, ninth in 1956, sixth in 1960, and second in 1964. During his last five competitive years, 1961–1965, he won nine medals in international competition, including European titles from 1962 through 1964, and the world title in 1965.

Calmat remained active in figure skating for many years as a world judge and referee and was honored as the person selected to light the Olympic flame at Grenoble in 1968. He served in the French government as the minister of sports. *See also* FRANCE.

CAMBRIDGE, SADIE (?–1964) AND ENDERS, ALBERT (?–1976) (GBR). The husband-and-wife pair of Sadie Cambridge and Albert Enders were Australian expatriates and show skaters who won the **Open Professional Championships** of **Great Britain** from 1932 through 1937. They became coaches first in England and then in **Canada**. Among their students were **Mollie Phillips** of England and the Canadian pairs **Suzanne Morrow and Wallace Diestelmeyer** and **Frances Dafoe and Norris Bowden**.

CAMBRIDGE SKATING CLUB. The Cambridge (Massachusetts) Skating Club seems almost anachronistic in the 21st century, representing a slice of skating reminiscent of the 19th century. Founded in 1898, it continues to provide its members with an outdoor natural skating facility. It must depend on weather patterns for its cherished and carefully counted skating days. An average winter provides about 30. **Theresa Weld**, **Nathaniel Niles**, **Sherwin Badger**, **Roger Turner**, **Maribel Vinson**, **Joan Tozzer**, and **Bernard Fox** were among the top skaters who trained there before World War II. The Cambridge Skating Club is a member of the United States Figure Skating Association.

CANADA. Skating was a rapidly growing and popular sport in Canada by the last quarter of the 19th century. Clubs existed in many cities and competitions between and within them occurred frequently. The need for a governing body became apparent, and in 1888 a meeting was held in Montreal to deal with various issues. It resulted in the formation of the Amateur Skating Association of Canada, which regulated both speed skating and figure skating. At that time, speed skating was more popular. In 1913, a figure skating department was established within the parent organization, but not until 1939 was the name Canadian Figure Skating Association (CFSA) adopted. It was subsequently changed to **Skate Canada** in 2000.

In addition to national competitions, beginning in 1923 the biennial **North American Championships** were established to provide a competition between figure skaters from the **United States** and Canada. They continued through 1971, held alternately in the two countries. The early competitions included events for **fours**, a discipline unique to North America, but one in which Canadian fours dominated through most of the discipline's history. Between the world wars, Canadian skaters competed at just four **World**

Championships but beginning in 1924 at all of the **Olympic Winter Games**, collecting one silver and two bronze medals behind some of that era's greatest European skaters. At the World Championships, **Cecil Smith** placed second behind **Sonja Henie** in 1930, and **Constance Samuel** placed third behind Henie and **Fritzi Burger** in 1932. At the Olympic Winter Games in 1932, **Montgomery Wilson** placed third behind **Karl Schäfer** and **Gillis Grafström**.

Barbara Ann Scott traveled to Europe in 1947 and entered the first postwar European and World Championships, winning both competitions and becoming the first champion from North America. She returned a year later and won again. When she and **Dick Button** of the United States won European titles in 1948, they unwittingly served as the catalyst for a rule change that no longer allowed North Americans to enter the **European Championships**. Beginning in 1954, two outstanding Canadian pairs dominated their discipline, winning all but one world title through 1960. **Frances Dafoe and Norris Bowden** were world champions twice, in 1954 and 1955. **Barbara Wagner and Robert Paul** were world champions for four years, 1957–1960, and Olympic champions in 1960. Following the **plane crash**, which led to the cancellation of the 1961 World Championships, **Maria and Otto Jelinek** continued Canada's winning tradition, claiming the world title in 1962. That same year, **Donald Jackson** became the first Canadian man to win a world title. Since then, there have been world champions in all disciplines. In addition to Jackson, the men include **Donald McPherson** in 1963; **Brian Orser** in 1987; **Kurt Browning** from 1989 to 1991 and 1993; **Elvis Stojko** in 1994, 1995, and 1997; and **Jeffrey Buttle** in 2008. Lady champions include **Petra Burka** in 1965 and **Karen Magnussen** in 1973. Three pairs, **Barbara Underhill and Paul Martini** in 1984, **Isabelle Brasseur and Lloyd Eisler** in 1993, and **Jamie Salé and David Pelletier** in 2001 have claimed world titles. In **ice dancing, Shae-Lynn Bourne and Victor Kraatz** won in 2003, the first couple from North America to do so, and **Tessa Virtue and Scott Moir** won in 2010. Nexxice won the **synchronized skating** world title in 2009, the first time the title did not go to a Scandinavian country. Barbara Ann Scott in 1948 and pair skaters Wagner and Paul in 1960 won Olympic titles, but not since the plane crash in 1961 had any Canadian skater won an Olympic title until 2002, at the Salt Lake City Games, duplicate gold medals were awarded to Salé and Pelletier, a result of the judging **controversy**.

The discontinuance of the North American Championships after 1971 was a result of the CFSA's desire to implement an international invitational competition called **Skate Canada**. First held in 1973, it is the oldest of the events on the **Grand Prix Series**. Canada has been the host to nine World Championships, most recently at Calgary in 2006, and two

Olympic Winter Games, Calgary in 1988 and Vancouver in 2010. *See also* BEZIC, SANDRA; CHAN, PATRICK; COLLINS, TOM; CRANSTON, TOLLER; DOANE, PAULETTE AND ORMSBY, KENNETH; DORE, DAVID M.; DUBREUIL, MARIE-FRANCE AND LAUZON, PATRICE; GALBRAITH, SHELDON; GILCHRIST, DONALD; GRINER, WENDY; HISEY, JOYCE KORNACHER; JENKINS, DOROTHY AND McLENNAN, A. GORDON; KNIGHT, DONALD; McDOUGALL, MARION AND BANGS, CHAUNCEY; MANLEY, ELIZABETH; McCREATH, RALPH S.; McLACHLAN, WILLIAM; MORROW, SUZANNE AND DIESTELMEYER, WALLACE; ROGERS, MELVILLE; SAMUEL, CONSTANCE WILSON; SANDHU, EMANUEL; SMITH, CECIL EUSTACE; TAYLOR, DONNA AND LENNIE, BRUCE; THACKER, MARY ROSE; WILKES, DEBBI; WILSON, MONTGOMERY S.

CANADIAN FIGURE SKATING ASSOCIATION. *See* CANADA.

CANDELORO, PHILIPPE (1972–) (FRA). Philippe Candeloro is remembered more for his exhibitions and as a showman than for his competitive record. He was the French national champion for four years, 1994–1997. Competing for six years at the **European Championships**, he won silver medals in 1993 and 1997. Six efforts at the **World Championships** resulted in a silver medal in 1994 and a bronze medal in 1995. Competing at the **Olympic Winter Games** in 1994 and 1998 resulted in two bronze medals. Owing to his popularity with audiences, a result of his originality, he became a mainstay for eleven years on **Champions on Ice** tours.

ČÁP, VLADISLAV. *See* CZECHOSLOVAKIA.

CARNIVALS. Skating carnivals date from the 1870s in both North America and Europe. Traditionally, they have provided an opportunity for skaters from beginners to those more advanced to present shows for parents, family, and the general public. The shows sometimes become large and spectacular, such as the Grand Carnival held at New York's Madison Square Garden in 1879. Many carnivals were presented by the **Vienna Skating Club** in **Austria**. By the early 20th century, the number of carnivals had increased dramatically, the result of the development of **artificial ice**, the availability of covered and indoor ice rinks, and a growth in the number of skating clubs. Their heyday came during the years between the world wars. In 1924, the **United States Figure Skating Association** sponsored the first of three annual association-wide carnivals held consecutively in Boston, Philadelphia, and New York. By that time, carnivals often featured elite and sometimes professional skaters. Among those who appeared in the 1930s were **Gillis Grafström**, **Karl Schäfer**, **Sonja Henie**, and the pairs of **Ernst Baier and Maxi Herber** and the **Brunets**. By the late 1930s professional traveling shows were being formed. In the **United States**, they included the **Ice Follies**, **Hollywood Ice Review**, and **Ice Capades**. As those companies grew and benefitted from large production budgets, club carnivals suffered. Carnivals continued after the war, but their numbers gradually dwindled. A few have managed to survive to the present including ones presented by clubs in Boston and Dallas. "Ice Chips," presented annually since 1912 by the **Skating Club of Boston** is the oldest continuous carnival in existence.

CARRELL, JOHN. *See* DYER, LORNA, AND CARRELL, JOHN.

CARROLL, FRANK (1939–) (USA). Frank Carroll began skating as a teenager, and soon **Maribel Vinson** became his coach and mentor. Carroll did not compete beyond the junior level, where his best placement was second at the **United States** Championships in 1960. He then turned professional and toured for four years with the **Ice Follies**. Carroll's role in skating is as one of America's most successful coaches. Three of his students have become world champions: **Linda Fratianne**, **Michelle Kwan**, and **Evan Lysacek**. Other strong skaters he has coached include Christopher Bowman, **Tiffany Chin**, **Timothy Goebel**, **Nicole Bobek**, and **Angela Nikodinov**. Carroll was inducted into the **World Figure Skating Hall of Fame** in 2007.

CARRUTHERS, CAITLIN "KITTY" (1961–) AND PETER (1959–) (USA). The brother-and-sister pair of Caitlin and Peter Carruthers were **United States** champions for four years, 1981–1984. Competing at four **World Championships**, 1980–1983, their best placement was third in 1982. Two Olympic bids resulted in a fifth-place finish in 1980 and silver medals in 1984. During those years, they were cast members for **Champions on Ice** tours. After retiring from competitive skating, Caitlin became a coach. Peter became a successful and respected television commentator.

CARRUTHERS, PETER. *See* CARRUTHERS, CAITLIN AND PETER.

CATTANEO, ANNA AND ERCOLE. *See* ITALY.

CHAIT, GALIT. *See* CONTROVERSIES.

CHALFIN, MORRIS. *See* HOLIDAY ON ICE.

CHAMPIONS ON ICE. *See* COLLINS, TOM.

CHAMPIONS SERIES. *See* GRAND PRIX SERIES.

CHAN, PATRICK (1990–) (CAN). Patrick Chan was the Canadian novice champion in 2004, the junior champion in 2005, and the senior champion from 2008 through 2010. Internationally, he won the gold medal in 2009 in his only appearance at the **Four Continents Championships**. At the **World Championships** he placed ninth in 2008 and won silver medals in 2009 and 2010. He placed fifth at the **Olympic Winter Games** in 2010.

CHANDLER, EVELYN (USA). Evelyn Chandler from New York became the United States junior ladies' champion in 1929 but turned professional soon afterward, often performing between periods of hockey games at Madison Square Garden. During the early to mid-1930s, she barnstormed throughout the **United States**, taking her popular and often acrobatic style of skating to any venue available. Chandler is remembered especially for her trademark "Arabian Cartwheels." She performed at many club carnivals, variety shows, and fairs, including Chicago's Century of Progress Exposition. Chandler toured with her husband, Bruce Mapes, a skater who has been credited with inventing the flip jump. In 1939, Chandler and Mapes joined the **Ice Follies** and were mainstays with the company for eight years.

CHANG, MYUNG SU. *See* KOREA.

CHARLOTTE. *See* OELSCHLAGEL, CHARLOTTE.

CHARLOTTE STOP. *See* OELSCHLAGEL, CHARLOTTE.

CHEN, LU (1976–) (CHN). Lu Chen won the bronze medal at the **World Junior Championships** in 1991 and proceeded to the **World Championships** where she placed 12th. A year later in 1992, she won the bronze medal ahead of two more experienced skaters, **Tonya Harding** and **Surya Bonaly**, both of whom had placed ahead of her the previous month at the Albertville **Olympic Winter Games**. In 1993, Lu Chen won a second bronze medal at the World Championships. In 1994, she won the bronze medal at the Lillehammer Olympics but withdrew that year from the World Championships. In 1995, she became the world champion, but in 1996 settled for second behind **Michelle Kwan** in one of the most exciting finishes in figure skating history. A disappointing year followed. In 1997 Lu Chen did not survive the qualifying round at the World Championships, but in 1998 at the Nagano Olympics, she won a second Olympic bronze medal. Retiring after the games, Lu Chen entered the world of professional skating where her graceful style has served her well. She is currently a coach in **China**.

CHERKASOVA, MARINA (1964–) AND SHAKHRAI, SERGEI (1958–) (URS). Marina Cherkasova and Sergei Shakhrai made skating history at the **European Championships** in 1977 by performing the first quadruple twist lift, a feat made possible by enormous differences in their height and weight. Criticism of their size differential led to the **International Skating Union** adopting a rule that pairs be penalized when there is a "serious imbalance" in physical appearance. But Cherkasova and Shakhrai won the bronze medals that year and continued competing through 1981, collecting a total of eight medals: two bronze, four silver, and two gold. They were the European champions in 1979 and the world champions in 1981. Their silver medals at the Lake Placid **Olympic Winter Games** in 1980 were behind the unbeatable **Irina Rodnina** and Alexandr Zaitsev.

CHETVERUKHIN, SERGEI (1946–) (URS). Sergei Chetverukhin competed internationally for nine years beginning in 1965. In 1971, he became the first Soviet man to medal at the **World Championships**, claiming the bronze medal. Two years earlier he won the bronze medal at the **European Championships**. Chetverukhin never climbed to the top of the medal stand, but from 1971 through 1973, he competed at every European and World Championship and the Sapporo **Olympic Winter Games** collecting six silver medals, always behind the unbeatable **Ondrej Nepela**.

CHIN, TIFFANY (1967–) (USA). Tiffany Chin was one of the early champions coached by **Frank Carroll**. Although she was not a national champion as a junior, she won the world junior title in 1981 and did so after placing eighth in the **compulsory figures**. Interestingly, she placed second in both the short and long programs but won the event because of inconsistencies among her competitors. Chin placed fifth at the **United States** Championships in 1982 but afterward never failed to medal, collecting two bronze and one silver in addition to winning the national title in 1985. At the **World Championships**, her best results were bronze medals in 1985 and 1986. One Olympic effort, in 1984, resulted in a fourth-place finish, primarily a result of placing 12th in the compulsory figures. She placed second in the combined short and long programs. Chin suffered throughout her career with injuries, which may have affected her decision to retire after the 1986 season. She skated professionally and currently teaches skating in California.

CHINA. The Skating Association of the People's Republic of China became in 1956 the second Asian country to join the **International Skating Union**. **Japan** had joined 30 years earlier. Beginning in 1980 and continuing for four years, China fielded one entry each in the men's, ladies', and pairs' events at the **World Championships** but with little success. Similarly, one man and one lady competed at the Lake Placid **Olympic Winter Games** that first year. Skipping two years, a team returned in 1985 with ice dancers added to the roster. Success was still disappointing with all contestants placing near the bottom. China entered no skaters for the next five years. In 1991, it reentered skaters cautiously, first in the ladies' event, and one of the most artistic skaters of the 1990s appeared. **Lu Chen** placed 12th. Five years later in 2005, she became the ladies world champion. By the end of the decade, **Xue Shen and Hongbo Zhao**, who first appeared in 1994, had become China's first medal-winning pair, claiming the silver medals in 1999. They became world champions in 2002, 2003, and 2007 and China's first Olympic champions in 2010. Chinese pairs have been dominant in the 21st century. **Qing Pang and Jian Tong** won world titles in 2006 and 2010, and **Dan Zhang and Hao Zhang** won silver medals in 2006, 2008, and 2009. In fewer than 20 years China became a major player in competitive figure skating. The Cup of China, first held in 2003, is one of the six events currently on the **Grand Prix Series**. It has been held in Beijing every year except two. *See also* LI, CHENGJIANG.

CHRYSLER, PHILIP. *See* NORTH AMERICAN CHAMPIONSHIPS.

CINQUANTA, OTTAVIO (1938–) (ITA). Ottavio Cinquanta of **Italy**, the current president of the **International Skating Union** (ISU), like his predecessor **Olaf Poulsen**, was trained as a speed skater. He is the fifth speed skater to head the ISU. Collectively, speed skaters have led the ISU for 71 of its 118 years. Cinquanta's first office in the ISU was as a member of the short track speed skating technical committee on which he served for 17 years, 1975–1992, eight years as its chair. Elected then as the vice president for speed skating, he served for just two years before being elected the ISU's 10th president in 1994.

Cinquanta has overseen many changes, especially in figure skating. Following the **Kerrigan-Harding incident** in 1994 at the **United States** Championships, the year of his election to the presidency, figure skating enjoyed an unprecedented increase in popularity. During that period of heightened interest, the **Grand Prix Series** was established in 1996. The Junior Grand Prix Series and **Four Continents Championships** were established in 1999. More far reaching was the scandal resulting from the **pair skating** competition at the 2002 **Olympic Winter Games** in Salt Lake City. It precipitated a sweeping change in the history of figure skating, the establishment of a new judging system. The inclusion of **ice dancing** in the **World Championships** in 1952 and the Olympic Winter Games in 1976 affected only that discipline; the total elimination of **compulsory figures** in 1990 affected only singles skating; but the new judging system, adopted in 2004, affected all figure skating disciplines including **synchronized skating**, which had just become a world sport in 2000.

CLARKE, HERBERT J. (1879–1956) (GBR). Herbert J. Clarke participated in and tested in both **English style** and **international style** skating as a young skater. His relatively long competitive career in the international style was primarily at the national level although he did participate in singles at the **Olympic Games** in 1924, placing 10th. He was a longtime world judge and referee, serving almost annually during the years preceding World War II. Clarke became active in the **International Skating Union** (ISU) in 1925 when he succeeded G. Herbert Fowler, who had served since 1903, as the representative from **Great Britain**. Clarke was twice the vice president, 1927–1935 and 1937–1945, before assuming the presidency in 1945 and serving until 1953. His long and distinguished service to the ISU was acknowledged in 1955 when he was elected as an honorary president. Clarke was instrumental in reviving quickly the international championships following World War II with countries "not under the control of foreign forces" being allowed to participate, a stipulation established primarily because the prewar federations in those countries no longer existed. Both the European and **World Championships** were held in 1947. The rapid growth of the ISU in the years following the war was under Clarke's leadership for which he was honored in 1996 by induction into the **World Figure Skating Hall of Fame**.

CLARKE, VERONICA. *See* McCREATH, RALPH S.

CLAUDET, FRANCES. *See* McDOUGALL, MARION AND BANGS, CHAUNCEY.

CLERICETTI, GABI. *See* FRANCE.

COHEN, ALEXANDRA PAULINE "SASHA" (1984–) (USA). Sasha Cohen began competing at the juvenile level in 1996. She retired 10 years later in 2006 but returned in 2010, an Olympic year. Her potential as a talented, artistic, and extremely flexible skater was never completely realized owing to her inability to present two clean programs in the same competition, especially in world and Olympic competition. The result was the collecting of many bronze and silver medals. At six United States Championships as a senior, she collected one bronze and four silver medals before becoming the national champion in 2006; at five **World Championships** the medals included one bronze and three silver; and in two Olympics efforts her one medal was silver in 2006. The 2003 season began as her strongest with wins at three Grand Prix events—Trophée Lalique, **Skate Canada**, and **Skate America**—plus the **Grand Prix Finals**. But at the United States Championships the medal was bronze, and at the World Championships she placed fourth. Cohen had several top coaches as she sought to improve her consistency. Beginning with **John Nicks**, she later switched to **Tatiana Tarasova**, and then to Robin Wagner before returning to Nicks. Probably because one of her best outings was the **Olympic Winter Games** in 2006, at which she was the silver medalist, Cohen returned to competition for the 2010 season hoping to make the Olympic team, but her hopes were dashed after placing fourth at the United States Championships.

COI, DENNIS. *See* WORLD JUNIOR FIGURE SKATING CHAMPIONSHIPS.

COLE, KING. *See* DYER, LORNA AND CARRELL, JOHN.

COLLEDGE, CECILIA MAGDALENA (1920–2008) (GBR). In 1932 Cecilia Colledge became the youngest competitor ever to compete at the **World Championships**, 11 years and 83 days, and in the **Olympic Games**, 11 years and 75 days. She was coached first by **Eva Keats** and then by the renowned **Jacques Gerschwiler**. Colledge was the British ladies' champion from 1935 through 1939 and again after the war in 1946. She was three times the European ladies' champion, 1937–1939, and once the world ladies' champion, 1937. Her Olympic placements were eighth in 1932 and second in 1936. She won the British **Open Professional Championships** twice, 1947 and 1948, and she skated in various shows. Colledge was a fine free skater and is credited with several firsts, including the first camel **spin**, then called a "parallel spin," the first layback spin, and the first one-foot **Axel Paulsen jump** by a lady. She was also the first lady to execute a double jump in international competition, a **Salchow jump** at the **European Championships** in 1936. Colledge emigrated to the **United States** in 1951 where she became a highly respected and longtime coach in the Boston area. She was elected to the **World Figure Skating Hall of Fame** in 1980. *See also* GREAT BRITAIN.

COLLINS, TOM (1931–) (CAN). Tom Collins competed nationally in the 1940s. Upon turning professional, he toured with the **Hollywood**

Ice Review (1949–1951) and **Holiday on Ice** (1951–1962). Joining the management staff of Holiday on Ice in 1962, he eventually became a vice president and remained with the company until 1971. While employed by Holiday on Ice, Collins managed a tour of medalists from the 1969 **World Championships** held that year in Colorado Springs. World Championships at that time were held triennially in North America, and beginning in 1972, tours under Collins's own management company followed the championships held at Calgary in 1972, Colorado Springs in 1975, Ottawa in 1978, and Hartford in 1981. The **Olympic Winter Games** at Lake Placid in 1980 were also followed by a tour. Beginning in 1983, tours were conducted every year regardless of where the World Championships were held. Several name changes have occurred: The Tour of Champions in 1972, The World Figure Skating Tour from 1975 through 1983, The Tour of Olympic and World Figure Skating Champions from 1984 through 1988, The Tour of World Figure Skating Champions from 1989 through 1997, and Champions on Ice beginning in 1998. The last tour was in 2007. Collins was inducted into the **World Figure Skating Hall of Fame** in 1998.

COMMONWEALTH OF INDEPENDENT STATES. For one season after the breakup of the **Soviet Union** in 1992, some of its countries, primarily **Russia** and **Ukraine**, competed at **International Skating Union** (ISU) competitions and the **Olympic Winter Games** under the designation Commonwealth of Independent States. The following year in 1993, each country competed under its own banner as the federations became members of the ISU in their own right.

COMPULSORY DANCES. Dancing on ice in set patterns dates back to the 1880s and probably earlier in Vienna, **Austria**, where the American waltz and the Jackson Haines waltz were particularly popular. *Spuren auf dem Eise* in its second edition (1892) provides descriptions of a rapidly expanding list of dances being skated there. By century's end, the three-step waltz, reportedly first skated in Paris in 1894, had become a craze internationally and was responsible for an explosion in the popularity of **ice dancing** throughout Europe. The three-step waltz was easy and could be done effectively by skaters with limited skating ability. Most of the older dances included in *Spuren auf dem Eise* were soon forgotten. In addition to the three-step waltz, two other 19th-century dances survived, the ten-step, soon to become the fourteen-step with a repeated sequence of steps, and the kilian. Between the world wars, dance competitions at the local and national level became popular, especially in England, creating the need for additional dances. Competitions for new dances sponsored in 1932 by the

Ice Club, Westminster, and the *Skating Times* resulted in the invention of dances still included in national test structures and in ice dancing competitions. **Eva Keats and Erik van der Weyden** invented the foxtrot, rocker foxtrot, Viennese waltz, and Westminster waltz. **Reginald Wilkie and Daphne Wallis** invented the Argentine tango, paso doble, and quickstep. **Robert Dench** and Leslie Turner invented the blues. No additional dances were added until after ice dancing became a world sport in the 1950s. Compulsory dances are one of three events included in ice dancing competitions, the others being the original dance beginning in 1983 and the **free dance**. Like **compulsory figures**, the value of compulsory dances was gradually reduced from the 60 percent they counted in 1952 when ice dancing became a world discipline to 20 percent before being eliminated completely. Compulsory figures were discontinued in 1990, but compulsory dances remained a part of competition for another 20 years. At the International Skating Union Congress in 2010, they were discontinued permanently, and the original dance was replaced by a "short dance." Ice dancing again became a two-event competition.

COMPULSORY FIGURES. Figure skating prior to the 1890s consisted primarily in the tracing of specified diagrams or figures on the ice. The connection of individual figures into a cohesive program led to the development of **free skating**, but compulsory figures, often called "school figures," remained a part of competitive skating until their total elimination in 1990. They were figure eights or similar three-lobed figures that were traced three times. Judging was based largely on geometric perfection of the circles, quality of included turns, and accurate retracings of the figures. The **International Skating Union** (ISU) adopted its schedule of figures in the 1890s. They counted 60 percent of the score in men's and ladies' competitions but were never required of pair skaters or ice dancers. Changes were not made until after World War II. At the ISU's first postwar congress, the number of assigned figures to be prepared for competition was reduced from 12 to six with those skated done on alternating feet rather than both feet, but their value of 60 percent remained unchanged until 1967 when the value was reduced to 50 percent with the value of the free skating raised to 50 percent.

During the early 1970s, three talented ladies—**Trixi Schuba** of **Austria**, **Karen Magnussen** of **Canada**, and **Janet Lynn** of the **United States**—were competing against each other. Each had different strengths. Schuba was viewed as an outstanding practitioner of compulsory figures but whose free skating was weak; Lynn was viewed as an unusually fine free skater who traced relatively weak compulsory figures; Magnussen's skating was more balanced. Audiences, especially televison audiences, did not see or understand the importance of compulsory figures, which were not shown on television. What they viewed was entirely different from the actual results. That served as a catalyst for change which occurred in 1973 with a further reduction in the value of the compulsory figures to 40 percent, the addition of a **short program** counting 20 percent, and a reduction in the value of the free skating to 40 percent. In 1977, the number of figures prepared for competition was further reduced, and in 1990, compulsory figures were eliminated entirely.

CONTINENTAL STYLE. *See* INTERNATIONAL STYLE.

CONTROVERSIES. The potential for controversy is always present in any subjectively judged sport. Many minor controversies have occurred, often the result of disappointment or close scores in the final placements of skaters. A few more serious ones, usually involving dishonesty, have occurred throughout the history of figure skating. No system of judging can completely rid the sport from such controversies. Some, dating back as far as the 19th century, have resulted from incompetency in judging. The **International Skating Union** (ISU) has attempted continuously to establish clearly defined rules for competition, has implemented judges training and testing, and has created technical committees to oversee judging. This continuing effort has provided a system that assures competency in judging but not honesty. Over the years, sanctions have been placed against dishonest judges, and some have been banned from judging. The controversies have often resulted in rule changes. The most notorious of them are described briefly here with outcomes and requisite rule changes.

The third **European Championship** was held in Berlin in 1893, one year after the ISU was founded. The Berlin Skating Club, the host for the event, named **Henning Grenander** of **Sweden** as the champion. The German and Austrian Skating Association, the sponsoring organization, named the defending champion, **Eduard Engelmann Jr.** of **Austria** as the champion. The discrepancy resulted from differences in interpretation of the scoring rules which could cause a tie depending on one's interpretation of the rules. **Compulsory figures** served as the tie breaker, which Engelmann won, making him the champion. It is noted that one of the Austrian judges was badly out of line with the others, placing Grenander fifth in the compulsory figures, while the other six judges placed him first or second. But one of the German judges placed Grenander fifth in the free skating while the other six all placed him first or second. The problem was never resolved, and at the 1895 congress, the ISU declared the results invalid and annulled the competition. Rules were soon adopted, assuring that discrepancies related to scoring interpretation would not occur again.

The 1927 **World Championship** for ladies was held in Oslo, **Norway**. Of the five judges, three were from **Norway**, and one each was from **Austria** and **Germany**. **Herma Szabo** of Austria was a five-time and reigning world champion. **Sonja Henie** of Norway was the silver medalist the year before, a unanimous placement by all five judges. In Oslo, the three Norwegian judges placed Henie first, while the Austrian and German judges placed Szabo first. Henie won the first of 10 consecutive world titles. In response to the appearance and probability of bloc judging, the ISU adopted a rule allowing only one judge from a country.

The 1930 European Championship for men was held in Slovakia and was sponsored by the Czechoslovakian Federation. Although there was no overt dishonesty, irregularities occurred in the men's events. The referee was not ISU certified and the Yugoslavian judge, likewise not certified, served falsely as a replacement for a duly appointed and certified judge, a situation not discovered until after the events had been skated. The winner, **Josef Sliva**, who had not previously placed higher than fourth in international competition, defeated the reigning champion **Karl Schäfer**. Upon discovering the situation, the ISU ordered the events to be reskated a month later in Berlin. Schäfer won easily. Sliva did not compete.

In 1951, Adolf Rosdol of Austria was suspended from judging for two years for attempting to influence another judge in favor of an Austrian skater, a practice that had been occurring since 1949 and which continued during the period of his suspension and afterward. He was then elected an ISU office-holder in 1953 and served on the figure skating technical committee, eventually becoming its chair. Rosdol and another Austrian judge, Hans Grünauer, established what has been called a "calculation office." It computed throughout competitions the exact position of each competitor with each judge and then, by signals, indicated to the Austrian judge on the panel what marks should be awarded to Austrian skaters, a practice that continued for several years. At the ISU Congress in 1957, Rosdol and Grünauer both received lifetime suspensions. The ban for Rosdol was lifted after 20 years, in 1977, and he was again allowed to judge international competitions. Grünauer died in 1976.

Figure skating's most recent, infamous, and far reaching controversy came following the pairs' free skating at the Salt Lake City **Olympic Winter Games** in 2002. The short program had provided no surprises. **Elena Berezhnaya and Anton Sikharulidze** of **Russia** were in first place; **Jamie Salé and David Pelletier** of **Canada** were in second place. In the **free skating**, both pairs skated well, although Sikharulidze stepped out on the side-by-side **Axel Paulsen jumps**, an obvious mistake. Salé and Pelletier skated a totally clean program. Not atypically, judges from the Eastern European countries placed the Russians first; most of those from western countries placed the Canadians first. The French judge, Marie-Reine Le Gougne, became the swing judge. She stated in the judges' meeting following the event that she had been pressured by her federation to give advantage to the Russians. The situation was particularly blatant because of Le Gougne's admission of impropriety. A protest was filed by the Canadian Federation and pressure from the media led to the unprecedented awarding of duplicate gold medals to the Canadians. The judging scandal at Salt Lake City became more far-reaching than any previous controversy. It resulted in the adoption of a totally new judging system, which is employed in all disciplines. It has changed dramatically the dynamics of the sport.

A minor controversy occurred in the **ice dancing** competition at the World Championships in 2002, which served to underscore the problem of bloc judging clearly present in many previous championships. **Irina Lobacheva and Ilia Averbukh** of Russia easily won the title, placing first in the **compulsory dances**, the **original dance** and in the **free dance**. Likewise, **Shae-Lynn Bourne and Victor Kraatz** of Canada placed second in each event. The controversy came in the awarding of the bronze medals. Galit Chait and Sergei Sakhnovski of Israel placed fourth in the compulsory dances and the original dance. **Margarita Drobiazko and Povilas Vanagas** of Lithuania by a split decision of the judges placed fourth in the free dance, a result that proved to be contentious. The Lithuanian Federation filed a protest supported by a petition signed by more than 30 skaters and coaches. Although the protest was denied, bloc judging may have occurred. The judges from **Hungary**, Israel, **Italy**, Russia, and **Ukraine** placed the Israelis first; the judges from **Great Britain**, **France**, **Germany**, and the **United States** placed the Lithuanians first. Following the judging scandal of one month earlier at the Salt Lake City games, this added fodder to the urgent concern for the ISU to again evaluate its judging system, criteria, and safeguards.

COOLIDGE, THORNTON. *See* VINSON, MARIBEL YERBA.

COUSINS, ROBERT JOHN "ROBIN" (1957–) (GBR). At the national level, Robin Cousins was the novice champion in 1969, junior champion in 1972, and the senior champion for four years beginning in 1976. Competing at the international level from 1973 through 1979, he accumulated one silver and four bronze medals at the European and **World Championships**. In 1980, he won the European and Olympic titles. He never won a world title, primarily the result of weak **compulsory figures**. His strength was always in **free skating**. Retiring after the World Championships in 1980, Cousins sought out professional opportunities where his flair and talent served him well. In addition to touring with **Holiday on Ice** in Europe, he created his own shows, made guest appearances with **Ice Capades**, and competed in professional competitions. He was elected to the **World Figure Skating Hall of Fame** in 2004. *See also* GREAT BRITAIN.

CRANSTON, TOLLER (1949–) (CAN). Toller Cranston won the first of six consecutive Canadian titles in 1971. He placed second that year in the last holding of the **North American Championships** but twice won the succeeding **Skate Canada**. Although he competed at the **World Championships** from 1970 through 1976, his only medal was bronze in 1974. His one Olympic bid in 1976 also resulted in a bronze medal. Cranston was weak in **compulsory figures**. For his bronze medal at the World Championships, he placed first in both the short program and the free skating but eighth in the figures. For his Olympic medal, he placed first in the short program, second in the free skating, and seventh in figures. Cranston was perhaps the most avant garde skater in the history of the sport, one who judges did not always understand or appreciate. Thus, he is remembered not for his competitive record but rather for what he brought to the sport. Free skating was Cranston's strength. He was never a conventional skater but rather a bold modernist who employed angular body movements in a dramatic and highly interpretive style. Cranston's influence on the sport following his competitive career has been primarily through his work as a choreographer although he made appearances in various shows including **Holiday on Ice**. Cranston was elected to the **World Figure Skating Hall of Fame** in 2003.

CUP OF CHINA. *See* CHINA; GRAND PRIX SERIES.

CUP OF RUSSIA. *See* GRAND PRIX SERIES.

CURRY, JOHN ANTHONY (1949–1994) (GBR). Skating lessons for John Curry began at age seven, but he underwent a long period of development. He was 21 when he won the British men's title, 25 when he won his first international medal, and 27 when he won the triple crown, world, European, and Olympic titles in 1976. Curry suffered early in his career from poor jumping technique and weak **compulsory figures**. Recognizing that he had little chance of progressing without strong jumps and solid figures, he sought out two masters, **Gustave Lussi** for jumping, and **Carlo Fassi** for compulsory figures. Under their tutelage he improved dramatically, medaling at every competition in 1975 and winning every competition in 1976. Coupled with 20 years of artistic development, his then fine-honed technique provided a balance that created one of the greatest artists in the history of the sport. Turning professional, Curry formed small skating companies in which emphasis was placed on carefully choreographed and complex ensemble work skated to classical music and performed to exacting standards. Curry was inducted into the **World Figure Skating Hall of Fame** in 1991.

CZECHOSLOVAKIA. The Czechoslovak Figure Skating Association was founded in 1922 and joined the **International Skating Union** (ISU) in 1923. Two years later in 1925, Czech skaters entered both the men's and pairs' events at the **World Championships**. **Josef Sliva**, who placed fifth in the men's competition, later became involved in one of figure skating's most bizarre **controversies**. Elise and Oscar Hoppe placed last in the pairs' event but two years later became the first Czech skaters to win medals, bronze in 1927. Since World War II, several elite skaters have represented Czechoslovakia. **Alena Vrzáňová** appeared immediately after the war, competing for four years at the World Championships. In the final two, 1949 and 1950, she won Czechoslovakia's first gold medals. Another fine Czech skater, **Hana Mašková** won bronze medals in 1967 and 1968 at the World Championships and at the Grenoble **Olympic Winter Games**. Four Czech men have distinguished themselves. **Karol Divin** won three medals, one bronze and two silver in world and Olympic competition in the early 1960s. Czechoslovakia's most successful skater, **Ondrej Nepela**, a two-time European champion, won two silver followed by three consecutive gold medals, 1969–1973, at the World Championships plus the Olympic title in 1972. **Jozef Sabovčík**, the European champion twice, in 1985 and 1986, was the bronze medalist at the Olympic Winter Games in Sarajevo in 1984. Most recently, **Petr Barna** became the European champion in 1992, defeating **Viktor Petrenko** of **Ukraine**. Two pairs have carried home medals. **Věra Suchánková and Zdeněk Doležal** won gold medals at the **European Championships** in 1957 and 1958 and silver medals at the World Championships in 1958. **Radka Kovaříková and René Novotný** won silver medals at the European Championships in 1995 and gold medals at the World Championships that same year. Several influential ISU council members have been from Czechoslovakia, including Ladislav Fürst, Vladislav Čáp, and **Josef Dědič**. Dědič authored a technical book entitled *Single Figure Skating*, and with Čáp wrote the Judges' Handbook for **compulsory figures**. Both books were published by the ISU. Dědič was named an honorary vice president in 1994. *See also* ROMANOVÁ, EVA AND ROMAN, PAVEL; VERNER, TOMÁŠ.

CZECH REPUBLIC. *See* CZECHOSLOVAKIA.

D

DAFOE, FRANCES HELEN (1929–) AND BOWDEN, ROBERT NORRIS (1926–1991) (CAN). Frances Dafoe and Norris Bowden were national pair champions for four years, 1952–1955. They became world champions in 1954 and repeated the following year, but in 1956, they slipped to second behind the Austrians **Elisabeth Schwarz and Kurt Oppelt** at both the **World Championships** and the **Olympic Winter Games**. The Olympic results were hotly debated, partly because Dafoe and Bowden had consistently defeated Schwarz and Oppelt for four years. An indirect result of the debate over the next several years was movement toward a short or technical program. **Pair skating** at that time was decided on the basis of a single free skate. Following retirement, Dafoe and Bowden continued to serve their sport as world judges. They were honored with election to the **World Figure Skating Hall of Fame** in 1984. *See also* CANADA.

DANZER, EMMERICH (1944–) (AUT). Emmerich Danzer competed internationally for eight consecutive years as a strong and consistent competitor, a fine free skater who also traced excellent **compulsory figures**. He won the European title four times, 1965–1968, and the world title three times, 1966–1968. Danzer placed fifth at the Innsbruck **Olympic Winter Games** in 1964. He was expected to win the gold medal at the Grenoble games in 1968 but was upset by his compatriot **Wolfgang Schwarz** who he had defeated consistently in 12 national and international competitions. Schwarz won the gold medal, while Danzer slipped to fourth in spite of winning the free skating, the result of an uncharacteristically poor showing in the compulsory figures. Following retirement from competitive skating, Danzer skated in various shows including **Holiday on Ice** and worked as a coach at Lake Placid in the United States. *See also* AUSTRIA.

DAVIES, NESTA. *See* WEIGHT, PAMELA AND THOMAS, PAUL.

DAVIS, MARGARET. *See* FOURS; ROGERS, MELVILLE.

DAVIS, MERYL (1987–) AND WHITE, CHARLIE (1987–) (USA). Meryl Davis and Charlie White began skating together at age nine and became the **United States** junior **ice dancing** champions in 2006. They proceeded to win bronze medals at the **World Junior Championships** that year. Their first national senior title was won in 2009, a year when the reigning U.S. champions **Tanith Belbin and Benjamin Agosto** did not compete because of an injury, but a year later they defeated Belbin and Agosto to win their second title. Three appearances at the **Four Continents Championships** resulted in silver medals in 2008 and gold medals in 2009. They were the bronze medalists at the **Grand Prix Finals** in 2009. Four consecutive appearances at the **World Championships** show annual improvement in the rankings: seventh in 2007, sixth in 2008, fourth in 2009, and second behind **Tessa Virtue and Scott Moir** of **Canada** in 2010 in an extremely close competition. The results had been the same at the **Olympic Winter Games** one month earlier.

DAVOS, SWITZERLAND. In the days before **artificial ice**, devotees of figure skating with the means to do so sought winter vacation spots that could provide opportunities to practice their sport. Three to four months of skating were assured in the Swiss Alps. The most important resorts were at Davos and **St. Moritz**. Davos is located in a valley at an elevation of 5,100 feet. It provides an excellent balance of long skating seasons, much sun, and natural protection from strong winds. There are reports of skating there by the Dutch, Germans, and Russians as early as the 1860s. The Hotel Belvedere opened an ice rink in 1877 that was dominated by British skaters and became known as the English rink. A second rink soon opened, primarily to accommodate German and Russian skaters. In 1880, the Davos Skating Club was formed with more than 200 members throughout the skating world. Davos later served as the site for 11 World Championships in figure skating, sometimes for just one discipline. Pairs' and ladies' competitions before World War II were often held at different locations from the men's competitions.

DEAN, CHRISTOPHER COLIN. *See* TORVILL, JAYNE AND DEAN, CHRISTOPHER COLIN.

DEATH SPIRAL. Death spirals are exciting **pair-skating** moves first done in the 1920s. They are required elements in **short programs**. The man pivots on his toe pick as the lady clasps his hand and spins around him with her body parallel to the ice either on an inside or an outside edge skating forward or backward. A minimum of one complete revolution is required. For short programs, pairs do a specific death spiral prescribed for that season by the **International Skating Union**. Death spirals are usually included in **free-skating** programs as well, with those done being selected by the skaters. Some pairs include multiple death spirals in their free-skating programs. The

Protopopovs occasionally included all four sequentially. **Fours** skaters in the 1990s have done quad death spirals in which the ladies skate close together, almost on top of each other, around the men's closely placed pivots.

DĚDIČ, JOSEF (1924–1993) (CZE). Josef Dědič was a national champion but competed only once internationally, at the **European Championships** in 1948, placing ninth. His contributions to the sport came later through service to the **International Skating Union** (ISU) as a member and chair of the figure skating technical committee, as a council member, and as a vice president. In 1994, he was elected as an honorary vice president. Dědič was a respected world judge and referee. He wrote a definitive book on skating technique and was coauthor of two of the ISU's judges' handbooks. Dědič was elected to the **World Figure Skating Hall of Fame** in 1998. *See also* CZECHOSLOVAKIA.

DE LEEUW, DIANNE (1955–) (NED). Dianne de Leeuw, the daughter of Dutch nationals, was born in Orange County, California, and thus enjoyed the citizenship of two countries. She chose to skate for the **Netherlands**, which provided the opportunity to compete at the **European Championships**. Her international career began in 1971. From 1972 through 1976, she competed at every world, European, and Olympic championship demonstrating steady improvement without medaling for three years after which she medaled at every competition entered, two bronze, three silver, and two gold. She won the world title in 1975 and the European title in 1976. At the Innsbruck **Olympic Winter Games** in 1976, she claimed the silver medal. Following retirement from competitive skating, de Leeuw toured with **Holiday on Ice** and the **Ice Follies**, and she has worked as a skating coach.

DEL MONTE, MRS. *See* FRANCE.

DELOBEL, ISABELLE (1978–) AND SCHOENFELDER, OLIVIER (1977–) (FRA). In a senior career that spanned 14 years, Isabelle Delobel and Olivier Schoenfelder were the French national **ice dancing** champions for six consecutive years, 2003–2008. Competing at 10 **European Championships**, they accumulated one medal of each color, winning the title in 2007. At 11 **World Championships**, they won the title in 2008 but acquired no other medals. Competing at three **Grand Prix Finals**, they won bronze medals in 2008 and gold medals in 2009. Delobel and Schoenfelder competed twice at the **Olympic Winter Games**, placing fourth in 2006 and sixth in 2010.

DE NANCE, WILLIAM, JR. *See* HISEY, JOYCE.

DEMMY, LAWRENCE. *See* WESTWOOD, JEAN AND DEMMY, LAWRENCE.

DENCH, ROBERT (1908–1975) (GBR). Robert Dench with his partner, Lesley Turner, invented the "blues" during the 1930s, a time when one-fourth of the **compulsory dances** still employed were invented by three British couples. The others two couples were **Reginald J. Wilkie and Daphne B. Wallis** and **Eva Keats and Erik van der Weyden**. Dench and his wife, Rosemarie Stewart, who he married in 1938, published a still valuable book, *Pair Skating and Dancing on Ice*. Stewart had earlier competed in pairs with Ernest H. C. Yates. They placed 10th at the 1936 **Olympic Winter Games**. **Ice dancing** did not become an international discipline until 1950, two years before the first world championship. As professionals, Dench and Stewart skated in the first **Ice Capades** tour, 1940–1941, and remained with the company for many years as skaters and coaches.

DENKOVA, ALBENA (1974–) AND STAVISKI, MAXIM (1977–) (BUL). Ice dancer Albena Denkova competed internationally for four years, 1992–1995, with Christo Nikolov. She did not compete in 1996 but reappeared in 1997 with her new partner, Maxim Staviski. They competed for 11 years and, as is often characteristic of ice dancers, improved gradually but steadily. Denkova and Staviski never captured a European title but won silver medals twice. Of significance are their two consecutive world titles won in 2006 and 2007. They became **Bulgaria**'s first world champions in any discipline. Denkova and Staviski also won the **Grand Prix Finals** title in 2007. Denkova serves as president of the Bulgarian Federation. *See also* BULGARIA.

DENNY, DOREEN. *See* JONES, COURTNEY J. L.

DEWHIRST, JOAN (1935–) AND SLATER, JOHN E. (c. 1928–1989) (GBR). Joan Dewhirst and John Slater were the silver medalists at the first two **World Championships** in **ice dancing**, 1952 and 1953, behind their countrymen, **Jean Westwood and Lawrence Demmy**. Turning professional and marrying the following year, they entered the **Open Professional Championships**, winning that competition six times, 1955–1957 and 1959–1961. Their son Nicky Slater and his partner Karen Barber became British ice dancing champions in the 1980s and bronze medalists at the **European Championships** in 1983. During the same years in which she won ice dancing medals, 1952 and 1953, Joan Dewhirst was a champion in the **English style**. It is rare for skaters to compete in both styles, and no other skater has been both an English and **international style** champion at the same time. She won the Cobb Cup, a junior competition, in 1953 and was a part of teams that won the Bear Challenge Cup for combined skating in 1952 and 1953.

DIESTELMEYER, FLORIANE. *See* MORROW, SUZANNE AND DIESTELMEYER, WALLACE.

DIESTELMEYER, WALLACE. *See* MORROW, SUZANNE AND DIESTELMEYER, WALLACE.

DIJKSTRA, SJOUKJE ROSALINDE (1942–) (NED). Sjoukje Dijkstra first appeared on the international scene in 1954 and placed 19th at the **European Championships**. She improved each year and in 1959 medaled for the first time, carrying home a silver medal from the European Championships and a bronze medal from the **World Championships**. A year later the medals were gold and silver, and she also won a silver medal at the Squaw Valley **Olympic Winter Games**. Thereafter she was not defeated, winning every world, European, and Olympic competition from 1961 through 1964. Following retirement, she toured with **Holiday on Ice**. *See also* NETHERLANDS.

DILLINGHAM, CHARLES. *See* OELSCHLAGEL, CHARLOTTE.

DIMITROVA, MARGARITA. *See* BULGARIA.

DISNEY ON ICE. *See* ICE FOLLIES.

DIVIN, KAROL (1936–) (CZE). Karol Divin was the first of two Czechoslovakian men who were major contenders internationally from the mid-1950s through the mid-1970s. **Ondrej Nepela** was the second. Competing at the **European Championships** in 1954, his first year on the international scene, Divin won the bronze medal. Six additional appearances all resulted in medals, two bronze, two silver, and two gold. Equal success did not occur at the **World Championships**. In seven appearances through 1964, he garnered just two medals, silver in 1962 and bronze in 1964. Three Olympic appearances earned him a silver medal in 1960. One of his most disappointing competitions occurred in 1962 at the World Championships in Prague. Divin was comfortably in first place after the compulsory figures, but in the free skating he did not do well, being placed third or fourth by every judge. Canadian **Donald Jackson** skated a near perfect program, which included the first completed triple **Lutz jump** in competition. All judges placed Jackson first, and he became the world champion. *See also* CZECHOSLOVAKIA.

DMITRENKO, DMITRI (1973–) (UKR). Competing internationally for 10 years, Dmitri Dmitrenko had his most successful outing during his first year, 1993, winning the gold medal at the **European Championships**. Although his placement was always in the top eight in the ensuing years, his only other medal was bronze in 2000. At the 1999 **World Championships**, his best placement was 11th; at the 1998 **Olympic Games** he placed 14th.

DMITRIEV, ARTUR (1968–) (URS/RUS). Artur Dmitriev is one of two pair skaters, both from **Russia**, who have won Olympic gold with two partners, the other being **Irina Rodnina**. For five years beginning in 1990, Dmitriev skated internationally with Natalia Mishkutenok (1970–). They capped their career with the triple crown, European, Olympic, and world titles in 1994 for a career total international medal count of two bronze, one silver, and four gold. They skated professionally for a year before Dmitriev returned to the amateur ranks in 1996 and competed for three years with a second partner, Oksana Kazakova (1975–). Kazakova and Dmitriev capped their career with Olympic gold in 1998. They had placed second at the **European Championships** that year but were unable to compete at the **World Championships** owing to food poisoning contracted by Dmitriev. Their record also includes the European title in 1996 and bronze medals at the World Championships in 1997.

DOANE, PAULETTE (1953–) AND ORMSBY, KENNETH (1942–) (CAN). Ice dancers Paulette Doane and Kenneth Ormsby were the Canadian junior champions in 1961 and the senior champions for two years, 1963 and 1964. Competing twice at the biennial **North American Championships**, they collected bronze medals in 1961 and won the title in 1963. They competed for three years at the **World Championships**, placing fifth in 1962, third in 1963, and second in 1964 behind the four-time champions **Eva Romanová and Pavel Roman**.

DOLEŽAL, ZDENĚK. *See* SUCHÁNKOVÁ, VĚRA AND DOLEŽAL, ZDENĚK.

DOMNINA, OKSANA (1984–) AND SHABALIN, MAXIM (1982–) (RUS). Oksana Domnina and Maxim Shabalin, both of whom had competed nationally with previous partners, won the world junior **ice dancing** title in 2003. As seniors, they were national champions in 2005 and 2007. Competing at the **Grand Prix Finals** for three years, they won medals of each color, bronze in 2007, gold in 2008, and silver in 2009. At the **European Championships**, they won medals twice, silver in 2007 and gold in 2008, and at the

World Championships once, gold in 2009. Domnina and Shabalin competed at the **Olympic Winter Games** in 2006 placing ninth and in 2010 winning the bronze medals.

DORE, DAVID M. (1940–) (CAN). David Dore competed nationally beginning in 1964. He won no singles' titles but was a member of a **four** including Bonnie Anderson, Laura Maybee, and Gregory Folk. They won the Canadian national title in 1964. It was a significant event historically because fours events, once so popular in **Canada**, were not held again until 1986. Dore became active in the **Canadian Figure Skating Association** (CSFA), serving as vice president from 1976 until 1980 and as president from 1980 until 1984. He was then hired for the position of program director in 1985, and in January 1986 became the association's first director general, a position he held for 18 years. Dore was elected in 2002 as the **International Skating Union**'s (ISU) vice president for figure skating, a position he still holds. He was also a world judge, serving at several **World Championships** and at the **Olympic Winter Games** of 1984.

DRIANO, SUZANNE. *See* FASSI, CARLO.

DROBIAZKO, MARGARITA (1971–) AND VANAGAS, POVILAS (1973–) (LTU). Ice dancers Margarita Drobiazko and Povilas Vanagas first appeared on the international scene in 1993. The Lithuanian Figure Skating Association had joined the **International Skating Union** (ISU) just two years earlier in 1991. Drobiazko and Vanagas won bronze medals at both the European and **World Championships** in 2000, a notable achievement. They received no further medals but continued competing through the 2002 season. In three Olympic efforts, their best placement was fifth in 2002. At the World Championships that year, the result was mildly contentious. Drobiazko and Vanagas were in third place entering the **free dance** with an Israeli couple, Galit Chait and Sergei Sakhnovski in fourth. By a split decision of the judges, the Israelis defeated the Lithuanians, placing third. The Lithuanian Federation filed a protest, and about 30 skaters signed a petition stating their discomfort with the result saying that the Lithuanians had skated a medal-winning performance and were not justly rewarded. The protest was rejected by the ISU.

DU BIEF, JACQUELINE (1930–) (FRA). Jacqueline du Bief competed at four **European Championships**, winning one bronze and two silver medals, and at four **World Championships**, winning one silver medal before becoming the ladies' world champion in 1952. She remains **France**'s only lady world champion. At the **Olympic Winter Games** in 1952, she claimed the bronze medal. Always an outgoing crowd pleaser as a competitor, du Bief readily answered the call of show skating. Turning professional, she moved to the United States and skated for many years with **Ice Capades**. Her book, *Thin Ice*, written four years into her professional career, provides valuable information on show skating in the 1950s.

DUBREUIL, MARIE-FRANCE (1974–) AND LAUZON, PATRICE (1975–) (CAN). Marie-France Dubreuil and Patrice Lauzon became **ice dancing** partners in 1995. They won their first national title in 2000, a year when the eight-time champions **Shae-Lynn Bourne and Victor Kraatz** did not compete. With the return of Bourne and Kraatz, they placed second for three years, 2001–2003, but after Bourne and Kraatz retired, they won the title each of their last four years of competitive skating, 2004–2007. Dubreuil and Lauzon qualified for the **Grand Prix Finals** in three consecutive years, placing fifth in 2005, third in 2006, and second in 2007. They competed at the **Four Continents Championships** on five occasions and won four medals including the title in 2007. Competing at eight **World Championships**, they won medals in 2006 and 2007, both of which were silver. In three Olympic efforts, they placed 12th in 2002, withdrew after a fall in the **original dance** in 2006, and placed sixth in 2010.

DUCHESNAY, ISABELLE (1963–) AND PAUL (1961–) (FRA). Isabelle and Paul Duchesnay, a French Canadian sister-and-brother **ice dancing** couple, competed for **France**. Their first year on the international scene, 1986, resulted in an eighth-place finish at the **European Championships** and a 12th-place finish at the **World Championships**. Competing and improving each year, their best results were silver medals at the European Championships in 1991, gold medals at the World Championships in 1991, and silver medals at the **Olympic Winter Games** in 1992 after which they turned professional. In addition to skating in shows, including **Holiday on Ice**, they became coaches.

DUCHESNAY, PAUL. *See* DUCHESNAY, ISABELLE AND PAUL.

DUNFIELD, PETER. *See* KLOPFER, SONYA.

DUNGJEN, JASON. *See* INA, KYOKO.

DUNN, JOHN EDWARD POWELL "JACK" (1917–1938) (GBR). Jack Dunn placed second at the British national championships in 1934 and 1935. In two appearances at the **European Championships** those same years, he placed fourth and sixth. His results at two **World Championships** were second and fourth in 1935 and 1936. Competing at the last **Olympic Winter Games** before the war in 1936, he placed sixth. Dunn is remembered as an excellent free skater and as one of **Sonja Henie**'s skating partners. Henie moved to the **United States** in 1936, following her eligible career. Dunn followed and skated in shows with her as Henie crossed the country on her way to Hollywood. He contracted tularemia, an infectious disease, and died in July 1938 in Hollywood.

DURASOVA, TATIANA. *See* WORLD JUNIOR FIGURE SKATING CHAMPIONSHIPS.

DWYER, RICHARD (1935–) (USA). Richard Dwyer, almost better known as "Mr. Debonair," appeared on the competitive scene as a student of **Eugene Turner** just after World War II. He won the **United States** novice men's title in 1948 as a 12-year-old, the junior title a year later, and the bronze medal in his first year as a senior in 1950, but he ended his amateur career that year at age 14 when Eddie Shipstad and Oscar Johnson offered him a contract with the **Ice Follies**, an arrangement that lasted for 30 years. Always the showman and never tiring of skating for audiences, Mr. Debonair continued performing in other shows including **Ice Capades**. Durability is represented in his education as well. For 22 years, he pursued a college degree during summers at the University of San Francisco, receiving his bachelor's degree at age 39. Dwyer, one of the most important and successful show skaters in the history of figure skating, was elected into the **World Figure Skating Hall of Fame** in 1993.

DYER, LORNA (1945–) AND CARRELL, JOHN (USA). Lorna Dyer and John Carrell competed as an **ice-dancing** couple for five years, 1963–1967. She had previously competed with King Cole, and they placed third at the United States Championships in 1962. Dyer and Carrell won medals each year at the national championships, two bronze, two silver, and gold in 1967, their final season. They also claimed North American titles in 1965 and 1967. Competing annually at the **World Championships**, they progressed consistently, placing eighth in 1963 and fifth a year later. Two bronze medals followed in 1965 and 1966 before their final year, 1967, when they won silver medals behind the four-time British champions, **Diane Towler and Bernard Ford**. *See also* UNITED STATES.

E

EDGES. A skate blade, which is less than an eighth of an inch wide, is sharpened on each side with a curved hollow space between. Almost all skating is done with the skater leaning so that only one edge of the blade is in contact with the ice. When the outer edge is employed, the skater is skating on an outside edge; when the inner edge is employed, the skater is skating on an inside edge. Outside and inside edges can be done on either foot, forward or backward.

EDINBURGH SKATING CLUB. The Edinburgh Skating Club held the distinction of being the only 18th-century skating club. Its organizational date has been in dispute, but it was probably established in 1744. The **London Skating Club**, formed in 1830, copied much of its organizational bylaws and rules directly from the Minute Books of the Edinburgh club. Admission to the Edinburgh club was by election. A skating test employed in the 19th century required candidates to skate complete circles on both feet and to jump over hats placed on top of each other. Women were not allowed and could not participate with men in combined skating until the late 19th century. Membership was an honor and club pins were worn proudly.

EIGEL, HANNA (1938–) (AUT). Hanna Eigel was one of three outstanding Austrian ladies who competed in the late 1950s, all of whom became national champions, European champions, and world silver medalists. In 1957, they swept the medals at the **European Championships**: Eigel, gold; **Ingrid Wendl**, silver; and **Hanna Walter**, bronze. Eigel competed just three times each at the European and **World Championships**. She placed sixth in her first European effort before winning the title twice in 1955 and 1957. She placed seventh in her first world effort before winning bronze and silver medals, also in 1955 and 1957. At the **Olympic Winter Games** in 1956, she placed fifth. Upon retirement from competitive skating in 1959, Eigel joined **Holiday on Ice**.

EILEN, CHRISTIANE. *See* GUHEL, CHRISTIANE AND JEAN PAUL.

EILERS, LUDOWIKA ANTJE MARGARETA (1884–1968) (FIN/GER) AND JAKOBSSON, WALTER ANDREAS (1882–1957) (GER). Pair skaters Ludowika Eilers of **Finland** and Walter Jakobsson of **Germany** first competed internationally as a couple in 1910 representing their respective countries, a procedure then possible under **International Skating Union** (ISU) rules. Following their marriage in 1911, they represented Finland. Competing before and after the war at every **World Championship** through 1923, the Jakobssons were silver medalists four times and claimed three world titles, 1911, 1914, and 1923. They added an Olympic title to their laurels in 1920. Walter Jakobsson served the ISU as a council member from 1927 through 1929 and again from 1931 through 1947.

EISLER, LLOYD. *See* BRASSEUR, ISABELLE AND EISLER, LLOYD.

ELDREDGE, TODD (1971–) (USA). For 20 years, 1989–2008, Todd Eldredge was the only American man to win a world title and from 1990 to 2001 the only one to win a silver medal. His long international career spanned 16 years. He won the world junior title in 1986 and the senior title 10 years later. He did not compete every year at the **World Championships** but accumulated in addition to his title in 1996 one bronze and three silver medals. Only at his first world effort in 1992 did he fail to medal. His best result in three Olympic appearances was fourth in 1998. At the national level, only the seven titles of **Roger Turner** and **Dick Button** surpass Eldredge's six. Eldredge skated into the era of quadruple jumps, a feat he was unable to accomplish successfully but one in which his younger opponents excelled. His artistry, which was always recognized, made him popular with the American public. After the Salt Lake City **Olympic Winter Games** in 2002, he turned professional and joined **Stars on Ice**.

ELSON, SANDRA. *See* TORVILL, JAYNE AND DEAN, CHRISTOPHER.

ELTSOVA, MARINA (1970–) AND BUSHKOV, ANDREI (1969–) (RUS). Pair skaters Marina Eltsova and Andrei Bushkov won the European title on their first try in 1993 but placed sixth at the **World Championships**. The results for the remainder of their eligible career were somewhat inconsistent. At the **European Championships**, they garnered two fourth-place finishes and a second gold medal in 1997. At the World Championships between 1994 and 1997, they garnered a fourth-place finish plus a medal of each color with their world title coming in 1996. In their final year of eligible competition, 1998, they placed well down in the rankings, seventh at the **Olympic Winter Games** and sixth at the World Championships. *See also* RUSSIA.

ENDERS, ALBERT. *See* CAMBRIDGE, SADIE AND ENDERS, ALBERT.

ENGELMANN, EDUARD, JR. (1864–1944) (AUT). Eduard Engelmann Jr., a member of an important Viennese skating family, competed at the **Great International Skating Tournament** in 1882 and placed second. A master of **special figures**, he is remembered for his unique figure the "Engelmann star." Engelmann competed at the **European Championships** and won for three consecutive years, 1892–1894, although the results of the 1893 competition, which provided figure skating's first major **controversy**, were declared invalid and annulled by the **International Skating Union** in 1895. Engelmann never competed at a **World Championship**.

ENGELMANN, HELENE (1898–1985) (AUT). Helene Engelmann, a member of an important Viennese skating family, was active in the **Vienna Skating Club**. She competed in pairs with two partners becoming a world champion with both of them, one before and one after World War I. With Karl Mejstrik (1895–?) she won the world title in 1913, their first effort internationally. They slipped to second a year later behind **Ludowika Eilers and Walter Jakobsson**, a couple they had narrowly defeated in 1913. Following the war, Engelmann partnered with Alfred Berger (1894–1966), and they were unbeatable, winning gold medals at the World Championships in 1922 and 1924 and at the Chamonix **Olympic Winter Games** in 1924. *See also* AUSTRIA.

ENGLAND. *See* GREAT BRITAIN.

ENGLISH STYLE. Prior to the establishment of the **International Skating Union** (ISU) in 1892, there were three prevalent styles of skating: English style, **American style**, and **international style**. The ISU adopted the international style. The American style disappeared quickly, but the English style continued into the 21st century. English style is unique owing to a prescribed body position and carriage. It is perfectly suited for combined skating, which was practiced in the American style as well, and also for **hand-in-hand skating**. Those disciplines were important in the 19th century, especially in **England**. The body position includes a straight skating leg with the free leg close behind, the heels nearly together, the toe of the free foot just off the ice and pointing down. Arms are held relative to the corresponding legs, the arm relative to the employed leg held slightly up but not too much with the other arm hung easily down. Arms and legs are not used to assist with turns as they are in the international style, an important distinction. Although many British skaters adopted the international style during the 1890s, others continued their national tradition. Separate test structures and competitions were adopted by the **National Skating Association**, and they remain in effect today. Skaters rarely practice or compete in both styles, a notable exception being **Joan Dewhirst** who won world medals in **ice dancing** in 1952 and 1953 and was that year a champion in English style skating. Two early champions in the English style, **Madge Syers** and **Phyllis Johnson**, adopted the international style and became champions in it as well. Only skaters in the **Royal Skating Club** still practice English style today, and the discipline will probably disappear with this generation. It is remarkable that the English style has survived for more than a century after the ISU adopted the international style. The last competition was held in 2001, and the last coach in English style skating, Gerald Spain, a former champion, died in September 2007.

ERRATH, CHRISTINE (1956–) (GDR). Christine Errath had just turned 12 when she competed at the **European Championships** in 1969 and placed 18th. She did not compete internationally in 1970 but thereafter competed every year through 1976 at both the European and the **World Championships**. She won three European titles, 1973–1975, and the world title in 1974. Her one Olympic effort in 1976 resulted in a bronze medal. Errath's total medal count from international competitions is four bronze, one silver, and four gold. She is remembered for her athleticism and for being a fearless jumper. *See also* GERMANY.

EUROPEAN FIGURE SKATING CHAMPIONSHIPS. The combined German and Austrian Figure Skating Association, founded in 1888, organized the first European Figure Skating Championship, which was held in Hamburg, **Germany**, January 23–24, 1891. Seven men competed in the event that included only **compulsory figures**. All competitors were from Germany or **Austria**. The winner was **Oskar Uhlig** of Germany. The second European Championship was held in Vienna, Austria, a year later, January 1892. It included **free skating** as well as compulsory figures. The eight competitors included one from **Hungary**, **Tibor von Földváry**, who placed second. He became the European champion in 1895. The winner was **Eduard Engelmann Jr.** of **Austria**. The European Championships have continued and are today the oldest international competition. The scoring of the 1893 competition, now under the newly established **International Skating Union** (ISU), resulted in a major **controversy**, causing the ISU to annul the competition. The European Championships were not held in 1896 or 1897, a result of the newly established **World Championships** held for the first time in 1896. They were canceled in 1902 and 1903 owing to a lack of ice and for seven years each during the two world wars. The European Championships were open, prior to World War II, to skaters from all federations and clubs belonging to the ISU. No skater from a non-European country competed except for four Japanese skaters in 1936, none of whom placed higher than seventh. But when competition resumed in 1947, **Barbara Ann Scott** of **Canada** and **Gretchen Merrill** of the **United States** entered. Scott won and Merrill placed second in a field of 20 ladies. A year later in 1948, Scott won a second European title. Merrill did not compete. Two men from the United States competed that year as well. John Lettengarver placed fifth in a field of nine, but **Dick Button** won the competition. As a result, the ISU closed the European Championships to skaters from non-European countries. North Americans had won three of the six titles awarded in 1947 and 1948. Originally for men only, ladies' and pairs' events were added in 1930 and **ice dancing** events in 1954. The 100th holding of the European Championships occurred at Zagreb, Croatia, in 2008. See Appendix G for a list of all European medalists.

EWELL, RICHARD. *See* FAIRBANKS, MABEL.

F

FADEEV, ALEXANDR (1964–) (URS). Alexandr Fadeev first appeared at the **World Junior Championships** in 1979 and won the bronze medal. A year later, he won the title. As a senior, he was the Soviet national champion for six years. He competed internationally for 10 seasons. At the **European Championships** in addition to two bronze medals, he won gold medals in 1984 and again from 1987 to 1989. At the **World Championships**, he collected three bronze medals and won the world title in 1985. His two Olympic efforts resulted in a seventh-place finish in 1980 and a fourth-place finish in 1988. Today Fadeev is a coach in the **United States**. *See also* RUSSIA.

FAIRBANKS, MABEL (1916–2001) (USA). Living in New York City, Mabel Fairbanks at age 10 received a pair of ice skates from her parents. In the 1930s and for three decades afterward, opportunities were denied to blacks in the **United States**, which included skating in public rinks regardless of their talent. Fairbanks was allowed to skate in one New York rink, primarily because she was a child. **Maribel Vinson** recognized her talent and reportedly gave her lessons without charge. By the mid-1940s, her skating had blossomed, but she could not compete because she did not belong to a skating club. Skating with professional touring companies was likewise not an option for an African American. Moving to California, Fairbanks ultimately became a respected teacher and coach. She had many students, the most famous being **Tai Babilonia and Randy Gardner**. Many of her students became fine skaters. Atoy Wilson in 1966 was the first African American to become a U.S. novice champion. After retiring from competitive skating in 1971, he toured with **Ice Capades** and **Holiday on Ice**. Other African American students included Leslie Robinson, also a Holiday on Ice star; Richard Ewell III, the national junior champion in 1970; and Michelle McCladdie, who, skating with Ewell, won the 1972 junior pair title. McCladdie and Ewell toured with Ice Capades. Fairbanks was elected to the United States Figure Skating Hall of Fame in 1997.

FALK, PAUL. *See* BARAN, RIA AND FALK, PAUL.

FASSI, CARLO (1929–1997) (ITA). By winning the bronze medal in 1952 Carlo Fassi became the first of just three singles skaters from **Italy** who have medaled at the **World Championships**. The American-born Suzanne Driano won the bronze medal in 1978, and **Carolina Kostner** won the silver medal in 2008. Competing for six years at the **European Championships**, beginning in 1949, Fassi advanced consistently in the rankings from fourth place that year through two bronze, one silver, and gold medals in 1953 and 1954. Fassi's importance, however, is not found in his competitive record but rather in his role as one of the most respected and successful coaches in the history of the sport. Emigrating to the **United States** in 1961, he devoted his life, assisted by his wife Christa, to teaching and coaching. World and Olympic champions **Peggy Fleming**, **John Curry**, **Dorothy Hamill**, **Robin Cousins**, and **Jill Trenary** were among his students. Fassi has left his ideas and methodology in written form in *Figure Skating with Carlo Fassi*. He was elected posthumously into the **World Figure Skating Hall of Fame** in 1997.

FAVART, JACQUES (1920–1980) (FRA). Jacques Favart, the eighth president of the **International Skating Union** (ISU), served for 13 years, 1967–1980. Favart competed in singles and in pairs. He was the French men's champion in 1942 and with his wife, Denise, the pairs champion from 1946 through 1950. They competed at the European and World Championships in 1947 and the **Olympic Winter Games** in 1948. Following his competitive years, he became a judge and referee at both the national and international level. Favart served as president of the Fédération Française des Sports de Glace, 1968–1969, while contemporaneously serving as president of the ISU. His service to the ISU included two terms on the Figure Skating Technical Committee, 1955–1959, the second as its chairperson. From 1959 to 1967, he was a vice president after which he served as president until his death in 1980. During his presidency, **ice dancing** became an Olympic sport. Like other presidents during the postwar years, Favart found it necessary to deal with difficult Cold War issues. In 1978 he oversaw the one-year suspension of all judges from the **Soviet Union**, a result of several years of demonstrably biased judging. For his devoted and effective leadership, in 1982 the ISU posthumously elected him as an honorary president and established the Favart Trophy, which is awarded annually to both speed skaters and figure skaters in recognition of their contributions to the sports.

FEDERAL REPUBLIC OF GERMANY. *See* GERMANY.

FENTON, GERALDINE. *See* McLACHLAN, WILLIAM.

FINLAND. Finland's most successful skaters were the pair of **Ludowika Eilers and Walter Jakobsson** who medaled at seven consecutive **World Championships** beginning in 1910, five before and two after the war. Several Finnish men competed between the world wars, the most successful being Marcus Nikkanen who competed in seven World Championships beginning in 1929. His best placement was third in 1934. Since World War II, medals in World competition have been won by the pair of **Susanna Rahkamo and Petri Kokko**, bronze in 1994 and silver in 1995. In figure skating's newest discipline, **synchronized team skating**, which became a world discipline in 2000, Finland has won 14 of the 33 medals awarded, including four bronze, five silver, and five gold. Four times Finnish teams have won two medals. No other country has won multiple medals in the same year. In only one year, 2007, has a Finnish team failed to medal. Several World Championships have been held in Helsinki including the men's events in 1914, the pairs' events in 1934, and all events in 1983 and 1999. The synchronized skating championships, always held separately, were held in Helsinki in 2001. Walter Jakobsson held important positions in the International Skating Union from 1927 through 1929 and again from 1931 through 1947. *See also* LEPISTÖ, LAURA.

FLAMING LEAVES INTERNATIONAL COMPETITION. *See* SKATE AMERICA; SKATE CANADA.

FLEMING, PEGGY GALE (1948–) (USA). Following the **plane crash** in Belgium in 1961, which took the lives of the entire world team on its way to the championships in Prague, the **United States**, which had dominated singles skating since World War II, had to rebuild. The first lady world champion following the crash became one of America's most popular skaters. Peggy Fleming was a surprise winner at the United States Championships in 1964, her first year as a senior. She had not won the junior title. Fleming proceeded to place sixth at the **Olympic Winter Games** and seventh at the **World Championships** that year. She remained the national champion for five years. Her first world medal was bronze in 1965. For the next three years, 1966–1968, all of Fleming's medals at every competition, national, North American, world, and Olympic were gold, and all were won decisively. Her senior career was under the tutelage of **Carlo Fassi**. In her free-skating program at the Grenoble Winter Olympics, she included a combined element frequently associated with Fleming, a double **Axel Paulsen jump** approached and finished in a **spread eagle** position. Upon turning professional, Fleming toured with the **Ice Follies**, skated in television specials, and performed in exhibitions into the 1990s. She also served as a television commentator on ABC beside **Dick Button** and

Terry Gannon. Fleming was honored in 1976 as the youngest of 20 persons in the initial class elected to the **World Figure Skating Hall of Fame**.

FLIP JUMP. The flip jump is a toe assisted jump approached on a relatively shallow backward inside edge with a landing on a backward outside edge on the opposite foot. The jump is attributed to Bruce Mapes, an American skater of the 1920s who had turned professional by the 1930s. He and his wife **Evelyn Chandler** were featured skaters with the **Ice Follies**. *See also* JUMPS.

FÖLDVÁRY, TIBOR VON (HUN). Tibor von Földváry competed at the **European Championships** for three consecutive years beginning in 1893, the year for which the **International Skating Union** declared the competition invalid owing to a **controversy** which resulted from differing interpretations of the scoring rules. Földváry placed fourth. In the two ensuing years he won silver and gold medals. Földváry never competed at the **World Championships**. *See also* HUNGARY.

FOLK, GREGORY. *See* DORE, DAVID M.

FORD, BERNARD. *See* TOWLER, DIANE, AND FORD, BERNARD.

FOTHERINGILL, JUDIANNE AND JERRY. *See* KAUFFMAN, CYNTHIA DIANE AND RONALD LEE.

FOUR CONTINENTS CHAMPIONSHIPS. After 1948, the **European Championships** were closed to non-European skaters. Skaters from **Canada** and the **United States** at that time competed in the biennial **North American Championships**, which were held alternately in the two countries but were discontinued after the 1971 championships. By then, other non-European skaters were entering world competitions, especially ones from **Japan**. Skaters from European countries had the advantage of a major international competition not open to skaters from other parts of the world. To provide equal opportunities to those skaters, in 1999 the **International Skating Union** (ISU) established the Four Continents Championships for skaters from North America, Asia, Australia, and Africa. At that time, there were no ISU members from South America. See Appendix F for a list of Four Continents medalists and Appendix A for a list of ISU members.

FOURS. Fours skating is a discipline no longer contested that lasted in its heyday just over a generation. It was immensely popular in **Canada** and the **United States**. Dating from the first decade of the 20th century, it began as an innovation of Canadian skating clubs. Fours is specifically for two mixed couples and incorporates most of the moves of **pair skating** as well as others unique to the discipline. Fours was an important event at the **North American Championships** with Canadian fours dominating through most of its competitive history. The most successful team, representing the Minto Skating Club in Ottawa, was Margaret Davis, Prudence Holbrook, Guy Owen, and **Melville Rogers**. They won the North American Championships three consecutive times beginning in 1933 and are the only team in the history of the event to repeat as champions. Not until 1941 did an American team prevail. **Janette Ahrens**, Mary Louise Premer, Robert Uppgren, and Lyman Wakefield Jr. represented the St. Paul Skating Club. Since World War II, fours competitions have been held only infrequently, most recently in 1997 at Canada's national championships.

FOWLER, G. HERBERT. *See* CLARKE, HERBERT J.

FOX, BERNARD. *See* TOZZER, JOAN AND FOX, BERNARD.

FRANCE. France has a long history in figure skating. The second major book on the sport, *Le vrai patineur* (The True Skater) by Jean Garcin, published in 1813, describes an advanced level of skating for that time. Emphasis was placed on artistry, a French characteristic that continued throughout the century. The three-step waltz, the first ice dance to feature speed and flow across the ice in a waltz position was reportedly first skated in Paris in 1894. Within a year it had become a craze throughout Europe, a defining moment in the history of **ice dancing**. In spite of its long history in figure skating, France was not an original member of the **International Skating Union** (ISU). The Fédération Française des Sports de Glace, not founded until 1903, joined the ISU in 1908. Its first president, Louis Magnus, was also an important writer on the sport. His book *Le patinage artistique* was published in 1914.

Magnus and Mrs. del Monte entered the pairs' event at the 1912 **World Championships**, the first French skaters to appear in international competition and the only ones before World War I. They placed fifth in a field of eight. Simone and Charles Sabouret competed in the pairs' event at the **Olympic Winter Games** in Antwerp in 1920, placing seventh in a field of eight. They never competed at the World Championships. One of the most successful pairs in the history of the discipline, **Andrée Joly and Pierre Brunet** won bronze medals at the 1924 Olympic Winter Games held in Chamonix, France. Ultimately, they won three world and two Olympic titles. Early in their career, both skaters competed in singles as well. Otherwise, the first male competitor from France was Jean Henrion who placed last at the

World Championships in 1927. The first lady competitor was Gabi Clericetti who placed eighth at the European Championships in 1932. In addition to Joly and Brunet, French skaters who became world champions include **Jacqueline du Bief** in 1952, **Alain Giletti** in 1960, **Alain Calmat** in 1965, and **Brian Joubert** in 2007. Ice dancers include **Isabelle and Paul Duchesnay** in 1991 and **Marina Anissina and Gwendal Peizerat** in 2000. Anissina and Peizerat also won the Olympic title in 2002. The 1924 Olympic Games were held in Paris with winter events—figure skating, speed skating, ice hockey, skiing, and bobsledding—contested in Chamonix. In 1926, two years later, the International Olympic Committee designated the 1924 events as the first Olympic Winter Games. France also hosted the Winter Games of 1968 in Grenoble and of 1992 in Albertville. *See also* BONALY, SURYA; CANDELORO, PHILIPPE; DELOBEL, ISABELLE AND SCHOENFELDER, OLIVIER; FAVART, JACQUES; GUHEL, CHRISTIANE AND JEAN PAUL; STENUF, HEDY.

FRATIANNE, LINDA SUE (1960–) (USA). Linda Fratianne alternated world titles with **Anett Pötzsch** of the **German Democratic Republic** during the four years leading up to and including the 1980 **Olympic Winter Games** at Lake Placid. Fratianne won in odd-numbered years, 1977 and 1979, Pötzsch in even-numbered years, 1978 and 1980. Fratianne was a roller skater before taking up ice skating at age 10. In her first year as a senior, 1975, she placed seventh at the **United States** Championships. A year later, she was the silver medalist, earning a place on the 1976 world and Olympic teams. She placed fifth and eighth. World and Olympic efforts for her last four competitive years resulted in one bronze, two silver, and two gold medals. Fratianne was coached throughout her career by **Frank Carroll** and was the first of his students to become a world Champion. Her professional career included 10 years with **Disney on Ice**.

FREE DANCE. The first **World Championship** in **ice dancing** was held in 1952, although the **International Skating Union** (ISU) held dance competitions at the World Championships in 1950 and 1951. Originally ice dancers skated four prescribed **compulsory dances** which counted for 60 percent of the score and a free dance of three minutes duration, later increased to four minutes, which counted 40 percent. ISU regulations called for a "nonrepetitive performance of novel movements and variants of known dances or parts thereof, combined into a program with originality of design and arrangement." There were strict limitations on moves associated with **pair skating**, specifically **jumps**, **spins**, and **lifts**. The rules dealt extensively with what couples could not do, assuring that the discipline was clearly distinctive from pair skating. Several subsequent adjustments reduced the number of compulsory dances and their value, and in 1967 the "original set pattern dance," soon called the original dance, was added, making ice dancing a three-event competition. The free dance then counted 50 percent of the score. Ice dancing today has become technically more demanding as couples have gradually "stretched the rules" making spins and lifts more complex and including much separation of the partners, which was not allowed originally. The rules have been relaxed, tending to move ice dancing away from its original concept of taking ballroom dancing to the ice and making it more like pairs. A further step in that direction occurred at the 2010 ISU Congress which voted to remove compulsory dances from competition and to replace the original dance with a "short dance," making ice dancing again a two-event championship.

FREE SKATING. Competitions for all disciplines are today divided into two parts, a short or technical program followed by free skating, often called the long program. The length and value of the free-skating programs has changed over time. For men and pairs it is now four and a half minutes in length, for ladies four minutes, and counts for two-thirds of the total score. There are no required elements, although there are regulations regarding what can be included, moves not allowed, and repetition of elements within programs. Free-skating programs are choreographed to music selected by the skaters who connect skating elements into cohesive programs constructed to interpret the music. Free skating has been a part of competition throughout the history of the **International Skating Union** (ISU). In singles skating **compulsory figures** and free skating were the two parts of competition through 1972. The **short program** was added in 1973 creating a three-part competition until compulsory figures were eliminated after 1990. **Pair skating**, first contested in world and Olympic competition in 1908, included only free skating through 1963, after which a short program was added. Pair skating never required compulsory figures. **Ice dancing** was originally a two-part competition, compulsory dances and free dance, but became a three-part competition with the inclusion of an original dance in 1967. At the 2010 Congress, the ISU eliminated the compulsory dances and substituted a "short dance" for the original dance. Synchronized team skating has always been a two part competition, a technical program and free skating.

FREEDOM BLADES. *See* WEISS, MICHAEL.

FREY, LEOPOLD (AUT). Leopold Frey, a student of **Jackson Haines**, was probably an original member of the **Vienna Skating Club**. In 1882, he won the **Great International Skating Tournament**, the most important skating competition held prior to the establishment of the **International Skating Union** in 1992. Frey defeated **Eduard Engelmann Jr.**, who placed second, and **Axel Paulsen**, who placed third.

FRICK AND FRACK. *See* GROEBLI, WERNER.

FRICK, MR. *See* GROEBLI, WERNER.

FRICK, WILLIE (1896–1964) (GER). Willie Frick was one of many skaters who had their amateur careers cut short or eliminated by the world wars and the resulting cancellation of the European and **World Championships**. Frick gave exhibitions in Europe before moving to the **United States** in 1920. Known as "the boy wonder of Berlin," he continued giving exhibitions and participating in **carnivals** in America both in singles and in pairs with his wife Catherine Pope. He taught skating for 40 years at the **Skating Club of Boston**. Although Frick was recognized as a master of **compulsory figures**, he was successful in turning out balanced skaters, many of whom became national and international champions. Skaters from **Theresa Weld Blanchard** through **Tenley Albright** were coached by him. Frick was elected to the **World Figure Skating Hall of Fame** posthumously in 1981.

FROTHINGHAM, CLARA. *See* BADGER, SHERWIN CAMPBELL.

FUCHS, GILBERT (1871–1952) (GER). Gilbert Fuchs became figure skating's first world champion in 1896. His long and distinguished career began a year earlier with a third-place finish at the **European Championships** in 1895. Fuchs competed in but did not win at four European and **World Championships** during the next nine years. He reclaimed the world title in 1906 but again was unable to defend it, placing third in 1907. Fuchs's career record over 15 years, competing at 10 European and **World Championships**, includes three bronze medals, five silver medals, and two world titles. He also won an international competition for **special figures** held in Munich in 1903. Fuchs is remembered as a technician who was especially strong in **compulsory figures**. His book *Theorie und Praxis des Kunstlaufes am Eise* (Theory and Practice of Figure Skating on Ice) provides a valuable resource for skating technique at the beginning of the 20th century. *See also* GERMANY.

FUSAR-POLI, BARBABA (1972–) AND MARGAGLIO, MAURIZIO (1974–) (ITA). Ice dancers Barbara Fusar-Poli and Maurizio Margaglio appeared on the world scene in 1993 and progressed steadily toward their first medals, silver at the **World Championships** in 2000. They won at the **Grand**

Prix Finals in 2001 and proceeded to win the world title that year. That created tremendous pressure for them to become the first Italian figure skaters to win an Olympic title in 2002, but a strong field of ice dancers in Salt Lake City placed in the same order for all events, **compulsory dances**, **original dance**, and **free dance**. Fusar-Poli and Margaglio won the bronze medals behind **Marina Anissina and Gwendal Peizerat** of **France**, the gold medalists, and **Irina Lobacheva and Ilia Averbukh** of **Russia**, the silver medalists. Fusar-Poli and Margaglio did not compete at the World Championships that year. They returned in 2006, not having competed internationally for four years, to compete at the **Olympic Winter Games** held in Torino, their own country, and placed sixth. *See also* ITALY.

G

GALBRAITH, MURRAY. *See* GALBRAITH, SHELDON.

GALBRAITH, SHELDON (1922–) (CAN). Sheldon Galbraith moved with his family from **Canada** to the **United States**, first to Los Angeles, then to Tacoma, Washington, and finally to San Francisco where he and his brother, Murray, took up figure skating. Both competed successfully at the national level. The brothers then joined the **Ice Follies** and toured for three years. Returning to Canada, Sheldon began his teaching career at the Minto Skating Club in Ottawa where **Barbara Ann Scott** became one of his first students. She retired with two European titles, two world titles, and an Olympic gold medal as North America's first world and Olympic champion. Moving to Toronto, Galbraith taught many other Canadian champions, including pair skaters **Frances Dafoe and Norris Bowden**, **Barbara Wagner and Robert Paul**, and singles skater **Donald Jackson**, all of whom became world champions. Galbraith was inducted into the **World Figure Skating Hall of Fame** in 1996.

GALINDO, RUDY. *See* YAMAGUCHI, KRISTI.

GAMGEE, JOHN. *See* ARTIFICIAL ICE.

GANNON, TERRY. *See* FLEMING, PEGGY GALE.

GARDNER, RANDY. *See* BABILONIA, TAI AND GARDNER, RANDY.

GAVRILOV, ALEXANDR. *See* ZHUK, TATIANA.

GERMAN DEMOCRATIC REPUBLIC. *See* GERMANY.

GERMANY. Germany has a long tradition in figure skating, and it was one of six countries represented at the congress in Scheveningen, **Netherlands**, in 1892 which resulted in the establishment of the **International Skating Union** (ISU). At the first **European Championship**, held in Hamburg a year earlier in 1891, five of the seven competitors were from Germany. **Oskar Ulhig** became the first European champion. His compatriots, A. Schmitson and Franz Zilly, placed second and third. At the first **World Championship** held in St. Petersburg, **Russia**, in 1896, **Gilbert Fuchs** of Germany, one of four competitors, became the world champion. He won a second title 10 years later, in 1906. When **pair skating** became a world and Olympic sport in 1908, Anna Hübler and **Heinrich Burger** became the first world champions. Germany produced no further champions in any discipline until the pair of **Ernst Baier and Maxi Herber**, the last European, world, and Olympic champions before World War II, although there were medalists of other colors and in all disciplines. German skaters competed at all World Championships between the wars except in 1930, the year they were held in New York City, and at all European Championships except in 1928 and 1934.

Germany held national championships during the first two years of World War II, 1940 and 1941. Following the war, they could not immediately reenter international competitions because the ISU issued invitations only to countries "not under the control of foreign forces." The Federal Republic of Germany (FRG), usually referred to as West Germany, was admitted to the ISU in 1951. The German Democratic Republic (GDR), usually referred to as East Germany, was created as an independent nation in 1949. It joined the ISU in 1953. Both the ISU and the International Olympic Committee refused at first to differentiate between the two Germanies in competition. Thus, **Gundi Busch**, the lady champion at the European and World Championships in 1954, represented the FRG but is listed officially as being from "Germany." That continued for only one year in ISU competitions but continued through 1964 at the **Olympic Winter Games**. The reunification of Germany in 1990 returned the country to its prewar status.

The first post–World War II champions were pair skaters **Ria Baran and Paul Falk**, world champions in 1951 and 1952 and Olympic champions in 1952. Notable skaters from the FRG during the period of the divided Germany include Gundi Busch, **Manfred Schnelldorfer**, both of whom were world and Olympic champions in 1964, and the pair of **Marika Kilius and Hans-Jürgen Bäumler**, world champions in 1963 and 1964. The GDR made its remarkable presence felt internationally during the 1970s and 1980s when four outstanding lady champions won nine world and three Olympic titles: **Gabriele Seyfert**, world champion in 1969 and 1970; **Christine Errath**, world champion in 1974; **Anett Pötzsch**, world Champion in 1978 and 1980 and Olympic champion in 1980; and **Katarina Witt**, world champion in 1984, 1985, 1987, and 1988 and Olympic champion in 1984 and 1988. In men's competitions, **Jan Hoffmann** won world titles in 1974 and 1980; in pairs, **Sabine Baess and Tassilo Thierbach** won the world title in 1982.

Since reunification, Germany has fielded champions only in pair skating. **Mandy Wötzel and Ingo Steuer** were European champions in 1995 and world champions in 1997. **Aliona Savchenko and Robin Szolkowy** were European champions for three years, 2007–2009, and world champions in 2008 and 2009.

No fewer than eight German cities have hosted 28 European and World Championships beginning with the European Championship of 1891 in Hamburg and most recently with the World Championships of 1991 in Munich. The Olympic Winter Games of 1936 were held in Garmisch-Partenkirchen. *See also* BAUER, INA; BUCK, ANGELIKA AND ERICH; EILERS, LUDOWIKA AND JAKOBSSON, WALTER; FRICK, WILLIE; FUCHS, GILBERT; GROSS, MANUELA AND KAGELMANN, UWE; GROSSMANN, EVELYN; KERMER, ROMY AND ÖSTERREICH, ROLF; LEISTNER, CLAUDIA; MAGER, MANUELA AND BEWERSDORFF, UWE; MÜLLER, JUTTA; RENDSCHMIDT, ELSA; RITTBERGER, WERNER; SCHRAMM, NORBERT.

GERSCHWILER, ARNOLD (1914–2003) (SUI). Arnold Gerschwiler, the younger brother of **Jacques Gerschwiler**, followed his brother to England in 1931, took lessons from him, and turned professional a year later. As his brother had done, Arnold entered the **Open Professional Championships** of **Great Britain**, placing fourth in 1935 and third in 1936. He joined the teaching staff at the Richmond Ice Rink in 1938 and remained there throughout his long career. Among his earliest students was **Daphne Walker**, who followed **Cecilia Colledge** and **Megan Taylor** as the last of three young British phenoms who dominated ladies' skating following the retirement of **Sonja Henie** in 1936. Upon reestablishment of competitions after the war, Arnold coached his nephew, **Hans Gerschwiler**, to European and world titles in 1947. In a rare distinction, his students, **Ede Király**, **Aja Vrzáňová**, and the pair of **Marianna and László Nagy**, won all three disciplines at the **European Championships** in 1950. Many successes followed. He was the coach of Olympic champion and three-time world champion **Sjoujke Dijkstra** throughout her career. Arnold Gerschwiler was inducted into the **World Figure Skating Hall of Fame** in 1985.

GERSCHWILER, HANS (1920–) (SUI). Hans Gerschwiler, the nephew of Arnold and **Jacques Gerschwiler**, was trained primarily by Arnold, first in **Switzerland** but after the war also in **England**. He was a five-time Swiss champion; 1938, 1939, and 1947–1949. His only international competition before World War II was the **European Championships** of 1939 where he placed fifth. When competition resumed in 1947, he became the European and world champion, defeating **Dick Button** of the **United States** at the **World Championships** in a close competition in which Button was placed first by all five judges in the free skating. Gerschwiler placed first in the **compulsory figures**. A year later, Button defeated Gerschwiler decisively at both the European and World Championships as well as at the **Olympic Winter Games**. Gerschwiler retired from competition in 1948 and taught skating first in **Canada** and then in the United States.

GERSCHWILER, JACQUES (1898–2000) (SUI). Jacques Gerschwiler is the older brother and teacher of **Arnold Gerschwiler**. As a competitive skater, he medaled at the **Open Professional Championships** of **Great Britain** in 1933 and 1934, but it is as a teacher that he is most important. He moved to England in the late 1920s where he taught world ladies' champion **Cecilia Colledge** throughout her competitive career. Under his guidance, Colledge became the inventor of the camel spin, then called the parallel spin. Following the war, Gerschwiler coached another great British champion, **Jeannette Altwegg,** who won the world title in 1951 and the Olympic title in 1952. Gerschwiler was inducted into the **World Figure Skating Hall of Fame** with the original class in 1976.

GIAMMONA, BONA. *See* ITALY.

GILCHRIST, DONALD (1922–) (CAN). Donald Gilchrist competed first as a **fours** skater, later as a pair skater. He was a member of winning fours three times at the Canadian championships before and during World War II, each of which included different skaters. The 1939 team included Gillian Watson, Sandy McKechnie, Ruth Hall, and Gilchrist. They also placed second at the **North American Championships**. The 1941 team included Theresa McCarthy, Gilchrist, Virginia Wilson, and Michael Kirby. They too placed second at the North American Championships. The 1942 team included only one substitution. Eleanor O'Meara replaced Theresa McCarthy. After the war, Gilchrist paired for two years with Marlene Smith. They won the Canadian pair title twice, in 1949 and 1950. At the **World Championships** in 1950, they placed ninth. Gilchrist was twice the vice president and from 1973 until 1974 the president of the **Canadian Figure Skating Association**. He was an officeholder in the **International Skating Union** (ISU) for many years, serving on the figure skating technical committee as a substitute member three different times for a total of six years, and as a regular member twice for a total of nine years before being elected to the council on which he served from 1980 until 1992. He was that year elected as an honorary member of the ISU. Gilchrist was a world judge and referee. In recognition of his dedication to the sport, Gilchrist was elected to the **World Figure Skating Hall of Fame** in 2004.

GILETTI, ALAIN (1939–) (FRA). Alain Giletti was the first man from **France** to medal in world or Olympic competition. A national champion from age 12, his international career spanned a decade. Beginning with a fourth-place finish in 1952, he went on to garner four silver and five gold medals at the **European Championships**, but eight appearances at the **World Championships** resulted in just two bronze medals prior to 1960. He was probably the best skater in Europe during the 1950s, but with strong American men competing during the postwar period, sometimes called the "golden age" of American skating, top placements could not be achieved. The indefatigable Giletti outlasted them, winning the world title in 1960. The leading American contenders all retired after the Squaw Valley **Olympic Winter Games**, not proceeding to the World Championships. Giletti's professional career included tours with **Holiday on Ice**.

GÖBL, MARGRET. *See* KILIUS, MARIKA.

GODWIN, ALDEN. *See* JENKINS, DOROTHY AND McCLENNAN, A. GORDON.

GOEBEL, TIMOTHY (1980–) (USA). Timothy Goebel became the U.S. novice champion at age 13, the junior champion at age 15, and the senior champion at age 19. He won two **Grand Prix** events, **Skate America** twice, 2000 and 2001 and Cup of China in 2003. At the **World Championships**, he was twice the silver medalist, in 2002 and 2003. At the **Olympic Winter Games** he claimed the bronze medal in 2002. Goebel is remembered primarily for his facile ability at quadruple jumps, being dubbed as "the quad king." He was the first person to land one in Olympic competition, but he is most often remembered for completing three quadruple jumps in his free-skating program at Skate America in 1999. Goebel was coached early in his career by **Carol Heiss** and later by **Frank Carroll**.

GONCHAROV, RUSLAN. *See* BULGARIA; UKRAINE.

GORDEEVA, EKATERINA (1971–) AND GRINKOV, SERGEI (1967–1995) (URS/RUS). Ekaterina Gordeeva and Sergei Grinkov, one of figure skating's most popular pairs, began skating together in 1982. After winning the world junior title in 1985, they won the world title in 1986, their first year as seniors, by defeating the reigning champions, **Elena Valova and Oleg**

Vasiliev. The results were the same in 1987. In the Olympic year, 1988, Gordeeva and Grinkov continued their winning streak in Calgary, but a month later, Valova and Vasiliev reclaimed the world title. Both couples then retired. Gordeeva and Grinkov ended their relatively short international career with a cumulative record in European, world, and Olympic competition of two silver and nine gold medals. Their popularity as amateurs carried forward to a successful professional career in shows, primarily **Stars on Ice**. They reinstated in 1994 and competed at the Lillehammer games where they won a second Olympic title, the only reinstated skaters to win, after which they returned to show skating. While rehearsing for a Stars on Ice tour in November 1995, Grinkov collapsed on the ice and could not be revived. At age 28, he died of a heart attack. After a short period in her native Russia, Gordeeva returned to the **United States** and rejoined Stars on Ice, where she developed a second career as a singles skater. Gordeeva and Grinkov were inducted into the **World Figure Skating Hall of Fame** in 1995.

GORELIK, ALEXANDR. *See* ZHUK, TATIANA.

GORSHKOV, ALEXANDR. *See* PAKHOMOVA, LIUDMILA AND GORSHKOV, ALEXANDR.

GRAFSTRÖM, GILLIS (1893–1938) (SWE). Gillis Grafström first appeared at the **World Championships** in 1914 and placed seventh. After the war, he developed a reputation that led his contemporaries to consider him the greatest skater of all times. He entered competitions only selectively, including three widely spaced World Championships, 1922, 1924, and 1929, all of which he won. He never entered a **European Championship**. In three consecutive Olympic efforts, beginning in 1920, he claimed the gold medals. Grafström entered the games for a fourth time in 1932, where, suffering from a leg injury, he settled for a silver medal behind another outstanding skater, **Karl Schäfer** of **Austria**. Grafström is one of only two singles skaters to hold three Olympic titles, the other being a near contemporary, **Sonja Henie** whose titles beginning in 1928 were likewise won consecutively. Grafström was also one of the last great practitioners of **special figures**. He was elected into the **World Figure Skating Hall of Fame** in 1976. *See also* CANADA; SWEDEN.

GRAND PRIX FINALS. *See* GRAND PRIX SERIES.

GRAND PRIX SERIES. The **International Skating Union** (ISU) implemented the Grand Prix Series, originally called the ISU Champions Series, in the 1996 skating season. It consists of six qualifying competitions plus the

Grand Prix Finals for the top point winners in the qualifying competitions. The series provides skaters from throughout the world with opportunities to present and perfect their programs early in the competitive season, actually during the previous fall, and often to compete against those skaters with whom they may compete at the **World Championships**. Grand Prix events are held essentially for six consecutive weeks beginning in October with skaters entered by their federations in no more than three of them. Points from placement in two of the competitions, designated in advance, qualify competitors for the Grand Prix Finals. Originally, the series included only five events held in as many countries: **Skate Canada**, **Skate America**, Bofrost Cup on Ice (Germany), Trophée Eric Bompard (France), and the NHK Trophy (Japan). For the second season, the Cup of Russia was added. For the 2003 season, the Cup of China replaced the Bofrost Cup on Ice. A Junior Grand Prix series was implemented in 1999. See Appendix I for a list of medalists at the Grand Prix Finals and Appendix K for a list of medalists at the Junior Grand Prix Finals.

GRANDJEAN, SILVIA (1934–) AND MICHEL (1931–) (SUI). Pair skaters Silvia and Michel Grandjean competed internationally for four years beginning in 1951. Three appearances at the **European Championships** include fourth-place finishes for two years. After skipping a year, they won gold medals in 1954. At the **World Championships**, competing every year, their placements were seventh, sixth, and fourth before claiming the silver medals in 1954. One Olympic effort resulted in a seventh-place finish. Following their competitive career, they skated in shows including **Ice Capades** and **Holiday on Ice**.

GRANDJEAN, MICHEL. *See* GRANDJEAN, SILVIA AND MICHEL.

GRAPEVINES. Grapevines, which probably originated in Canada by the third quarter of the 19th century, are the most American of all figures. Their uniqueness results from both feet remaining of the ice through the duration of the figure doing similar moves but not in unison while creating interesting chain-like designs on the ice. Grapevines entered both **English style** and **international style** skating for short periods of time. English skaters experimented with them in the 1890s, and they were required in the first class test. Grapevines, which are described in detail in Irving Brokaw's book, *The Art of Skating*, were still employed in free-skating programs into the 1920s.

GREAT BRITAIN. England is the birthplace of figure skating. The tradition dates from the restoration of the monarchy in 1660 with descriptions of the future James II skating on bladed skates. A century later, in 1772, the first book on skating, Robert Jones's *The Art of Skating*, describes figures then being done in England and presumably in Scotland. The first skating club was established in Edinburgh in 1744. By the mid-19th century, skating had advanced significantly with many new figures being done, the term figure skating being first employed, and the **English style** being developed. In 1879, the **National Skating Association** (NSA) was formed to regulate speed skating, but within a year figure skating was added. The English style was employed exclusively until the last decade of the century. In 1992, the NSA became a charter member of the **International Skating Union** (ISU). Many British skaters converted to the **international style**, which was adopted by the ISU, but many others, a majority at first, continued the English style. The NSA established separate test structures and competitions for the two styles, and they still exist today.

The first lady world and Olympic champion was **Madge Syers**, who had previously been a champion English style skater. The world pair champions in 1909 and 1912 were **Phyllis and James Johnson**. Phyllis Johnson had also been a champion in the English style. Great Britain had no further world or Olympic champions until just before World War II when world titles were won by **Cecilia Colledge** in 1937, **Megan Taylor** in 1938 and 1939, and **Graham Sharp** in 1939. During the 1930s, however, British skaters advanced significantly in **ice dancing**, which did not become a world championship discipline until 1952.

After the war, **Jeannette Altwegg** won the world ladies' title in 1951 and the Olympic title in 1952. **Jennifer and John Nicks** won the world pair title in 1953. British dominance came in **ice dancing** when it became a world discipline in 1952. British couples won the title every year through 1960. **Jean Westwood and Laurence Demmy**, 1952–1955, **Pamela Weight and Paul Thomas**, 1956, **Courtney Jones** with two partners, June Markham, 1957 and 1958, and Doreen Denny, 1959 and 1960. Later champions include **Diane Towler and Bernard Ford** who won four titles beginning in 1966 and **Jayne Torvill and Christopher Dean** who won four titles beginning in 1981. After Altwegg, no British skaters won Olympic titles in any discipline until John Curry in 1976 and **Robin Cousins** in 1980. Four years later, Torvill and Dean won the ice dancing title. Since 1984, British skaters have won no world or Olympic titles in any discipline.

Great Britain has furnished several leaders in the ISU, including **Herbert J. Clarke** who served for more than 20 years including the presidency from 1937 to 1945. Among former champions who have served the ISU in various roles are Lawrence Demmy and Courtney Jones. Both served on the ice dancing technical committee, Demmy from 1965 to 1984, 14 years as its chair and Jones from 1998 to 2010. Demmy also served as the vice president for figure skating from 1993 to 1998 and was named an honorary vice president in 1998. Jones was named an honorary member in 2010. *See also* CALLAWAY, BETTY; CAMBRIDGE, SADIE AND ENDERS, ALBERT; DENCH, ROBERT; DEWHIRST, JOAN AND SLATER, JOHN; DUNN, JOHN; HOGG, GLADYS MARGARET; JEPSON-TURNER, GLADYS; KEATS, EVA AND WEYDEN, ERIK VAN DER; OSBORN, VALDA; PHILIPPS, MOLLIE; RICHARDSON, THOMAS DOW; SAWBRIDGE, JANET; SHARP, HENRY GRAHAM; SHEARMAN, LINDA AND PHILLIPS, MICHAEL; SYERS, EDGAR; TOMLINS, FREDERICK; WALKER, DAPHNE; WILKIE, REGINLD AND WALLIS, DAPHNE.

GREAT INTERNATIONAL SKATING TOURNAMENT. The Great International Skating Tournament, held in Vienna in 1882, was the first major international skating competition. Sponsored by the **Vienna Skating Club**, it attracted many elite skaters. Leopold Frey, a student of **Jackson Haines**, was the winner. **Eduard Engelmann Jr.**, who became the European Champion in 1893, placed second. Both were members of the Vienna Skating Club. **Axel Paulsen** of **Norway**, who placed third, offered for his **special figure** the jump that bears his name.

GREEN, HILARY. *See* MOISEEVA, IRINA AND MINENKOV, ANDREI.

GRENANDER, HENNING (1874–1958) (SWE). Henning Grenander won the world title in 1898, the only year he entered the competition. He entered the **European Championships** just once, and won the silver medal in 1893, but the result was declared invalid by the **International Skating Union** (ISU) in one of figure skating's early **controversies**. Grenander moved to **England** in 1898 and became an active member of the **National Skating Association**. He was deeply involved with planning for figure skating events held at the **Olympic Games** in 1908 and served as a judge for two disciplines, men's and **special figures**. *See also* SWEDEN.

GRINER, WENDY (1944–) (CAN). Wendy Griner was the Canadian national ladies' champion for four consecutive years, 1960–1963. Competing twice at the biennial **North American Championships**, she won the silver medal in 1961 and the gold medal in 1963. At the **World Championships**, her best result was winning the silver medal in 1962, the first medal of any color for a Canadian lady since **Barbara Ann Scott** in 1947 and 1948. Griner competed at two **Olympic Winter Games**, placing 12th in 1960 and 10th in 1964.

GRINKOV, SERGEI. *See* GORDEEVA, EKATARINA AND GRINKOV, SERGEI.

GRISHCHUK, OKSANA (1971–) AND PLATOV, EVGENY (1967–) (URS/RUS). Oksana Grishchuk and Evgeny Platov of Russia were the most successful ice dancers of the 1990s. They progressed steadily from fifth place at the **World Championships** in 1990 to world and Olympic titles in 1994. **Torvill and Dean**, who had reinstated for the Olympic year in 1994, defeated Grishchuk and Platov at the **European Championships** in an extremely close competition, but Grishchuk and Platov were never defeated again. Their competitive record includes three European, four world, and two Olympic titles. They were also the first winners at the **Grand Prix Finals** in 1996, and two years later, they won that title again. They are the only ice dancers to win Olympic gold twice. **Controversy** followed the win at Nagano in 1998 with accusations of bloc judging, but actionable evidence was not available. The judges unanimously placed Grishchuk and Platov first in the free dance. Grishchuk and Platov skated in various shows including **Champions on Ice**.

GROEBLI, WERNER (1915–2008) (SUI). Better known as Mr. Frick, Werner Groebli, the Swiss junior champion in 1934, turned professional in 1937. He and his skating partner, Hans-Rudi Mauch (1919–1979), Mr. Frack, took their comedy routine to **England**, performing in Brighton and at Covent Garden in London. Traveling next to the **United States**, they performed at skating centers throughout North America. In 1942 they joined the **Ice Follies** where Frick and Frack became perhaps the best known names in show skating. Owing to a crippling illness, Frack was forced to retire in 1953, but Frick continued as a solo act until his own retirement in 1980. In addition to tours with the Ice Follies, Frick and Frack appeared in two full-length movies with **Belita**, *Silver Skates* and *Ladies Let's Dance*. They are best remembered for their cantilever spread eagle, invented by Frick, which they did solo and together. During his career, Frick appeared in more than 15,000 performances, a record that will surely never be duplicated. He supported eligible skating throughout his life by attending international skating competitions in support of young skaters. Groebli was inducted into the **World Figure Skating Hall of Fame** in 1984.

GROGAN, JAMES (1931–2000) (USA). The period from World War II through 1960 has been called the "golden age" of American skating. All four Olympic titles, and all but two world titles, 1947 and 1960, were won by **Dick Button**, **Hayes Jenkins**, and his brother **David Jenkins**. The depth of American skating was notable. Olympic and world silver medalists, all of whom failed to win national, world, or Olympic titles, include James Grogan, **Ronald Robertson**, and **Tim Brown**. Grogan, the oldest of the three, won silver medals at four United States Championships, always behind Button. At four consecutive World Championships, 1951–1954, he won silver medals twice behind Button and twice behind Hayes Jenkins. At three consecutive **North American Championships** beginning in 1947 he won silver medals, again behind Button. His only other medal was bronze at the **Olympic Winter Games** in 1952 behind Button and **Helmut Seibt** of **Austria**. Upon turning professional, Grogan joined **Ice Capades**. *See also* ITALY.

GROSS, MANUELA (1957–) AND KAGELMANN, UWE (1950–) (GDR). Manuela Gross and Uwe Kagelmann were among several early pairs from the **German Democratic Republic** who became dominant competitors internationally during the 1970s and early 1980s. Gross and Kagelmann competed annually from 1969 through 1976 and were national champions for three years. Their first of six international medals was won at the **European Championships** in 1972. All of their medals from the European and World Championships were bronze as were those from their Olympic efforts in 1972 and 1976.

GROSSMANN, EVELYN (1971–) (GDR). Evelyn Grossmann competed internationally for just three years. She placed seventh at both the European and **World Championships** in 1989. Gold and silver medals followed the next two years at the **European Championships**. At one additional world effort in 1990 she placed eighth. Grossmann did not compete at the **Olympic Winter Games**.

GRÜNAUER, HANS. *See* CONTROVERSIES.

GRUSHINA, ELENA. *See* BULGARIA; UKRAINE.

GUERASSIMOVA, LIDIA. *See* BAKUSHEVA, NINA AND ZHUK, STANISLAV.

GUHEL, CHRISTIANE (NEE EILEN) AND JEAN PAUL (FRA). Christiane and Jean Paul Guhel, a married couple, became in 1962 the first non-British ice dancers to win a European title. In the two previous years, they had placed second behind Doreen Denny and **Courtney Jones**. Jean Paul and a previous partner, Fanny Besson, were the first French ice dancers to compete internationally. Their best results were fourth at the **European Champion-**

ships and fifth at the **World Championships** in 1956. Christiane Eilen had competed for one year, 1957, with Claude Lambert. They placed sixth at the European Championships and 10th at the World Championships. The Guhels competed together for five years beginning in 1958. In addition to their European medals, one bronze, two silver, and one gold, they won bronze medals in 1960 and silver medals in 1962 at the World Championships.

GUHEL, JEAN PAUL. *See* GUHEL, CHRISTIANE AND JEAN PAUL.

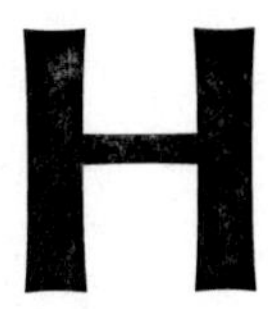

HAINES, JACKSON (1840–1875). Jackson Haines is figure skating's first superstar. There is much legend surrounding his life, activities, and accomplishments, but his importance and influence cannot be denied. He was born in New York City. Leaving home as a teenager, he became an itinerant actor, dancer, and entertainer, working in Philadelphia and other places in New England. As an entertainer, Haines took dance to the ice. Following a performance in Toronto in 1864, he departed for Europe where he spent the next several years. Most important were two stays in Vienna beginning in 1865 and 1870. There he taught skating and influenced a generation of skaters. Haines has been called the "father of the Viennese school," which ultimately developed into the **international style** of skating. He was in **Finland**, presumably returning from **Russia**, when he died in 1875, probably from pneumonia, and is buried in Gamla-Karleby. Haines is the inventor of the sit spin, sometimes called the Jackson Haines spin. *See also* AUSTRIA.

HALL, RUTH. *See* GILCHREST, DONALD.

HAMILL, DOROTHY STUART (1956–) (USA). Dorothy Hamill, one of America's best-known and most popular skaters, capped her eligible career in 1976 with a third national title, an Olympic title, and a world title. While still a junior skater, she introduced the layover camel sit spin that bears her name, the "Hamill camel," and that foretold the artistry that has always been associated with her. Hamill's youthful persona thrilled audiences, leading young girls to copy her wedge-cut hair style, typically called the "Dorothy Hamill haircut." Her popularity as an eligible skater resulted in a lucrative contract with **Ice Capades**, and it continued to soar as she enjoyed an unusually long professional career including shows and professional competitions. She was a mainstay with **Champions on Ice** for many years. Hamill was elected to the **World Figure Skating Hall of Fame** in 2000. *See also* UNITED STATES.

HAMILTON, SCOTT SCOVELL (1958–) (USA). Scott Hamilton suffered a life-threatening illness as a child. Physical benefits from skating probably contributed to his cure. His development as a skater was slow but consistent. He placed last in his first novice event at age 14 and seventh in his first junior event at age 16. He became the junior champion a year later. His first senior event resulted in a ninth-place finish. A year later, he placed third and was named to the world team. Through the Olympic year, 1980, Hamilton's best results were bronze medals at two national championships and fifth-place finishes that year at the **Olympic Winter Games** and the **World Championships**, but during the next Olympic cycle, 1981–1984, Hamilton was unbeatable. He claimed all four national and world titles in addition to capturing the Olympic gold medal. Hamilton's greatest strength was in free skating, but he also performed well in the **compulsory figures**. His athletic prowess and on-ice personality made him extremely popular with the skating public. A natural showman, he loved audiences and revealed his enthusiasm when performing for them. Upon retirement from eligible skating, Hamilton became one of the most popular show skaters in the history of the sport. After two years with **Ice Capades**, he created his own show, which became **Stars on Ice**, and performed with the company through 2001. Because of his personality and knowledge of the sport, he became a successful television commentator. In 1990, Hamilton was elected to the **World Figure Skating Hall of Fame**. *See also* UNITED STATES.

HAN, SOO BONG. *See* KOREA.

HAND-IN-HAND SKATING. As early as 1836, the Oxford Skating Society had a simple program of club figures suitable for hand-in-hand skating, but further references to the activity come much later in the century. It became an important activity, especially in **England**, as more women became participants in figure skating. It was a natural social activity in recreational skating, but more advanced skaters soon employed specific dance-like patterns suitable for use in the growing number of skating rinks. Our major source for this activity is Norcliffe G. Thompson's book *Hand in Hand Figure Skating* dating from 1896. Thompson describes 106 figures, most of which are suitable for rink skating. In England it was done in the **English style** and eventually became a competitive discipline.

HARDING, TONYA (1970–) (USA). Tonya Harding is forever linked to other skaters, primarily **Nancy Kerrigan** but also **Kristi Yamaguchi**. These three talented skaters, rival competitors in the early 1990s, swept the medals at **World Championships** in 1991. Yamaguchi won the title with Harding and Kerrigan claiming the silver and bronze medals. Harding was the most athletic of the three but also the most inconsistent, and that is important when attempting to understand the attack on Nancy Kerrigan at the **United States** Championships in 1994. Harding appeared on the national scene at the senior level two years before Kerrigan. They first competed against each other in 1988. Harding placed fifth, Kerrigan 12th. A year later they advanced to third and fifth. The year 1990 proved disastrous to Harding. She slipped to seventh as their roles reversed, and Kerrigan advanced to fourth. But in 1991, the scrappy Harding returned and celebrated her best outing. She won the national title ahead of Kerrigan and Yamaguchi, the result of a strong free-skating program which included the first triple **Axel Paulsen jump** done by an American lady. But in 1992, Harding settled for the bronze medal behind Yamaguchi and Kerrigan. In 1993, a dismal fourth place kept her off the world team. With 1994 being an Olympic year, Harding was determined to not be denied the opportunity to participate. With Kerrigan out, following the attack at the national championships, Harding won the title. Harding competed at the Lillehammer **Olympic Winter Games**, having not yet been found guilty of wrongdoing, but she skated poorly, placing eighth. As a result of the **Kerrigan-Harding incident**, the **United States Figure Skating Association** banned Harding for life and stripped her of the 1994 title.

HARRIS, JOHN H. (1901–1969). John H. Harris was the founder and first president of **Ice Capades**. As an arena owner in Pittsburgh and recognizing the popularity of **Sonja Henie** during the late 1930s, Harris submitted a proposal to the Arena Managers Association in 1940 to establish an ice show that could play at various member arenas in their association. The name Ice Capades was selected. Under Harris's leadership, the company flourished and continued for 24 seasons before it was purchased by Metromedia in 1964.

HARTSHORNE, HAROLD (1891–1961) (USA). Ice dancing was not contested as a world discipline until 1952 or an Olympic discipline until 1976, but some countries, including **Canada**, the **United States**, and **Great Britain**, had held national competitions since the 1930s. Harold Hartshorne was an early U.S. competitor. With three partners, he competed every year from 1936 through 1944. His first partner, Nettie Prantel, had won two titles with Roy Hunt before partnering with Hartshorne for four years. Prantel and Hartshorne placed second in 1936 and first for the next three years. Changing partners, Hartshorne competed with Sandy McDonald for three years. They placed first in 1940 and 1941 and second in 1942. He then returned to his former partner, Nettie Prantel, and they placed third in 1943. Competing for yet another year, Hartshorne and a third partner, Kathe Mehl, placed second in 1944. Hartshorne served as chair of the **United States Figure Skating Association** dance committee from 1938 through 1941 and three times as a member of the executive committee: 1949–1950, 1952–1955, and 1959–1961. He served on the **International Skating Union**'s ice dancing technical committee from 1959 until his death in the **plane crash** in 1961. As a world judge in ice dancing, he officiated at the **World Championships** in 1959.

HARVEY, RAYMOND. *See* LOUGHRAN, BEATRIX S.

HÄSLER, BEAT. *See* HÄSLER, GEORG.

HÄSLER, GEORG (c. 1907–1985) (SUI). Prior to 1947 the headquarters of the **International Skating Union** (ISU) was always in the country of the president with the secretary chosen from that country as well. In 1947, a permanent headquarters was established in **Davos, Switzerland**. Georg Häsler of Davos was appointed as the honorary secretary. He remained in that position for 28 years until his retirement in 1975. His son Beat Häsler, who had served as the executive secretary for 10 years, moved into his father's position, which he retained until 1996. Thus, the two Häslers served the ISU continuously for 50 years. During Georg's 28 years as honorary secretary, five championships in speed skating and five in figure skating were held at Davos. As a historian and writer, Häsler, on the occasion of the 75th anniversary of the ISU, compiled and published the complete records of ISU championships in both speed and figure skating. Upon his death in 1985 and in recognition of his dedication and service to the ISU, the Georg Häsler Medal was established to be awarded annually to skaters, speed or figure, and to administrators for their contributions to the sports. Häsler was elected to the **World Figure Skating Hall of Fame** in 1993.

HEISS, CAROL ELIZABETH (1940–) (USA). From childhood, Carol Heiss studied skating with **Pierre and Andrée Brunet**. In just five years, she began a rapid climb through the national ranks: novice champion at age 12, junior champion at age 13, and senior competitor at age 14, winning the silver medal for the first of two times. She then became a four-time national champion. At the international level, Heiss won five consecutive world titles, 1956–1960, the only lady since World War II to do so, plus Olympic gold in 1960. She pursued a short professional career, including appearances in ice shows and a role in a Hollywood film. Heiss married the 1956 men's Olympic champion, **Hayes Alan Jenkins**. She later became a successful coach in the Cleveland area. Her students have included **Tonia**

Kwiatkowski and **Timothy Goebel**. Heiss was a member of the first class to be inducted into the **World Figure Skating Hall of Fame** in 1976. *See also* UNITED STATES.

HEITZER, REGINA (1944–) (AUT). Regina Heitzer competed in every European, world, and Olympic championship from 1958 through the **European Championships** in 1966. She was twice the European champion, 1965 and 1966, but never the world champion. Her second Olympic bid in 1964 resulted in a silver medal. In international competition, she amassed a career total of two bronze, eight silver, and two gold medals.

HENIE, SONJA (1912–1969) (NOR). Sonja Henie dominated ladies' skating for a decade. She began skating at age five, won a children's competition at age eight, became **Norway**'s junior champion at age nine and senior champion a year later. As an 11-year-old national ladies' champion, she entered the 1924 **Olympic Winter Games** at Chamonix and placed eighth. In 1926, she competed at the **World Championships** and placed second behind five-time champion **Herma Szabo**. After that she was never to be defeated, although the world title in 1927 in which she defeated Szabo resulted in a **controversy**. Her record of 10 consecutive world titles, 1927–1936, and three Olympic gold medals cannot be matched by any singles skater. Henie is remembered especially for her artistry, but her athleticism was also impressive. She displayed faster spins with more revolutions than other skaters, and she did all the jumps including the **Axel Paulsen** in her programs. Upon retiring from amateur skating in 1936, Henie moved to the **United States** where she had a brilliant and distinguished professional career as a show skater anchoring the popular **Hollywood Ice Review** in addition to a successful acting career with Twentieth Century Fox, producing nine films over a period of seven years. Henie was elected into the **World Figure Skating Hall of Fame** in 1976. *See also* AUSTRIA; BELGIUM; CANADA.

HENRION, JEAN. *See* FRANCE.

HERBER, MAXI. *See* BAIER, ERNST.

HERBERT, HOWARD D. *See* SHUMWAY, F. RITTER.

HERBOS, GEORGETTE AND WAGEMANS, GEORGES. *See* BELGIUM.

HERZ, ERNST (AUT). Ernst Herz competed during a period when national championships were not held in Austria, but internationally he competed four times, always medaling. Three appearances at the **European Championships**, 1906–1908, resulted in a medal of each color. His only appearance at the **World Championships**, in 1909, resulted in a bronze medal.

HERZ, JENNY. *See* HUNGARY.

HICKINBOTTOM, DAVID. *See* SAWBRIDGE, JANET.

HICKOK, WILLIAM O., IV "BILL" (1905–1957) (USA). Although **ice dancing** was a part of figure skating as early as the 1870s in Vienna, **Austria**, and in other places by the end of the century, it did not become an internationally regulated sport until the 1950s. England had become the predominant leader in the 1930s, developing new dances and establishing national level competitions. The **International Skating Union** (ISU), acting on a proposal by **Great Britain** in 1947, appointed an ice dancing standardization committee of three members including **Reginald J. Wilkie** of Great Britain, Marcel Nicaise of **Belgium**, and Hickok. They completed their work in two years, and in 1949, the ISU adopted the committee's comprehensive proposal without change. ISU competitions were held in connection with the **World Championships** in 1950 and 1951, and ice dancing became a world championship discipline in 1952. Bill Hickok took up skating after completing his Ph.D. degree from Yale University and joining his family's business. He became a national judge by 1934, was elected a member of the **United States Figure Skating Association**'s executive committee in 1939, and was appointed chair of the dance committee in 1941. In that position, Hickok did much to improve the standards for ice dancing. In 1947, he was named to the ISU's ice dance standardization committee, and in 1949 to the first ice dancing technical committee on which he served until his death in 1957. As one of the first international ice dancing judges, he officiated at the 1950 competition. In 1951, he was named a world championship referee. Hickok was elected to the **World Figure Skating Hall of Fame** posthumously in 1981.

HILL, GEORGE. *See* VINSON, MARIBEL YERBA.

HIRAMATSU, JUNKO. *See* JAPAN.

HISEY, JOYCE KORNACHER (1929–) (CAN). Joyce Hisey competed as an ice dancer at the national level with William de Nance Jr., placing second in the 1952 Canadian senior dance events. Although she did not compete internationally, Hisey was involved with the **International Skating Union**

(ISU) in an official capacity, serving as a world judge and referee from 1972 to 1994 and as a council member for 10 years, 1992–2002. She served as a technical delegate at many ISU championships and Olympic Winter Games. In recognition of her many years of service to figure skating, Hisey was elected to the **World Figure Skating Hall of Fame** in 2009.

HOCKETTES. *See* PORTER, RICHARD.

HOFFMANN, JAN (1955–) (GDR). Jan Hoffmann began his 13-year international career at the **European Championships** in 1968 at age 13. He placed 21st. During his first five years, his best placements were fourth in 1971 at both the European and **World Championships**. From 1973 to 1980, excluding1975, he competed at every European, world, and Olympic competition and medaled at all except the 1976 **Olympic Winter Games**, where he placed fourth, collecting a total of five bronze, four silver, and six gold medals. He holds four European titles as well as world titles from 1974 and 1980. His second Olympic effort in 1980 produced a silver medal. Since retirement, Hoffmann has served his sport as a championship referee. *See also* GERMANY.

HOGG, GLADYS MARGARET (?–1985) (GBR). Gladys Hogg began skating on rollers at age 12 and became a British roller skating dance champion with John G. Blauer. She also competed on ice. Turning professional in 1930, she entered the **Open Professional Championships** with Ronald S. Baker. They won the pairs and the **ice dancing** titles in 1947. In 1950, she competed with a new partner, Bernard Spencer, and they won the ice dancing title. Hogg became a leading and one of the most successful ice dancing coaches in England. Among skaters she coached are World champion ice dancers **Jean Westwood and Lawrence Demmy**; **Courtney Jones** and his two partners, June Markham and Doreen Denny; and **Diane Towler and Bernard Ford**. She also coached **Great Britain**'s only pair champions since World War II, Jennifer and **John Nicks**. Hogg was elected to the **World Figure Skating Hall of Fame** in 1999.

HOLBROOK, PRUDENCE. *See* FOURS; ROGERS, MELVILLE.

HOLIDAY ON ICE. Named for the season, Holiday on Ice began on Christmas day in 1943 as an ice review in Toledo, Ohio. A second edition followed in 1944. In 1945, now under the direction of entrepreneur Morris Chalfin, the third edition was taken on tour. Holiday on Ice was able to compete with the established ice shows, the **Ice Follies**, the **Hollywood**

Ice Review, and **Ice Capades**, by using portable ice-making equipment, allowing it to perform in communities not available to the other companies. In 1947, a tour to Central America, South America, and Cuba was undertaken, and in 1950 Holiday on Ice crossed the Atlantic Ocean, performing in **Belgium**, **Switzerland**, **France**, **Austria**, and **Germany**. In 1958, Holiday on Ice represented the **United States** at the Brussels World Fair and in 1959 traveled to **Russia** under the newly established Cultural Exchange Program. Like the Ice Follies and Ice Capades, Holiday on Ice featured many world and Olympic champions including among others **Dick Button**, **Hayes Alan Jenkins**, **Alain Giletti**, **Sjoukje Dijkstra**, **Donald McPherson**, **Emmerich Danzer**, **Tim Wood**, **Trixi Schuba**, and **Denise Biellmann**. The company was purchased in 1996 by Endemol Entertainment, a European conglomerate. It continues to produce shows, primarily in Europe.

HOLLYWOOD ICE REVIEW. Upon retirement from competitive skating in 1936, **Sonja Henie** moved to the **United States** and under the management of Chicago businessman Arthur Wirtz embarked on a tour across the country which culminated in a spectacular show at the Polar Palace in Hollywood. That success is credited with Henie's ability to negotiate a highly favorable contract with Twentieth Century Fox, resulting in nine films during the next seven years. The contract stipulated that filming be done in the summer, allowing Henie to tour with the Hollywood Ice Review during the winter season. Under Wirtz's management the Hollywood Ice Review lasted until 1950 when Henie decided to dissolve the highly successful arrangement and manage her own shows. Wirtz continued the Hollywood Ice Review, but ultimately both companies failed. Henie joined forces for a short time with **Holiday on Ice**, opening in Paris in 1953. Henie's relationship with Holiday on Ice ended after a tour to South America in 1956. She rarely skated afterward.

HOLOVSKY, HILDE (1918–1933) (AUT). Hilde Holovsky was one of 10 ladies who placed second behind **Sonja Henie** during her 10-year reign as world champion. Three of them were from **Austria**, a country that produced many fine skaters between the wars. Holovsky was the Austrian national champion in 1932 and 1933. A year earlier in 1931, at age 13 she won the bronze medal at the **European Championships** and the silver medal behind Henie at the **World Championships**. Many thought she had the talent to upset Henie, but tragically, she died at age 15 following the 1933 season.

HOLTHE, OSCAR. *See* NORWAY.

HONDA, TAKESHI (1981–) (JPN). Takeshi Honda, a five-time national champion, became the first Japanese man to win a medal at the 2002 **World Championships** since 1977 when **Minoru Sano** won the country's first. Both were bronze. Honda won a second bronze medal in 2003. In another first, Honda won the gold medal at the first holding of the **Four Continents Championships** in 1999. He won silver medals in 2001 and 2002 and a second gold medal in 2003. His two Olympic efforts resulted in a 15th-place finish in 1998 and a fourth-place finish in 2002. Honda retired from competition after a fifth-place finish at the Japanese nationals in 2006. *See also* JAPAN.

HOPPE, ELISE AND OSCAR. *See* CZECHOSLOVAKIA.

HORNE, PERI. *See* JONES, COURTNEY.

HORNUNG, ILSE (1908–?) (AUT). Ilse Hornung was one of a distinguished group of Austrian ladies who were dominant competitors during the period between the world wars. They include also **Herma Szabo**, **Gisela Reichmann**, **Fritzi Burger**, **Melitta Brunner**, **Hilde Holovsky**, **Liselotte Landbeck**, and **Emmy Putzinger**, all of whom medaled in international competition. Collectively, they stood on the medal stand almost every year. Hornung won two medals at the Austrian national championships, bronze in 1930 and silver in 1931. She competed at the first holding of the **European Championship** for ladies in 1930 and won the silver medal behind Fritzi Burger. A year later in her second and only other European effort, she placed seventh. Hornung competed once at the **World Championships** in 1929, placing fourth, and once at the **Olympic Games** in 1928, placing eighth.

HORVÁTH, OPIKA VON MÉRAY (c. 1888–1977) (HUN). Opika von Méray Horváth had a brief international career lasting just four years. In her first effort at the **World Championships** in 1911, she won the silver medal behind her countryman, **Lily Kronberger**. For the next three years, until World War I, with Kronberger retired, Horváth was an unbeatable world ladies' champion. At age 34 when competition resumed after the war, she no longer competed.

HÜBLER, ANNA. *See* BURGER, HEINRICH.

HÜGEL, GUSTAV (1876–1954) (AUT). Gustav Hügel won the silver medal at the first **World Championship** in 1896 and became the world champion a year later. Hügel's record includes one European title in 1901, and world titles in 1897, 1899, and 1900. Other than at his first international competition, the **European Championships** in 1892 at which he placed sixth, Hügel never placed lower than second in any competition. At an international competition for **special figures** held in conjunction with the World Championship in St. Petersburg, **Russia**, in 1896, he received the gold medal. *See also* AUSTRIA.

HUGHES, SARAH (1985–) (USA). Sarah Hughes became the **United States** junior champion in 1998 at age 12. She competed as a senior for five years, collecting two bronze and two silver medals. Sent to the **World Championships** for the first time at age 13, she placed seventh. Her best placement in three efforts was third in 2001. At the Salt Lake City **Olympic Winter Games** in 2002, Hughes managed a dramatic upset by defeating more experienced skaters including **Irina Slutskaya** and **Michelle Kwan** to win the Olympic title. Hughes competed through 2003 but then retired to attend college. After her freshman year, she spent a year touring with **Stars on Ice** and then returned to Yale University.

HULTÉN, VIVI-ANNE (1911–2003) (SWE). Vivi-Anne Hultén was the Swedish national champion for five years, but internationally she had the misfortune of being one of several ladies who competed during the 10-year reign of the unbeatable **Sonja Henie** of **Norway**. Between 1930 and 1937, Hultén collected one silver and six bronze medals in European, world, and Olympic competition. The silver medal was won at the **World Championships** in 1933. Her one Olympic medal was bronze behind Henie and **Cecilia Colledge** of **Great Britain** in 1936. *See also* BELGIUM; SWEDEN.

HUNGARY. Hungary was one of the five original members of the **International Skating Union** (ISU), founded in 1892. **Tibor von Földváry** competed at the **European Championships** for four years beginning in 1892, claiming three medals and the title in 1895. Hungarian skaters did not compete at the **World Championships** until the first ladies' competition in 1906. **Lily Kronberger** placed third twice behind **Madge Syers** of **Great Britain** and Jenny Herz of **Germany** before becoming a four-time lady world champion, 1908–1911. She was followed by **Opika von Méray Horváth** who won the last three titles before World War I, 1912–1914. Between the world wars, the Hungarian pair of **Emilia Rotter and László Szollás** won four world titles, 1931 and 1933–1935. Following World War II, another outstanding Hungarian pair, Andrea Kekéssy and **Ede Király**, won the title in 1949. Hungarian men have not yet won a world title, but in **ice dancing Krisztina Regóczy and András Sallay** became world champions in 1980. No skater from Hungary has yet won an Olympic title in any discipline. Judges from Hungary have officiated at numerous ISU competitions, and several Hungarians have served the ISU in important roles. They include **Emerich von Szent-Györgyi**, a council member beginning in 1895 and a vice president from 1921 to 1925; Elemér Terták, who served in several capacities including terms on the council for more than 30 years; and Zoltán Balázs, who received the Häsler Medal in 1987. Szent-Györgyi was elected as an honorary president in 1933. *See also* ORGONISTA, OLGA AND SZALAY, SÁNDOR.

HUNT, ROY. *See* HARTSHORNE, HAROLD.

HUTCHESON, MICHAEL. *See* TORVILL, JAYNE AND DEAN, CHRISTOPHER.

I

ICE CAPADES. In February 1940, a group of arena owners met in Hershey, Pennsylvania, to plan an ice show that would play in their arenas during the coming season. They selected the name Ice Capades. The company debuted in New Orleans and performed also in Atlantic City and Philadelphia while rehearsing for its premier season. Ice Capades of 1941, boasting a cast of 75, began a tour of 25 cities on November 5, 1940. **John Harris**, the original president, managed the company through 24 highly successful seasons as it expanded to include two casts and tours abroad. Ice Capades was purchased in 1963 by Metromedia and subsequently by the International Broadcasting Corporation. The company continued to prosper, but the industry was changing as the age of spectacular ice shows for general audiences gradually passed. By the early 1990s, Ice Capades could no longer operate profitably. While under Chapter 11 bankruptcy laws, the assets of Ice Capades were purchased by the just-established corporation **Dorothy Hamill** International. Profitability could not be restored, and within a year the company was sold to International Family Entertainment, resold again soon afterward, and then disbanded.

ICE DANCING. Although ice dancing has a long history in figure skating, it did not become a world discipline until 1952 and an Olympic discipline until 1976. **Jackson Haines** is often associated with the early history of dancing on ice, although French skaters were employing dance steps and movements even earlier in the 19th century. Our earliest knowledge of specific dances comes from the Viennese school during the last quarter of the 19th century, following Haines's two periods of residency there. They are described in detail in *Spuren auf dem Eise* (Tracings on the Ice). The Viennese dances were relatively static with the skaters remaining in a confined space, and most fell into disuse by the end of the century. The first dance featuring flow across the ice as in modern ice dancing was the three-step waltz reportedly first skated in Paris in 1894. It rapidly became a craze throughout Europe. By World War I, the ice dances being done were primarily the three-step waltz, the ten-step, and the kilian. During the years between the world wars many new dances were invented by British skaters, the result of competitions sponsored by the Ice Club, Westminster, and the *Skating Times* specifically to increase the repertoire of ice dances. Nearly one fourth of the compulsory dances still done today were invented during the 1930s. Establishing ice dancing as an international discipline was a high priority for the **International Skating Union** (ISU) after World War II. Competitions called "international dance competitions" were held in connection with the **World Championships** for two years beginning in 1950, before the first World Championship in ice dancing was held in 1952. **Jean Westwood and Lawrence Demmy** won the first four world titles. **Pamela Weight and Paul Thomas** won in 1956. **Courtney Jones** with two partners, June Markham and Doreen Denny, won from 1957 through 1960. In the early competitions, four **compulsory dances** were required in addition to a **free dance**. The compulsory dances, like **compulsory figures** in singles skating, counted 60 percent of the score. For the free dance, strict limitations were imposed to assure that ice dancing was distinctly different from **pair skating**.

British ice dancers dominated during the early years, winning every world title through 1960. A Czechoslovak brother and sister, **Eva Romanová and Pavel Roman**, then won for four years, 1962–1965, before another British couple, **Diane Towler and Bernard Ford**, reclaimed the title and held it for four years, 1966–1969. Since then, **Jayne Torvill and Christopher Dean**, 1981–1984, are the only British skaters who have won world titles. Soviet ice dancers became dominant in the 1970s. **Liudmila Pakhomova and Alexandr Gorshkov** won five world titles, 1970–1974, and in 1976 became the first Olympic champions as well. Except for Torvill and Dean, one Hungarian, and two French couples, each of whom won one title each, Soviet and Russian ice dancers won every world and Olympic title through the end of the century.

The discipline of ice dancing has experienced significant changes in the latter half of the 20th century. Originally it was viewed as taking ballroom dancing to the ice. In the 1980s it became more interpretive, largely the result of Torvill and Dean's choreography. The importance of compulsory dances was significantly diminished with fewer required in competition and reductions in their scoring value. An "original set pattern dance," now called the "original dance," was added in 1983, lowering the value of the compulsory dances and making ice dancing a three-part competition. Rules originally designed to keep ice dancing different from pair skating, such as separation of the partners and lifts, were gradually relaxed as emphasis has moved toward technical difficulty. At the ISU Congress in 2010, compulsory dances were removed completely from competition, and the original dance was replaced with a "short dance," making ice dancing again a two-part competition.

ICE FOLLIES. The Ice Follies, the first major touring ice show in the **United States**, was an effort begun in 1936 by three skaters from St. Paul, Minnesota, Roy and Eddie Shipstads and Oscar Johnson. The company had presented shows for more than 40 years when it was purchased by Feld Entertainment and joined forces with **Holiday on Ice**. For two seasons, it produced shows under the banner of Ice Follies and Holiday on Ice. Then, under an agreement with the Walt Disney Company, the Ice Follies revamped its show and marketed itself toward children. Disney on Ice undertook its first tour in 1981. From the Ice Follies' first tour in 1936, skating's oldest show continues to prosper today as Disney on Ice as the last major touring show in the United States with a full ensemble of skaters.

ICE RESURFACING MACHINES. *See* ZAMBONI, FRANK J.

INA, KYOKO (1972–) (USA). Kyoko Ina was born in **Japan** and competed nationally in that country as a singles skater before moving to the **United States** where she had a successful career in pairs with two partners. For five years, 1994–1998, she competed with Jason Dungjen (1967–). At the U.S. Championships, they won three silver and two gold medals. In international competition, their best placements were fourth at the **World Championships** in 1997 and the **Olympic Winter Games** in 1998. Changing partners, Ina competed with John Zimmerman (1973–) for four years. At the U.S. Championships, they won one silver medal followed by three gold medals, 2000–2002. In international competition, their best year was 2002, winning bronze medals at the World Championships and placing fifth at the Olympic Games.

INOUE, RENA (1976–) AND BALDWIN, JOHN, JR. (1973–) (USA). Rena Inoue and John Baldwin Jr. first competed as a pair in 2001. He was 27; she was 24. Both skaters had previous competitive careers in singles as well as in pairs. Inoue, who was born in **Japan**, placed fifth at the **World Junior Championships** in 1994, two years before moving to the **United States** in 1996. Baldwin was the novice men's champion in 1987. As a pair, Inoue and Baldwin won medals at the United States Championships for eight years, collecting three bronze and three silver, and then gold in 2004 and 2006. Their international medals at **Grand Prix** events include three silver and one gold in 2006 at **Skate America**. At the **Four Continents Championships**, they won gold in 2006 and bronze in 2007. Their best placement at the **World Championships** was fourth in 2006. Their Olympic effort in 2006 resulted in a seventh-place finish. Inoue and Baldwin are the first pair to have completed a throw triple **Axel Paulsen jump** in competition, having landed the jump at both the United States Championships and at the **Olympic Winter Games** in 2006.

INTERNATIONAL JUDGING SYSTEM. Following the judging **controversy** at the 2002 **Olympic Winter Games** in Salt Lake City, a move spearheaded by **Ottavio Cinquanta**, president of the **International Skating Union** (ISU), to change the traditional 6.0 and placement judging system to a point-based system resulted ultimately in the adoption at the 2004 Congress of the International Judging System (IJS). The system had been tested in 2002–2003 and employed for the Grand Prix events in 2003–2004. The intent of the IJS is to reduce outside influence on judges. A separate part of the system is the anonymity of judges which are randomly selected from an enlarged panel. The use of the IJS is employed for all ISU events but is not a requirement for national competitions, although countries, including the **United States**, have adopted it.

Under the IJS, all elements employed in all disciplines of figure skating are assigned a base value depending on their level of difficulty. A technical specialist and an assistant identify each element and its level of difficulty according to established criteria while it is being skated. Judges then determine the quality of each element performed and assign a grade from –3 to +3 to its assigned base value. In addition to the technical evaluation, points are awarded by the judges for five program components, specifically skating skills, transitions/linking footwork and movement, performance/execution, composition/choreography, and interpretation. They are combined with the technical score to determine the total score.

Under the previous 6.0 and placement system, a goal of all skaters, in addition to winning titles, was the achievement of earning the perfect 6.0. That does not exist in the IJS, although a new and continuous goal replaces it, the receipt of a score higher than the skater has previously received, which is referred to as a "personal best."

INTERNATIONAL PROFESSIONAL SKATERS ASSOCIATION. *See* OPEN PROFESSIONAL CHAMPIONSHIPS.

INTERNATIONAL SKATING UNION. The International Skating Union (ISU), the governing body for speed skating and figure skating, was founded in 1892. A meeting called by the Dutch Federation was held in Scheveningen, **Netherlands**, in July with representatives of federations and clubs from the Netherlands, **Great Britain**, **Germany**, **Austria**, **Sweden**, and **Hungary** in attendance. Letters of interest were received from **Norway**, **Russia**, and the **United States**. At that first biennial congress, **Willem J. H. Mulier** of the Netherlands was elected president. Significant legislation adopted was related solely to speed skating, although a committee was appointed to develop rules for figure skating.

The **European Championships**, which had been sponsored twice by the German and Austrian Figure Skating Association, now came under the jurisdiction of the ISU. The championship in 1893 resulted in the union's first major **controversy**, a result of the application of conflicting scoring rules. As a result the congress scheduled for 1894 could not be organized. Mulier announced his intention not to run for reelection. By a mail vote in 1895, **Viktor G. Balck** of Sweden was elected the new president. Balck served for 30 years, and under his leadership the ISU developed into a strong and permanent governing organization. The **World Championships**, the ISU's premier championship in figure skating, were first held in 1896. It replaced the European Championships for two years, but in 1898 the European Championships were reinstated and both competitions have been held ever since. The early competitions were for men only. At the World Championships, competitions for ladies were added in 1906 and for pairs in 1908, but events for women and pairs were not added to the European Championships until 1930.

The ISU's permanency was tested with the outbreak of World War I, which resulted in seven years without European or World Championships, but 20 European and 19 World Championships had been held before the War. From that solid foundation the sport rebounded quickly. The first congress after the war was held in October 1921, and dates for resumption of the championships were scheduled for early 1922. Fifteen nations were still members, and within a year, participation in the championships equaled that of the prewar years. By the end of the 1920s, membership in the union had increased by more than 50 percent. Permanency was tested again with the onset of World War II. For a second time, championships were suspended for seven years, but again, the union survived and soon developed into an even stronger organization.

No problem has plagued the ISU more than controversies related to the problem of judging the sport subjectively. From the conflicting rules interpretations at the 1893 European Championships, which resulted in the annulment of the competition, to the dishonest judging in the pairs' event at the 2002 **Olympic Winter Games**, which resulted in the establishment of a new judging system, the ISU has attempted through legislation to establish rules that address the problem.

The official language of the ISU is English, which was adopted after World War II. Originally, it was German, the name of the organization being the Internationale Eislauf-Verein. A permanent headquarters was established in **Switzerland** in 1947. The current address is Chemin de Primerose 2, 1007 Lausanne, Switzerland.

In the year 2010, World Championships were held for the 100th time, and the European Championships were held for the 102nd time. Current ISU membership includes two clubs and 81 federations for speed and figure skating from 65 countries and six continents, most recently South America. See Appendix A for a list of all ISU figure skating members.

INTERNATIONAL SKATING UNION OF AMERICA. *See* UNITED STATES.

INTERNATIONAL STYLE. Prior to the establishment of the **International Skating Union** (ISU) in 1892, there were three prevalent styles of skating, **English style**, **American style**, and international style. The ISU adopted the international style. The American style disappeared quickly. Although the English style has continued into the 21st century with separate test structures and competitions, many British skaters adopted the international style during the 1890s and by the post–World War I era it had become dominant. The international style, called the "continental style" by British skaters, is a continuation and expansion of the Viennese style, which evolved in Vienna after **Jackson Haines**'s two periods of residency there. It was a flowing style in which movement across the ice was as important as the figures traced on the ice. Elements of dance were present. The use of the arms was important for their aesthetic value as well as an aid in executing turns. A monumental book, *Spuren auf dem Eise* (Tracings on the Ice), dating from 1881, describes in detail the use of the arms as well as figures then being skated. Free-skating programs eventually evolved from the connection of various figures.

ITALY. The Federazione Italiana Sport del Ghiaccio was formed in 1926 and joined the **International Skating Union** (ISU) in 1927. Prior to World War II, just one lady and one pair competed internationally. Renée Volpato competed at the **European Championships** twice, 1931 and 1932, placing 10th both times. Pair skaters Anna and Ercole Cattaneo placed sixth at the European Championships in 1937. Proceeding to the **World Championships** they again placed sixth. Continuing for an additional year, they placed 10th. After the war, Italy demonstrated quickly its skating capabilities with entries in international championships every year beginning in 1949. Most notable of the postwar skaters was **Carlo Fassi** who placed fourth at the European Championships in 1949 and then proceeded incrementally through medals of each color, winning gold in 1953 and 1954. At the World Championships, Fassi was the only Italian to compete through 1953. That year, in his fourth appearance, he won the bronze medal behind **Hayes Alan Jenkins** and **James Grogan** of the **United States**. In addition to Fassi, Grazia Barcellona placed 16th in the ladies' events at the European Championships in 1949 and with Fassi placed ninth in the pairs' event. The previous year at the first postwar **Olympic Winter Games**, Fassi had placed 15th, Barcellona 24th, and together in pairs they placed 13th.

Italian ice dancers first competed internationally in 1954 at the European Championships. Bona Giammona and Giancarlo Sioli placed fourth, being defeated by three couples from **Great Britain** who swept the medals. They competed at the World Championships in 1955, placing 10th. Not since Fassi in 1954 had Italian skaters won a European title when in 2001 ice dancers **Barbara Fusar-Poli and Maurizio Margaglio** did so and proceeded that year to win the country's first world title in any discipline. **Carolina Kostner** became in 2007 Italy's first lady European champion. She won two consecutive titles. No Italian skater has yet won an Olympic title in any discipline. Italy has hosted three European and two World Championships in addition to two holdings of the Olympic Winter Games, Cortina in 1956 and Torino in 2006. The current ISU president, **Ottavio Cinquanta**, is from Italy. *See also* BIANCHETTI, SONIA.

ITO, MIDORI (1969–) (JPN). Midori Ito, a jumping sensation, became **Japan**'s first world ladies' champion. Ito competed at the **World Championships** beginning in 1984, but through the Olympic year, 1988, she placed no better than sixth, primarily owing to relatively poor **compulsory figures**. Her strength was in athleticism, especially jumping. In her first Olympic effort, the 1988 Calgary Winter Games, she completed a triple **Axel Paulsen jump**, the first lady to successfully land one in competition. She placed third in the **free skating** but 10th in the compulsory figures for an overall placement of fifth. A year later at the 1989 World Championships, she placed a career best sixth in the compulsory figures which she coupled with first place in the free skating to win the title. In 1990, at her last world competition, she claimed the silver medal. Returning for the Winter Olympics at Albertville in 1992, Ito completed her amateur career with a silver medal. Turning professional, she skated in shows, primarily in Japan, and served as a commentator for Japanese television. Ito was inducted into the **World Figure Skating Hall of Fame** in 2003.

J

JACKSON, DONALD (1940–) (CAN). For four consecutive years, 1959–1962, Donald Jackson was the Canadian national champion. In 1961, he won the **North American Championships**, and in 1962 he became the first Canadian man to win a world title. It was a historic event. Competing in Prague against the hometown favorite **Karol Divin**, who held a substantial lead after the **compulsory figures**, Jackson completed the first ever triple **Lutz jump** in world competition. He received seven 6.0 marks from the judges, all of whom placed him first in the **free skating**. Jackson had won silver medals at two previous **World Championships** and a bronze medal at the 1960 **Olympic Winter Games**. Retiring immediately after winning the world title, Jackson toured with the **Ice Follies** through the 1960s and won professional competitions in 1965 and 1970. He was inducted into the **World Figure Skating Hall of Fame** in 1977. *See also* CANADA.

JACOBY-ANDERSON, ANDREE AND JACOBY, DONALD. *See* McLACHLAN, WILLIAM.

JAKOBSSON, WALTER ANDREAS. *See* EILERS, LUDOWIKA ANTJE MARGARETA AND JAKOBSSON, WALTER ANDREAS.

JAPAN. Japan joined the **International Skating Union** (ISU) in 1926 and twice before World War II entered skaters in world and Olympic competitions. Two men competed in 1932, four men and one lady in 1936. After the war, Japanese men competed in 1951, but a quarter century passed before **Minoru Sano** in 1977 claimed their first medal. It was bronze. Japanese ladies competed in 1957, but nearly a quarter century passed before **Emi Watanabe** in 1979 claimed their first medal, also bronze. A decade later, **Midori Ito** became Japan's first world ladies' champion. Japanese ladies have since excelled. Those winning world titles include **Yuka Sato** in 1994, **Shizuka Arakawa** in 2004, **Miki Ando** in 2007, and **Mao Asada** in 2008 and 2010. Arakawa claimed Japan's first Olympic title in any discipline in 2006. Although she lacks a world title, **Fumie Suguri** has won three titles at the **Four Continents Championships**, 2001, 2003, and 2005. Both Suguri and Asada have won at the **Grand Prix Finals**. In 2010 **Takeshi Honda** became the first Japanese man to win a world title. He had previously won titles at the Four Continents Championships in 1999 and 2003. **Nobunari Oda** also won a Four Continents title in 2006. Many international competitions have been held in Japan. Tokyo has hosted the **World Championships** five times and the Grand Prix Finals twice. Osaka has hosted the Four Continents Championships. The **Olympic Winter Games** were held in Sapporo in 1972 and in Nagano in 1998. Japanese judges have officiated at numerous competitions. Junko Hiramatsu, a former national ladies' champion, was appointed to the ISU figure skating technical committee in 2002 and to the council in 2010. *See also* OTA, YUKINA; SATA, NOBUO; TAKAHASHI, DAISUKE.

JELINEK, MARIA (1942–) AND OTTO (1940–) (CAN). The brother-and-sister pair of Maria and Otto Jelinek was born in Prague, **Czechoslovakia**, children of a prosperous family. Following the communist takeover in 1948, they made a daring escape to **Austria**. The family then moved to **Canada**. Otto and Maria Jelinek won the Canadian junior title in 1955. Their first of two senior titles came six years later in 1961, following the retirement of **Barbara Wagner and Robert Paul**. They also won the **North American** title that year. The 1962 **World Championships** were held in Prague, the city of the Jelineks' birth from which they had escaped as children. There they won the world title after which they retired from competitive skating. Their one Olympic effort in 1960 resulted in a fourth-place finish. The Jelineks toured for several years with **Ice Capades**. Otto served in the Canadian Parliament and held appointments in two ministries, sports and finance. He also served as a figure skating analyst for Canadian television. Both siblings currently reside in Prague.

JELINEK, OTTO. *See* JELINEK, MARIA AND OTTO.

JENKINS, DAVID WILKINSON (1936–) (USA). David Jenkins, the younger brother of **Hayes Alan Jenkins**, won the national junior title in 1953. Following his brother's retirement, he became a four-time national champion beginning in 1957 and the North American champion that year. At the **World Championships**, he won two bronze medals before becoming a three-time champion, 1957–1959. He competed at the **Olympic Winter Games** twice, medaling both times, bronze in 1956 and the gold in 1960. Jenkins skated with **Ice Capades** for a short time before proceeding to medical school followed by a career as a thoracic surgeon. *See also* UNITED STATES.

JENKINS, DOROTHY AND McLENNAN, A. GORDON (CAN). Dorothy Jenkins and Gordon McLennan of **Canada** won the pairs' title at the first holding of the **North American Championships** in 1923. Jenkins was also the Canadian ladies' champion in singles for two years, 1922 and 1923. McLennan competed with three pair partners, winning national titles with two of them but not with Jenkins. In 1913, he won the title with Muriel Burrows and in 1922 with Alden Godwin.

JENKINS, HAYES ALAN (1933–) (USA). Hayes Jenkins, the older brother of **David Jenkins**, began skating nationally as a novice in 1946, placing fourth. Two years later he was the junior champion. As a senior, he competed for four years before becoming a four-time national champion, 1953–1956. He was twice the **North American** champion, 1953 and 1955. At the **World Championships**, Jenkins won two bronze medals before becoming a four-time world champion, 1953–1956. In Olympic competition he placed fourth in 1952 and won the title in 1956. Jenkins skated professionally for a short time with **Holiday on Ice** before proceeding to law school and to his subsequent career as a corporate counsel. He married the five-time world ladies' champion and 1960 Olympic champion **Carol Heiss**. Jenkins and Heiss were both elected into the **World Figure Skating Hall of Fame** with the initial class in 1976. *See also* ITALY; UNITED STATES.

JEPSON-TURNER, GLADYS LYNNE (1923–2005) (GBR). Internationally, Gladys Lynne Jepson-Turner competed only at the Berlin **Olympic Winter Games** in 1936 where she placed 16th. She was 13. Turning professional at age 14, she adopted the stage name Belita. Her popularity soared when she skated in two special ice ballets at the Royal Opera House at Covent Garden in 1937. *The Brahmin's Daughter* and *Enchanted Night* were extravagant productions, each with a cast of 120 skaters supported by a 50-piece orchestra. Moving to the **United States** early in the war years, Belita became a headliner with **Ice Capades**, billed as the "world's greatest skater." After the war, she left Ice Capades and returned to England where she continued her career as a show skater. The popular Belita was also a talented actress, pianist, ballerina, and swimmer. She appeared in several films, the most important of which was a 1953 MGM release, *Never Let Me Go*, with Clark Gable. Belita is also known, especially in England, by her married name, Mrs. Joel Riordan.

JOHNSON, JAMES HENRY. *See* JOHNSON, PHYLLIS WYATT AND JAMES HENRY.

JOHNSON, LYNN-HOLLY (1958–) (USA). Lynn-Holly Johnson was the novice silver medalist at the United States Championships in 1974, her best competitive result. She toured with **Ice Capades** in 1977 and subsequently pursued an acting career. Her first major effort was the 1978 skating film, *Ice Castles*. She was nominated for a Golden Globe award. Also notable was her role of Bibi Dahl opposite Roger Moore in the 1981 James Bond film *For Your Eyes Only*.

JOHNSON, OSCAR. *See* ICE FOLLIES.

JOHNSON, PHYLLIS WYATT (1886–1967) AND JAMES HENRY (1874–1921) (GBR). Phyllis and James Johnson of England were twice the world pair champions and in 1908 the Olympic silver medalists. Phyllis Wyatt Squire was a champion **English style** skater before marrying James Johnson in 1904. She then adopted the **international style** and competed in pairs with her husband. Three times they competed against Anna Hübler and **Heinrich Burger**, always to second-place finishes, but following Hübler and Burger's retirement, the Johnsons won world titles twice, 1909 and 1912. James did not compete after 1912, but beginning that year, Phyllis, who was 12 years younger, competed in ladies' events for three years, 1912–1914, winning one silver and two bronze medals at the World Championships. She appeared after the war at the Antwerp **Olympic Winter Games** in 1920, placing fourth, but retired before the **World Championships** were reinstated in 1922. At the Antwerp Games, she competed also in pairs with Basil Williams. They placed third. The Johnsons wrote a valuable article on **pair skating** which was published in Irving Brokaw's book of 1910, *The Art of Skating*.

JOLY, ANDRÉE. *See* BRUNET, ANDRÉE AND PIERRE.

JONES, COURTNEY J. L. (1933–) (GBR). Courtney Jones holds a unique position in the history of **ice dancing** as a world champion for four consecutive years, twice with each of two partners. June Markham (1939–), his first partner, retired following gold medal performances in 1957 and 1958. Jones quickly selected Doreen Denny (1941–) as his next partner. Two additional gold medals followed in 1959 and 1960. Jones and his two partners continued the dominance of British skaters in ice dancing since it had become a world discipline in 1952. **Jean Westwood and Lawrence Demmy** were the champions from 1952 through 1955, and they were followed by **Pamela Weight and Paul Thomas** in 1956. Jones had a long and distinguished career that crossed disciplines. His competitive career began in 1947, five years before ice dancing was contested at the **World Champion-**

ships. As an ice dancer, he competed in local and national competitions with several partners; as a pair skater he competed successfully at the national level; and as a singles skater, he won several national competitions. Continuing to skate after retirement, with a later partner, Peri Horne, he invented two **compulsory dances**, the Silver Samba and the Starlight Waltz. After his long competitive career, Jones served the International Skating Union as a judge and referee for ice dancing and in various other capacities through 2010, including membership on the ice dancing technical committee and as a council member. Jones was elected to the **World Figure Skating Hall of Fame** in 1986. *See also* GREAT BRITAIN.

JOSEPH, VIVIAN LAUREEN (1948–) AND RONALD BERT (1944–) (USA). Brother and sister Vivian and Ronald Joseph, the **United States** junior pair champions in 1961, competed for four years as seniors, progressing from bronze medals in 1962 through silver medals for two years before winning gold medals in 1965. At the biennial **North American Championships**, they were bronze medalists in 1963 and gold medalists in 1965. Competing at the **World Championships** for three years, beginning in 1963, they placed eighth and fourth before winning silver medals behind the **Protopopovs** in 1965. Their one Olympic effort in 1964 resulted in a fourth-place finish. The Josephs turned professional after the 1965 skating season.

JOUBERT, BRIAN (1984–) (FRA). Brian Joubert, the national champion for six consecutive years, 2003–2008, became in 2004 the first man from **France** to win the European title since **Alain Calmat** 40 years earlier and in 2007 the world title for the first time since Calmat won it in 1965. From 2002 through 2010, Joubert medaled at every **European Championship**, a total of four bronze, two silver, and gold in 2004, 2007, and 2009. He competed those same years at the **World Championships**, winning a total of six medals, two bronze, three silver, and gold in 2007. Joubert competed at three **Olympic Winter Games**, placing 16th in 2002, sixth in 2006, and 14th in 2010. He won the title at the **Grand Prix Finals** in 2007 and qualified again in 2008 but had to withdraw due to an injury.

JUMPS. A jump can be defined simply as a leap into the air in which both feet leave the ice and the skater rotates at least a half revolution. This popular element of figure skating is relatively recent in the history of the sport, not having a major role in free skating programs until the 1930s. Jumping was not viewed as artistic in the 19th century, but hops, jumps without rotation, had a practical application as a safety factor owing to impediments found on natural ice. Jumping had no place in **English style** skating. Skaters on the continent experimented with jumps from the ice during the last quarter of the century, but not extensively. **Axel Paulsen** was tremendously progressive when in 1882 he did as a **special figure** the jump that today bears his name. Most jumps in the standard repertoire today were invented between the world wars. They are required elements in tests at all levels and in competitive programs for singles skaters and pair skaters.

Jumps are divided into groups known as edge jumps and toe-pick assisted jumps. Edge jumps leave the ice from any of the four possible **edges**, and the lift is achieved from the spring gained by straightening of a bent knee in combination with a swing of the free leg. The most important edge jumps are the **loop**, the **Salchow**, and the Axel Paulsen. Toe-pick assisted jumps achieve lift from the ice partially by pressing the toe pick into the ice on takeoff, allowing greater height than in an edge jump. The most important toe-pick assisted jumps are the **toe loop**, the **flip**, and the **Lutz**.

Jumps are also classified by the number of revolutions. Single jumps, except for the Axel Paulsen, include one revolution, double jumps include two revolutions, and so on. The single Axel Paulsen includes one and one-half revolutions, the double Axel Paulsen two and one-half revolutions, and so on. All jumps have established values of difficulty employed in evaluating programs. **Split jumps**, which are not required elements, all have a half revolution. They add variety to programs and are particularly attractive when done in sequence.

Pair skaters employ two categories of jumps. Side-by-side jumps are those described previously in which the two skaters do the jumps in unison and side by side. Unique to **pair skating** are throw jumps, being the described jumps in which the lady who does the jump is assisted and propelled by her partner.

KACHLER, FRITZ (1888–1973) (AUT). Fritz Kachler enjoyed a competitive career that spanned 15 years, including four years before and four years after World War I. His appearances at three European and seven **World Championships** resulted in as many medals, one bronze, four silver, and five gold. He did not compete at the **Olympic Winter Games**. Remaining active in the sport for many years, Kachler served the **International Skating Union** in various capacities, including two years, 1957–1959, as the vice president for figure skating. *See also* AUSTRIA.

KADAVY, CARYN JAMI (1967–) (USA). Caryn Kadavy, a medalist for three years at the **United States** Championships, 1986–1988, was sent to the **World Championships** those years where her best result was a bronze medal in 1987. She was unable to compete at the Calgary **Winter Olympic Games** owing to a serious bout with the flu, which also affected her ability to perform well at the World Championships a month later. Kadavy is remembered for her musical and graceful free skating, which ultimately served her well as a professional show skater.

KAGELMANN, UWE. *See* GROSS, MANUELA AND KAGELMANN, UWE.

KAISER, OTTO. *See* SCHOLZ, LILY AND KAISER, OTTO.

KARPONOSOV, GENNADI. *See* LINICHUK, NATALIA AND KARPONOSOV, GENNADI.

KASPAR, FELIX (1915-2003) (AUT). Felix Kaspar was three times the Austrian national champion, and twice each the European and World Champion. All except his first national title were in 1937 and 1938, years he won every competition entered. At the **Olympic Winter Games** in 1936, he claimed the bronze medal. Kaspar retired after the 1938 season and embarked on a professional skating career in **Australia** and subsequently in the **United States**. He is remembered for his athleticism. It has been reported that his **Axel Paulsen jump** reached four feet above the ice and a distance of 25 feet from takeoff to landing. Kaspar was elected to the **World Figure Skating Hall of Fame** in 1998.

KAUFFMAN, CYNTHIA DIANE (1948–) AND RONALD LEE (1946–) (USA). Siblings competing as pairs is not unusual, but in the 1960s, three American sister-and-brother pairs competed against each other and in 1964 claimed all the medals at the United States Championships. In addition to Cynthia and Ron Kauffman the pairs include Judianne and Jerry Fotheringill and **Vivian and Ronald Joseph**, all of whom became national pair champions. The Kauffmans were the junior champions in 1963. As seniors, they claimed the bronze medals in 1964 and the silver medals in 1965. For the next four years, 1966–1969, they were the national pair champions. Competing at the World Championships, they won three consecutive bronze medals, 1966–1968. At two Olympic efforts, their best placement was sixth in 1968. The Kauffmans competed at three of the biennial **North American Championships**, winning silver medals in 1965 and gold medals in 1967 and 1969. They turned professional after the 1969 skating season.

KAUFFMAN, RONALD LEE. *See* KAUFFMAN, CYNTHIA DIANE AND RONALD LEE.

KAZAKOVA, OKSANA. *See* DMITRIEV, ARTUR.

KEATS, EVA AND WEYDEN, ERIK VAN DER (GBR). Eva Keats and Erik van der Weyden were British dance champions on roller skates in the early 1920s after which they turned professional and taught both roller skating and ice skating. During the 1930s, van der Weyden and Eva Keats, now his wife, entered contests for new ice dances sponsored by the Ice Club, Westminster and the *Skating Times*. Three dances of their invention, the foxtrot, rocker foxtrot, and Viennese waltz, were to become **compulsory dances** when the **International Skating Union** made **ice dancing** a world discipline in the 1950s. Van der Weyden wrote an authoritative book entitled *Dancing on Ice*.

KÉKESSY, ANDREA. *See* KIRÁLY, EDE.

KELLEY, H. KENDALL (c. 1897–1980) (USA). H. Kendall Kelley served skating nationally and internationally. He was the treasurer of the **United States Figure Skating Association** (USFSA) from 1945 to 1948. Although never a vice president, he served one term as president, 1952–1955. Kelley was elected an honorary member of USFSA in 1955 and an honorary member of the executive committee, now called the board of directors, in 1966. He served the **International Skating Union** as a substitute member of the **ice dancing** technical committee for two years, 1961–1963, replacing **Harold Hartshorne** who had died in the plane crash in 1961, and then as a voting member from 1963 until 1967. He previously served as a world judge, officiating at both the **World Championships** and the **Olympic Winter Games** in 1956.

KENNEDY, KAROL ESTELLE (1932–2004) AND MICHAEL EDWARD "PETER" (1927–) (USA). In 1950, the brother and sister Karol and Peter Kennedy became the first pair from the **United States** to win a world title, and it was another 29 years before **Tai Babilonia and Randy Gardner** did so again. The Kennedys were the U.S. champions five times, 1948–1952, after having won the silver medal in 1947. That same year they won silver medals in their first effort at the **World Championships**. They slipped to fourth place in 1948, won silver medals again in 1949, and claimed the gold medals in 1950. The following year, a dominant German couple, **Ria Baran and Paul Falk**, appeared on the scene, and in 1951 and 1952 the Kennedys settled for silver medals at both the World Championships and the **Olympic Winter Games**. At the 1952 World Championships, an incident occurred in which Peter assaulted a press photographer. Although there was provocation, he was convicted. Both the **International Skating Union** and the **United States Figure Skating Association** suspended him permanently.

KENNEDY, MICHAEL EDWARD. *See* KENNEDY, KAROL ESTELLE AND MICHAEL EDWARD "PETER."

KERMER, ROMY (1956–) AND ÖSTERREICH, ROLF (1952–) (GDR). Romy Kermer and Rolf Österreich, a talented pair from the **German Democratic Republic**, had the misfortune of skating during the reign of the unbeatable **Irina Rodnina** and her second partner, Alexandr Zaitsev. During their first year on the international stage in 1973, Kerner and Österreich placed sixth at the **European Championships** and fourth at the **World Championships**. For the next three years at those competitions and the 1976 **Olympic Winter Games**, they collected one bronze and six silver medals behind Rodnina and Zaitsev. Following their competitive career, Kermer and Österreich skated in various shows, including **Champions on Ice**.

KERRIGAN-HARDING INCIDENT. At the 1993 United States Championships, **Nancy Kerrigan** won the gold medal and for the first time defeated **Tonya Harding** who slipped to a dismal fourth place, a result which kept her off the World team. Kerrigan had become the new American "ice princess." Her elegant style and popularity weighed on Harding as she entered the 1994 season. Determined not to be excluded again, especially in an Olympic year, Harding became involved in figure skating's most sinister plot, one intended to ensure her position on the world and Olympic teams. At the national championships in Detroit, following a practice session, a man approached Kerrigan, who had just exited the ice, and struck her above her landing knee with a metal baton. Damage to Kerrigan's leg was severe but not permanent. Withdrawing from nationals was necessary, but skating at the Olympics was possible. Suspicion soon turned to Harding, a skater with so much raw talent but an inconsistent record and someone who had much to gain without Kerrigan as a competitor. At first, Harding claimed innocence of wrongdoing as well as lack of knowledge regarding a plot against Kerrigan, but at a news conference three weeks after the attack, she admitted learning that "persons close to me" might have been involved. Those persons included her husband Jeff Gillooly, his friends Shawn Eckardt, Derrick Smith, and Shane Stant, the actual attacker. All were implicated as the plot unraveled. In a plea bargain, Gillooly implicated Harding. She was not incarcerated but ultimately performed 400 hours of public service, paid fines totaling $160,000, and was placed on probation. Her eligible skating career ended when the **United States Figure Skating Association** banned her for life and stripped her of the 1994 national title.

KERRIGAN, NANCY (1969–) (USA). Nancy Kerrigan was only once the national ladies' champion and never a world or Olympic champion, but she became one of America's favorite skaters in the early 1990s, partly a result of the **Kerrigan-Harding incident**. Kerrigan competed at a time when outstanding ladies from several countries were also seeking international titles. They included **Tonya Harding** and **Kristi Yamaguchi** from the **United States**, **Oksana Baiul** from Ukraine, **Surya Bonaly** from **France**, **Lu Chen** from **China**, and **Yuka Sato** from **Japan**. Kerrigan's record against such talented skaters is good, medaling twice at the **World Championships**, in 1991 and 1992, and twice at the **Olympic Winter Games**, 1992 and 1994. Only once, in 1993, did she not medal. Turning professional after the games in 1994, Kerrigan entered a few professional competitions and skated in various shows. She is currently a television commentator on IceNetwork.

KHOKHLOVA, JANA (1985–) AND NOVITSKI, SERGEI (1981–) (RUS). Ice dancers Jana Khokhlova and Sergei Novitski began skating together in 2002. At the Russian Championships, they placed fourth in 2004, third for the next two years, and second in 2007 before becoming national champions in 2008 and 2009. Competing at the **European Championships** from 2006 through 2009, they won bronze medals in 2008 and gold medals in 2009. At the **World Championships** during the same years, their best success was as the bronze medalists in 2008. Khokhlova and Novitski entered the **Olympic Winter Games** twice, placing 12th in 2006 and ninth in 2010.

KILIUS, MARIKA (1943–) (FRG). Pair skater Marika Kilius enjoyed an international career that spanned 10 years and included two partners. From 1955 through 1957, she paired with Franz Ningel (1936–). They won bronze medals at the **European Championships** in 1955 and 1956. Those same years they won bronze and silver medals at the **World Championships** and placed fourth at the 1956 **Olympic Winter Games**. Changing partners, both skaters continued to compete. With placements ranging from second to fifth, Ningel and his new partner Margret Göbl (1938–) consistently placed behind Kilius and her new partner Hans-Jürgen Bäumler (1942–) as they captured six European titles, 1959–1964, world titles in 1963 and 1964, and Olympic silver medals in 1960 and 1964. The pairs event at Innsbruck has been called "the story" of the 1964 Games. As reigning European and world champions and silver medalists at the 1960 Olympics, Kilius and Bäumler were strongly favored to win, but by a decision of five judges to four, **Liudmila Belousova and Oleg Protopopov** upset them to claim the **Soviet Union**'s first Olympic gold medals. Enterprising merchants had been so sure of the outcome that souvenirs proclaiming the Germans as champions had gone on sale before the event was skated. Turning professional, Kilius and Bäumler appeared in **Holiday on Ice** shows as did Göbl and Ningel. *See also* GERMANY; RUSSIA.

KIM, YU NA (1990–) (KOR). Yu Na Kim, **Korea**'s first and only medalist in figure skating, won every major title—**Grand Prix Finals**, Four Continents, worlds, and Olympics—by age 19. She held her national title continuously beginning in 2003 and won the world junior ladies' title in her second try in 2006. Competing twice at the **Four Continents Championships**, she won the title in 2009 after having withdrawn the previous year because of an injury. At four consecutive **World Championships**, 2007–2010, Kim won the title in 2009, and claimed one silver and two bronze medals in the other years. The silver medal in 2010 was behind **Mao Asada** of **Japan** who Kim had defeated the previous month to become the 2010 Olympic ladies' champion. Earlier that season Kim won at the Grand Prix Finals.

KIRÁLY, EDE (1926–2009) (HUN). Ede Király had a short but successful international career as a singles skater which lasted just three years,

1948–1950, and as a pair skater with Andrea Kékessy (1926–) for two of those years, 1948 and 1949. Király became the European champion in 1950 after winning the silver medal in 1949 and placing fourth the year before. At the **World Championships** with the American men present, his record of one bronze followed by two silver medals is excellent. He placed fifth at the **Olympic Winter Games** in 1948. During the two years he competed in pairs with Kékessy, he medaled at the World Championships in both disciplines, a rare feat. Kékessy and Király's record as a pair includes gold medals at the **European Championships** both years, silver and gold medals at the World Championships, and silver medals at the Olympic Winter Games. Kékessy, like Király, skated singles but not as successfully. At the European Championships she placed seventh in 1948 and 10th in 1949. In one effort at the World Championships, she placed ninth.

KIRBY, MICHAEL. *See* GILCHRIST, DONALD.

KIRK, JENNIFER "JENNY" (1984–) (USA). Jenny Kirk's best success was as a junior. She placed second at the Junior Grand Prix Finals in 1999 and won the world junior ladies' title in 2000. As a senior, Kirk won the **Four Continents Championships** in 2002, but at the **United States** Championships, her best result was a bronze medal in 2004. At the **World Championships** that year, she placed 18th. In her final competitive year, 2005, she placed fourth at the national championships, which kept her off the world team. Through 2002, Kirk was coached by Mary and Evy Scovold. Changing coaches, she trained with **Richard Callaghan** for two years before making a second change to **Frank Carroll** for her final competitive year.

KISSELE, TURII. *See* BAKUSHEVA, NINA AND ZHUK, STANISLAV.

KLIMOVA, MARINA (1966–) AND PONOMARENKO, SERGEI (1960–) (URS). Marina Klimova and Sergei Ponomarenko are one of several Soviet couples who dominated **ice dancing** following the retirement of **Jayne Torvill and Christopher Dean** in 1984 and continuing through the 1990s. **Natalia Bestemianova and Andrei Bukin**, their compatriots, had been European, world, and Olympic champions for four years culminating with the **Olympic Winter Games** and **World Championships** in 1988. Klimova and Ponomarenko did likewise through the games in 1992, winning every competition except the World Championships in 1991 when a French couple, **Isabelle and Paul Duchesnay**, defeated them in an unexpected upset. Klimova and Ponomarenko were an appealing couple who typically displayed a more classic style than their predecessors. Upon retirement, they skated in shows for several years including **Champions on Ice**. They are currently teaching skating in the United States. Klimova and Ponomarenko were inducted into the **World Figure Skating Hall of Fame** in 2000.

KLOPFER, SONYA (1934–) (USA). Sonya Klopfer became the U.S. junior ladies' champion in 1949. Her short senior career lasted just three years, 1950–1952, after which she turned professional and became a show skater, primarily in England. As a senior competitor, she entered just two national championships, placing second in 1950 and winning the title in 1951. At three **World Championships**, 1950–1952, she placed fifth, third, and second. Those were years of tremendous talent among the ladies nationally and internationally. At the 1952 **Olympic Winter Games** in Oslo, **Norway**, Klopfer placed fourth behind **Jeannette Altwegg** of **Great Britain**, **Tenley Albright** of the **United States**, and **Jacqueline du Bief** of **France**, all of whom were or would become world champions. Klopfer worked for many years as a coach with her husband, Peter Dunfield.

KNIGHT, DONALD (1947–) (CAN). Donald Knight became the Canadian junior champion in 1961. Four years later, he won the first of three consecutive senior titles, 1965–1967. Knight competed during a period when two other strong Canadian men with the same given name, **Donald Jackson** and **Donald McPherson**, became world champions. He competed also against the modernist **Toller Cranston,** whose best placement at the **World Championships** was as the bronze medalist. Knight competed at five World Championships, 1963–1967, and like Cranston, his best placement was as the bronze medalist in 1965. His one Olympic effort in 1964 resulted in a ninth-place finish. Knight won two medals at the biennial **North American Championships**, bronze in 1965 and gold in 1967.

KOCH, JAMES (c. 1904–1982) (SUI). Dr. James Koch capably led the **International Skating Union** (ISU) from 1953 through 1967, the early years of the Cold War. He had been active in the Swiss Federation during World War II, and in 1947 he became a world judge and referee. Koch subsequently served at both the **Olympic Winter Games** and the **World Championships** in 1948 and many other events over the next several years. He was elected to the ISU's figure skating technical committee in 1949, to the vice presidency for figure skating in 1953, and then ascended to the presidency that same year following the resignation of **Herbert L. Clarke**. During the 1950s, attempts to influence the outcome of competitions by various means, including bloc judging, a product of the Cold War, tested Koch's administrative skills. Suspensions of persons involved with the attempted manipulations occurred and formal procedures to eliminate or check bloc judging were established. Koch's influence and accomplishments were recognized in 1994 with his induction into the **World Figure Skating Hall of Fame**. *See also* SWITZERLAND.

KOKKO, PETRI. *See* RAHKOMO, SUSANNA AND KOKKO, PETRI.

KOREA. The Republic of Korea joined the **International Skating Union** in 1948. Twenty-five years later, in 1973, they sent Myung Su Chang, their first lady competitor, to the **World Championships**. She competed for two years. Other Korean ladies have appeared annually except in 1992. The first Korean man to compete, Soo Bong Han, appeared in 1977, and he too competed for two years. Unlike the ladies, men did not compete every year. Ice dancers first appeared in 1987, pair skaters in 1992. Placements were always low in the rankings. No Korean skater placed higher than 17th in any discipline until 2007. That year at her first World Championship, **Yu Na Kim** carried home the bronze medal. She repeated the next year, winning a second bronze medal. Kim became the lady world champion in 2009 and the Olympic champion in 2010.

KORPI, KIIRA. *See* LEPISTÖ, LAURA.

KOSTNER, CAROLINA (1987–) (ITA). Carolina Kostner is a four-time national champion, although her titles are not consecutive. She was the first lady from **Italy** to win the European ladies' title, winning it three times, 2007, 2008, and 2010. Her best placement at the **World Championships** was as the silver medalist in 2008. She was the bronze medalist in 2005. Kostner has won two **Grand Prix** events, the NHK Trophy in 2007 and the Cup of Russia in 2009. At the **Grand Prix Finals** she was the bronze medalist in 2008 and 2009. Two Olympic efforts resulted in a ninth-place finish in 2006 and a disappointing 16th place in 2010, largely the result of a poor showing in the free skating.

KOSTOMOROV, ROMAN. *See* NAVKA, TATIANA AND KOSTOMAROV, ROMAN.

KOVALEV, VLADIMIR (1953–) (URS). During a nine-year international career Vladimir Kovalev was twice a world champion. His first appearance on the world stage in 1972 resulted in a bronze medal. Kovalev was strong in the **compulsory figures**, but nerves frequently affected his performances in the free skating. He did not compete internationally in 1973 but returned in 1974 to place fourth at both the European and **World Championships**. For the remainder of his career, 1975 through the **European Championships**

in 1980, he medaled at all but the 1979 World Championships, winning the European title in 1975 and the world title in 1977 and 1979. His other medals include one bronze and six silver. At the Olympic Games in 1976, he won the silver medal. *See also* RUSSIA.

KOVAŘÍKOVÁ, RADKA (1975–) AND NOVOTNÝ, RENÉ (1963–) (CZE). Radka Kovaříková and René Novotný are the only pair skaters from the **Czech Republic** to become world champions. Their tenure in international competition was short, just three years. First appearing in 1993, they placed fourth at both the European and **World Championships**. In the Olympic year, 1994, they again placed fourth at the **European Championships** but slipped to fifth at the World Championships. Their Olympic effort resulted in a sixth-place finish. In 1995, they won medals at both competitions, silver at the European Championships before becoming the world pair champions. They then retired.

KOZUKA, TAKAHIKO. *See* SATO, NOBUO.

KRAATZ, VICTOR. *See* BOURNE, SHAE-LYNN AND KRAATZ, VICTOR.

KRISTOFICS-BINDER, CLAUDIA (1961–) (AUT). Claudia Kristofics-Binder competed internationally for seven years beginning in 1976. In the tradition of her compatriot **Beatrix Schuba**, she became a master of **compulsory figures**. During her final two years of competition, 1981 and 1982, she consistently placed first in the compulsory figures, and like Schuba, she placed lower in free-skating events. All four of her medals came during that two-year period, three bronze medals at the European and **World Championships** and a gold medal at the **European Championships** in 1982. In two Olympic efforts, her best placement was seventh in 1980. Following her eligible career, she skated in shows including **Holiday on Ice**.

KROH, ALEXANDER. *See* NORWAY.

KRONBERGER, LILY (1890–1974) (HUN). Lily Kronberger became the second lady world champion. She competed at the **World Championships** for six years beginning with their inception in 1906 but did not compete at the **Olympic Games** in 1908. Twice, she placed third behind **Madge Syers** and **Jenny Herz** of **Austria**, but after their retirement, Kronberger won four consecutive world titles, 1908–1911. Kronberger is remembered for lavish costumes and was an early advocate for attention to interpretation of the music. She was elected to the **World Figure Skating Hall of Fame** in 1997.

KRYLOVA, ANJELIKA (1973–) AND OVSIANNIKOV, OLEG (1970–) (RUS). In their first year on the international stage, in 1995, ice dancers Anjelika Krylova and Oleg Ovsiannikov won bronze medals at the **European Championships** and placed fifth at the **World Championships**. Beginning the next year and continuing through the **Olympic Winter Games** in 1998, they claimed silver medals behind another Russian couple **Oksana Grishchuk and Evgeny Platov**, but following Grishchuk and Platov's retirement, Krylova and Ovsiannikov became world champions in 1998 and 1999 and European champions in 1999. They also won the title at the **Grand Prix Finals** in 1999. Although they announced their intention to continue competing through the next Olympic cycle, they retired in 2000 and skated in various shows including **Champions on Ice**.

KULIK, ILIA (1977–) (RUS). Ilia Kulik was the Olympic champion in 1998. He is the most recent of four men who have won Olympic gold medals but not world titles. The others are **Wolfgang Schwarz** in 1968, **Robin Cousins** in 1980, and **Alexei Urmanov** in 1994. Kulik was the Russian national champion in 1997 and 1998, and he won the title at the **Champions Series Final** in 1997. Two years earlier in 1995, he was the world junior champion and the European champion. Turning professional after winning the Olympic title in Nagano, Kulik joined **Stars on Ice**. *See also* RUSSIA.

KUTSCHERA, HANS (AUT). Hans Kutschera, an ice dancer, competed during the 1950s. At the Austrian national championships, seven medals, two bronze, two silver, and three gold, were won with three different partners. The bronze medals were won with Luise Lehner in 1950 and 1953, the silver medal with Ilse Reitmeyer in 1952, and one silver, followed by three gold medals with Edith Peikert, 1954–1957. Kutschera competed each year at the **World Championships** beginning with the first holding of the dance competition in 1952 and continuing through 1957 for one year each with Reitmeyer and Lehner and then for five years with Peikert, always placing well down in the rankings. Those were years in which British ice dancers dominated, winning 18 of the 27 medals awarded through 1960 including all of the gold medals. Kutschera served the **International Skating Union** for 29 years beginning in 1967 through membership on the **ice dancing** technical committee as a substitute member for two years, as a voting member from 1969 until 1984, and as the chair from 1984 until 1986.

KWAN, MICHELLE (1980–) (USA). Michelle Kwan is perhaps the best-known and most-loved skater of the past 15 years. She began her rise to fame immediately following the **Kerrigan-Harding incident** in 1994 and benefitted from the rapid growth in popularity of the sport that followed. Her fans watched her compete through her teen years and beyond as she developed unusually fine artistry and tremendous media appeal. Through most of her career, she was coached by **Frank Carroll**. Kwan nine times won the United States Championship, tying the record set 70 years earlier by **Maribel Vinson**. She was the world junior champion in 1994. As a senior she accumulated five world titles, tying the records of **Herma Szabo** in the early 1920s and **Carol Heiss** in the late 1950s. In her Olympic efforts, she was the silver medalist behind **Tara Lipinski** in 1998 and the bronze medalist behind **Sarah Hughes** and **Irina Slutskaya** in 2002. Kwan's five world medals were not continuous, as Szabo's and Heiss's had been, a result of the talented competition against which she skated. She first won in 1996. A year later, a major rival, Tara Lipinski, defeated her, primarily because of a technically more difficult program including a triple loop–triple loop combination jump. Kwan won again in 1998, but a Russian skater who could never be ignored, **Maria Butyrskaya**, slipped past her and won the title in 1999. For the next two years Kwan was not denied, but in 2002, her second major rival, Irina Slutskaya, defeated her. Kwan won her last world title in 2003. She was also the first winner of the **Grand Prix Finals**, which were established in 1996. Kwan has skated in many shows, especially **Champions on Ice**. Unable to continue with her college education while competing, she returned and completed her degree in 2009 at the University of Denver. She is currently a graduate student at Tufts University.

KWIATKOWSKI, TONIA (1971–) (USA). Tonia Kwiatkowski's record fails to demonstrate completely her strength. Coached by **Carol Heiss** from age nine through her long eligible career, she in many ways embodied her coach's sophistication, always exhibiting feminism and maturity in her performances, and she is one of few skaters in recent years who has attended college and completed a degree while competing. Others include **Debi Thomas** and **Paul Wylie**. Kwiatkowski claimed the bronze medal in 1987 at the junior national championships. During her 11 years as a senior, competing every year, her best finish was a silver medal in 1996 at age 24. She was named to world teams three times where her best result was sixth in 1998, her last year of competitive skating. Kwiatkowski coaches figure skating in the Cleveland, Ohio, area.

L

LABIN, ERNST (? –1967) (AUT). Ernst Labin was an official in the Austrian Federation and a World Championship referee. He served the **International Skating Union** (ISU) as its president for less than two months in 1967 owing to his unexpected death just six weeks after being elected. Prior to his presidency, Labin served the ISU for many years. He became a substitute council member in 1959 and a council member for figure skating in 1963. Labin was elected an honorary member posthumously in 1969.

LAMBERT, CLAUDE. *See* GUHEL, CHRISTIANE AND JEAN PAUL.

LAMBIEL, STÉPHANE (1985–) (SUI). Stéphane Lambiel won world titles in 2005 and 2006. He is just the third skater from **Switzerland** to win a world title. **Hans Gerschwiler** won in 1947, and **Denise Biellmann** won in 1981. Lambiel won the **Grand Prix Finals** twice, in 2006 and 2008, but did not win either a European or an Olympic title. His best placements were second at the **European Championships** in 2008 and second at the **Olympic Winter Games** in 2006. He retired in October 2008 owing to an injury.

LANDBECK, LISELOTTE (1916–) (AUT). Liselotte Landbeck was one of several talented ladies from **Austria**, primarily members of the **Vienna Skating Club**, who during the 1920s and 1930s dominated ladies' skating. From 1922 through 1934 they stood on the medal stand at the **World Championships** every year except one. The others include **Herma Szabo**, **Gisela Reichmann**, **Fritzi Burger**, **Melitta Brunner**, and **Hilde Holovsky**. Twice the Austrian national ladies' champion, Landbeck's medal count at the European and World Championships includes one bronze and two silver. During her last competitive year, 1936, Landbeck competed for **Belgium**, placing fourth at both the **European Championships** and the **Olympic Games**. She was also a champion speed skater, setting several records.

LANE, JON. *See* SAWBRIDGE, JANET.

LANG, NAOMI (1978–) AND TCHERNYSHEV, PETER (1971–) (USA). Ice dancers Naomi Lang and Peter Tchernyshev won bronze medals at their second national championship in 1998 and followed with five consecutive titles, 1999–2003. Competing at five **Four Continents Championships**, they medaled each time, bronze twice, silver once, and gold in 2000 and 2002. Their best result at the **World Championships** was eighth. In their one Olympic effort, in 2002, they placed 11th. Tchernyshev is Russian; Lang is a Native American, the second of two who have become national champions. The other is Gorsha Sur who with Renée Roca won national **ice dancing** titles in 1993 and 1995. Lang and Tchernyshev toured with **Champions on Ice**.

LANNOY, MICHELINE (1925–) AND BAUGNIET, PIERRE (1925–) (BEL). Little is known about pair skaters Micheline Lannoy and Pierre Baugniet. They did not compete internationally before World War II, but when the European and **World Championships** were revived in 1947, Lannoy and Baugniet appeared at both events and easily won the gold medals. They competed again in 1948 at the World Championships and the Olympic Winter Games but not the **European Championships**, collecting additional gold medals in their second and last year of competition. They retired never having lost an international competition. *See also* BELGIUM.

LAPONTE, JULIE. *See* SALÉ, JAMIE AND PELLETIER, DAVID.

LAUZON, PATRICE. *See* DUBREUIL, MARIE-FRANCE AND LAUZON, PATRICE.

LAWRENCE, JIMMY. *See* ATWOOD, DONNA.

LEBEDEV, ALEXEI (RUS). Alexei Lebedev was a master of **special figures**. He won two of the three gold medals awarded at an international competition held at St. Petersburg in 1890, one for special figures and the other for "specialties." **Louis Rubenstein** of **Canada** won the third gold medal for basic figures. Lebedev is remembered especially for his tracing of a treble clef sign as a special figure. Although he never competed in either the European or **World Championships**, he occasionally served as a judge for men's events at the early competitions.

LEE, ROBIN H. (1919–1997) (USA). Robin Lee is one of two American men who have won five consecutive national titles: **Sherwin Badger**, 1920–1924, and Lee, 1935–1939. Three men have won more than five titles;

most recently, **Todd Eldredge** won six that were not consecutive, spanning the years 1990–2002. **Roger Turner** won seven, all consecutive, 1928–1934, as did **Dick Button**, 1946–1952. Lee's three efforts in international competitions did not result in medals. At the **World Championships**, he placed ninth in 1932 and eighth in 1936. At the **Olympic Winter Games** in 1936, he placed 12th.

LEFSTAD, JOHANN. *See* NORWAY.

LE GOUGNE, MARIE-REINE. *See* CONTROVERSIES; SALÉ, JAMIE AND PELLETIER, DAVID.

LEHNER, LUISE. *See* KUTSCHERA, HANS.

LEISTNER, CLAUDIA (1965–) (FRG). Claudia Leistner did not compete at the **World Junior Championships** but was a contender internationally at the senior level for eight years, 1982–1989, winning the European title in her final year. She had won bronze medals in 1983 and 1985. Her best results at the **World Championships** were silver medals won six years apart, 1983 and 1989. Between the silver medals there were one fourth and three sixth-place finishes. In 1984 she placed ninth at the **Olympic Winter Games**. In 1988, she was sixth. In her early competitions, Leistner suffered from poor **compulsory figures**, but they improved dramatically. At both the European and World Championships in 1989, she placed first in the compulsory figures.

LENNIE, BRUCE. *See* TAYLOR, DONNA AND LENNIE, BRUCE.

LEPISTÖ, LAURA (1988–) (FIN). Laura Lepistö won the Finnish junior ladies' title in 2005 and twice the senior title, in 2008 and 2010. She was second behind Susanna Pöykiö in 2007 and behind Kiira Korpi in 2009. These three skaters—Lepistö, Pöykiö, and Korpi—demonstrate the current quality of skating in Finland. They claimed the three medals at the Finnish national championships in 2010. Lepistö became in 2009 the first singles skater from **Finland** to win a European or world title, claiming the gold medal at the **European Championships**. In three years of international competition as a senior she medaled at **Grand Prix** events and won a medal of each color at the European Championships. In 2010 she placed sixth at the **Olympic Winter Games** and won the bronze medal at the **World Championships**.

LETTENGARVER, JOHN. *See* EUROPEAN FIGURE SKATING CHAMPIONSHIPS.

LI, CHENGJIANG (1979–) (CHN). Chengjiang Li, who won six national titles, had a relatively long international career spanning 13 years, from 1997 through 2009. His best results came early in his career. At the **Four Continents Championships**, he won silver medals in his first two attempts, 1999 and 2000, before winning the title in 2001, a significant win because it was the first international title won by a Chinese man. He entered the competition four additional times and claimed two medals, bronze in 2003 and silver in 2005. Competing at eight **World Championships**, beginning in 2000, his best placement was fourth in 2003. Two Olympic efforts, in 2002 and 2006, resulted in ninth- and 16th-place finishes. Li won the bronze medal at the **Grand Prix Finals** in 2005.

LIASHENKO, ELENA. *See* UKRAINE.

LIFTS. Lifts became an important part of **pair skating** as the discipline became more athletic in the early 1930s, and they are today the most exciting elements in pairs programs. Many variations on basic lifts have been developed as skaters have increased the difficulty level by changing positions of the lady at full extension and by dramatic dismounts. Lifts are of two basic types, overhead lifts in which the man presses the lady into an overhead position, and twist lifts in which the man tosses the lady into the air and catches her on the way down. There are many varieties of overhead lifts. They are best understood by the lift itself, what the lady does at full extension, and the dismount. Lifts can be categorized by the way the partners hold each other at the takeoff. The easiest is the armpit hold in which one hand is under the lady's armpit while the other clutches the lady's hand. The two-hand hold is what the name indicates. In the hand to body hold, the man's hands are placed either on the lady's hips or waist. The partners can be skating the same direction, usually backward, or facing each other prior to the lift. In all overhead lifts, the man must turn at least a half but no more than three revolutions. The lady can assume various positions in the air. When more than one position is employed, it is called a combination lift. In some lifts one hand is released, increasing the difficulty level. There are many varieties of dismounts. The man's strength is often shown by employing just one hand. A twist lift is a hand to waist lift in which the lady is tossed into the air, remains vertical, rotates up to three and one-half times, and is caught by the man on the descent. Women will sometimes go into a split position before rotating, making it a split twist lift. A more difficult variation is a lateral twist lift in which the lady rotates after assuming a position parallel to the ice.

LIGNE-GEURTS, YVONNE DE. *See* BELGIUM.

LINICHUK, NATALIA (1956–) AND KARPONOSOV, GENNADI (1950–) (URS). Natalia Linichuk and Gennadi Karponosov competed in **ice dancing** internationally for eight years beginning in 1974, collecting bronze medals in their first year at both the European and **World Championships**. They continued by medaling every year at the **European Championships**, accumulating five bronze, one silver, and two gold medals. Medaling at five of seven World Championships, their medal count is two bronze, one silver, and gold in 1978 and 1979. Linichuk and Karponosov competed at the **Olympic Winter Games** twice, placing fourth in 1976, the first year ice dancing was contested, and winning the title in 1980. Karponosov, six years older than Linichuk, had competed from 1969 through 1972 with Elena Zharkova. Their best result at the **European Championships** was sixth. At the World Championships, competing for three years, 1970–1972, they consistently placed eighth. Linichuk and Karponosov are currently coaches in the **United States**.

LIPINSKI, TARA (1982–) (USA). In her first year as a senior, 1996, Tara Lipinski placed third at the **United States** Championships, and it was a year in which the United States qualified to send three ladies to the **World Championships**. There, Lipinski had a disappointing first outing, placing 22nd in the short program. Her free skate was much stronger, raising her to 15th overall. The tiny Lipinski was a facile jumper, but in 1997, she also displayed much improved artistry. The results were surprising and remarkable. **Michelle Kwan**, the reigning U.S. and world ladies' champion, defeated Lipinski in the first competition of the season, **Skate America**, but in three following head-to-head battles, the Champions Series Finals, the United States Championships, and the World Championships, Lipinski consistently held Kwan to silver medals. In the 1998 Olympic year, the two Americans met only twice. Kwan regained the U.S. title, but at the Nagano Games, Lipinski skated more aggressively than Kwan and included her triple loop–triple loop combination jump. She became the youngest ever Olympic ladies' champion. Electing not to proceed to the World Championships that year, Lipinski retired from competitive skating and joined **Stars on Ice**, remaining with the company for several seasons before injuries forced her retirement.

LISOVSKY, IGOR. *See* VOROBIEVA, IRINA AND LISOVSKY, IGOR.

LITHUANIA. *See* DROBIAZKO, MARGARITA AND VANAGAS, POVILAS.

LOBACHEVA, IRINA (1973–) AND AVERBUKH, ILIA (1973–) (RUS). Ice dancers Irina Lobacheva and Ilia Averbukh, a husband-and-wife couple, competed at the **World Championships** for 10 consecutive years beginning in 1994, medaling in the last three: bronze in 2001, gold in 2002, and silver in 2003. In the Olympic year 2002, they were the silver medalists at the games behind their longtime rivals, **Marina Anissina and Gwendal Peizerat**, a couple they never defeated. Anissina and Peizerat did not continue to the World Championships after the games, allowing Lobacheva and Averbukh to win the world title. In 2003, they won gold medals at the **Grand Prix Finals** and were the silver medalists at the **European Championships**. Averbukh had previously competed and won the world junior title with Anissina, but that partnership ended when he married Lobacheva and competed with her.

LONDON SKATING CLUB. The London Skating Club is today the oldest skating club in existence. Formed in 1830, it is associated specifically with the development of **English style** skating. In 1929, one year before its centennial celebration, it joined forces with the Wimbledon Skating Club, which dated from 1871. In 1932, by Royal decree from King George V, it became the Royal Skating Club. The club still functions today and is the only club that continues the practice of the **English style**, figure skating's oldest tradition.

LONG PROGRAM. *See* FREE SKATING.

LOOP JUMP. The loop jump has a takeoff from a backward outside edge with a landing on the same foot and the same backward outside edge. The jump is attributed to **Werner Rittberger** of **Germany**, silver medalist at the **World Championships** three times, 1910–1912. In Europe it is sometimes called the Rittberger jump. When the takeoff is assisted by a toe pick it is called a toe loop. A variation of the loop jump is the half loop jump, which is frequently seen in combination with other jumps. It has a takeoff from a backward outside edge, as does a loop jump, but the landing is on a backward inside edge on the opposite foot and same circle. In Europe the half loop jump is sometimes called the Thorén jump, named after world and Olympic bronze medalist **Per Thorén** of **Sweden**. The first triple jump done in competition was a triple loop jump landed by **Dick Button** at the Oslo **Olympic Winter Games** in 1952. *See also* JUMPS.

LORENZ, BIRGIT. *See* SELEZNEVA, LARISA AND MARAKOV, OLEG.

LOUGHRAN, BEATRIX S. (1900–1975) (USA). Beatrix Loughran was the junior ladies' champion at the last holding of the **International Skating Union of America** Championships in 1921. As a senior, she won silver medals behind **Theresa Weld Blanchard** for three years before becoming a three-time U.S. champion, 1925–1927. Traveling abroad in 1924, she won the silver medal at the **Olympic Winter Games** and the bronze medal at the **World Championships**. It was the first world medal won by a North American skater. Four years later at the games in **St. Moritz**, she won an Olympic bronze medal. Loughran also competed in pairs, first with Raymond Harvey. They placed second at the United States Championships in 1927. Beginning in 1928, she skated with **Sherwin Badger**, and they were national champions for three consecutive years, 1930–1932. Their international medals include bronze medals at the World Championships in 1930 and 1932 and silver medals at the Olympic Games in 1932. *See also* UNITED STATES.

LUDINGTON, RONALD EDMUND (1934–) (USA). Ron Ludington competed in pairs with Nancy Irene Rouillard, who later became his wife. They won the U.S. junior title in 1956 and the senior title for four consecutive years, 1957–1960. Competing at the **World Championships** each of those years, they won bronze medals in 1959. They also won medals at the **North American Championships**, bronze in 1957 and silver 1959. At the 1960 **Olympic Winter Games**, they were the bronze medalists. Both skaters became coaches. Ron Ludington has been for many years connected with the skating club at the University of Delaware and in that role has taught many skaters. Most successful of his students were **Caitlin and Peter Carruthers**. Ludington was inducted into the **World Figure Skating Hall of Fame** in 1999.

LUSSI, GUSTAVE (1898–1993) (SUI). Gustave Lussi moved to the **United States** after suffering a skiing accident and taught skating. One of his first and most notable students was **Dick Button**, America's first world and Olympic champion. Lussi was among the first coaches to analyze jumping and spinning from the standpoint of physics, leading to the significantly increased athleticism associated with the "golden age" of American skating, 1948–1960. Button's followers, brothers **Hayes Alan Jenkins** and **David Jenkins** were also Lussi's students early in their careers. Lussi has left his methods in written form, *Championship Figure Skating*. He was a member of the original class of inductees into the **World Figure Skating Hall of Fame**.

LUTZ, ALOIS. *See* LUTZ JUMP.

LUTZ JUMP. The Lutz jump, named after Alois Lutz, an obscure Austrian skater of the 1920s, is the most difficult jump other than the **Axel Paulsen jump**. It is a toe-pick assisted jump approached on a backward outside edge with rotation in the air opposite to that of the approach edge. The landing is on a backward outside edge on the opposite foot. The first triple Lutz was done by **Donald Jackson** of **Canada** at the **World Championships** in 1962. The first lady to land a triple Lutz in competition was **Denise Biellmann** of **Switzerland** at the World Championships in 1978. *See also* JUMPS.

LYNN, JANET (1953–) (USA). Janet Lynn became the U.S. junior champion in 1966 at age 13. Three years later she won the senior title and held it for five consecutive years, 1969–1973, equaling the records of **Tenley Albright** and **Peggy Fleming**. Two prewar skaters, **Maribel Vinson** and **Gretchen Merrill** won six consecutive titles. **Michelle Kwan** now holds the record with eight consecutive titles beginning in 1998. Lynn competed at the **World Championships** for six years beginning in 1968, placing ninth the first year. Medals came from the last two, bronze in 1972 and silver in 1973. She also carried home the bronze medal from the **Olympic Winter Games** in 1972. Lynn's strength was in free skating, her weakness the **compulsory figures**. It was a time when the relative value of compulsory figures, 50 percent, was being questioned by officials, coaches, and skaters, as well as fans, and Lynn became unwittingly a catalyst for change, which included implementation of the short or technical program in 1973. Lynn was expected to win the world ladies' title that year, but owing to an uncharacteristically poor performance in the new short program, including falls on two jumps, she placed second to her longtime rival **Karen Magnussen** of **Canada**. In spite of an inspired free-skating performance in which she placed first and received two 6.0 marks from the judges, she ended her career never having won a world or Olympic title, but Lynn holds an all-time record among singles skaters in world and Olympic competition for the most perfect scores for artistic impression. During her final three competitive years, she received two 6.0s at each of the World Championships and one at the Olympic Winter Games. Upon turning professional, Lynn skated for two years with the **Ice Follies** and then after an absence of five years returned for three more. She was elected into the **World Figure Skating Hall of Fame** in 2001.

LYSACEK, EVAN (1985–) (USA). In 2010 Evan Lysacek became the sixth American man to win an Olympic gold medal, the others being **Dick Button**, **Hayes Jenkins**, **David Jenkins**, **Scott Hamilton**, and **Brian Boitano**. He had placed fourth at the previous games. Lysacek was the national champion twice, 2007 and 2008. He won four medals at the **Four Continents Championships** including gold medals in 2005 and 2007. Lysacek competed at the **World Championships** from 2005 through 2009 and was the bronze medalist twice, 2005 and 2006, before becoming the world champion in 2009. He did not defend his world title after winning his Olympic title in 2010. Lysacek was also the winner at the **Grand Prix Finals** in 2010.

MAGER, MANUELA (1962–) AND BEWERSDORFF, UWE (1958–) (GDR). Pair skaters Manuela Mager and Uwe Bewersdorff appeared internationally the year after their compatriots with the same given names, **Manuela Gross and Uwe Kagelmann** retired from the competitive scene. Mager and Bewersdorff's brief career together, 1977–1980, was made even shorter by an injury that kept them out of international competition in 1979. During their first year, they placed fourth and fifth at the European and **World Championships**. Mager was just age 14. This was followed in 1978 by bronze medals at the **European Championships** and silver medals at the World Championships. For their final season, following the missed year, they did not compete at the European Championships but claimed the bronze medals at the **Olympic Winter Games** and the silver medals at the World Championships.

MAGNUS, LOUIS. *See* FRANCE.

MAGNUSSEN, KAREN (1952–) (CAN). Karen Magnussen won the Canadian junior title in 1965 and the senior title three years later. Suffering from stress fractures in her legs, she placed second at the national championships in 1969 and withdrew from the **World Championships**. She regained her national title in 1970 and held it for four years. At the World Championships, she improved annually moving incrementally from fourth in 1970 to a world title in 1973. At the **Olympic Winter Games**, she won the silver medal in 1972. Magnussen was involved in a rivalry among three skaters with different strengths and styles. **Beatrix Schuba** of **Austria**, the oldest of the group, is remembered as one of the finest exponents of **compulsory figures** but as a relatively weak free skater, and at that time, the compulsory figures counted 50 percent of the total score. **Janet Lynn**, the youngest of the three is remembered as an unusually musical and gifted free skater, but one whose compulsory figures were weak. The free skating counted just 40 percent. Magnussen typically traced better figures than Lynn, and her **free skating** was stronger than that of Schuba. This typically placed Schuba on top followed by Magnussen, then Lynn. After Schuba retired in 1972, the value of the compulsory figures was reduced and a **short program** was implemented. With that change, it was believed that Lynn would win in 1973, but in an uncharacteristically poor performance, she fell twice in the short program. Magnussen became the world champion and then retired. She is now a coach. *See also* CANADA.

MAKAROV, OLEG. *See* SELEZNEVA, LARISA AND MAKAROV, OLEG.

MARIGOLD ICE UNITY. *See* SYNCHRONIZED SKATING.

MALININA, TATIANA (1973–) (UZB). Uzbekistan joined the **International Skating Union** in 1993 and by 1999 had an international medal winner. Tatiana Malinina competed at the **World Championships** annually from 1994 through 2002 with a best finish of fourth in 1999. In addition to her fourth-place finish at the World Championships, she began that season by winning at the **Grand Prix Finals** and then becoming the **Four Continents** champion at the first holding of that competition. At the **Olympic Winter Games** in 1998, she placed eighth.

MANLEY, ELIZABETH (1965–) (CAN). Elizabeth Manley was one of the most vivacious skaters of the 1980s and always a crowd pleaser. The three-time Canadian champion competed at the **World Championships** from 1982 through 1988 except in 1983. Improving steadily throughout her career, she claimed her only medals, silver, at both the World Championships and the **Olympic Winter Games** in 1988. The media driven **Battle of the Carmens** at the games in Calgary between **Katarina Witt** and **Debi Thomas** resulted in gold and bronze medals for the two rivals. Manley slipped in between them and claimed the silver medal. Upon retirement, she skated in shows, including **Champions on Ice**, and competed in various professional and **pro-am competitions**.

MAPES, BRUCE. *See* CHANDLER, EVELYN; FLIP JUMP.

MARGAGLIO, MAURIZIO, *See* FUSAR-POLI, BARBARA AND MARGAGLIO, MAURIZIO.

MARININ, MAXIM. *See* TOTMIANINA, TATIANA AND MARININ, MAXIM.

MARKHAM, JUNE. *See* JONES, COURTNEY.

MARTINI, PAUL. *See* UNDERHILL, BARBARA AND MARTINI, PAUL.

MAŠKOVÁ, HANA (1949–1972) (CZE). Hana Mašková competed internationally for 10 years, 1960–1969, including every European and **World Championship** as well as three **Olympic Winter Games**. She placed well in her first year, 1960, fifth at the **European Championships**, sixth at the World Championships, and fourth at the Squaw Valley Olympics. The next year, 1961, she won the bronze medal at the European Championships, but the World Championships were canceled owing to the **plane crash**. Mašková then regressed for four years, but during her final three years, 1966–1969, she realized the promise shown at the beginning of her career. She collected two silver and in 1968 a gold medal at the European Championships, two bronze medals at the World Championships, and a bronze medal at the 1968 Winter Games in Grenoble. *See also* CZECHOSLOVAKIA.

MAUCH, HANS-RUDI. *See* GROEBLI, WERNER.

MAUROY-JULIN, MAGDA (1894–1990) (SWE). Magda Mauroy-Julin became an Olympic champion in 1920. She is one of only two ladies to hold Olympic titles without holding a world title, the other being **Sarah Hughes**, the Olympic champion 82 years later in 2002. The **World Championships** were not reinstated after World War I until 1922. Mauroy-Julin was then nearly 28 years of age and did not compete. The only other known international competition in which she competed was the World Championships of 1913 at which she placed sixth.

MAYBEE, LAURA. *See* DORE, DAVID M.

McCARTHY, NORAH. *See* McCREATH, RALPH S.

McCARTHY, THERESA. *See* GILCHRIST, DONALD.

McCLADDIE, MICHELLE. *See* FAIRBANKS, MABEL.

McCLENNAN, A. G. *See* NORTH AMERICAN CHAMPIONSHIPS.

McCREATH, RALPH S. (1919–1997) (CAN). Ralph McCreath was the Canadian junior champion in 1936 and the senior champion three times, 1940, 1941, and 1946. He won the title at the **North American Championships** in

1941, culminating 18 years of domination by Canadian men. Melville Rogers had won twice, in 1925 and 1927, followed by Montgomery Wilson who won six times beginning in 1929. McCreath also distinguished himself in **pair skating**, winning national titles for six years with three partners, Veronica Clarke, 1936–1938, Norah McCarthy, 1939–1940, and Eleanor O'Meara in 1941. Clarke and McCreath won the North American title in 1937; O'Meara and McCreath did likewise in 1941. Neither McCreath nor any of his three pair partners competed at the World Championships in singles or pairs. In 1963, as television contracts were being negotiated, the **Canadian Figure Skating Association** retained McCreath, an attorney, as its counsel.

McDONALD, SANDY. *See* HARTSHORNE, HAROLD.

McDOUGALL, MARION AND BANGS, CHAUNCEY (1901–1942) (CAN). Marion MacDougall and Chauncey Bangs were gold medalists at the third holding of the biennial **North American Championships** in 1927. They were also the national pair champions that year and the next. In 1931, Bangs, skating with a new partner, Frances Claudet, won an additional national title. In 1932, Claudet and Bangs competed at the **World Championships**, held in Montreal, and at the **Olympic Winter Games**, held in Lake Placid, New York, placing sixth at both competitions.

McGEAN, MICHAEL. *See* WARING, LOIS.

McKECHNIE, SANDY. *See* GILCHRIST, DONALD.

McLACHLAN, WILLIAM (1938–) (CAN). Ice dancer William McLachlan of Canada, like his contemporary **Courtney Jones** of **Great Britain**, is a tale of two partners. McLachlan with Geraldine Fenton was the national champion for three years, 1957–1959 and the North American champion in 1957 and 1959. With his second partner, Virginia Thompson, he was the national champion for another three years, 1960–1962 and the North American champion in 1961. He competed with both partners at the **World Championships**. Fenton and McLachlan placed second in 1957 and 1958 behind June Markham and Jones, and third in 1959 behind Doreen Denny and Jones and Andree Jacoby-Anderson and Donald Jacoby of the **United States**. Thompson and McLachlan placed second in 1960 behind Denny and Jones, and third in 1962 behind **Eva Romanová and Pavel Roman** of **Czechoslovakia** and **Christiane Guhel and Jean Paul Guhel** of **France**.

McLENNAN, A. GORDON. *See* JENKINS, DOROTHY AND McLENNAN, A. GORDON.

McMULLIN RULE. *See* McMULLIN, STACI.

McMULLIN, STACI (1967–) (USA). Staci McMullin won the silver medal at the United States Junior Championships in 1982. She competed for three additional years at the senior level. It was as a junior, however, that McMullin's name became permanently connected to the sport. At the **World Junior Championships** held in Sarajevo in 1983, she was sent as the alternate. Lorilee Pritchard was injured after the draw that established the skating order, but McMullin could not compete under an existing rule that did not allow substitutions after the draw. The rule was subsequently changed to allow a substitution in the event of injury or illness. The rule has come to be known as the "McMullin Rule." Turning professional, McMullin toured for two years with **Ice Capades** after which she became a figure skating coach.

McPHERSON, DONALD (1945–2001) (CAN). Donald McPherson won the Canadian junior title in 1959. His short career at the international level lasted just four years, 1960–1963. He competed at three **World Championships**, placing eighth in 1960, fourth in 1962, and winning the title in 1963. The championships were not held in 1961 owing to the **plane crash**. His one Olympic bid in 1960 resulted in a 10th-place finish. Following his short competitive career, McPherson joined **Holiday on Ice** and enjoyed a long and distinguished career as a show skater. *See also* CANADA.

MEHL, KATHE. *See* HARTSHORNE, HAROLD.

MEISSNER, KIMBERLY "KIMMIE" (1989–) (USA). Kimmie Meissner was the U.S. novice ladies' champion in 2003 and the junior ladies' champion in 2004. As a senior she progressed through the medals, bronze in 2005, silver in 2006, and gold in 2007. She placed sixth at the **Olympic Winter Games** in 2006 and a month later was the surprise winner at the **World Championships**. In 2007 she won the gold medal in her only appearance at the **Four Continents Championships**. In her final year of competitive skating, 2008, she slipped to seventh at both the U.S. and World Championships.

MEJSTRIK, KARL. *See* ENGELMANN, HELENE.

MENO, JENNI (1970–) AND SAND, TODD (1963–) (USA). Jenni Meno and Todd Sand, one of the most popular American pairs, first competed against each other with former partners, Meno with Scott Wendland and Sand with Natasha Kuchiki. Kuchiki and Sand, the national champions in 1991, won bronze medals at the **World Championships**. Meno and Wendland, the bronze medalists at the national championships that year, placed 10th at the World Championships. In the Olympic year, 1992, Kuchiki and Sand were the bronze medalists at the national championships. They placed eighth at the World Championships and sixth at the Olympics. Meno and Wendland were the silver medalists at the national championships that year. They placed 11th at both the World Championships and the Olympics. Meno and Sand joined forces immediately after the 1992 season ended, and in 1993 they were the silver medalists at the national championships and placed fifth at the World Championships. Continuing through 1998 they won three national titles, 1994–1996, and two world bronze medals, 1995 and 1996. At the Olympics, they placed fifth in 1994 and eighth in 1998. Their persona on the ice was romantic and musical. The couple married in 1995. Meno and Sand were coached by **John Nicks**. Like many skaters, they toured with **Champions on Ice**.

MERRILL, GRETCHEN (1925–1965) (USA). Gretchen Merrrill competed during the war years, which limited her international opportunities. At the national level, she holds an outstanding record of six consecutive ladies' titles at the United States Championships. **Theresa Weld Blanchard** also holds six national titles, but they are not consecutive. Only two ladies hold more titles. **Maribel Vinson** holds nine with six of them consecutive, and **Michelle Kwan** also holds nine with eight of them consecutive. Merrill placed second to **Barbara Ann Scott** at the **North American Championships** in 1945. Competing internationally after the war, she placed second at the **European Championships** and third at the **World Championships** in 1947. Her Olympic effort in 1948 resulted in an eighth-place finish.

MILLNS, JAMES G., JR. *See* O'CONNOR, COLLEEN M. AND MILLNS, JAMES G. JR.

MINENKOV, ANDREI. *See* MOISEEVA, IRINA AND MINENKOV, ANDREI.

MINTO SKATING CLUB. *See* NORTH AMERICAN CHAMPIONSHIPS.

MISHIN, ALEXEI. *See* MOSKVINA, TAMARA AND MISHIN, ALEXEI.

MISHKUTENOK, NATALIA. *See* DMITRIEV, ARTUR.

MOIR, SCOTT. *See* VIRTUE, TESSA AND MOIR, SCOTT.

MOISEEVA, IRINA (1955–) AND MINENKOV, ANDREI (1954–) (URS). From 1965 through 1978, Soviet skaters dominated **pair skating**, winning every world and Olympic title. Beginning in 1970 and continuing through 1979, they did likewise in **ice dancing**. The first and most successful ice dancers were **Liudmila Pakhomova and Alexandr Gorshkov**, six-time world champions and in 1976 the first Olympic champions. Owing to a serious bout with pneumonia suffered by Gorshkov in 1975, the champions were sidelined. Irina Moiseeva and Andrei Minenkov, who had first appeared on the international scene two years earlier, placed fourth at the **European Championships** and in a come-from-behind victory at the **World Championships** won the title ahead of two couples, Hilary Green and Glyn Watts of **Great Britain** and **Natalia Linichuk and Gennadi Karponosov** of the **Soviet Union**, who had defeated them at the European Championships. In 1976, Pakhomova and Gorshkov returned for a final year, holding Moiseeva and Minenkov to silver medals at the European and World Championships and the Olympic Games, but with the former champions retired, Moiseeva and Minenkov won a second world title in 1977. They won no further world titles but won their second European title in 1978. From the World Championships in 1975 through their retirement in 1982, competing at every European, world, and Olympic competition, Moiseeva and Minenkov never failed to medal, accumulating six bronze, seven silver, and four gold medals. Upon turning professional, they skated in various shows including **Champions on Ice**.

MOROZOV, NIKOLAI. *See* NAVKA, TATIANA AND KOSTOMAROV, ROMAN.

MORPHY, CECIL R. *See* NORTH AMERICAN CHAMPIONSHIPS.

MORRIS, KELLY. *See* BLUMBERG, JUDY AND SEIBERT, MICHAEL.

MORROW, SUZANNE (1930–2006) AND DIESTELMEYER, WALLACE (1926–1999) (CAN). Pair skaters Suzanne Morrow and Wallace Diestelmeyer, the first Canadian pair to medal at the **World Championships**, had a relatively short career. They were national champions twice, in 1947 and 1948, and North American champions once, in 1947. Their world and Olympic efforts in 1948 resulted in bronze medals. Both skaters had competed nationally with other partners before or during the war, Morrow with **Norris Bowden** and Diestelmeyer with two partners, his sister Floriane and Joyce Perkins. Morrow followed her **pair skating** career with a second career in singles, becoming a national champion three times, 1949–1951. Competing at the World Championships for four years beginning in 1950, she placed fourth three times and fifth once. Morrow remained active in the sport for many years. She was a World Championship judge and held leadership roles in the **Canadian Figure Skating Association**. Diestelmeyer became a successful coach.

MOSKVIN, IGOR. *See* MOSKVINA, TAMARA AND MISHIN, ALEXEI.

MOSKVINA, TAMARA (1941–) AND MISHIN, ALEXEI (1941–) (URS). Soviet domination of **pair skating** began with the **Protopopovs** who won gold medals at the Olympic Winter Games in 1964 and 1968, and continued with **Irina Rodnina** and her two partners through the Lake Placid Games in 1980, winning three Olympic titles and 10 world titles. Throughout that period, several other Russian pairs competed successfully, often winning bronze or silver medals. Among them were Tamara Moskvina and Alexei Mishin, whose time on the international scene was short but notable. Competing at the European and **World Championships** for three years, they accumulated bronze medals once and silver medals twice. Upon retirement they completed studies in pedagogical sciences and became coaches for many of the next generation of Soviet skaters. Moskvina coauthored with Igor Moskin an **International Skating Union** publication, *Pair Skating as Sport and Art*. Moskvina was elected to the **World Figure Skating Hall of Fame** in 2004.

MOUNTAIN CUP INTERNATIONAL COMPETITION. *See* ADULT SKATING.

MULIER, WILLEM J. H. *See* INTERNATIONAL SKATING UNION.

MÜLLER, INES. *See* WÖTZEL, MANDY AND STEUER, INGO.

MÜLLER, JUTTA (1928–) (GDR). Jutta Müller competed at the national level immediately after World War II with her best result being the bronze medalist in 1953. She was a champion in 1949 in the unusual women's pair event, held specifically to accommodate women who wanted to do pairs at a time when few men were available. Müller's importance in skating is as one of the sport's most successful coaches, guiding skaters from the German Democratic Republic into the top ranks of competitive skating. Her first success was her daughter **Gabriele Seyfert**, a world champion in 1969 and 1970. Other world champions she coached include **Jan Hoffmann** in 1974 and 1980, **Anett Pötzsch** in 1978 and 1980, and **Katarina Witt** in 1984 and

1985 and again in 1987 and 1988. Pötzsch and Witt became Olympic champions as well, Pötzsch in 1980 and Witt in 1984 and 1988. Witt was just the second lady to win multiple Olympic titles. Other elite skaters who Müller coached include Günter Zöller, Sonja Morgenstern, and **Evelyn Grossmann**. In recognition of her success, Müller was inducted into the **World Figure Skating Hall of Fame** in 2003.

MURDOCH, RODNEY M. *See* PHILLIPS, MOLLIE.

MYUNG SU CHANG. *See* KOREA.

NAGY, LÁSZLÓ. *See* NAGY, MARIANNA AND LÁSZLÓ.

NAGY, MARIANNA (1929–) AND LÁSZLÓ (1927–2005) (HUN). Pair skaters Marianna and László Nagy competed in the years just after World War II, first appearing at the **European Championships** in 1948 and placing sixth. They placed seventh at the **World Championships** and the **Olympic Winter Games**. During the next 10 years, they claimed medals in all but three competitions entered. At the European Championships they collected one bronze and four silver medals in addition to winning the titles in 1950 and 1955. They won bronze medals at three World Championships and at the Olympics in 1952 and 1956.

NAM, NAOMI NARI. *See* NICKS, JOHN ALLEN WISDEN.

NATIONAL ICE SKATING ASSOCIATION OF THE UNITED KINGDOM. Organized to regulate speed skating, the National Skating Association (NSA) was founded in 1879, but within a year, figure skating was added. It is the oldest existing national regulatory body for figure skating. Almost immediately, a progressive test structure was implemented with proficiency levels through gold medals, all in the **English style**. During the 1890s, when the **international style** invaded the British Isles, separate test structures were added. Still today, test structures are in place for both styles of skating. The NSA supported the establishment of the **International Skating Union** in 1892, and **Great Britain** is one of the original six members. The NSA also regulated roller skating for many years. In 1990, the name was changed to the National Ice Skating Association of Great Britain, and soon thereafter it went through a second name change to the National Ice Skating Association of the United Kingdom (NISA).

NATIONAL SKATING ASSOCIATION. *See* NATIONAL ICE SKATING ASSOCIATION OF THE UNITED KINGDOM.

NAUMOV, VADIM. *See* SHISHKOVA, EVGENIA AND NAUMOV, VADIM.

NAVKA, TATIANA (1975–) AND KOSTOMAROV, ROMAN (1977–) (RUS). Ice dancers Tatiana Navka and Roman Kostomarov won the **Grand Prix Finals** three times, the **European Championships** three times, the **World Championships** in 2004 and 2005, and the **Olympic Winter Games** in 2006. Navka had competed internationally with Nikolai Morozov for two years, 1997–1998, representing **Bulgaria**. In 1999, she competed for one year with Kostomarov representing **Russia** but did not compete in 2000. Kostomarov competed with a new partner, Anna Semenovich, before returning to Navka in 2001. Navka and Kostomarov placed ninth and 12th that year in the European and World Championships. Through 2003, their best placement was third at the European Championships. In a remarkable leap forward they received only gold medals during their final three years, 2004–2006. They capped their competitive careers winning Olympic gold medals in Torino.

NEPELA, ONDREJ (1951–1989) (CZE). Ondrej Nepela was the second of two talented men who competed for **Czechoslovakia** in the 1960s and early 1970s. The first was **Karol Divin** who won many medals but never a world or Olympic title. His successor, Nepela, competed internationally for 10 years, 1964–1973, and became the first and only Czech skater to win those titles. From 17th place at his first world competition, Nepela demonstrated five years of improvement before winning silver medals in 1969 and 1970 and gold medals from 1971 through 1973. At the **European Championships**, he medaled for eight years, 1966–1973, winning three bronze followed by five gold medals. Nepela won the Olympic gold medal in 1972. Upon retirement, he skated in shows in Europe and North America.

NETHERLANDS. A national skating federation was founded in the Netherlands in 1882. Ten years later, it took the initiative of calling a meeting held in Scheveningen to establish the **International Skating Union** (ISU). Five countries sent representatives and became charter members. Three others sent letters of support. **Willem J. H. Mulier** of the Netherlands became the first president of the ISU and served until 1895. A significant number of Netherlanders have since served the ISU in various roles, including **Gerrit W. A. van Laer**, president 1937–1945, and his son Hermann van Laer, a council member for speed skating. Gustavus F. C. Witt was vice president for figure skating, 1949–1953, and was elected as an honorary member in 1953. Hendrik Roos was the vice president for speed skating, 1971–1977, and was elected as an honorary vice president in 1977. Speed skating has been the area of greatest success for Netherlander skaters. In the area of figure skating there has been a small number of champions. Most important is **Sjoukje Dijkstra**, a three-time ladies' world champion, 1962–1964, and the Olympic champion in 1964. Their only other world champion is **Dianne de Leeuw** who won her gold medal in 1975.

NEUMANN, CURT. *See* OELSCHLAGEL, CHARLOTTE.

NEXXICE. *See* SYNCHRONIZED SKATING.

NHK TROPHY. *See* GRAND PRIX SERIES.

NICAISE, MARCEL. *See* BELGIUM; HICKOK, WILLIAM O.

NICHOLSON, HOWARD (1896–1978) (USA). Howard Nicholson began his professional career as a show skater in the **United States**. Moving to Europe after World War I, he continued exhibiting and competing. In 1932, he became the first **Open Professional Champion** of **Great Britain** and repeated the following year. He also developed a reputation as an outstanding teacher and coach in England and **Switzerland**. He began teaching the 11-year-old **Sonja Henie** in 1924 and guided her through her competitive career. Returning to the United States shortly before World War II, he continued his teaching career. Among his many students were **Carlo Fassi** of **Italy** and **Toller Cranston** of **Canada**. Nicholson was a member of the first class elected to the **World Figure Skating Hall of Fame** in 1976.

NICKS, JENNIFER MARY. *See* NICKS, JOHN ALLEN WISDEN.

NICKS, JOHN ALLEN WISDEN (1929–) (GBR). John Nicks was the British junior champion in 1947 and that same year the senior pair champion with his sister Jennifer Mary (1932–1980). They proceeded to the **European Championships** and placed sixth. The Nicks accumulated six national titles. Internationally from 1950 through retirement in 1953, they won four bronze and two silver medals before becoming European and world champions in 1953. Their best placement at the Olympic Games was fourth in 1952. The siblings skated in a few shows in London, South Africa, and elsewhere. Jennifer became the British **Open Professional Champion** twice, 1955 and 1956. They both moved to Canada in 1960 and became coaches. John later moved to California where he became over many years an outstanding and highly respected coach. Most successful of the pairs he has coached are **Tai Babilonia and Randy Gardner**, the 1979 world champions, **Alicia Jo Starbuck and Kenneth Shelley**, the world bronze medalists in 1971 and 1972, and **Jenni Meno and Todd Sand**, the 1998 world silver medalists. Among singles skaters who have benefitted from his tutelage, are **Tiffany Chin**, **Sasha Cohen**, and Naomi Nari Nam (1985–). Nicks was inducted into the **World Figure Skating Hall of Fame** in 2000. *See also* GREAT BRITAIN.

NIKKANEN, MARKUS. *See* FINLAND.

NIKODINOV, ANGELA (1980–) (USA). Angela Nikodinov, over a period of seven years, 1996–2002, carried home bronze medals twice from the United States Championships. Competing at the **World Championships** for three years beginning in 1999, her best placement was fifth in 2001. Nikodinov won the gold medal at the **Four Continents Championships** in 2000.

NIKOLOV, CHRISTO. *See* DENKOVA, ALBENA AND STAVISKI, MAXIM.

NILES, NATHANIEL WILLIAM. *See* BLANCHARD, THERESA WELD.

NINGEL, FRANZ. *See* KILIUS, MARIKA.

NOEL, JOHN. *See* BIRD, DENNIS.

NORDIC GAMES. The Nordic Games held in Stockholm, **Sweden**, had for 25 years a close relationship with the **World Championships** in figure skating. Owing to the death of Queen Victoria in 1901, the championships, scheduled for London that year, were moved to Stockholm and held in connection with the Nordic Games. **Viktor Balck** of Sweden, president of the **International Skating Union** from 1895 to 1925, has been called the "Father of the Nordic Games." During his tenure as president, several World Championships were held contemporaneously with the Nordic Games, the last being the ladies' championship in 1926.

NORÉN, SVEA (1895–1985) (SWE). Svea Norén was the Swedish national champion in odd-numbered years from 1913 through 1919. At her first **World Championships** in 1913 she carried home the bronze medal. The World Championships were not held from 1914 through 1921 because of the war, but when they were reinstated in 1922, Norén reappeared, the only prewar skater to do so, and won the silver medal. It was her final year of competitive skating, She also won the silver medal at the 1920 **Olympic Winter Games**.

NORTH AMERICAN CHAMPIONSHIPS. Through cooperation between the Amateur Figure Skating Association of Canada and the **United States Figure Skating Association**, a biennial competition was established between the two countries with sites for the events alternating between the two countries.

The first North American Championships were held in Ottawa, Ontario, in 1923. Events were held for men, ladies, pairs, and **fours**. The first singles champions were **Sherwin Badger** and **Theresa Weld Blanchard** both from the **United States**. **Dorothy Jenkins and Gordon McLennan** from **Canada** won the pairs event. Elizabeth Blair, Florence Wilson, Philip Chrysler, and Cecil Morphy from the Minto Skating Club in Ottawa won the fours event. The North American Championships were continuous through 1971 except in 1943 when they were not held due to the war. Just a ladies' event was held in 1945. At a planning meeting in 1972 for what would have been the 50th anniversary of the championships, delegates from Canada announced their immediate withdrawal from the championships, presumably owing to their planned implementation of **Skate Canada** in 1973. The **Four Continents Championships** might be viewed as a replacement for the North American Championships, but they were not established until 1999, more than a quarter of a century later.

NORWAY. The **International Skating Union** (ISU) was formed in 1892 with six members: **Netherlands**, **Great Britain**, **Germany**, **Austria**, **Sweden**, and **Hungary**. The first noncharter member was Norway, which joined later that first year. Johann Lefstad of Norway entered the **European Championship** in January 1897. As with other men and pairs, he competed prior to World War I, and all won medals. In addition to Lefstad's two medals, bronze at the World Championship in 1897 and silver at the European Championship in 1898, Oscar Holthe won bronze medals at the European Championships in 1898 and 1900. Martin Stixrud won the bronze medal at the European Championship in 1912 as did Alexander Kroh in 1914. The pair of Alexia and Yngvar Bryn won bronze medals at the World Championships in 1912. Norwegian skaters did not compete at the London **Olympic Games**. No ladies competed before the war, but between the world wars, beginning in 1927, ladies' figure skating was dominated by the unbeatable **Sonja Henie** from Oslo. She won 10 world titles, 1927–1936 and three Olympic gold medals during that period. Since Henie's last year of competition in 1936, no Norwegian figure skater in any discipline has won a medal at the European or World Championships. Norway has hosted six European and World Championships, always at Oslo, the last in 1956. The Olympic Winter Games have twice been held in Norway: Oslo in 1952 and Lillehammer in 1994. The ISU's ninth president, **Olaf Poulsen**, had presided over the Norwegian Federation for four years, 1969–1973 before holding positions in the ISU and serving as its president from 1980 through 1994.

NOVITSKI, SERGEI. *See* KHOKHLOVA, JANA AND NOVITSKI, SERGEI.

NOVOTNÝ, RENÉ. *See* KOVAŘÍKOVÁ, RADKA AND NOVOTNÝ, RENÉ.

O'CONNOR, COLLEEN M. (1951–) AND MILLNS, JAMES G., JR. "JIM" (1949–) (USA). Ice dancers Colleen O'Connor and Jim Millns placed third at the United States Championships in 1973 before winning the title from 1974 through 1976 and being sent to the **World Championships** each year. They placed seventh in 1974, but in 1975, with the reigning champions **Liudmila Pakhomova and Alexander Gorshkov** not competing because of illness, O'Connor and Millns claimed the silver medals behind **Irina Moiseeva and Andrei Minenkov**, passing two couples who had defeated them the year before. In 1976, O'Connor and Millns won the bronze medals when Pakhomova and Gorshkov returned and reclaimed the title. Moiseeva and Minenkov won the silver medals. At the **Olympic Winter Games** that year, the first to include ice dancing, the order of medalists was the same as at the World Championships.

ODA, NOBUNARI (1987–) (JPN). Nobunari Oda, the Japanese junior champion in 2005, proceeded to win the world junior title that year. He won the national senior title in 2009. In his first of two trips to the **Four Continents Championships**, in 2006 he won the gold medal. Three years later in 2009, he placed fourth. Oda has competed at three **World Championships** where his best placement was fourth in 2006. He placed seventh in 2007 and 2009. At the 2010 **Olympic Winter Games**, he placed seventh. In **Grand Prix** events, Oda has won gold medals twice, **Skate America** in 2007 and the NHK Trophy in 2009. He was the silver medalist at the **Grand Prix Finals** in 2010.

OELSCHLAGEL, CHARLOTTE (1898–1984). Charlotte Oelschlagel was skating's first theatrical star. She participated in an ice show at age 10 and just two years later began appearing in "ice ballets" produced at the Admirals Platz in Berlin, **Germany**. The popular productions were described as a kind of pantomime and musical comedy on ice. Soon after the outbreak of war in 1914 and armed with an attractive offer from American entrepreneur Charles Dillingham, Oelschlagel and 20 members of the company traveled to America for the reopening of New York's Hippodrome. Their ice ballet, which served as the climatic closing act to a musical review entitled *Hip-Hip-Hurray!* enthralled audiences for a run of 425 performances in 300 days, a record at that time. Oelschlagel's hard-to-pronounce surname was dropped. New York's newfound theatrical star was billed simply as "Charlotte." Charlotte was the first woman to include an **Axel Paulsen jump** in her programs, but a move she invented is most associated with her today. A spectacular spiral in which the body is brought forward until the head is near the ice with the free leg extended very high is called the "Charlotte stop." After its New York run, the ice ballet was taken to other U.S. cities. Charlotte then returned to Berlin but was soon back in New York for another Dillingham production. *Get Together*, which was almost as successful as *Hip-Hip-Hurray!*, had a run of nearly 400 performances. During the 1920s and 1930s, Charlotte appeared throughout Europe and North America. In 1925, she married her skating partner, Curt Neumann. They are credited with inventing the backward outside **death spiral**. Charlotte was the first skater to appear in cinema. *The Frozen Warning* was a six-part serial filmed in 1916. In 1939, the couple returned to Berlin for the funeral of her mother and were trapped, unable to leave for the duration of World War II. After the war, Charlotte lived in West Berlin where she taught skating for many years. She was elected to the **World Figure Skating Hall of Fame** in 1985.

OKAWA, KUMIKO. *See* SATO, NOBUO.

OLYMPIC WINTER GAMES. The modern Olympic Games were first held in Athens in 1896. The games of the IVth Olympiad were held in London, England, in 1908. Through the efforts and influence of the local figure skating community and the availability of indoor **artificial ice**, figure skating became the first winter Olympic sport. Events were held for men, ladies, pairs, and **special figures**. The games of the next Olympiad were held in Stockholm, **Sweden**, in 1912, but skating events were not included, possibly due to a lack of artificial ice. The games of 1916 were canceled because of the war. The games of 1920 were held in Antwerp, **Belgium**. Figure skating events were again held, and ice hockey was added. The games of 1924 were held in Paris, **France**, with winter events held at Chamonix earlier that year. In addition to figure skating and ice hockey, events were held in speed skating, skiing, and bobsledding. Two years later, the International Olympic Committee (IOC) voted to call the Chamonix events the first **Olympic Winter Games**. Separate winter games have since been held every four years except for 1940 and 1944 when they were canceled during World War II. Summer and winter games were held in the same years through 1992 when the IOC moved the winter games ahead two years to be held between the summer games, resulting in the next winter games being held in 1994. Special figures were contested only at the London Games in 1908. To the three remaining events, men, ladies, and pairs, **ice dancing** was added in 1976. There has been discussion about making **synchronized team skating** an Olympic sport. *See* Appendix H for a list of Olympic medalists in figure skating.

O'MEARA, ELEANOR. *See* GILCHRIST, DONALD; McCREATH, RALPH.

OPEN PROFESSIONAL CHAMPIONSHIPS. The prototype of professional figure skating competitions, which were to become commonplace in the 1980s, was the Open Professional Championships of **Great Britain** held under the auspices of the **National Skating Association** (NSA) beginning in 1932. Except for the war years, 1939–1945, they were continuous until 1957 at which time sponsorship moved to the International Professional Skaters Association (IPSA) for 14 years, through 1970. They continued for another three years but without sponsorship. In 1974, the championships were moved to Jaca, Spain, where under local sponsorship they survived for another 17 years. During the early years, while under NSA sponsorship, competitors were primarily British skaters. Just seven of 53 titles awarded went to non-British skaters. Only one former world champion won the title, largely the result of many skaters turning professional during the 1930s because of the difficult and worldwide economic conditions. **Cecilia Colledge** won twice in 1947 and 1948. Wider participation occurred under the management of the IPSA in the postwar era. Former world champions who won titles include **Donald McPherson** of **Canada**, **Emmerich Danzer** of **Austria**, **Donald Jackson** of Canada, and ice dancers **Eva Romanová and Pavel Roman** of **Czechoslovakia**. The Open Professional Championships remained the only major professional competition until **Dick Button** established the **World Professional Figure Skating Championships** in 1973.

OPPELT, KURT. *See* SCHWARZ, ELISABETH AND OPPELT, KURT.

ORGONISTA, OLGA (1901–1978) AND SZALAY, SÁNDOR (1893–1965) (HUN). Olga Orgonista and Sándor Szalay were the first champions when **pair skating** was added to the **European Championships** in 1930. They won again in 1931. Three efforts at the **World Championships** resulted in two medals, bronze in 1929 and silver in 1931. At the **Olympic Winter Games** in 1932, their final year of competition, they placed fourth.

ORIGINAL DANCE. When **ice dancing** became a world discipline in 1952, the two-part competition included four **compulsory dances** counting 60 percent and a free dance counting 40 percent. In 1967, an "original set pattern dance" done to a rhythm and tempo selected by the skaters replaced one of the compulsory dances and assumed its value of 15 percent. The remaining three compulsory dances counted 45 percent. Its value was soon changed to 20 percent, with the compulsory dances being reduced to 30 percent and the free dance increased to 50 percent, a ratio that remained in effect until 1988 when the number of compulsory dances was reduced to two with a reduction in value to 20 percent. The value of the original set pattern dance was increased to 30 percent. An additional change followed, reducing the number of compulsory dances skated to one. In 1991, the term original set pattern dance was changed to "original dance." With the change in value of the original set pattern dance, the **International Skating Union** (ISU) began specifying the rhythms and tempos for the dance which changed annually. Ice dancers chose their own music, and vocal music was allowed. At the ISU Congress in 2010, two changes made ice dancing again a two-part competition. The compulsory dances were eliminated, and a new "short dance" replaced the original dance.

ORMSBY, KENNETH. *See* DOANE, PAULETTE AND ORMSBY, KENNETH.

ORSER, BRIAN (1961–) (CAN). Brian Orser became the Canadian novice champion at age 15, junior champion at age 17, and senior champion at age 19. He held the senior title for eight years, 1981–1989, and represented **Canada** at the **World Championships** each of those years. Owing to weakness in the **compulsory figures** and often competing against skaters much stronger in that part of the competitions, especially **Scott Hamilton** and **Alexandr Fadeev**, Orser, who was a strong free skater, accumulated only one gold medal but multiple silver medals. His medal count at the World Championships is one bronze, four silver, and one gold won in 1987. His two Olympic efforts also resulted in silver medals. The head-to-head battle with **Brian Boitano** at the Calgary Games in 1988, known as the **Battle of the Brians**, provided one of the most exciting skating competitions in history. Orser, who was always a crowd pleaser, has had an excellent professional career as a skater and recently as a coach. **Yu Na Kim**, the 2010 Olympic champion, is his student. He was elected to the **World Figure Skating Hall of Fame** in 2009.

OSBORN, VALDA ROSEMARY (1934–) (GBR). Valda Osborn, a student of **Arnold Gerschwiler**, first competed internationally in 1949, placing ninth at the European and 12th at the **World Championships**. She competed for the next three years without medaling, but during her final competitive year, 1953, she won the European title and the bronze medal at the World Championships. She then turned professional, skating in shows in England and teaching skating for a few years. Her only Olympic effort in 1952 resulted in an 11th-place finish.

ÖSTERREICH, ROLF. *See* KERMER, ROMY AND ÖSTERREICH, ROLF.

OTA, YUKINA (1986–) (JPN). Yukina Ota bounded onto the competitive scene in 2002, placing third at the Japanese national championships, sixth at the Junior Grand Prix Finals, and ninth at the Junior World Championships. The next year, 2003, she again placed third at the national junior championships but won the ladies' title at World Junior Championships. In her first year as a senior, 2004, she placed fifth at the national championships and won the title in her only appearance at the **Four Continents Championships**. Ota did not compete for the next two years owing to aggravated skeletal problems. She tried **ice dancing** for a year but returned to singles, reappearing at the Japanese championships in 2007 and 2008, placing 12th and seventh respectively, after which she retired from competitive skating.

OVSIANNIKOV, OLEG. *See* KRYLOVA, ANJELIKA AND OVSIANNIKOV, OLEG.

OWEN, GUY. *See* FOURS; ROGERS, MELVILLE; VINSON, MARIBEL YERBA.

OWEN, LAURENCE ROCHON (1944–1961) (USA). Laurence Owen, the daughter of **Maribel Vinson** of the **United States** and Guy Owen of **Canada**, was coached by her mother. She won the U.S. junior ladies' title in 1959. As a senior, she claimed the bronze medal in 1960 and was one of three ladies sent to the **Olympic Winter Games** where she placed sixth and to the **World Championships** where she placed ninth. Owen was expected to continue the winning tradition established by **Tenley Albright** and **Carol Heiss**. The new year, 1961, confirmed her readiness as she won both the national title and the North American title. But tragedy followed on February 15. En route to the World Championships scheduled for Prague, **Czechoslovakia**, Laurence, her mother, her older sister Maribel Jr. (1940–1961) and pair partner Dudley Richards (1932–1961), and the entire U.S. world team were lost in the crash of Sabena Airlines flight 548 while attempting a landing at Brussels, Belgium. The World Championships of 1961 were canceled in respect to the U.S. team.

OWEN, MARIBEL VINSON. *See* VINSON, MARIBEL YERBA.

OWEN, MARIBEL Y. *See* VINSON, MARIBEL YERBA.

P

PAIR SKATING. The early history of pair skating is the least understood of figure skating's disciplines. It was first contested at both the **World Championships** and the **Olympic Games** in 1908, but few mentions of it exist prior to that time, and it was rarely a competitive activity. Descriptions of skating by the earliest pairs show significant differences in their styles. Prior to World War I, **spirals** were the most important elements. Beginning in the late 1920s, the discipline became more athletic with **lifts** and **death spirals** being included in programs of the best pairs. Pair skaters were not required to do **compulsory figures**, and competitions were judged solely on a single free-skating program. A short program of eight required elements was added in 1964. They include a side-by-side jump, a throw jump, a side-by-side spin, a pair spin, an overhead lift, a twist lift, a death spiral, and a footwork sequence.

The first **International Skating Union** (ISU) pair skating champions were Anna Hübler and **Heinrich Burger** of **Germany**. They competed just three times internationally, claiming gold medals at the World Championships in 1908 and 1909 and gold medals at the 1908 Olympic Games. **Phyllis and James Johnson** of **Great Britain**, who always placed behind Hübler and Burger but won world titles in 1909 and 1912, wrote an important article on pair skating which is included in **Irving Brokaw**'s *The Art of Skating* published in 1910. Significantly increased athleticism came with the **Brunets** of **France** beginning in the late 1920s and with **Ernst Baier and Maxi Herber** of Germany in the late 1930s. The **Protopopovs** of the **Soviet Union**, world and Olympic pair champions in the mid-1960s, adopted a more balletic style, reflecting the Russian tradition in ballet. Soviet and Russian pairs dominated for the next 35 years, winning all but six world titles through the end of the century and every Olympic gold medal through 2006. Most successful of the Soviet pair skaters was **Irina Rodnina** who, with two partners, Alexei Ulanov and Alexandr Zaitsev, won 10 world titles and three Olympic gold medals, a record equaled only by singles skater **Sonja Henie** in the 1930s. Since 2006, Aliona Savchenko and Robin Szolkowy of Germany and two Chinese couples, Qing Pang and Jian Tong, and Xue Shen and Hongbo Zhao, have won world titles. Shen and Zhao won the 2010 Olympic title as well.

PAKHOMOVA, LIUDMILA (1946–1986) AND GORSHKOV, ALEXANDR (1946–) (URS). Liudmilla Pakhomova and Alexandr Gorshkov of the **Soviet Union** became in 1976 the first Olympic champions in **ice dancing**. During nine years of international competition, missing only one World Championship owing to illness, they won six European titles, 1970–1971 and 1973–1976, and six world titles, 1970–1974 and 1976, a record not yet duplicated in ice dancing. They received 29 perfect 6.0s from the judges, the second highest number in the record books. The tango romantica, their **original dance** introduced in 1974, was adopted as a **compulsory dance** just a year later. Upon retirement from competitive skating, Pakhomova became head of the Department of Sports Choreographers at the Theater Arts Institute in Moscow. Gorshkov became a championship judge and referee and served the International Skating Union as a member and later chair of the ice dancing technical committee. Pakhomova and Gorshkov were honored with election to the **World Figure Skating Hall of Fame** in 1988.

PANG, QING (1979–) AND TONG, JIAN (1979–) (CHN). Qing Pang and Jian Tong are the second of three Chinese pairs who became dominant competitors in the early 21st century. **Xue Shen and Hongbo Zhao** had first entered the **World Championships** in 1994. They competed through the 2010 **Olympic Winter Games**, which they won, and they won three world titles as well. Pang and Tong first appeared in 1999, and they won their first world title in 2006. **Dan Zhang and Hao Zhang** appeared in 2005, adding depth to Chinese **pair skating**, and by 2010, they had placed second at the World Championships three times. With two entries in the World Championships each year for 12 years, these three pairs won collectively 15 of 24 medals awarded from 1999 when Shen and Zhao won their first silver medals through the 2010 skating season when Pang and Tong won the gold medals, a combined total of three bronze, seven silver, and five gold medals. Pang and Tong's record includes three national titles, **Four Continents** titles in 2006, 2008, and 2009, the **Grand Prix Finals** title in 2009, and world titles in 2006 and 2010. In their Olympic efforts, they placed fourth in 2006 and second behind Shen and Zhao in 2010. *See also* CHINA.

PANIN, NIKOLAI (1871–1956) (RUS). Nikolai Kolomenkin owing to his status in Russian society competed as a figure skater under the name Nikolai Panin. He is best known as a master of **special figures**, but he also competed successfully in singles events. Special figures were contested at the 1908 **Olympic Games** in London where figure skating became the first winter Olympic sport. Panin won by a wide margin being placed first by all five judges. As a singles skater, he competed twice at the **European Championships** and once at the **World Championships**, claiming one bronze and two silver medals. Later activities in figure skating included coaching Soviet skaters, including **Oleg Protopopov**. Panin was elected to the **World Figure Skating Hall of Fame** in 2009. *See also* RUSSIA.

PAPEZ, IDI AND ZWACK, KARL (AUT). Pair skaters Idi Papez and Karl Zwack, the Austrian national champions for three years, 1933–1935, first competed internationally at the **European Championships** in 1930 and placed fifth. During the remaining five years of their eligible career, they collected international medals every year. At the European Championships they won one bronze and two silver medals in addition to winning the title in 1933. At the **World Championships**, they won one bronze and two silver medals. Papez and Zwack never competed in the **Olympic Winter Games**. Upon retirement from competitive skating, they skated in various shows.

PAUL, ROBERT. *See* WAGNER, BARBARA AND PAUL, ROBERT.

PAULSEN, AXEL (1855–1938). Axel Paulsen of **Norway** was a speed skater as well as a figure skater. He and another speed skater, Carl Werner, are credited with designing a radically new and lighter skate. In figure skating, Paulsen placed third behind **Leopold Frey** and **Eduard Engelmann Jr.** at the **Great International Skating Tournament** held in 1882 and sponsored by the **Vienna Skating Club**. For his **special figure**, he did the jump that has immortalized his name. Paulsen toured widely in Europe and made trips to **Canada** and the **United States**. He was honored in 1976 as one of the original inductees into the **World Figure Skating Hall of Fame**.

PAUSIN, ILSE (1919–1999) AND ERICH (1920–1997) (AUT). A talented sister-and-brother pair, Ilse and Erich Pausin placed second at the Austrian national championships in 1935 and proceeded to the **European Championships** where they placed fourth. She was 14; he was 13. A month later, they placed second at the **World Championships**, defeating skaters who had defeated them a month earlier. Competing for another four years, until international competitions were canceled for World War II and missing only one, the Pausins consistently won silver medals, always placing second to the older and unbeatable **Ernst Baier and Maxi Herber** of Germany. The Pausins were national champions for six years, 1936–1941.

PAUSIN, ERICH. *See* PAUSIN, ILSE AND ERICH.

PAWLIK, EVA (1927–1983) (AUT). Eva Pawlik was the Austrian national ladies' champion for four consecutive years, 1946–1949. Her international career spanned just two years. In 1948, she placed second at the European and **World Championships** and at the **Olympic Winter Games**, always behind **Barbara Ann Scott** of **Canada**. In 1949 she competed only at the **European Championships** and won the ladies' title. Pawlik then turned professional to join the Vienna Ice Review. She later served as a television commentator.

PEIKERT, EDITH. *See* KUTSCHERA, HANS.

PEIZERAT, GWENDAL. *See* ANISSINA, MARINA.

PELLETIER, DAVID. *See* SALÉ, JAMIE AND PELLETIER, DAVID.

PERKINS JOYCE. *See* MORROW, SUZANNE AND DIESTELMEYER, WALLACE.

PETERS, CAROL ANN (1932–) AND RYAN, DANIEL (1930–1961) (USA). Carol Peters and Daniel Ryan won the U.S. junior **ice dancing** title in 1950. A year later, as seniors, they won bronze medals at the national championships and placed fourth at the second of two **International Skating Union** (ISU) competitions held as preludes to the inauguration of ice dancing as a world championship discipline. Competing for two more years, 1952 and 1953, Peters and Ryan won silver and then gold medals at the United States Championships and bronze medals both years at the **World Championships**. They twice competed at the biennial **North American Championships**, claiming the silver medals in 1951 and winning the title in 1953.

PETKEVICH, JOHN MISHA (1949–) (USA). John Misha Petkevich was the U.S. junior champion in 1966. At the senior level, he won the national title once in 1971, and that same year he became the North American champion at the last holding of that competition. He represented America for four years at the **World Championships**, 1969–1972, placing fifth three times before a career best of fourth in 1972. His two Olympic efforts resulted in sixth- and fifth-place finishes. Invariably, Petkevich's **free skating** was stronger than his **compulsory figures**. In 1989, he wrote the book *Figure Skating Championship Techniques* for Sports Illustrated which has gone through several reprintings.

PETRENKO, VIKTOR (1969–) (UKR). Viktor Petrenko was born in Odessa, **Ukraine**, where he began skating at age five. Four years later, he began working with his only coach, Galina Zmievskaya. His first international title came at the **World Junior Championships** in 1984. He won the first of three European titles in 1990 and claimed both the world and Olympic titles in 1992. With the collapse of the **Soviet Union**, Ukraine and Russia entered competitors for one year only, in 1992, under the designation **Commonwealth of Independent States**. Petrenko retired after 1992 but was reinstated for the 1994 season, winning his third European title and placing fourth at the **Olympic Winter Games**. Moving to the **United States** after the games, he toured with **Champions on Ice** for 20 years. Petrenko is a coach and also serves the International Skating Union as a **technical specialist**. *See also* CZECHOSLOVAKIA.

PETROVA, MARIA (1977–) AND TIKHONOV, ALEXEI (1971–) (RUS). Early in her career, Maria Petrova competed with Anton Sikharulidze. They were twice the world junior pair champions, but in senior competition their best placement was fifth at the **European Championships** in 1996. Petrova appeared with her new partner, Alexei Tikhonov, in 1999. They won the European title that year and proceeded to the **World Championships** where they placed fourth. A year later in 2000, they placed second at the European Championships and won the world title. The win resulted from the disqualification of their compatriots **Elena Berezhnaya and Anton Sikharulidze** who had won the gold medals at the European Championships that year but were disqualified when Berezhnaya failed her doping test. This resulted in the mandatory revocation of the title, and it kept them out of the World Championships. Although they won no additional European or world titles, during their final seven years of competition, 2001 through 2007, Petrova and Tikhonov proved to be consistent and solid competitors, winning three silver medals and six bronze medals. In their two Olympic efforts, they placed sixth in 2002 and fifth in 2006.

PHILADELPHIA SKATING CLUB AND HUMANE SOCIETY. The Skating Club of the City and County of Philadelphia, founded in 1849, was the first in the **United States**. Twelve years later in 1861, it joined forces with the local humane society and incorporated as the Philadelphia Skating Club and Humane Society. It remains an active club more than 160 years later. In 1921, it was one of five charter members of the **United States Figure Skating Association**. A relatively small number of national champions have represented the Philadelphia club, but among them are two of America's best-known skaters. Although he is from New Jersey and trained in Lake Placid, New York, **Dick Button** represented the Philadelphia Club until his college years at Harvard when he represented the **Skating Club of Boston**. **Scott Hamilton**, although originally from Ohio, represented the Philadelphia Club during the four years of his world titles. Philadelphia has served as the site of seven national championships and the **North American Championships** in 1941 and 1949.

PHILLIPS, MICHAEL. *See* SHEARMAN, LINDA LESLEY AND PHILLIPS, MICHAEL.

PHILLIPS, MOLLIE (1907–1994) (GBR). Mollie Phillips, a student of **Howard Nicholson**, competed internationally as a singles skater each year from 1932 through 1936. Her best placements were seventh at the **European Championships** in 1933 and ninth at the **World Championships** and the **Olympic Winter Games** in 1936. She also competed in pairs with Rodney M. Murdoch in 1932 and 1933. They won bronze medals at the European Championships in 1933. Phillips served terms on the **National Skating Association** council and on its Ice Figure Committee. She became a national and international judge, officiating at World Championships in all disciplines, serving almost every year during the 1950s and continuing, although less frequently, into the 1970s.

PLANE CRASH. On 15 February 1961, Sabena Airlines flight 548 crashed near the Brussels, **Belgium**, airport after an aborted landing attempt. On board was the entire U.S. world figure skating team, including referees, judges, coaches, and family members en route to Prague, **Czechoslovakia**, for the **World Championships**, all of whom perished. Although the president of the **United States Figure Skating Association** (USFSA), **F. Ritter Shumway**, requested that the championships continue, **James Koch**, president of the **International Skating Union** (ISU), announced the following day that the ISU Council had voted for cancellation "as a sign of mourning over the deaths of our United States comrades."

PLATOV, EVGENY. *See* GRISHCHUK, OKSANA AND PLATOV, EVGENY.

PLUSHENKO, EVGENY (1982–) (RUS). Evgeny Plushenko won the world junior title in 1997. Nine years in the senior ranks culminated with an Olympic title in 2006. His career results include seven national titles, five European titles, and three world titles. In addition, he is the only man to have won four titles at the **Grand Prix Finals**. From 1998 through 2002, one of the great rivalries in modern skating occurred between Plushenko and his countryman, **Alexei Yagudin**. In four head-to-head battles at the **World Championships**, each skater won twice. At the **Olympic Winter Games** in

2002, Yagudin won the gold medal. From age 11 and throughout his career, Plushenko was coached by Alexei Mishin. Since winning the Olympic title in 2006, he has skated in various shows, including **Champions on Ice**. In 2010, the Olympic year, Plushenko returned to competition and won his sixth European title. At the games in Vancouver, following a short program in which the top three skaters were within one point of each other, Plushenko won the silver medal behind the Olympic champion, **Evan Lysacek** of the **United States**. **Daisuke Takahashi** of **Japan** won the bronze medal and was the only one of the three medalists who proceeded to the World Championships, which he won. *See also* RUSSIA.

PODUSKOV, NICOLAI (?–?) (RUS). Little is known about Nicolai Poduskov, one of four competitors at the first **World Championship** held in 1896 in St. Petersburg, **Russia**. He and his compatriot, **Georg Sanders**, are the only Russians who competed at the European or World Championships until **Nikolai Panin** in 1903. The four competitors at St. Petersburg in order of placement were **Gilbert Fuchs** of **Germany**, **Gustav Hügel** of **Austria**, Sanders, and Poduskov.

PONOMARENKO, SERGEI. *See* KLIMOVA, MARINA AND PONOMARENKO, SERGEI.

POPE, CATHERINE. *See* FRICK, WILLIE.

PORTER, RICHARD (1913–1997). Dr. Richard Porter, a member of the Ann Arbor, Michigan, figure skating club can be considered the father of **synchronized team skating**. In 1954 he organized a group of 16 girls into a team called the Hockettes, which practiced and performed regularly, often between the periods of University of Michigan hockey games, with crisp routines in a discipline then called precision team skating. Its popularity grew and expanded nationally and then internationally as the activity evolved into the discipline today called synchronized team skating and became a world discipline. The first World Championship was held in Minneapolis, Minnesota, in 2000.

PÖTZSCH, ANETT (1960–) (GDR). Anett Pötzsch was a strong and consistent skater who first appeared internationally in 1973 at age 12, placing eighth at the **European Championships** and 14th at the **World Championships**. She presented excellent **compulsory figures** but was not yet a solid free skater. Her first medal, won at the European Championships in 1975, was bronze. A year later she won the silver medal, and that was followed with four consecutive gold medals, 1977–1980. During those last four years, she won medals, silver or gold, at every World Championship, where a strong rivalry existed between her and **Linda Fratianne** of the **United States**. In odd-numbered years, Fratianne won; in even-numbered years, Pötzsch won. Competing in two **Olympic Winter Games**, Pötzsch placed fourth in 1976 and won the title in 1980. In her final year of competition, Pötzsch won all three major events, claiming European, world, and Olympic titles. *See also* GERMANY.

POULSEN, OLAF (1920–2008) (NOR). Olaf Poulsen of **Norway**, a speed skater, became active in the sport administratively in his home club in Oslo and then in the Norges Skøyteforbund (Norwegian Skating Federation), serving as its president from 1969 until 1973. He held important offices in the **International Skating Union** (ISU) including terms as a council member, 1971–1977, vice president for speed skating, 1977–1980, and president, following the death of **Jacques Favart** in 1980, until retirement in 1994. He was elected as an honorary president that year. Poulsen also served on the program commission of the International Olympic Committee.

During Poulsen's presidency, ISU congresses were held outside Europe for the first time: Colorado Springs, Colorado, in the **United States** in 1984; Christchurch, New Zealand, in 1992; and Boston, Massachusetts, in the United States in 1994. At the congress in Colorado Springs, major revisions to the constitution were adopted, the first since 1951. He also worked for and oversaw the establishment of stricter doping regulations. The Berlin wall fell during Poulsen's presidency, resulting in countries in the former Soviet Bloc becoming separate members of the ISU. By the 100th anniversary celebration in 1992, as a result of the breakup of the former **Soviet Union**, the ISU had grown in membership by 30 percent in a two-year period.

POWELL, WALTER SHERMAN (1879–1961) (USA). Walter S. Powell was a world judge and referee, serving in the latter capacity at the **Olympic Winter Games** in 1952, 1956, and 1960. He held offices in the **United States Figure Skating Association** (USFSA) during the war years as second vice president, 1939–1940, first vice president, 1940–1943, and president, 1943–1946. After the war, Powell became the first U.S. officeholder in the **International Skating Union** (ISU), serving as a council member from 1947 until 1949, when the council was divided into separate bodies for speed skating and figure skating, and then as a figure skating council member from 1949 until 1961. Powell was on board the Sabena Airlines plane that crashed while attempting a landing at the Brussels, **Belgium**, airport en route to the 1961 **World Figure Skating Championships** scheduled for Prague, **Czecho-**

slovakia. He was made an honorary member of the USFSA in 1960 and was posthumously elected an honorary member of the ISU in 1961.

PÖYKIÖ, SUSANNA. *See* LEPISTÖ, LAURA.

PRANTEL, NETTIE. *See* HARTSHORNE, HAROLD.

PRECISION TEAM SKATING. *See* SYNCHRONIZED SKATING.

PREMER, MARY LOUISE. *See* AHRENS, JANETTE; FOURS; WRIGHT, BENJAMIN T.

PREUSCH, ARTHUR. *See* AHRENS, JANETTE.

PRINS, ARY. *See* INTERNATIONAL SKATING UNION.

PRITCHARD, LORILEE. *See* McMULLIN, STACI.

PRO-AM COMPETITIONS. In 1992, the **International Skating Union** approved a one-time reinstatement of ineligible skaters to full eligibility, allowing them to compete at the European and **World Championships** as well as in the **Olympic Winter Games** in 1994. The rule change led also to the establishment of pro-am competitions in the **United States** which were popular for several years and drew major sponsorships during the era of heightened interest in the sport following the **Kerrigan-Harding incident**. The first was the Chrysler Concord Pro-Am Figure Skating Challenge held in November 1992. Others that followed include the Hershey's Kisses Pro-Am Championships, April 1993; the AT&T U.S. Pro-Am Figure Skating Challenge, December 1993; the Thrifty Car Rental International Challenge, November 1994; and the U.S. Postal Service Challenge, December 1994.

PROFESSIONAL SKATERS ASSOCIATION. In 1938, 14 coaches joined together to form the American Skaters Guild. Following an inaugural meeting held at Lake Placid, New York, **Willy Böckl** was elected the first president. The guild was inactive during World War II but became functional again in 1946. In 1950, the name was changed to the Professional Skaters Guild of America. Its first newsletter, published in 1951, was distributed to an expanded membership numbering about 50. The organization has since grown steadily. In 1956, job placement services were first offered; in 1972, its first annual trade show was held. Expanding into competition in 1980, the first U.S. Open Professional Championships were held. They served as qualifying events for entrance into the **World Professional Championships** in Jaca, Spain. In 1985, the newsletter was replaced by a bimonthly magazine, *The Professional Skater*. In 1990, **Ronald Ludington** was named the first annual "Coach of the Year." In 1995, the name was changed to the Professional Skaters Association (PSA). In 2000, the PSA moved into a new building on its own property in Rochester, Minnesota. The organization, which began with 14 coaches in 1938, now maintains a membership of nearly 6,000 coaches, technicians, and patron members, who are primarily interested nonprofessionals. The PSA serves as the official coaching arm of U.S. Figure Skating.

PROFESSIONAL SKATERS GUILD OF AMERICA. *See* PROFESSIONAL SKATERS ASSOCIATION.

PROSKURIN, GEORGI. *See* TARASOVA, TATIANA.

PROTOPOPOVS. *See* BELOUSOVA, LIUDMILA AND PROTOPOPOV, OLEG.

PUNSALAN, ELIZABETH (1971–) AND SWALLOW, JEROD (1966–) (USA). Elizabeth Punsalan and Jerod Swallow were the U.S. junior **ice dancing** champions in 1988. As seniors they placed eighth and fifth before becoming national champions in 1991 and winning the title four additional times, but not consecutively. They won bronze medals twice and silver medals once before capping their career with gold medals from 1996 through 1998. Punsalan and Swallow competed at the **World Championships** five times with best placements of sixth in 1997 and 1998 and at the **Olympic Winter Games** twice with a best placement of seventh in 1998. They were popular performers for many years with **Champions on Ice**.

PUTZINGER, EMMY (1921–) (AUT). Emmy Putzinger was the last of a distinguished group of Austrian ladies who were dominant competitors during the period between the world wars. They include also **Herma Szabo**, **Gisela Reichmann**, **Fritzi Burger**, **Melitta Brunner**, **Hilde Holovsky**, **Liselotte Landbeck**, and **Ilse Hornung**, all of whom medaled in international competition. Collectively, they were on the medal stand almost every year. Putzinger was the Austrian national champion for three years, 1936–1939, and the European bronze medalist for two years, 1937 and 1938.

RADA, EDI (1922–?) (AUT). Edi Rada was the Austrian national champion from 1938 through 1949 excepting one year in which he did not compete. In international competition before the war, he placed seventh at the European and **World Championships** in 1938, and fourth at those events in 1939. After the war, Rada won the bronze medal at the **European Championships** in 1948 but withdrew after the **compulsory figures** at the World Championships. In his final year of competition, 1949, he won the European title and the bronze medal at the World Championships. Moving to Canada, Rada coached for many years. Most notable among his students was **Karen Magnussen**.

RAHKAMO, SUSANNA (1965–) AND KOKKO, PETRI (1966–) (FIN). Ice dancers Susanna Rahkamo and Petri Kokko, the European champions in 1995, were the first skaters from **Finland** to win a major international title since the Jakobssons won their last pair title at the **World Championships** in 1923. Finland claimed no further titles until their synchronized skating team, Marigold Ice Unity, won its first world title in 2002. Rahkamo and Kokko first appeared at the **European Championships** in 1986 and placed 18th. For the next nine years they competed at every European, world, and Olympic championship, and as was typical for ice dancers at that time, they continually improved in the standings until winning the European title in their last year of competitive skating. At the World Championships in their final two years, 1994 and 1995, they won bronze and silver medals. At the **Olympic Winter Games** in 1994, they placed fourth. Their original dance, "Finn step," first skated at the European Championships in 1995, was accepted as a new compulsory dance in 2009.

RATCH, EDITH. *See* BADGER, SHERWIN CAMPBELL.

RAUSCHENBACH, AXEL. *See* WÖTZEL, MANDY AND STEUER, INGO.

REICHMANN, GISELA (?–?) (AUT). Gisela Reichmann was the Austrian national ladies' champion from 1913 through 1918. At the last holding of the

World Championships before the war in 1914, she placed fifth. Reichmann was the first of a talented group of Austrian ladies who were dominant competitors during the period between the world wars. Others include **Herma Szabo**, **Fritzi Burger**, **Melitta Brunner**, **Hilde Holovsky**, **Liselotte Landbeck**, **Ilse Hornung**, and **Emmy Putzinger**, all of whom medaled. Reichmann won the silver medal at the World Championships in 1923 and placed fourth the following year. She did not compete at the **Olympic Winter Games**.

RENDSCHMIDT, ELSA (1886–1969) (GER). Elsa Rendschmidt was one of five ladies who competed at the first **World Championship** for ladies held at **Davos, Switzerland**, in 1906. She placed fourth. Rendschmidt competed annually through 1910 missing just one year and won two silver medals. She competed also at the **Olympic Winter Games** in 1908 and won the silver medal.

REGÖCZY, KRISZTINA (1955–) AND SALLAY, ANDRÁS (1953–) (HUN). Krisztina Regöczy and András Sallay were among the challengers to the dominant Soviet ice dancers who were only once defeated during the 1970s at the **European Championships** and never at the **World Championships** or the **Olympic Winter Games**. Regöczy and Sallay first appeared at the European Championships in 1970 and placed 13th. She was 14, and he had just turned 16. From 1973 through 1980, they never missed a competition, European, world, or Olympic, consistently improving in the rankings. Their first medals came in 1973 at the European Championships. During their last three years of competing, 1978–1980, they medaled in every competition accumulating gold medals once, silver medals twice, and bronze medals three times. The gold medals were won at the World Championships in 1980, breaking the Soviet run of 10 consecutive titles.

REITMEYER, ILSE. *See* KUTSCHERA, HANS.

REVELL, GUY. *See* WILKES, DEBBI AND REVELL, GUY.

RICHARD, MONSIER. *See* FRANCE.

RICHARDS, DUDLEY. *See* VINSON, MARIBEL YERBA.

RICHARDSON, THOMAS DOW (1887–1971) (GBR). T. D. Richardson's competitive career as a pair skater and ice dancer was primarily at the national level, but he competed in pairs at the 1924 **Olympic Winter Games** with his wife, Mildred Allingham, placing eighth. Richardson began as an **English style** skater but converted to the **international style** in 1905. Throughout his life, he was active in the **National Skating Association**, holding several important positions. He became a world judge and served at the Olympic Winter Games in 1928. He is most remembered today for several books on skating, including *Modern Figure Skating*. He was made an officer of the Order of the British Empire (OBE) in 1955 for his service to figure skating. Richardson was inducted into the **World Figure Skating Hall of Fame** with the initial class in 1976.

RIORDAN, MRS. JOEL. *See* BELITA.

RITTBERGER, WERNER (1891–1975) (GER). For three consecutive years, Werner Rittberger was the silver medalist at the **World Championships** behind two of the sport's earliest stars, **Ulrich Salchow** in 1910 and 1911, and **Fritz Kachler** in 1912. Rittberger is most remembered as an early jumper and the inventor of the **loop jump**. In Europe, it is sometimes referred to as the Rittberger jump. Rittberger was a world judge and served the **International Skating Union** as chair of the figure skating technical committee from 1953 until 1955 and as a substitute member of the committee from 1955 until 1957.

RIZHKIN, VICTOR. *See* RUSSIA.

ROBERTSON, RONALD FREDERICK (1937–2000) (USA). Ronald Robertson won the U.S. junior title in 1952 but never the senior title. He competed during the "golden age" of American skating and was one of three strong Americans who consistently placed behind **Dick Button** and the Jenkins brothers at the national and international level, the others being **James Grogan** and **Tim Brown**. For two years in succession, in 1955 and 1956, the Americans, **Hayes Alan Jenkins**, Robertson, and **David Jenkins**, swept the medals at the **World Championships**. Robertson is remembered for unusually fast and exciting spins. Upon retirement from competitive skating, Robertson toured as a principal with **Ice Capades** for six years and then with **Holiday on Ice** for seven years. He was elected to the **World Figure Skating Hall of Fame** in 1993.

ROBINSON, LESLIE. *See* FAIRBANKS, MABEL.

ROCA, RENÉE. *See* LANG, NAOMI AND TCHERNYSHEV, PETER.

RODNINA, IRINA (1949–) (URS). Irina Rodnina is a tale of two partners. The success of Soviet pair skaters had begun with the **Protopopovs** who in

1964 won their first Olympic title and for the next four years, 1965–1968, won all of the European and world titles plus a second Olympic title. Rodnina and her two partners continued that tradition through the 1970s. Rodnina and Alexei Ulanov (1947–) first appeared at the **European Championships** in 1968 and placed fifth. A year later, 1969, they won the European and world titles, defeating the Protopopovs. Through that Olympic cycle they claimed all of the European and world titles and the Olympic gold medals in 1972. The partnership then dissolved. Ulanov began skating with **Liudmila Smirnova** who later became his wife. Rodnina chose as her next partner Alexandr Zaitsev (1952–) who became her husband. Their career together spanned two Olympic cycles during which they won every competition entered. Not competing in 1979 owing to Rodnina's pregnancy, they returned for their final season in 1980, winning additional European and Olympic titles, but they did not compete at the **World Championships**. Rodnina with her two partners won 11 European, 10 world, and three Olympic titles, a record equaled only by one other skater, **Sonja Henie**, who likewise won 10 world and three Olympic titles. Henie won just six European titles because ladies' events were not implemented until 1930. Rodnina worked as a coach for many years in the **United States** but then returned to her native **Russia**. She was elected to the **World Figure Skating Hall of Fame** in 1989.

ROGERS, GLADYS. *See* ROGERS, MELVILLE.

ROGERS, MELVILLE (1899–1973) (CAN). Melville Rogers was the Canadian national men's champion first in 1923 and again for four consecutive years, 1925–1928. He and his sister, Gladys, were the pair champions in 1925. At the biennial **North American Championships**, he was twice the champion, 1925 and 1927, and with his sister the silver medalist in pairs in 1925. Rogers competed abroad at the 1924 **Olympic Winter Games** in Chamonix and placed seventh. In the 1930s, he was a part of the most successful **four** in the history of that discipline. Rogers, Guy Owen, Prudence Holbrook, and Margaret Davis, known as the Minto Four, were five times the national champions, 1933–1937 and three times the North American champions, 1933, 1935, and 1937. Rogers served the **Canadian Figure Skating Association** as vice president, 1934–1936, and president, 1936–1938. He was also a longtime world judge.

ROMAN, PAVEL. *See* ROMANOVÁ, EVA AND ROMAN, PAVEL.

ROMANOVÁ, EVA (1946–) AND ROMAN, PAVEL (1943–1972) (CZE). Eva Romanová and Pavel Roman won world dance titles in each of their four efforts, 1962–1965. The talented sister and brother first competed internationally in 1959 at the **European Championships** in two disciplines, **pair skating** and **ice dancing**. They placed 12th in pairs but seventh in ice dancing. She was 10; he was 13. They never again competed in pairs. In 1960, they placed seventh in ice dancing; in 1961 they were fifth. During their last four years, 1962–1965, they advanced through the medal ranks, one bronze, one silver, and two gold at the European Championships. They did not compete at the **World Championships** until 1962, but skating in their hometown, Prague, they won the world title in an unexpected upset, having placed third at the European Championships a month earlier. Three additional world titles followed. Romanová and Roman toured with **Holiday on Ice** after retirement from competitive skating.

ROOS, HENDRIK. *See* NETHERLANDS.

ROSDOL, ADOLF. *See* CONTROVERSIES.

ROTCH, EDITH. *See SKATING* MAGAZINE.

ROTTER, EMILIA (1906–2003) AND SZOLLÁS, LÁSZLÓ (1907–1980) (HUN). The Hungarian pair Emilia Rotter and László Szollás competed internationally for six years appearing first at the **European Championships** in 1930, the first year a pairs event was included, and winning silver medals. In 1931, they again won silver medals but did not compete for the next two years. Reappearing in 1934, they claimed the European title. Competing at the **World Championships** every year from 1931 through 1935, they won gold medals except in 1932. The **Brunets**, the three-time and reigning world champions, did not compete in 1931 owing to the birth of a child, but returned in 1932 to win their fourth title. Rotter and Szollás won their last three titles after the Brunets retired. At the **Olympic Winter Games**, Rotter and Szollás won bronze medals in 1932 and 1936.

ROUILLARD, NANCY IRENE. *See* LUDINGTON, RONALD EDMUND.

ROYAL SKATING CLUB. *See* LONDON SKATING CLUB.

RUBENSTEIN, LOUIS (1861–1931) (CAN). Louis Rubenstein, **Canada**'s first important figure skater, won the Championship of Montreal in 1878 and the National Amateur Skating Association Championship in New York in 1888. For the occasion of the 25th anniversary of the St. Petersburg Skating Club in 1890, he traveled to **Russia** where he won one of three gold medals awarded. Rubenstein is the first North American known to have competed in an important European competition and, other than **Irving Brokaw**, who competed at the **Olympic Games** in London in 1908, the only North American competitor prior to World War I. Rubenstein was an active participant in the organization of the Amateur Skating Association of Canada in 1887, a national regulatory body and the direct predecessor of the **Canadian Figure Skating Association**, today **Skate Canada**. Rubenstein was elected to the **World Figure Skating Hall of Fame** in 1984.

RUSSIA. Among the earliest international skating competitions was one held at St. Petersburg, Russia, in 1890 on the occasion of the 25th anniversary of the Neva Skating Association (St. Petersburg Skating Club). Among the competitors was **Louis Rubenstein** of Canada, the first figure skater from North America to compete at a major competition in Europe. By the late 19th century Russia had become one of the most advanced skating countries. Their skaters were especially strong in **special figures**. Two Russian skaters, **Georg Sanders** and **Nicolai Poduskov**, competed at the first **World Championships** held at St. Petersburg in 1896. They placed third and fourth. Championships were held there again in 1903 and 1908. The **European Championships** began in 1891, for the first several years including primarily skaters from **Germany**, **Austria**, and **Hungary** and were held in those countries. After the **International Skating Union** (ISU) reinstated the European Championships in 1898, skaters from other countries participated regularly and the competitions were held in other places, including St. Petersburg in 1911. Prior to World War I, 13 men, one lady, and one pair from Russia competed at various European and World Championships. Most successful was **Nikolai Panin** who placed third at the World Championships in 1903 and third and second at the European Championships in 1904 and 1908. Panin was the only Russian to enter figure skating events at the **Olympic Games** held in London in 1908. He withdrew from the men's competition after the **compulsory figures** but won the special figures event solidly. Although Russia was a leading country in figure skating in the days of czarist rule, the Bolshevik revolution in 1917 brought that phase of Russian skating to an end. No Russian skater competed in ISU competitions during the period between the world wars.

In 1948, the Union of Soviet Socialist Republics Skating Federation joined the ISU, but not until 1956 did Soviet skaters appear in international competition. Three men and two pairs competed at the European Championships. A year later in 1957, four men and one pair competed, including **Nina Bakusheva and Stanislav Zhuk** who placed sixth in a field of 13 pairs. In 1958, ice dancers appeared for the first time, but of more importance, the now married couple of Nina and Stanislav Zhuk won the Soviets' first international medal. It was silver. Also that year, Soviet skaters first competed at the World Championships. The Zhuks placed eighth. **Liudmila Belousova and Oleg Protopopov**, who were to become the Soviet Union's first world and Olympic champions, placed 13th. At the Olympic Games in 1960, the Zhuks placed sixth, the Protopopovs ninth. In a period of just four years, 1957–1960, Soviet skaters became major contenders in **pair skating**, a discipline they would soon dominate. Four years later, the Protopopovs defeated **Marika Kilius and Hans-Jürgen Bäumler** of the **Federal Republic of Germany** at the 1964 Olympic Winter Games, an unexpected upset that marked the beginning of a Russian dynasty that continued through the century. Not until 2010 did a non-Soviet or Russian pair win an Olympic title in pairs. At the World Championships from 1965 through the end of the century, only five of the 36 titles were won by non-Soviet or Russian pairs. Those who won both world and Olympic titles after Belousova and Protopopov include **Irina Rodnina** with her two partners, **Elena Valova and Oleg Vasiliev**, **Ekaterina Gordeeva and Sergei Grinkov**, Natalia Mishkutenok and **Artur Dmitriev**, Oksana Kazakova and Artur Dmitriev, and **Elena Berezhnaya and Anton Sikharulidze**.

Soviet ice dancers entered the European Championships in 1958, placing last. They did not reappear until 1965. Then in 1966, **Liudmila Pakhomova** and Victor Rizhkin competed at both the European and World Championships, placing seventh and 10th. A year later, in 1967, Pakhomova appeared with a new partner, **Alexandr Gorshkov**, and they became the first great Soviet **ice dancing** couple, winning five consecutive world titles, 1970–1974. When ice dancing became an Olympic discipline in 1976, they claimed that title as well. As in pair skating, it marked the beginning of a Soviet dynasty in ice dancing. From 1970 through the end of the century, Soviet ice dancers won 24 world and six Olympic titles. Those who won both world and Olympic titles after Pakhomova and Gorshkov include **Natalia Linichuk and Gennadi Karponosov**, **Natalia Bestemianova and Andrei Bukin**, **Marina Klimova and Sergei Ponomarenko**, and **Oksana Grishchuk and Evgeny Platov**.

In singles skating, **Sergei Volkov** won the Soviets' first world title in 1975. Other champions include **Vladimir Kovalev**, **Alexandr Fadeev**, **Alexei Yagudin**, and **Evgeny Plushenko**. Russian men won four consecutive titles at the Olympic Games: **Alexei Urmanov** in 1994, **Ilia Kulik** in 1998, Yagudin in 2002, and Plushenko in 2006. **Maria Butryskaya** became the first Russian lady world champion in 1999. **Irina Slutskaya** has since won twice, 2002 and 2005. No Soviet or Russian lady has won an Olympic title.

The Union of Soviet Socialist Republics Skating Federation was renamed the Figure Skating Federation of Russia following the breakup of the Soviet Union. For one year only, in 1992, competitors, primarily from Russia and **Ukraine**, entered unified teams in ISU events under the banner Commonwealth of Independent States. Since 1993, all former Soviet republics have held separate membership in the ISU. *See also* BAKUSHEVA, NINA AND ZHUK, STANISLAV; BOBRIN, IGOR; CHERKASOVA, MARINA; CHETVERUKHIN, SERGEI; DOMNINA, OKSANA AND SHABALIN, MAXIM; ELTSOVA, MARINA AND BUSHKOV, ANDREI; KHOKLOVA, JANA AND NOVITSKI, SERGEI; KRYLOVA, ANJELIKA AND OVSIANNIKOV, OLEG; LEBEDEV, ALEXEI; LOBACHEVA, IRINA AND AVERBUKH, ILIA; MOISEEVA, IRINA AND MINENKOV, ANDREI; MOSKVINA, TAMARA AND MISHIN, ALEXEI; NAVKA, TATIANA AND KOSTOMAROV, ROMAN; PETROVA, MARIA AND TIKHONOV, ALEXEI; PODUSKOV, NICOLAI; SANDERS, GEORG; SELEZNEVA, LARISA AND MAKAROV, OLEG; SHISHKOVA, EVGENIA AND NAUMOV, VADIM; SMIRNOVA, LIUDMILA; TOTMIANINA, TATIANA AND MARININ, MAXIM; USOVA, MAIA AND ZHULIN, ALEXANDR; VOROBIEVA, IRINA AND LISOVSKI, IGOR; ZHUK, TATIANA.

RYAN, DANIEL. *See* PETERS, CAROL ANN AND RYAN, DANIEL.

S

SABOURET, SIMONE AND CHARLES. *See* FRANCE.

SABOVČÍK, JOZEF (1963–) (CZE). Jozef Sabovčík competed at the **International Skating Union**'s Junior Figure Skating Championships held in Megave, **France**, in 1976, the first of two trial competitions for junior level skaters before the **World Junior Figure Skating Championships** were established in 1978. He did not compete internationally for the next two years, but from 1979 through 1986, he competed at every European and **World Championship**. Sabovčík never medaled at the World Championships, but at the **European Championships** he won the bronze medal in 1983 and gold medals in 1985 and 1986. His one Olympic effort in 1984 resulted in a bronze medal. Upon retirement, Sabovčík, known as "Jumpin' Joe," became a popular show skater. *See also* CZECHOSLOVAKIA.

ST. MORITZ, SWITZERLAND. In the days before **artificial ice**, devotees of figure skating with the means to do so sought winter resorts that could provide opportunities to practice their sport. In the Swiss Alps, three to four months of skating were assured. The most important locations were **Davos** and St. Moritz. In the 1870s, skaters from England traveled to St. Moritz, a mountainside resort. The Engadine Hotel at that time was not equipped for winter residence, but by special arrangement it was opened for them. The hotel overlooked a large lake at an elevation of 6,900 feet. Annual pilgrimages began, and like Davos, St. Moritz became a major skating center, eventually an important site for international competition. Twice the **Olympic Winter Games** have been held there, in 1928 and 1948.

SAKHNOVSKI, SEREI. *See* CONTROVERSIES.

SALCHOW JUMP. The Salchow jump is named for its inventor, **Ulrich Salchow**. It has a takeoff from a backward inside edge with a landing on a backward outside edge on the opposite foot. *See also* JUMPS.

SALCHOW, ULRICH (1877–1949) (SWE). Although Danish by birth, Ulrich Salchow moved to **Sweden** as a youngster. There he became a junior champion and three times, 1895–1897, the senior champion. Salchow won the European title at his first effort in 1898 and a year later placed second at his first **World Championship**. Over a long international career, 1897 through 1913, competing at 24 European and world championships, Salchow won a remarkable 20 gold medals. Other medals included one bronze and three silver. Salchow became the first Olympic champion in 1908. He competed again in the 1920 Games and at age 41 placed fourth. His record of 10 world titles has not been equaled among the men. Salchow was a master of **compulsory figures**, but his free skating was strong as well. He is most remembered today for the jump he invented, which bears his name. At the conclusion of his competitive career, Salchow became active in the **International Skating Union**, serving for 12 years, 1925–1937, as president during a period of significant growth for the union. Salchow was a member of the original class elected to the **World Figure Skating Hall of Fame** in 1976.

SALÉ, JAMIE (1977–) AND PELLETIER, DAVID (1974–) (CAN). Jamie Salé and David Pelletier were both Canadian junior pair champions with other partners, Salé with Jason Turner in 1992 and Pelletier with Julie Laponte in 1993. Salé followed her junior pairs career with an attempt at singles skating, while Pelletier competed with two additional partners. In 1998, Salé and Pelletier began their career together and a year later won their first international title at **Skate America**. At their first **World Championships** in 2000, they placed fourth, but in all other competitions through their retirement from eligible skating in 2002, they carried home only silver and gold medals. In addition to winning the **Four Continents Championships** twice, 2000 and 2001, and the **Grand Prix Finals** twice, 2001 and 2002, they won the world title in 2001. Salé and Pelletier were at the center of the judging **controversy** at the Salt Lake City **Olympic Winter Games** in 2002. They placed second in a split decision of the judges, but owing to a statement by the French judge, Marie-Reine Le Gougne, that she had been "pressured" to favor the Russian pair, **Elena Berezhnaya and Anton Sikharulidze**, a protest was filed by the Canadian Federation. That ultimately resulted in the awarding by the International Olympic Committee of duplicate gold medals and provided the stimulus for a new judging system adopted by the **International Skating Union** two years later. Electing not to defend their world title in 2002, Salé and Pelletier retired from eligible skating. They have since skated in many shows. *See also* CANADA.

SALLAY, ANDRÁS. *See* REGÖCZY, KRISZTINA AND SALLAY, ANDRÁS.

SAMUEL, CONSTANCE WILSON (1908–1953) (CAN). Constance Wilson won the Canadian ladies' national title nine times between 1924 and 1935 and at the **World Championships** won a bronze medal in 1932. Beginning in 1929, she competed under her married name, Constance Wilson Samuel. She also competed in pairs with her brother, **Montgomery Wilson**. They won five national titles and represented **Canada** at two World Championships held in North America, placing fourth in 1930 and sixth in 1932. The Wilson siblings dominated the biennial **North American Championships**. Beginning in 1929, Constance won four consecutive titles; Montgomery won six consecutive titles; and together they won three consecutive pair titles. *See also* BELGIUM.

SAND, TODD. *See* MENO, JENNI AND SAND, TODD.

SANDAHL, GÖSTA (1893–1963) (SWE). Gösta Sandahl was a four-time Swedish national champion. He competed twice at prewar international competitions, both of which he won, the **European Championship** in 1912 and the **World Championships** in 1914. The scores in both cases show his strength to be in the **compulsory figures**. At the championships in 1914, he competed against a strong field of younger skaters, including **Fritz Kachler**, the silver medalist, and **Willy Böckl**, the bronze medalist. In Sandahl's only postwar competition, the World Championships of 1923, he competed against the same skaters. Kachler won the gold medal, Böckl the silver medal, and Sandahl the bronze medal. Sandahl did not compete in the Olympics. *See also* SWEDEN.

SANDERS, GEORG (RUS). Georg Sanders was one of four competitors at the first **World Championship** held in 1896 at St. Petersburg, **Russia**. The others were **Gilbert Fuchs**, **Gustav Hügel**, and **Nicolai Poduskov**. Sanders won the bronze medal. He competed in no other **International Skating Union** competitions. Sanders, who is remembered primarily for his skill in **special figures**, wrote a chapter on them for **Irving Brokaw's** monumental book of 1910, *The Art of Skating*.

SANDHU, EMANUEL (1980–) (CAN). Emanuel Sandhu competed internationally from 1998 through 2007 including eight **World Championships**. His best placement was fifth in 2006. He was sent to the **Olympic Winter Games** in 2002 but had to withdraw owing to an injury. Sandhu's best outing was at the Grand Prix Finals in 2004 where he won the gold medal by defeating **Evgeny Plushenko** and **Michael Weiss**.

SANO, MINORU (1955–) (JPN). Minoru Sano was **Japan**'s first world medalist. He appeared on the international scene in 1973, the same year as his compatriot, **Emi Watanabe**. Four years later, in 1977, he won the bronze medal at the **World Championships** after which he retired. Watanabe proceeded to win the bronze medal in 1979, the first medal won by a Japanese lady. Sano placed ninth at the **Olympic Games** in 1976. Although Japan had joined the **International Skating Union** (ISU) in 1926, Japanese skaters appeared infrequently at the World Championships prior to 1960 but have since appeared at all World Championships as Japan has evolved into the first Asian powerhouse in figure skating.

SANTEE, DAVID (1957–) (USA). David Santee became the U.S. junior men's champion in 1971. Competing for eleven years as a senior, he compiled a total of four bronze and four silver medals but never became the national champion. Santee competed at the **World Championships** for seven consecutive years, 1976–1982, where his best placement and only medal was silver in 1981.

SATO, NOBUO (1942–) (JPN). Nobuo Sato was the Japanese national champion for 10 consecutive years, 1957–1966. He first competed at the **World Championships** in 1960 and placed 12th. The championships were not held in 1961 because of the **plane crash**, but Sato returned in 1961 and competed annually through 1966. His best placement was fourth in 1965. At the **Olympic Winter Games**, he placed 14th in 1960 and 18th in 1964. His wife Kumiko Okawa was also a world and Olympic competitor during the 1960s. Since retirement from competing Sato has served as a coach to many Japanese skaters, several of whom became ladies' world champions. They include **Yuka Sato**, his daughter, in 1994, **Shizuka Arakawa** in 2004, and **Miki Ando** in 2007. Arakawa also won Japan's first Olympic title in 2006. Other outstanding skaters he coached include **Fumie Suguri** and Takahiko Kozuka. Sato has served as association chief in the Japanese Skating Federation and as the executive in the Japanese Professional Coaches Association. He was elected into the **World Figure Skating Hall of Fame** in 2010.

SATO, YUKA (1973–) (JPN). Yuka Sato became the world junior champion in 1990. As a senior, her only medal in four efforts at the **World Championships** was gold in 1994. She had placed fifth at the **Olympic Winter Games** a month earlier, but she was now skating in her homeland. The gold and silver medalists at the games, **Oksana Baiul** and **Nancy Kerrigan**, had retired, and the bronze medalist, **Lu Chen**, withdrew. **Surya Bonaly**, who placed fourth at the games was favored to win the world title, but Sato was not to be denied. Bonaly placed second as she had the previous year. Sato, who is remembered for her artistry, turned professional after winning the world title and competed in many professional competitions, winning several of them. They include both the **World Professional Figure Skating Championships** and the **Challenge of Champions**. She is currently working as a coach. *See also* JAPAN.

SAVAGE, JOSEPH. *See* SCHWOMEYER, JUDY AND SLADKY, JAMES.

SAVCHENKO, ALIONA (1984–) AND SZOLKOWY, ROBIN (1979–) (GER). Aliona Savchenko and Robin Szolkowy are consistent pair skaters who medaled in every competition entered from 2007 through 2010. They began skating together in 2003 and won the German national title for the next six years, 2004–2009. Their international career began in 2005 with a fourth-place finish at the **European Championships**. They proceeded to win silver medals in 2006, gold medals for the three years, 2007–2009, and silver medals again in 2010. At the **World Championships** during those same years, two sixth-place finishes were followed by bronze medals in 2007, gold medals in 2008 and 2009, and silver medals again in 2010. Competing at the **Olympic Winter Games**, they placed sixth in 2006 and won bronze medals in 2010. Qualifying for the **Grand Prix Finals** in three consecutive years, 2008–2010, they won gold medals the first year and bronze medals for the next two years. *See also* GERMANY.

SAWBRIDGE, JANET (1947–) (GBR). Janet Sawbridge, competing with David Hickinbottom, represented the hoped for continuation of British domination in **ice dancing** in the early 1960s, but they competed during the four years in which the Czech skaters **Eva Romanová and Pavel Roman** proved unbeatable. Competing from 1963 through 1965, Sawbridge and Hickinbottom won bronze medals once and silver medals twice at the **European Championships**. They placed fourth and then won bronze and silver medals at the **World Championships**. Sawbridge competed for an additional two years but less successfully with Jon Lane. As a coach for several years, she is most remembered for pairing together **Jayne Torvill and Christopher Dean**.

SAWYER, JILL. *See* WORLD JUNIOR FIGURE SKATING CHAMPIONSHIPS.

SCHÄFER, KARL (1909–1976) (AUT). Two men claimed the five Olympic gold medals awarded between the world wars. **Gillis Grafström** won the first three; Karl Schäfer, **Austria**'s most successful skater, won the next two in 1932 and 1936. Schäfer was the national champion eight times, 1929–1936. Competing at the European and **World Championships** for the first time in 1927, he won the bronze medals. In 1928 they were silver; in 1929 gold and silver. For the next seven years, 1930–1936, without missing a national, European, world, or Olympic competition, Schäfer's medals were all gold. The multitalented Schäfer was also an Olympic swimmer. Following retirement, he was featured in **carnivals** and ice shows in the **United States**, and he taught skating on both sides of the Atlantic Ocean. Schäfer was one of the original inductees into the **World Figure Skating Hall of Fame** in 1976. *See also* CANADA.

SCHMITSON, A. *See* GERMANY.

SCHNELLDORFER, MANFRED (1943–) (FRG). Manfred Schnelldorfer was 10 times the **Federal Republic of Germany** champion. His first international effort was at the **European Championships** in 1955. He placed 10th. At his first **World Championships** in 1956, he withdrew after the **compulsory figures**. Beginning in 1957, he competed at both competitions through 1964, missing only the World Championships of 1959. He medaled at five consecutive European Championships beginning in 1960, three bronze followed by two silver. His first medal at the World Championships was bronze in 1963. His final season, 1964, began with a silver medal at the European Championships, but at the **Olympic Winter Games**, he managed a surprising upset, defeating **Alain Calmat** and **Karol Divin** to become the champion. He then proceeded to defeat the same skaters decisively at the 1964 World Championships. Schnelldorfer skated professionally for a short time.

SCHOENFELDER, OLIVIER. *See* DELOBEL, ISABELLE AND SCHOENFELDER, OLIVIER.

SCHOLDAN, EDI (1910–1961) (AUT). Edi Scholdan competed internationally through 1933 before turning professional to teach skating. He entered the **Open Professional Championships** twice, placing fourth in 1934 and seventh in 1935. In England he became a member of the teaching staff at Brighton in Sussex, then an important skating center. Scholdan emigrated to the **United States** in 1938 and taught in Boston through the war years. In 1946, he moved to Colorado Springs where he established the summer school at The Broadmoor and further developed his reputation as an outstanding teacher. Among his students were the Jenkins brothers, Hayes Alan and David, both of whom became world and Olympic champions. Scholdan was on the airplane that crashed in Brussels, **Belgium**, on its way to the **World Championships** in 1961. The entire U.S. world team was lost. Scholdan was inducted into the **World Figure Skating Hall of Fame** in 1976.

SCHOLZ, LILY (1903–?) AND KAISER, OTTO (1901–1977) (AUT). Lily Scholz and Otto Kaiser, four times the Austrian national pair champions, competed at the World Championships for five years beginning in 1925, claiming medals each year, bronze once, silver three times, and gold once. **Herma Szabo** and **Ludwig Wrede** and the **Brunets** were the only pairs to defeat them. In 1929, the year of Scholz and Kaiser's gold medals, Szabo and Wrede had retired, and the Brunets did not compete. At the **Olympic Winter Games** in 1928, Scholz and Kaiser won silver medals behind the Brunets. *See also* AUSTRIA.

SCHÖNBAUER, GERLINDE. *See* BIETAK, WILHELM "WILLY."

SCHOOL FIGURES. *See* COMPULSORY FIGURES.

SCHRAMM, NORBERT (1960–) (FRG). Norbert Schramm competed at the first **World Junior Championships** in 1976 and placed fourth. In 1979 he appeared at his first European and **World Championships**, placing 11th and 16th. He did not compete in the Olympic year, 1980, but competed throughout the next Olympic cycle, 1981–1984. At the **European Championships** he won two bronze medals in addition to gold medals in 1982 and 1983. At the World Championships he won silver medals in 1982 and 1983. His one Olympic effort in 1984 resulted in a ninth-place finish. Upon retiring from competitive skating, Schramm joined **Holiday on Ice**.

SCHUBA, BEATRIX "TRIXI" (1951–) (AUT). Trixi Schuba was the Austrian national champion for six years, 1967–1972. She competed those same years at every European, world, and Olympic competition. At age 15 in 1967, she placed fifth at the **European Championships** and ninth at the **World Championships**. A year later she advanced to third and fourth at those competitions and placed fifth at the **Olympic Winter Games**. One bronze and three silver medals were won in 1969 and 1970, but during her final two competitive years, 1971 and 1972, all medals were gold. Schuba is remembered as a master of **compulsory figures** whose free skating was not outstanding. She competed at a time when **Janet Lynn** of the United States, whose compulsory figures were weak but whose free skating was outstanding, and **Karen Magnussen** of Canada, who demonstrated more balanced skating, were sharing the ice. Skating audiences, especially television audiences, saw only the free-skating portions of competitions and could not understand the results which gave titles to Schuba. This provided a catalyst for changes in the scoring system. In 1973, the **International Skating Union** reduced the value of compulsory figures and added a **short program**. It is sometimes forgotten that Schuba was a competent free skater, which was demonstrated by a six-year professional career with **Ice Capades** and **Holiday on Ice**.

SCHUBERT, KNUT. *See* SELEZNEVA, LARISA AND MAKAROV, OLEG.

SCHWARZ, ELISABETH "SISSY" (1936–) AND OPPELT, KURT (1932–) (AUT). Sissy Schwarz and Kurt Oppelt were the only skaters who defeated the Canadians during the years they dominated **pair skating**, 1954–1962. As the Austrian national champions for five years, 1952–1956, Schwarz and Oppelt appeared at every European, world, and Olympic competition except the 1955 **European Championships**. They won all three of the competitions in 1956. Their other medals include silver at the European Championships in 1954 and bronze and silver successively at the **World Championships** in 1954 and 1955. Upon turning professional, Schwarz and Oppelt skated in shows on both sides of the Atlantic Ocean. *See also* AUSTRIA.

SCHWARZ, WOLFGANG (1947–) (AUT). Wolfgang Schwarz is the first of just four men who hold an Olympic title but not a world title. The others are **Robin Cousins**, **Alexei Urmanov**, and **Ilia Kulik**. Schwarz's nemesis during a relatively short international career was his compatriot **Emmerich Danzer**. In five head-to-head matchups at the European and **World Championships** prior to the 1968 **Olympic Winter Games**, the results were always Danzer first and Schwarz second, but at the games, Danzer placed fourth, the result of poor scores in the **compulsory figures**. Schwarz retired after winning the gold medal, not proceeding to the World Championships where Danzer with a better effort in the compulsory figures won his third consecutive title. Schwarz's Olympic victory provided his only national or international title. He entered the world of show skating, touring with **Ice Capades** and **Holiday on Ice**.

SCHWOMEYER, JUDY (1948–) AND SLADKY, JAMES (1947–) (USA). In 1968 Judy Schwomeyer and James Sladky became the first of four American couples who have won five consecutive national ice dancing titles. The others are **Judy Blumberg and Michael Seibert**, 1981–1985, **Naomi Lang and Peter Tchernyshev**, 1999–2003, and **Tanith Belbin and Benjamin Agosto**, 2004–2008. During that same period, **Elizabeth Punsalan and Jerod Swallow** won five titles but they were not consecutive, 1991,

1994, and 1996–1998. Over a period of 42 years these five couples won 25 national **ice dancing** titles. Three earlier ice dancers—Joseph Savage, **Harold Hartshorne**, and **Lois Waring**—also won five titles, but each did so with two different partners. Schwomeyer and Sladky competed in six World Championships, 1967–1972, collecting three bronze medals and in 1970 the silver medal, a record not duplicated until Belbin and Agosto won their fourth world medal, which was silver, in 2009.

SCOTT, BARBABA ANN (1928–) (CAN). Barbara Ann Scott won the Canadian junior ladies' title in 1940 and for the first of four times the senior title in 1944. She was the North American champion twice, 1945 and 1947. When international competition was resumed in 1947, she became the first North American lady to win European and world titles. In 1948, she won them again and added Olympic gold to her laurels. The **European Championships** were closed after 1948 to non-Europeans. No Canadian lady has since won an Olympic ladies' title, and only two, **Petra Burka** in 1965 and **Karen Magnussen** in 1973, have won world titles. Turning professional, Scott skated for five years with **Ice Capades** and the **Hollywood Ice Review**. She was inducted into the **World Figure Skating Hall of Fame** in 1979. *See also* CANADA.

SCOVOLD, MARY AND EVA. *See* KIRK, JENNY.

SEBO, SUSAN. *See* BROWN, TIMOTHY TUTTLE.

SEIBERT, MICHAEL. *See* BLUMBERG, JUDY AND SEIBERT, MICHAEL.

SEIBT, HELMUT (1929–1992) (AUT). Helmut Seibt and **Edi Rada** were the leading Austrian men after World War II. They continued but could not equal the strong tradition established before the war by **Karl Schäfer** and **Felix Kaspar**. At the national championships, Seibt placed second behind Rada for four years, 1946–1949, but upon Rada's retirement, Seibt won the title for the next three years. Neither Seibt nor Rada won a world title, although both skaters claimed one bronze medal, Rada in 1949 and Seibt in 1951. That was the "golden age" of the American men. At the **European Championships**, with the Americans not present after 1948, Rada won the title in 1949, Seibt in 1951 and 1952. At the **Olympic Winter Games** in 1952, Seibt claimed the silver medal behind **Dick Button**.

SELEZNEVA, LARISA (1963–) AND MAKAROV, OLEG (1962–) (URS). Larisa Selezneva and Oleg Makarov won bronze medals at the **Olym-**

pic Winter Games in 1984, their first year on the international stage, defeating two pairs, **Sabine Baess and Tassilo Thierbach**, and Birgit Lorenz and Knut Schubert, who had defeated them one month earlier at the **European Championships**. In 1985, they carried home silver medals from the European and **World Championships**. During their remaining competitive years, 1986–1990, additional medals include silver in 1988 and 1990 and gold in 1987 and 1989 at the European Championships and bronze in 1988 at the World Championships.

SEMENOVICH, ANNA. *See* NAVKA, TATIANA AND KOSTOMAROV, ROMAN.

SEYFERT, GABRIELE "GABBY" (1948–) (GDR). Gabriele Seyfert, the first skater from the **German Democratic Republic** to medal at the **World Championships**, was the daughter of the country's leading coach, **Jutta Müller**. In 1961 at age 13, Seyfert entered the European and World Championships, placing 21st at both competitions. She skipped the World Championships for the next three years, but at the **European Championships**, she placed 12th in 1962 and 10th in 1963. In 1964, she competed only at the **Olympic Winter Games** and placed 19th. For the next six years, Seyfert competed at every European, world, and Olympic championship. Following fifth-place finishes in 1965, she never failed to medal, collecting two silver and three gold medals at the European Championships, three silver followed by two gold medals at the World Championships, and silver at the 1968 Olympics. Her silver medals at the World Championships and the Olympic Games were behind American **Peggy Fleming**, but when Fleming retired, Seyfert became a worthy successor. Seyfert was a member of the original **Champions on Ice** tour in 1969.

SHABALIN, MAXIM. *See* DOMNINA, OKSANA AND SHABALIN, MAXIM.

SHAKHRAI, SERGEI. *See* CHERKASOVA, MARINA AND SHAKHRAI, SERGEI.

SHARP, HENRY GRAHAM (1917–1995) (GBR). In 1939 Graham Sharp became the first British man to win either a European or world title. He was eight times the national champion. At his first world competition in 1934, he placed sixth. A year later, he advanced to fourth. For the next three years, he placed second at both the European and **World Championships** behind the dominant Austrian skaters, **Karl Schäfer** in 1936 and **Felix Kaspar** in 1937 and 1938. After they retired, Sharp won both competitions at their last holdings before the war. Following service in the military during the war, Sharp competed again in 1948, placing sixth at the World Championships and seventh at the **Olympic Winter Games**. He later taught skating in the **United States**. *See also* GREAT BRITAIN.

SHEARMAN, LINDA LESLEY (1944–) AND PHILLIPS, MICHAEL (1942–) (GBR). Linda Shearman and Michael Phillips were British ice dance champions in 1961 and 1962. They competed internationally for just three years, 1961–1963, an unusually short competitive career, winning successively bronze, silver, and gold medals at the **European Championships**. The **World Championships** were canceled in 1961 owing to the **plane crash**, but in the ensuing years, Shearman and Phillips placed fourth in 1962 and won silver medals in 1963. They then turned professional. Phillips became a coach in England.

SHELLEY, KENNETH GENE. *See* STARBUCK, ALICIA JO AND SHELLEY, KENNETH GENE.

SHEN, XUE (1978–) AND ZHAO, HONGBO (1973–) (CHN). Xue Shen and Hongbo Zhao, **China**'s first internationally successful pair skaters, appeared at the **World Championships** in 1994 and placed 21st. Four years later they placed fourth. For the remainder of their eligible career, 1999 through 2007, they never failed to medal. At the World Championships they accumulated bronzes, three silvers, and golds in 2002, 2003, and 2007. When the **Four Continents Championships** were implemented in 1999, they became the first champions. Three additional efforts resulted in silver medals once and gold medals twice. Finding success also at the **Grand Prix Finals**, they accumulated two bronze, one silver, and five gold medals. No other skaters in any discipline have won five gold medals at the Grand Prix Finals. Their Olympic efforts resulted in two bronze medals. China had joined the **International Skating Union** in 1956. Its first champion was **Lu Chen** who won the bronze medal at the World Championships in 1992 and the gold medal in 1995. Shen and Zhao demonstrated that China had become a major player in international figure skating. They retired from competitive skating in 2007 but returned in 2010 and won the formerly illusive and China's first Olympic gold medal. They did not compete at the following World Championships.

SHERMAN, YVONNE (1930–2005) (USA). Yvonne Sherman was one of three talented American ladies who competed during World War II and continued skating with the revival of international competition afterward, the others being **Gretchen Merrill** and **Sonya Klopfer**. All were national ladies' champions who medaled also at the **World Championships**. At the United States Championships, Sherman placed second behind Merrill in 1948 but defeated her in 1949. She won again in 1950 after Merrill had retired. Sherman was the ladies' champion at the biennial **North American Championships** in 1949. At the World Championships she was the silver medalist in 1949 and the bronze medalist in 1950. At the **Olympic Winter Games**, she placed sixth in 1948. Sherman also competed in pairs with Robert J. Swenning (1924–). They were the national champions in 1947 and placed sixth at the Olympics in 1948.

SHIPSTADS, ROY AND EDDIE. *See* ICE FOLLIES.

SHISHKOVA, EVGENIA (1972–) AND NAUMOV, VADIM (1969–) (RUS). Pair skaters Evgenia Shishkova and Vadim Naumov became World champions in 1994. They had placed fourth at the Lillehammer Games the previous month, but the top two pairs, gold medalists **Ekaterina Gordeeva and Sergei Grinkov** and silver medalists Natalia Mishkutenok and **Artur Dmitriev**, chose not to compete at the **World Championships**. The bronze medalists **Isabelle Brasseur and Lloyd Eisler** who had soundly defeated Shishkova and Naumov at the games in a turnabout were themselves defeated soundly at the World Championships. Shishkova and Naumov first appeared at the World Championships in 1991 and placed fifth. Competing for six consecutive years, they won medals of each color: bronze in 1993, gold in 1994, and silver in 1995. At five **European Championships**, they amassed silver medals once and bronze medals three times. Shishkova and Naumov were the first winners at the **Grand Prix Finals** in 1996.

SHOEMAKER, JOHN R. (?–?) (USA). John Shoemaker served as president of the **United States Figure Skating Association** (USFSA) from 1964 through 1967. He had previously served as vice president, 1960–1963 and treasurer, 1963–1964. Upon retirement from the presidency, Shoemaker was appointed as chair of the President's Planning Committee, which had been established by his predecessor **F. Ritter Shumway**. He was named an honorary member of the USFSA in 1967 and 10 years later an honorary member of the executive committee. Shoemaker served the **International Skating Union** (ISU) as the vice president for figure skating from 1967 through 1980. He was the first and remains the only president or vice president of the ISU from the United States. In acknowledgment of his work and influence, he was elected as an honorary vice president in 1980.

Sonja Henie of Norway won three consecutive Olympic titles and is the only singles skater to have won 10 world titles as well (1928, 1932, 1936). Courtesy of the World Figure Skating Museum & Hall of Fame.

Katarina Witt of the German Democratic Republic was a popular skater of the 1980s and a fierce competitor. She was rarely defeated (1984, 1988). Courtesy of the World Figure Skating Museum & Hall of Fame.

Gillis Grafström of Sweden was the first repeat gold medalist in figure skating and is one of just two skaters who hold three Olympic titles (1920, 1924, 1928). Courtesy of the World Figure Skating Museum & Hall of Fame.

Karl Schäfer of Austria won his two Olympic titles at the last holdings of the Olympic Winter Games before World War II (1932, 1936). Courtesy of the World Figure Skating Museum & Hall of Fame.

Richard "Dick" Button of the United States was the first exponent of the more athletic skating following World War II, a period known as the "golden age of American skating" (1948, 1952). Courtesy of the World Figure Skating Museum & Hall of Fame.

Oksana Grishchuk and Evgeny Platov are among the Soviet and Russian ice dancers who dominated the discipline during the 20th century. They are the only ones to have repeated as Olympic champions (1994, 1998). Courtesy of the World Figure Skating Museum & Hall of Fame.

Andrée and Pierre Brunet of France, a husband-and-wife pair, advanced pair skating in the years following World War I, making it more athletic (1928, 1932). Courtesy of the World Figure Skating Museum & Hall of Fame.

Liudmila Belousova and Oleg Protopopov, a husband-and-wife pair, won the Soviet Union's first figure skating titles in any discipline at the 1964 World Championships and Olympic Winter Games (1964, 1968). Courtesy of the World Figure Skating Museum & Hall of Fame.

Irina Rodnina of the Soviet Union won three consecutive Olympic titles, the first with Alexei Ulanov (above) and the next two with Alexandr Zaitsev (below). Coupled with 10 world titles, four with Ulanov and six with Zaitsev, her record equals that of Sonja Henie (1972, 1976, 1980). Courtesy of the World Figure Skating Museum & Hall of Fame.

Ekaterina Gordeeva and Sergei Grinkov of the Soviet Union, a popular husband-and-wife pair, won their second Olympic title after reinstatement for the 1994 Games, They were the only reinstated skaters to win a second Olympic title (1988, 1994). Courtesy of the World Figure Skating Museum & Hall of Fame.

Artur Dmitriev of Russia holds Olympic titles with two partners, first with Natalia Mishkutenok (above) and later with Oksana Kazakova (below) (1992, 1998). Top photo courtesy of the World Figure Skating Museum & Hall of Fame; bottom photo courtesy of Paul Harvath.

SHORT PROGRAM. Short programs were first introduced into **pair skating** at the **European Championships** in 1963, the **World Championships** in 1964, and the **Olympic Winter Games** in 1968. Prior to their introduction, pair skaters presented only a **free-skating** program, which was clearly a weakness. A few controversial decisions during the 1950s served as a catalyst for change. Short programs, two minutes and 40 seconds in length, included eight required elements: a side-by-side jump, a throw jump, a side-by-side spin, a pair spin, two different **lifts**, a step sequence, and a **death spiral**. They counted for one-third of the total score.

The short program in singles skating was introduced in 1973. Prior to its introduction, singles skaters, men and women, traced a prescribed group of **compulsory figures** followed by a free-skating program. It was not unusual for individual skaters to be stronger in one area than the other. **Jeannette Altwegg** of **Great Britain** serves as an excellent example of a skater whose free skating was not as strong as her compulsory figures. But the skater who most influenced the addition of a short program was **Janet Lynn** of the **United States**, an outstanding free skater who suffered from relatively weak compulsory figures. She competed at a time when **Beatrix Schuba** of **Austria**, who was viewed as a master of compulsory figures, was competing. Although the value of the figures and the number required to be skated had already been reduced and further reductions were to come before their total elimination in 1990, the differences in the strengths of Schuba and Lynn led to the addition of a short program for men and women. As with pairs, short programs for singles skaters included eight required elements in a two-minute-and-40-second period: three jumps, one of which is a combination jump, three spins, one of which is a combination spin, and two-step sequences, one of which for the women is a spiral sequence.

Synchronized team skating, which was approved as a world discipline in 1990, likewise includes a short program. Synchronized routines include five elements or maneuvers, specifically circles, lines, blocks, wheels, and intersections, and they serve as the required elements for short programs.

SHUMWAY, F. RITTER (1906–1992) (USA). F. Ritter Shumway's interest in figure skating evolved as an adult skater with a special interest in **ice dancing**. He earned a master's degree in divinity from Oxford University in England and became an ordained Presbyterian minister. After a short time, he joined the Ritter Company, a manufacturer of dental and medical equipment founded by his grandfather. He became its president in 1953 and chief executive officer in 1965. Ritter served also as a director for the Xerox Corporation for 30 years. His administrative skills benefitted figure skating when in 1953 he became a member of the executive committee of the **United States Figure**

Skating Association (USFSA) and in 1956 the chair of the dance committee. In 1957 he was elected to the **International Skating Union**'s dance committee and served until 1959. Howard D. Herbert, president of the USFSA, died suddenly in January 1961. Shumway became the acting president, serving until 1964. On February 15, 1961, one month after Shumway became the acting president, the entire U.S. world team was lost in a **plane crash** in **Belgium** on its way to the **World Championships**. Appropriately, Shumway, as both the president of USFSA and an ordained minister, conducted the memorial service. At the following governing council meeting, he proposed the establishment of a memorial fund to remember those lost and to support the development of future U.S. skaters. Through the remainder of his life, Shumway devoted much effort to growth of the fund. He was inducted into the **World Figure Skating Hall of Fame** in 1986.

SIKHARULIDZE, ANTON. *See* BEREZHNAYA, ELENA AND SIKHARULIDZE, ANTON.

SIOLI, GIANCARLO. *See* ITALY.

SKÁKALA, EMIL. *See* CZECHOSLOVAKIA.

SKATE AMERICA. The **Olympic Games** for 1980 were scheduled for Lake Placid, New York. Regulations of the International Olympic Committee require that an international event be previously held at venues to be employed for the games. To satisfy the requirement, the **United States Figure Skating Association** (USFSA) held the Flaming Leaves International Competition in 1979. It was successful beyond expectations, leading the USFSA to establish in 1981 an annual event called Skate America. It later became one of the original competitions on the **International Skating Union's Grand Prix Series**.

SKATE CANADA. The name "Skate Canada" has two distinct meanings. It is the current name, adopted in 2000, of the Canadian Federation for figure skating, formerly known as the Canadian Figure Skating Association (CFSA). It is also the name of the oldest event on the **International Skating Union**'s **Grand Prix Series**. At a planning meeting held in 1972 for the 1973 **North American Championships** with representatives from the CFSA and the **United States Figure Skating Association** (USFSA) in attendance, the CFSA delegation announced its immediate withdrawal from the championships. Their purpose was to establish an international competition to be held annually in **Canada**. Skate Canada was first held in 1973. It became an annual event missing only 1979, a courtesy to the USFSA which held the Flaming Leaves International Competition that year in adherence to an International Olympic Committee requirement that a competition be held in the venue prior to the games scheduled for Lake Placid in 1980. Originally, events at Skate Canada were held for just men, ladies, and ice dancers, but pairs events were added in 1984.

SKATING CLUB OF BOSTON. The Skating Club of Boston (SCofB), the fourth oldest club in the United States, will celebrate its 100th anniversary in 2012. The New Haven, Connecticut, Skating Club was formed the same year but probably earlier. The **Philadelphia Skating Club and Humane Society** was formed in 1849, and the **Cambridge Skating Club** was formed in 1898. Initially the SCofB skated at the Boston Arena, rebuilt as the New Boston Arena after a fire in 1920, but in 1938, it built its own rink, which is still in use today. The SCofB is one of few **United States Figure Skating Association** (USFSA) member clubs that owns its own facility. National, world, and Olympic champions have trained there and represented the club. Among the most notable are **Theresa Weld Blanchard**, **Maribel Vinson**, **Tenley Albright**, **Roger Turner**, and **Dick Button**. **World Figure Skating Hall of Fame** members from the club include Albright and Button; three coaches, **Montgomery Wilson**, **Cecilia Colledge**, and **Willie Frick**; and the senior past president of USFSA, **Benjamin T. Wright**. Fifteen other club members or former club members are in the United States Figure Skating Hall of Fame. The SCofB presents annual **carnivals**, which, since World War II, have been called Ice Chips. The club is one of few that carries on this old and important tradition in figure skating. The SCofB is a charter member of the USFSA and has hosted many regional, sectional, and national championships over the years.

***SKATING* MAGAZINE.** Many skating magazines have been published in various languages by governing bodies and as commercial ventures, usually for short durations, but arguably, *Skating* magazine, the official publication of **U.S. Figure Skating**, is the most important over an extended period. Its first issue is dated December 1923, and it has been published continuously to the present, including the World War II years. In an article written for the occasion of the magazine's 50th anniversary, December 1973, Barbara R. Boucher referred to it as "the brainchild of four enthusiastic skaters," **Theresa Weld Blanchard**, Nathaniel W. Niles, and Edith Rotch, of the **Skating Club of Boston** and Paul Armitage of the New York Skating Club. Blanchard and Niles became the first editors of the magazine, but Blanchard eventually assumed the complete role and continued for 40 years. The magazine includes articles on skaters, skating technique, competition results both national and international, tests passed by skaters, and association news and records. From 1941 until 1968 it served also as the official publication of the **Canadian Figure Skating Association** and for a short time in the 1940s included information on roller skating. The magazine was issued three times annually from 1923 until 1927, four times annually until 1933, five times annually until 1936, six times annually until 1947, eight times annually until 1978, and 10 times annually to the present. For many years it was published in a 6" x 9" format. Between 1966 and 1969, an 8½" 11" format was tried in an attempt to increase readership among fans and other interested people by selling it on news stands, but the experiment was not successful. However, in 1993 the magazine was permanently changed to the larger format. Readership had expanded after 1976 when a subscription was included with the dues of all skaters who were members of U.S. Figure Skating.

SLACHOV, OLEG. *See* BEREZHNAYA, ELENA AND SIKHARULIDZE, ANTON.

SLADKY, JAMES. *See* SCHWOMEYER, JUDY AND SLADKY, JAMES.

SLATER, JOHN E. *See* DEWHIRST, JOAN AND SLATER, JOHN E.

SLATER, NICKY. *See* DEWHIRST, JOAN AND SLATER, JOHN E.

SLIVA, JOSEF (1898–?) (CZE). Josef Sliva was involved in a bizarre judging scandal at the **European Championships** in 1930. Two irregularities occurred in the men's competition. The referee was not certified by the **International Skating Union** (ISU) and a Yugoslavian judge served falsely under the name of a duly appointed judge without being detected until after the competition. Sliva defeated the reigning champion, **Karl Schäfer**. When the irregularities were discovered, the ISU nullified the results and ordered the event to be reskated. Schäfer won easily; Sliva did not compete. Other than the controversial competition of 1930, which was Sliva's only appearance at the European Championships, his international career of just five competitions included fourth- and fifth-place finishes at the **Olympic Winter Games** in 1924 and 1928, fifth-place finishes at the **World Championships** in 1925 and 1926, and a later world effort in 1931 in which he placed 12th. *See also* CZECHOSLOVAKIA.

SLUTSKAYA, IRINA (1979–) (RUS). Irina Slutskaya won the first of four national titles in 2000 after having already twice been the European ladies' champion. She had won the world junior title in 1995 and that same year competed at the European and **World Championships**, placing fifth and seventh. From 1996 through 2006, she never failed to medal at those competitions. She won seven European titles between 1996 and 2006 and holds two world titles, 2002 and 2005. Slutskaya won the **Grand Prix Finals** four times. No other lady has won more than twice. Competing at three **Olympic Winter Games**, she received two medals, silver at Salt Lake City in 2002 and bronze at Torino in 2006. A strong rivalry existed between Slutskaya and **Michelle Kwan** of the **United States**. Kwan holds five world titles but has won the Grand Prix Finals just once. Both skaters hold one bronze and one silver medal in Olympic competition. Slutskaya did not compete during the 2004 season owing to serious health problems. She was a popular skater for several years on **Champions on Ice** tours. *See also* RUSSIA.

SMIRNOVA, LIUDMILA (1949–) (URS). Pair skater Liudmila Smirnova was for five years the silver medalist behind **Irina Rodnina** at the **World Championships**, and her career is likewise a tale of two partners, one intertwined with Rodnina. From 1970 through 1972, Smirnova competed with Andrei Suraikin (1948–) at the European, world, and Olympic competitions, always placing second behind Rodnina and her first partner **Alexei Ulanov**. Following the 1972 season, Smirnova married Rodnina's partner, Ulanov, and competed with him for two additional years during which they placed second at the European and World Championships three times behind Rodnina and her new partner, Alexandr Zaitsev. Following their competitive career, Smirnova and Ulanov appeared in shows including **Holiday on Ice**.

SMITH, CECIL EUSTACE (1908–1997) (CAN). Cecil Smith, twice the national ladies' champion in 1925 and 1926, was the first Canadian lady to travel abroad and compete in the **Olympic Winter Games** in 1924. She placed sixth. Smith was accompanied by Melville Rogers who placed seventh in the men's event. Smith and Rogers also entered the pairs competition and placed seventh. In 1930, Smith became the first Canadian medalist at the **World Championships**, winning the silver medal in New York City. *See also* CANADA.

SOO BONG HAN. *See* KOREA.

SOVIET UNION. *See* RUSSIA.

SPAIN, GERALD. *See* ENGLISH STYLE.

SPECHT, BOBBY. *See* ATWOOD, DONNA.

SPECIAL FIGURES. Special figures evolved primarily during the last third of the 19th century, becoming an important competitive discipline by the 1890s. They were included in the 1908 **Olympic Games**, but they were never a discipline regulated by the **International Skating Union** (ISU) or included in ISU competitions. Special figures disappeared by the early 1930s. Owing to their evolution and long period of development in the 19th century, a definitive definition for special figures is difficult, but by the early 20th century they were typically closed figures skated on one foot, always unique, complex, and difficult. Specific designs were often connected to well-known skaters who created and performed them in competition. Earlier they were basically any new or unusual design traced on the ice, but **Axel Paulsen** left the ice for his special figure at the **Great International Skating Tournament** in 1882 resulting in the jump that bears his name and which is a required element in **short programs**. The interest in special figures was in the designs left on the ice. As the discipline evolved, they were characteristically closed geometric figures, often star-like figures. Special figures were particularly popular in North America, the Scandinavian countries, and **Russia**. **Nikolai Panin** of Russia, a master of special figures, easily won the event at the 1908 Olympic Games in London. Other skaters remembered for their special figures include **Eduard Engelmann Jr.** of **Austria** and **Gillis Grafström** of **Sweden**.

SPENCER, BERNARD. *See* HOGG, GLADYS MARGARET.

SPINS. From a physical standpoint spins can be defined simply as rotation of the body around a fixed axis. If done successfully, the skater will remain in one spot, called centering the spin. Specific spins are required elements in **short programs**, and spins are always included in **free-skating** programs. They are done in all disciplines although with specific limitations in **ice dancing** and **synchronized team skating**. Spins can be understood through useful classifications. Three basic positions are upright spin, sit spin, and camel spin. The sit spin was originally called the **Jackson Haines** spin, being named for its inventor. The camel spin was originally called the "parallel spin," the name given to it by **Cecilia Colledge** and her coach **Jacques Gerschwiler**, the inventors of the spin. It is not clear how the name "camel spin" became attached to it. Upright spins include two-foot spins, cross-foot spins, and one-foot spins. All spins can be done forward or backward, most easily recognizable by the foot on which the skater is spinning. For skaters rotating counterclockwise, the back spin is done on the right foot; for skaters rotating clockwise it is done on the left foot. A skater can jump into a spin in which case it is called a flying spin. The flying camel spin was first done by **Dick Button**. Some frequently seen spins have specific names such as the layback spin, the death drop, and the Biellmann spin, named for **Denise Biellmann**. There is an infinite variety of possible body positions whether an upright spin, a sit spin, or a camel spin. Spins are also done in combination, a requirement in short programs. Judges look especially for speed and innovative positions.

SPIRALS. Spirals, arabesques done on skates, are among the earliest described figures. Robert Jones in *The Art of Skating,* the first treatise on figure skating, published in 1772, describes the spiral, which was perhaps the most artistic figure of the 18th century. It was done only on forward outside **edges**. The skating leg was bent with the body leaning well forward but unlike the modern spiral in which the body is characteristically parallel to the ice with the free leg in a high extension. Spirals today are done on inside as well as outside edges backward and forward, and often in sequence. They were among the most frequently employed figures in the early days of competitive skating, especially in **pair skating** during the 1920s, and they continue to be important elements to the present. A spiral sequence was a required element in ladies' **short programs**. The Charlotte stop, an unusual backward spiral, was first done by **Charlotte Oelschlagel**. **Sonja Henie** included one in her 1936 Olympic program. **Michelle Kwan** resurrected it in her 1999 free-skating program, and it has since been done by other skaters including **Sasha Cohen** and **Sarah Hughes**.

SPLIT JUMP. The split jump usually consists of a takeoff from a backward edge with a landing on a forward edge after a half revolution. The legs are pulled up into a split position in the air. Two variations of the half revolution split jump include the stag jump, not frequently seen today, which is similar to the regular split jump but with the forward leg bent under rather than stretched out, and the Russian split jump, more often seen today, in which the legs form a V in a sit position with the hands reaching out and touching the toes. Split jumps are sometimes done in sequence. *See also* JUMPS.

SPREAD EAGLE. Spread eagles are employed primarily as connecting moves between elements in **free-skating** programs but can be tremendously effective when done in sequence. Both skates are kept on the ice with the feet pointed in opposite directions. They are done on inside and outside **edges** with the legs straight making an inverted V above the ice. The spread eagle, one of the sport's oldest figures, is described in 1772 by Robert Jones in *The Art of Skating*, our earliest treatise on figure skating, as being done on either an inside or outside edge, but unlike spread eagles today, the legs were bent significantly at the knees. Jean Garcin, writing in 1813, describes the figure in great detail, devoting more space to it than to any of the other 30 figures described. **Ina Bauer** invented a variation of the spread eagle figure frequently seen today in which the two feet trace parallel lines. Called the Ina Bauer or simply Bauer, the front leg is deeply bent while tracing a flat or a shallow forward outside edge. The body is bent backward so the other leg is on a parallel line, tracing a backward edge.

SQUIRE, PHYLLIS WYATT. *See* JOHNSON, PHYLLIS AND JAMES.

STAG JUMP. *See* SPLIT JUMP.

STARBUCK, ALICIA JO (1951–) AND SHELLEY, KENNETH GENE (1951–) (USA). Alicia Jo (JoJo) Starbuck and Kenneth Shelley were the **United States** junior **pair skating** champions in 1967 and the senior champions for three years beginning in 1970. They won gold medals at the last holding of the **North American Championships** in 1971. Five consecutive years at the **World Championships** concluded with bronze medals in 1971 and 1972. They placed 13th and fourth at the **Olympic Winter Games** in 1968 and 1972. Shelley was also the national men's champion in 1972, thus earning titles in two disciplines at the same championships. Starbuck and Shelley were included on the first **Champions on Ice** tour in 1969. Following retirement, they toured with **Ice Capades**.

STAVISKI, MAXIM. *See* DENKOVA, ALBENA AND STAVISKI, MAXIM.

STENUF, HEDY (1922–2010) (AUT/FRA/USA). Hedy Stenuf was Austrian, but she competed during a relatively short international career for three countries including **France** and the **United States**. In 1935, she represented **Austria**, placing seventh at the **European Championships** and fourth at the **World Championships**. In 1936, she represented France, placing sixth at the European Championships. One month later she represented Austria again, placing fourth at the **Olympic Winter Games**. She did not compete at the World Championships. In 1937, she represented France at the European and World Championships, placing fourth both times. She then moved to and competed for the United States for her final two competitive years, winning her only international medals, bronze and silver, at the World Championships in 1938 and 1939. Turning professional, she became a highly respected coach.

STEUER, INGO. *See* WÖTZEL, MANDY AND STEUER, INGO.

STEWART, ROSEMARIE. *See* DENCH, ROBERT.

STOJKO, ELVIS (1972–) (CAN). Elvis Stojko provides the culmination of an 11-year period in which three outstanding Canadian skaters, **Brian Orser**, **Kurt Browning**, and Stojko, won eight world titles. Only two Canadian men had previously won world titles, **Donald Jackson** in 1962 and **Donald McPherson** in 1963. Since Stojko's last title in 1997, only **Jeffrey Buttle** in 2008 has won a world title. No Canadian man has yet won an Olympic title. Stojko first appeared at the **World Championships** in 1990 and placed ninth. Two years later he won the bronze medal and the year after that the silver medal. World titles followed in 1994 and 1995. A fall in the short program and an uninspired free-skating program resulted in a fourth-place finish in 1996, but the following year, he won his third and last world title. Earlier that season he won at the **Grand Prix Finals**. His last major international title was won at the **Four Continents Championships** in 2000. Stojko is one of few skaters who has competed at four **Olympics**. Twice, in 1994 and 1998, he carried home silver medals. Since retiring from competitive skating, Stojko has appeared in many skating shows. He is currently coaching in Mexico. *See also* CANADA.

SUCHÁNKOVÁ, VĚRA (1932–) AND DOLEŽAL, ZDENĚK (1931–) (CZE). Pair skaters Věra Suchánková and Zdeněk Doležal of **Czechoslovakia** had a short international career of just four years. Their first outing, the **European Championships** in 1955, resulted in a remarkable second-place finish. Proceeding to the **World Championships** they placed sixth. In 1956 they placed fifth at the European Championships and eighth at the **Olympic Winter Games** but did not compete at the World Championships. Competing just three times during their final two years, 1957 and 1958, they won European titles both years and collected silver medals at the World Championships in 1958.

SUGURI, FUMIE (1980–) (JPN). Fumie Suguri won a silver medal for the second time at the Japanese junior ladies' championship in 1997. That same year she entered the senior championships and won the gold medal. During the next 12 years, her national record includes 10 additional medals, two bronze, four silver, and four gold. She was 28 in 2009, her last year of competitive skating. Other than her gold medal in 1997, all of Suguri's medals, national and international, were won between 2001 and 2006. They included gold medals at the **Four Continents Championships** in odd-numbered years, 2001, 2003, and 2005. She did not compete in the even-numbered years. Suguri won the gold medal at the **Grand Prix Finals** in 2004. She competed at nine **World Championships**, where her medals were bronze in 2002 and 2003 and silver in 2006. Two efforts at the **Olympic Winter Games** resulted in placements of fifth in 2002 and fourth in 2006. Suguri is remembered especially for her artistry, but by 2007, at age 26 she was one of the oldest ladies competing and that affected her placements when competing against the jumping prowess of younger skaters. *See also* JAPAN.

SUMNERS, ROSALYNN DIANE (1964–) (USA). Rosalynn Sumners advanced rapidly in the rankings during a relatively short international career. She became the world junior ladies' champion in 1980 at age 15. At the United States Championships as a senior, she placed fifth in her first try in 1981, and followed with three consecutive gold medals. She was on two world teams, placing sixth in 1982 and winning the gold medal in 1983. Her one Olympic bid in 1984 resulted in a silver medal after which she turned professional rather than proceed to the **World Championships**. She toured with **Disney on Ice** for two years and then joined **Scott Hamilton**'s company, which became **Stars on Ice**.

SUR, GORSHA. *See* LANG, NAOMI AND TCHERNYSHEV, PETER.

SURAIKIN, ANDREI. *See* SMIRNOVA, LIUDMILA.

SWALLOW, JEROD. *See* PUNSALAN, ELIZABETH AND SWALLOW, JEROD.

SWEDEN. A Swedish skating club, Stockholms/Göteborgs Skridskoklubb, was founded in 1883. It sent three representatives to the congress in Scheveningen, **Netherlands**, in 1892 where the **International Skating Union** (ISU) was formed and became one of the five original members. The name was later changed to Stockholms Almanna Skridskoklubb, and it is today one of just two club members of the ISU. The Swedish Federation, Svenska Konståkningsförbundet, was not formed until 1945. In 1895 **Viktor G. Balck**, one of the club's representatives to the first congress, became the second president of the ISU and served in that capacity for 30 years. He was succeeded by another member of the Stockholm club, **Ulrich Salchow**, who served for 12 years. Thus, two Swedes provided leadership for 42 of the ISU's first 45 years. Balck was elected as an honorary president in 1925.

Swedish men dominated the sport during the early years of international competition. World champions include **Henning Grenander** in 1898, Ulrich Salchow 1901 through 1905 and 1906 through 1911, **Gösta Sandahl** in 1914, and **Gillis Grafström** in 1922, 1924, and 1929. Swedes also won the first four Olympic titles: Salchow in 1908, and Grafström in 1920, 1924, and

1928. Swedish men have won no titles since Grafström's retirement. Three Swedish women distinguished themselves between the world wars. Magda Mauroy-Julin won the ladies' title at the 1920 Olympic Games but that was her last competition. She had competed once before the war at the World Championships in 1913. Svea Norén likewise competed in 1913 and was the only lady from before the war to reappear when the World Championships resumed in 1922. She claimed the bronze medal. **Vivi-Anne Hultén**, probably the strongest of the three skaters, competed during the 1930s, years the unbeatable **Sonja Henie** was competing. Hultén collected one silver and six bronze medals in European, world, and Olympic competition. Since World War II, no Swedish women, men, pairs, or ice dancers have won world or Olympic titles, but in figure skating's newest world discipline, **synchronized team skating**, Sweden has excelled. Team Surprise has won a total of five world titles, including the first in 2000. *See also* THORÉN, PER.

SWENNING, ROBERT J. *See* SHERMAN, YVONNE.

SWITZERLAND. Switzerland has a long history in figure skating, largely the result of resorts in the Swiss Alps at **Davos** and **St. Moritz** where serious skaters vacationed as early as the 1860s. Although the club at Davos was not an original member of the **International Skating Union** (ISU), it joined just four years later in 1896, as a club member. The Swiss Federation was founded in 1911 and joined the ISU that year. Leadership in the ISU has included several Swiss. **James Koch** served as president from 1953 until 1967. Hans Valär was involved in various capacities beginning in 1907 and eventually served as vice president in 1945–1946. **Georg Häsler** was honorary secretary from 1947 until 1975. In 1985, a medal was established in Häsler's memory to recognize his outstanding service and dedication to the union. It is awarded annually to skaters and administrators. Beat Häsler, his son, served as general secretary from 1975 until 1996. The headquarters of the ISU was permanently moved to Switzerland in 1947. It had previously been in the country of the presiding president. Three Swiss skaters have won world titles: **Hans Gerschwiler** in 1947, **Denise Biellmann** in 1981, and **Stéphane Lambiel** in 2005 and 2006. No Swiss skater has yet won an Olympic title. *See also* GERSCHWILER, ARNOLD; GERSCHWILER, HANS; GERSCHWILER, JACQUES; GRANDJEAN, SILVIA AND MICHEL; GROEBLI, WERNER; LUSSI, GUSTAVE.

SYERS, EDGAR MORRIS (1863–1946) (GBR). Edgar Syers was a dominant personality in British skating for more than a quarter of a century holding several positions in the **National Skating Association** (NSA) including a term as general secretary. He was one of several leaders who championed and fostered the movement from the established **English style** of skating to the **international style**, which the **International Skating Union** adopted after its formation in 1892. Syers was instrumental in attracting the **World Championship** of 1898 to London, and he was a strong influence in getting figure skating into the Olympics for the first time in 1908. The most important of his three books, *The Art of Skating (International Style)* was coauthored with his wife **Madge Syers**. He competed in a few NSA championships but only one international event as a singles skater. He placed third at the 1899 World Championship. Syers competed also with his wife in pairs. In their one international effort, they placed third at the 1908 Olympic Games. Syers had little involvement in figure skating after his wife's death in 1917.

SYERS, FLORENCE MADELEINE "MADGE" (1881–1917) (GBR). Madge Syers, née Florence Madeleine Cave, was a skater in the **English style** prior to her marriage in 1900 to **Edgar Syers**. She was a member of the team that won the Challenge Shield for combined skating in 1899. After her marriage, she competed only in the **international style**. In 1902, she shocked the skating world by entering the **World Championship** held that year in London. She placed second to **Ulrich Salchow**. The World Championship had been viewed as a competition for men only, but she was allowed to compete because there was no rule disallowing women. That led the **International Skating Union** to establish a competition for ladies beginning in 1906, which in 1924 became the Ladies World Championship. Still today, only men can become world champions. Madge Syers was the lady champion twice, in 1906 and 1907 as well as the first Olympic ladies' champion in 1908. She also competed in pairs with her husband at the 1908 Olympic Games, placing third. She was elected to the **World Figure Skating Hall of Fame** in 1981. *See also* GREAT BRITAIN.

SYNCHRONIZED SKATING. Originally called "precision team skating," the term synchronized skating was adopted in 1998 by the **International Skating Union** (ISU) when it was slated to become a **World Championship** discipline in 2000. Synchronized skating began 44 years earlier in Ann Arbor, Michigan, when in 1954 Dr. **Richard Porter** organized 16 girls into a team that presented crisp and polished routines like those done by drill teams. The popular activity expanded rapidly. The team, named the "Hockettes," performed locally at first, nationally later. Other skating clubs throughout the **United States** and **Canada** soon began forming teams. In 1974, an event for "drill teams" was held at the Central Pacific Regional Championships in the United States, and in 1976, the Ann Arbor Skating Club sponsored a precision team skating competition with teams from Canada and the United States participating.

Although precision skating was an American innovation, by the late 1970s Canadian teams had taken a leadership role, and by the early 1980s, both Canada and the United States were holding annual competitions. Later that decade, the discipline became international as teams were formed in **Australia** and **Japan**. Teams from **Finland** and **Sweden**, countries who would soon dominate the sport, were formed, and other European countries followed. The sport was officially recognized by the ISU in 1990, and several international competitions were held during the 1990s. Challenge Cups were held annually for four years beginning in 1996 as preparation for the first World Championship, which was held in Minneapolis, Minnesota, in 2000. Team Surprise of Sweden won three of the Challenge Cups, 1996, 1998, and 1999. Black Ice of Canada won in 1997. Scandinavian teams, Finnish and Swedish, have the best record, winning 10 of the 11 World Championships. Team Surprise has the best competitive team record of five gold medals. Two Finnish teams, Marigold Ice Unity and the Rockettes, equal that record with a combined total of five gold medals. In the total medal count, Finland has 14, Sweden 10, Canada seven, and the **United States** two.

Synchronized skating includes five basic maneuvers: circles, lines, blocks, wheels, and intersections, which serve as the specific elements required in **short programs**. Judging considerations include unison, difficulty, and presentation. The short program is two minutes and 50 seconds in duration and counts one-third of the total score. The **free-skating** program, which is four and one-half minutes in duration, includes an artistic balance of the five basic elements connected by intricate step sequences. The music must include at least one change of tempo and cannot be vocal. Interest exists in making synchronized skating an Olympic discipline.

SZABO, HERMA (1902–1986) (AUT). Herma Szabo moved ladies skating forward to a level of athleticism not possible with the long skirts previously worn. She had shortened her skirts by 1923, the first competitor in international competition to do so. Although remembered especially for her athleticism, Szabo was also a master of **compulsory figures**. She competed internationally as a singles skater for six years after World War I as the Austrian ladies' champion each of those years, 1922–1927. She was the lady world champion every year until her last year of competing, 1927, when she placed second behind **Sonja Henie**, a result that ended in **controversy**. Szabo was the Olympic lady champion in 1924. She competed also in pairs with **Ludwig Wrede** for three years, 1925–1927. At the **World Championships** they won bronze medals in 1926 and gold medals in 1925 and 1927, making Szabo a world champion in two disciplines in 1925, a feat never duplicated. She was inducted into the **World Figure Skating Hall of Fame** in 1982. *See also* AUSTRIA.

SZALAY, SÁNDOR. *See* ORGONISTA, OLGA AND SZALAY, SÁNDOR.

SZENT-GYÖRGYI, EMERICH VON (?–?) (HUN). Emerich von Szent-Györgyi was not in attendance at the first congress of the **International Skating Union** (ISU) held in 1892, although **Hungary** was one of the five organizing nations, but three years later in 1895, he was elected to the first council. He served in that capacity until 1907 and again from 1911 until 1921 when he was elected vice president, a position he held until 1925. As a highly respected colleague among ISU officeholders and having served faithfully for more than 30 years, he was elected as an honorary president of the ISU in 1933, the only person so designated who has not served as an actual president.

SZOLKOWY, ROBIN. *See* SAVCHENKO, ALIONA AND SZOLKOWY, ROBIN.

SZOLLÁS, LÁSZLÓ. *See* ROTTER, EMILIA AND SZOLLÁS, LÁSZLÓ.

TAKAHASHI, DAISUKE (1986–) (JPN). In his first try at the **World Junior Championships** in 2002, Daisuke Takahashi won the gold medal. During the next eight years as a senior at the Japanese national championships, he accumulated six medals, one bronze, one silver, and four gold. In international competition, his record includes bronze in 2005 and gold in 2008 at the **Four Continents Championships** and silver in 1908 at the **Grand Prix Finals**. Competing at the **Olympic Winter Games** twice, he placed eighth in 2006 and won the bronze medal in 2010. At the **World Championships**, Takahashi won the silver medal in 2007, becoming the first Japanese man to win a world medal since **Minoru Sano** won the bronze medal in 1977. Three years later, in 2010, Takahashi won the world title, the first Japanese man to do so. **Evan Lysacek** and **Evgeny Plushenko**, the two skaters who had placed ahead of him at the 2010 Olympics a month earlier, did not compete at the World Championships.

TANO LUTZ. *See* BOITANO, BRIAN.

TARASOVA, TATIANA (1947–) (URS/RUS). Tatiana Tarasova, one of the **Soviet Union**'s early pair skaters, competed internationally for just two years and with two different partners. In 1964 Tarasova and **Alexandr Gorelik** won silver medals behind the **Protopopovs** at the national championships, placed seventh at the **European Championships**, but did not compete at the **World Championships**. In 1965, Tarasova and Georgi Proskurin won silver medals behind **Tamara Moskvina** and **Alexandr Gavrilov** at the national championships. They placed sixth at the European Championships and seventh at the World Championships. Since her competitive career, Tarasova has become a highly respected and successful coach, especially of ice dancers. She has coached many members of Soviet and Russian national teams, including singles skaters **Irina Rodnina** and **Alexei Yagudin**, and ice dancers **Irina Moiseeva and Andrei Minenkov**, **Natalia Bestemianova and Andrei Bukin**, **Marina Klimova and Sergei Ponomarenko**, and **Oksana Grishchuk and Evgeny Platov**. Among those from other countries have been singles skaters

Shizuka Arakawa of **Japan**, **Sasha Cohen** and **Johnny Weir** of the **United States**, and ice dancers **Barbara Fusar-Poli and Maurizio Margaglio** of **Italy** and **Shae-Lynn Bourne and Victor Kraatz** of **Canada**. Tarasova was inducted into the **World Figure Skating Hall of Fame** in 2008.

TAYLOR, DONNA (1951–) AND LENNIE, BRUCE (1945–) (CAN). Donna Taylor and Bruce Lennie were the Canadian junior **ice dancing** champions in 1967 and the senior champions in 1969, after which they retired. They won gold medals at the **North American Championships** in 1969. Competing at the **World Championships** twice, in 1968 and 1969, they placed 13th and 11th.

TAYLOR, KATY (1989–) (USA). Katy Taylor placed second at the United States Championships as a novice lady in 2003 and as a junior lady in 2004. Her best result as a senior was fourth in 2006. She proceeded to the **Four Continents Championships** that year where she won her only national or international title. In 2007 Taylor placed eighth at the national championships after which, owing to an injury, she chose to retire.

TAYLOR, MEGAN DEVENISH (1920–1993) (GBR). Megan Taylor is one of several skaters who was coached by a parent. Her father Phil Taylor (1895–1959) was a stilt skater, showman, and barrel jumper. As a coach, he led his daughter and **Graham Sharp** to world titles in the same year, 1939, a rare occurrence in the coaching world. Megan Taylor became a national champion in 1932 at age 11. She ended her competitive career seven years later as the only British skater other than **Madge Syers** to become a two-time lady world champion. Taylor's international medal count includes one bronze and three silver at the **European Championships** and three silver and two gold, in 1938 and 1939, at the **World Championships**. She placed seventh at the 1932 **Olympic Winter Games** but did not compete in 1936. Taylor was an early star with **Ice Capades** after which she remained active as a skating coach until retirement in 1982. *See also* GREAT BRITAIN.

TAYLOR, PHIL. *See* TAYLOR, MEGAN.

TAYLOR, VERN. *See* AXEL PAULSEN JUMP.

TCHERNYSHEV, PETER. *See* LANG, NAOMI AND TCHERNYSHEV, PETER.

TEAM SURPRISE. *See* SYNCHRONIZED SKATING.

TECHNICAL SPECIALIST. *See* INTERNATIONAL JUDGING SYSTEM.

TERTÁK, ELEMÉR. *See* HUNGARY.

THACKER, MARY ROSE (1922–1993) (CAN). Mary Rose Thacker was the Canadian junior ladies' champion in 1937 and the senior ladies' champion three times, in 1939, 1941, and 1942. She was twice the North American ladies' champion, in 1939 and 1941 but competed in no other international competitions. Canadian ladies dominated the biennial **North American Championships** for eleven years before the war, **Constance Wilson Samuel** won four consecutive titles beginning in 1929 before **Maribel Vinson** of the **United States** won in 1937. Thacker followed Vinson winning the title twice, in 1939 and 1941. After the war, **Barbara Ann Scott** continued the Canadian domination, winning titles in 1945 and 1947.

THEATER ON ICE. Theater on Ice, called Ballet on Ice in Europe, is a competitive discipline in which teams of eight to 30 skaters combine aspects of the theater with figure skating. It can be seen as an extension of routines done in shows and carnivals but with specific requirements and limitations making it suitable for judging. Theater on Ice is a discipline for all levels of skating from juvenile to adult as well as for novice, junior, and senior skaters. For national and international competitions, a specific theme is selected annually with required movements specified for the season. Each team's routine is created to express that theme. Theater on Ice is the newest discipline for figure skating. In the **United States**, competitions are sanctioned by **U.S. Figure Skating**, but as a new and evolving discipline, competitions are currently under the jurisdiction of its Program Development Committee. Judging is based on technical merit and presentation with emphasis placed on originality, costuming, artistry, and musicality. Two programs are required, a short program and a free-skating program. Theater on Ice enjoyed its first international competition in 2010. It was held in Toulouse, **France**, with the winning team coming from France.

THIERBACH, TASSILO. *See* BAESS, SABINE AND THIERBACH, TASSILO.

THOMAS, DEBRA JANINE (1967–) (USA). Debi Thomas entered the United States Championships in 1983 at age 15 and placed 19th. Two years later, she was the silver medalist. She placed fifth at her first **World Championships** that year and by her retirement in 1988 had collected medals of every color. Thomas is the first and only African American who has become a world champion, and it was a momentous occasion. In 1986, she defeated **Katarina Witt**, a two-time and reigning world champion, in both the **compulsory figures** and the combined **short program** and **free skating**. Two years later at the Calgary **Olympic Winter Games**, Thomas and Witt both skated to music from Georges Bizet's opera *Carmen*, which the media called the **Battle of the Carmens**. Although Thomas won the short program and placed third in the **compulsory figures**, her placement of fourth in the **free skating** resulted in a bronze medal. Witt skated brilliantly in one of her most remembered programs, claiming her second Olympic title. **Elizabeth Manley** of **Canada** won the silver medal. During her amateur career, Thomas pursued an undergraduate premed program at Stanford University and is today a practicing orthopedic surgeon. For a short time after retiring, she toured with **Stars on Ice**.

THOMAS, PAUL. *See* WEIGHT, PAMELA AND THOMAS, PAUL.

THOMPSON, VIRGINIA. *See* MCLACHLAN, WILLIAM.

THORÉN, PER (1885–1962) (SWE). Per Thorén became the European champion in 1911 after having won three bronze medals. At the **World Championships** he won the bronze medal in his first effort, in 1905, after which his best placement was second behind **Ulrich Salchow** in 1909. At the London Olympic Games in 1908, he claimed the bronze medal. Thorén is most remembered as the inventor of the half loop jump. In Europe it is sometimes called the Thorén jump.

TICKNER, CHARLES F. (1953–) (USA). Charlie Tickner, a national champion from 1977 through 1980, competed at the **World Championships** each of those years, winning the title in 1978. It was an interesting result. He placed third in the **compulsory figures** and second in the combined **short program** and **free skating**, but each of the leading competitors had a major deficiency in one of the three parts. Tickner's one Olympic effort, in 1980, resulted in a bronze medal. For a short time, Tickner toured with **Ice Capades**.

TIKHONOV, ALEXEI. *See* PETROVA, MARIA AND TIKHONOV, ALEXEI.

TOE LOOP JUMP. *See* LOOP JUMP.

TOMLINS, FREDERICK (1919–1943) (GBR). Freddie Tomlins was one of three talented British men who competed in the mid to late 1930s, the others being **Jack Dunn** and **Graham Sharp**. Tomlins's best results were silver medals at the European and **World Championships** in 1939. He was a fine free skater who suffered continuously from weak **compulsory figures**. For example, at the 1939 World Championships, four of five judges placed him first in the **free skating**. Three placed him third in the compulsory figures, while one judge placed him as low as sixth. Tomlins died in service with the Royal Air Force in 1943.

TONG, JIAN. *See* PANG, QING AND TONG, JIAN.

TORVILL, JAYNE (1957–) AND DEAN, CHRISTOPHER COLIN (1958–) (GBR). Jayne Torvill and Christopher Dean are arguably the most famous ice dancers in the history of figure skating. Torvill began her career as a pair skater with Michael Hutcheson, winning British junior and senior titles in 1970 and 1971. After the partnership dissolved, Torvill tried singles skating for three years without significant success. Dean had competed in **ice dancing** with Sandra Elson, and they had become national junior champions. In 1975, Torvill and Dean were paired together by **Janet Sawbridge**, but beginning in 1978 and through most of their career together, they were coached by **Betty Callaway**, also the coach of **Krisztina Regöczy and András Sallay**. Their first appearances at the European and **World Championships** three years later in 1978, resulted in ninth and 11th-place finishes. In 1979, they placed sixth and eighth. In 1980, they placed fourth at those competitions and fifth at the **Olympic Winter Games**. Through the next Olympic cycle, 1981–1984, Torvill and Dean could not be defeated, winning three European, four world, and the Olympic titles. They did not compete at the European Championships in 1983 owing to an injury. During those years they accumulated a total of 75 perfect marks, 6.0s, at the World Championships and the Olympics, a phenomenal record. However, it is not their competitive record for which Torvill and Dean are most remembered but rather a dramatic change in the direction of ice dancing, the result of their program content, music, and choreography. Most famous of their programs was their free dance from 1984 set to music from Maurice Ravel's *Bolero*, a Spanish dance with intricate rhythms. Torvill and Dean interpreted the music as a story of two lovers, which they played out on the ice. The judges awarded them 12 out of 18 6.0s. International tours, television specials, and professional competitions followed their eligible careers. Dean has worked as a choreographer, including routines for world champions **Isabelle and Paul Duchesnay**. Torvill and Dean reinstated for the 1994 Olympic year. They won a fourth European title but garnered only bronze medals at the games. Afterwards, they returned to their professional careers. Torvill and Dean were elected to the **World Figure Skating Hall of Fame** in 1989. *See also* GREAT BRITAIN.

TOTMIANINA, TATIANA (1981–) AND MARININ, MAXIM (1977–) (RUS). Tatiana Totmianina and Maxim Marinin are **Russia**'s most successful pair since the turn of the 21st century. They first appeared on the international scene in 1999, placing fifth at the **European Championships** and seventh at the **World Championships**. Advancing quickly in the rankings, they received their first medals, silver, at the European Championships in 2001. For the next five years until retirement, they accumulated two additional silver medals at the World Championships, 2002 and 2003, but more remarkable, all other medals were gold, including five consecutive titles at the European Championships, 2002–2006, and two titles at the World Championships, 2004 and 2005. They capped their career with Olympic gold at Torino in 2006. Competing three times at the **Grand Prix Finals**, they collected silver medals in 2004 and gold medals in 2003 and 2006.

TOWLER, DIANE (1946–) AND FORD, BERNARD (1947–) (GBR). British ice dancers were preeminent from implementation of the discipline as a world championship sport in 1952 through 1960, winning every title and twice sweeping the medals, but at the **World Championships** in 1962, a Czechoslovak brother and sister **Eva Romanová and Pavel Roman** broke that tradition by claiming the title and holding it for four years. The title returned to the British when Diane Towler and Bernard Ford stepped to the top of the podium in 1966. Their first effort at the World Championships in 1964 had resulted in a 13th-place finish. A year later they were fourth, but in 1966, not having won an international medal of any color, they won both the European and world titles, a pattern that continued through 1969, the remainder of their eligible career. Following retirement, they appeared with **Holiday on Ice**, and both skaters became coaches in England. They were elected to the **World Figure Skating Hall of Fame** in 1993. *See also* GREAT BRITAIN.

TOZZER, JOAN (1921–) AND FOX, BERNARD (1916–?) (USA). Joan Tozzer and Bernard Fox won the U.S. junior title in pairs in 1936. After placing third as seniors in 1937, they won the title for three consecutive years, 1938–1940. They also won gold medals at the **North American Championships** in 1939 but competed at no other international competitions. Tozzer was the national ladies' champion those same years, 1938–1940 and at the North American Championships was the silver medalist in 1939. Fox won novice and junior titles but no senior medals in singles skating.

TRENARY, JILL ANN (1968–) (USA). Jill Trenary was an artistic skater whose **compulsory figures** were also strong. When the compulsory figures were discontinued, the year after Trenary's world title, she was one of a dwindling number of skaters who thought they should be retained. Trenary was a three-time U.S. champion. Four trips to the **World Championships** beginning in 1987 showed steady improvement: seventh, fifth, third, and first. At the World Championships in 1990, Trenary, the gold medalist, placed first in the compulsory figures but third in the other two parts. **Midori Ito**, the silver medalist, placed first in both the short and long programs but 10th in the compulsory figures. Trenary skated for many years on **Champions on Ice** tours. She currently coaches skating in Colorado Springs, Colorado.

TROPHÉE ERIC BOMPARD. *See* GRAND PRIX SERIES.

TURNER, EUGENE (1920–2010) (USA). Eugene Turner was one of many skaters whose amateur career was shortened by World War II. He was the U.S. champion in 1941 and 1942 and the silver medalist at the biennial **North American Championships** in 1941. He competed in pairs with **Donna Atwood**. They won the U.S. title and silver medals at the North American Championships in 1941. Turning professional, Turner skated for a short time with **Ice Capades** and for a year as **Sonja Henie**'s partner in the **Hollywood Ice Review**. Following service in the Army Air Corps, he taught skating for many years and wrote articles for ***Skating* magazine** under the heading "Turner's Turn."

TURNER, JASON. *See* SALÉ, JAMIE AND PELLETIER, DAVID.

TURNER, LESLEY. *See* DENCH, ROBERT.

TURNER, ROGER FELIX (1901–1993) (USA). Roger Turner was America's most successful male skater between the world wars, the only one to medal at the **World Championships**. He won seven consecutive national titles beginning in 1928. His world efforts produced silver medals in 1930 and 1931. In two Olympic efforts, 1928 and 1932, he was held to 10th- and sixth-place finishes. Turner served as a national judge for many years.

TUTT, WILLIAM THAYER (1912–1989). William Thayer Tutt's influence and immeasurable contributions to the sport of figure skating are administrative and organizational rather than as a direct participant, a result of his position at The Broadmoor Hotel in Colorado Springs, Colorado, from 1946 until his death. He was the company's president and an honorary chairman of the board. His father, Charles Tutt, opened the Broadmoor Ice Palace in 1938, which resulted in his son's interest in ice sports. Through Thayer's efforts, the Broadmoor Skating Club hosted five **World Championships** and a biennial congress of the **International Skating Union**, the first held outside Europe. The headquarters of the **United States Figure Skating Association** was moved to Colorado Springs in 1979, and the United States Olympic Committee headquarters and a training center were located at Colorado Springs. He exercised similar influences in ice hockey and golf, as The Broadmoor became an important resort complex with a strong dedication to sports. Thayer Tutt has received many accolades from sports organizations including being inducted into the **World Figure Skating Hall of Fame** in 1995.

UHLIG, OSKAR (?–?) (GER). Oskar Uhlig competed at the first **European Championship** in 1891 and won the title. Seven skaters competed in the event for **compulsory figures** only. Uhlig won by a significant margin, suggesting that he clearly was a master of compulsory figures, but he never again competed at the European or **World Championships**. *See also* GERMANY.

UKRAINE. With the breakup of the **Soviet Union**, Ukraine became an independent country and soon demonstrated its presence in figure skating as a separate entity, although for one year, in 1993, it fielded skaters with the Soviet Union under the designation **Commonwealth of Independent States** (CIS). Ukraine has produced several medal-winning skaters. **Viktor Petrenko** had already won his world and Olympic titles in 1992 and continued to skate afterward professionally. He was then reinstated and allowed to compete at the 1994 **Olympic Winter Games**. He was followed by a four-time national champion, **Viacheslav Zagorodniuk**, who won the bronze medal at the **World Championships** in 1994 and the gold medal at the **European Championships** in 1996. **Oksana Baiul**, skating under the CIS designation in 1993, became the lady world champion. Skating for Ukraine, she won the Olympic ladies' title in 1994. Baiul was followed by a six-time national champion, Elena Liashenko, who competed at the World Championships from 1994 through 2005, missing only one year. Her best placements were sixth in 1994 and 2002. In **ice dancing**, the five-time national champions, Elena Grushina and Ruslan Goncharov, won bronze medals at the World Championships in 2005. *See also* DMITRENKO, DMITRI.

ULANOV, ALEXEI. *See* RODNINA, IRINA.

UNDERHILL, BARBARA ANN (1963–) AND MARTINI, PAUL (1963–) (CAN). Barbara Underhill and Paul Martini became the Canadian junior pair champions in 1978. That same year, at the first **World Junior Championships**, Underhill and Martini became world junior pair champions. They competed at the senior level for five years, always winning their national titles. Improving incrementally at the **World Championships**, they medaled in their final two efforts, bronze in 1983 and gold in 1984. As professionals, Underhill and Martini were popular show skaters. Both served also as television analysts. They were elected into the **World Figure Skating Hall of Fame** in 2009. *See also* CANADA.

UNION OF SOVIET SOCIALIST REPUBLICS. *See* RUSSIA.

UNITED STATES OF AMERICA. The Skating Club of the City and County of Philadelphia, established in 1849, was the first in the United States. Twelve years later it joined with the Humane Society and became the **Philadelphia Skating Club and Humane Society**. The first national governing body, the American Skating Congress (ASC), founded in 1868, held its first competition that year and continued for at least three years before its demise. Although the organizational date is unknown, the next national governing body, the National Skating Association held its first competition in 1886, 15 years after the last known competition by the ASC. Possibly to avoid confusion with the governing body of the same name in **Great Britain**, the name was changed in 1887 to National Amateur Skating Association. It oversaw competitions for nearly two decades until its demise in 1905. Annual championships, now well established and eagerly awaited, continued for four years under the auspices of the New York Skating Club. In cooperation with Canadian skaters, the International Skating Union of America (ISUofA), a body of five regional organizations, was formed in 1907. It became the direct predecessor of the United States Figure Skating Association (USFSA). During its 14-year history, the ISUofA sponsored just four competitions, one before and three after World War I, the last being held in February 1921. Two weeks earlier, a proposal was made by Paul Armitage, the chair of the figure skating committee, to have figure skating in the United States governed by a figure skating association under the umbrella of the ISUofA. The proposal was adopted, and seven clubs became charter members. They included the Beaver Dam Winter Sports Club (Mill Neck, New York), the **Skating Club of Boston**, the Chicago Figure Skating Club, the New York Skating Club, the Philadelphia Skating Club and Humane Society, the Sno Birds of Lake Placid, and the Twin City (now Minneapolis) Figure Skating Club. The Skating Club of Lake Placid is the successor to the Sno Birds. The name United States Figure Skating Association was changed to U.S. Figure Skating in 2003.

The United States and **Canada** had a long and highly developed skating tradition in the 19th century known historically as the **American style**. Neither country was directly involved in the establishment of the **International Skating Union** (ISU), although the United States sent a letter of support to the organizing congress in 1892. Following its adoption by the ISU, both countries embraced the **international style**, and the American style disappeared rapidly. North Americans did not compete in ISU competitions prior to World War I, but between the world wars, skaters from Canada and the United States competed frequently, and twice the **World Championships** were held in North America, New York City in 1930 and Montreal in 1932. Skaters from the United States competed at all of the Olympic Games, including the 1908 Games at London. The 1932 **Olympic Winter Games** at Lake Placid, New York, were the first to be held in North America. **Beatrix Loughran** was the first American to win a medal at the World Championships, bronze in 1924. **Maribel Vinson** won a silver medal in 1928. In pairs Loughran and **Sherwin Badger** twice won bronze medals, 1930 and 1932. All of these skaters also won medals in Olympic competition.

The United States had its "golden age" after World War II, which continued through the 1950s. Three American men—**Dick Button**, **Hayes Jenkins**, and **David Jenkins**—won every world title from 1948 through 1959 and all of the Olympic titles through 1960. Two American women, **Tenley Albright** and **Carol Heiss**, won seven world and two Olympic titles. That era came to a tragic conclusion in 1961 with the **plane crash** in Brussels, **Belgium**, that killed the entire U.S. world team, but American men and ladies became dominant competitors again. The first was **Peggy Fleming**, a three-time world and an Olympic champion. Other ladies who have won both world and Olympic titles include **Dorothy Hamill**, **Kristi Yamaguchi**, and **Tara Lipinski**. Men who have won both include **Scott Hamilton** and **Brian Boitano**. Pair skaters have twice won world titles but not Olympic titles. No Americans have yet won a world or Olympic **ice dancing** title.

Since World War II, 10 World Championships have been held in the United States, more than in any other country. Five of them were held in Colorado Springs, Colorado. The United States has hosted four Olympic Winter Games, more than any other country: Squaw Valley in 1960, Lake Placid in 1932 and 1980, and Salt Lake City in 2002. One other international event is held annually in the United States. **Skate America**, the second oldest event on the **Grand Prix Series**, dates from 1981.

Synchronized skating is an American invention started in 1954 as an activity to keep young women interested in skating, but it developed into a competitive activity that crossed the border into Canada, then across both oceans to European and Asian countries. Although it became a world discipline in 2000, the United States has yet to win the world title. A team from Miami University won silver medals in 2007, and the Haydenettes from Massachusetts won bronze medals in 2010. *See also* ABBOTT, JEREMY; AHRENS, JANETTE; ALLEN, SCOTT; ATWOOD, DONNA; BABILONIA, TAI

AND GARDNER, RANDY; BEATTY, HENRY; BELBIN, TANITH AND AGOSTO, BENJAMIN; BOBEK, NICOLE; BODEL, CARMEL AND EDWARD; BROKAW, IRVING; BROWN, TIMOTHY; BROWNE, GEORGE; CALLAGHAN, RICHARD; CARROLL, FRANK; CARRUTHERS, CAITLIN AND PETER; CHANDLER, EVELYN; CHIN, TIFFANY; COHEN, SASHA; DAVIS, MERYL AND WHITE, CHARLIE; DWYER, RICHARD; DYER, LORNA AND CARRELL, JOHN; ELDREDGE, TODD; FRATIANNE, LINDA; GOEBEL, TIMOTHY; GROGAN, JAMES; HARDING, TONYA; HARTSHORNE, HAROLD; HICKOK, WILLIAM; HUGHES, SARAH; INA, KYOKO; INOUE, RENA AND BALDWIN, JOHN, JR.; JOHNSON, LYNN-HOLLY; JOSEPH, VIVIAN AND RONALD; KADAVY, CARYN; KAUFFMAN, CYNTHIA AND RONALD; KELLEY, H. KENDALL; KENNEDY, KAROL AND MICHAEL; KERRIGAN, NANCY; KIRK, JENNY; KLOPFER, SONYA; KWAN, MICHELLE; KWIATKOWSKI, TONIA; LANG, NAOMI AND TCHERNYSHEV, PETER; LEE, ROBIN; LUDINGTON, RONALD; LYNN, JANET; LYSACEK, EVAN; McMULLIN, STACI; MEISSNER, KIMBERLY; MENO, JENNI AND SAND, TODD; MERRILL, GRETCHEN; NICHOLSON, HOWARD; NIKODINOV, ANGELA; O'CONNOR, COLLEEN AND MILLNS, JAMES G., JR.; PETERS, CAROL AND RYAN, DANIEL; PETKEVICH, JOHN; POWELL, WALTER; PUNSALAN, ELIZABETH AND SWALLOW, JEROD; ROBERTSON, RONALD; SANTEE, DAVID; SCHWOMEYER, JUDY AND SLADKY, JAMES; SHERMAN, YVONNE; SHOEMAKER, JOHN; SHUMWAY, F. RITTER; STARBUCK, ALICIA JO AND SHELLEY, KENNETH; STENUF, HEDY; SUMNERS, ROSALYNN; TAYLOR, KATIE; THOMAS, DEBRA; TICKNER, CHARLES; TOZZER, JOAN AND FOX, BERNARD; TRENARY, JILL; TURNER, EUGENE; TURNER, ROGER; VISCONTI, GARY; WARING, LOIS AND BAINBRIDGE, WALTER H., JR.; WEIR, JOHNNY; WEISS, MICHAEL; WOOD, TIMOTHY; WRIGHT, BENJAMIN; WYLIE, PAUL; ZAYAK, ELAINE.

UNITED STATES FIGURE SKATING ASSOCIATION. *See* UNITED STATES OF AMERICA.

UPPGREN, ROBERT. *See* AHRENS, JANETTE; FOURS.

URMANOV, ALEXEI (1973–) (RUS). Alexei Urmanov competed internationally for nine years, 1991–1999. Appearing at the **European Championships** each year, he claimed one gold, one silver, and three bronze medals. At the **World Championships**, his only medal in eight attempts was bronze in 1993. Urmanov won three **Grand Prix** events and was the first winner at the **Grand Prix Finals** in 1996. His greatest achievement was becoming the Olympic champion in 1994. He is one of only four men who hold Olympic titles but not world titles, the others being **Wolfgang Schwarz**, **Robin Cousins**, and **Ilia Kulik**. Since retirement, Urmanov has skated in shows including **Holiday on Ice**. *See also* RUSSIA.

U.S. FIGURE SKATING. *See* UNITED STATES OF AMERICA.

USOVA, MAIA (1964–) AND ZHULIN, ALEXANDR (1963–) (URS). Maia Usova and Alexandr Zhulin, a married **ice dancing** couple from the **Soviet Union**, competed at the international level for seven years. Appearing first at the **European Championships** in 1988, they placed fourth. In ensuing years they never failed to medal, collecting one gold, two silver, and two bronze medals at the European Championships; one gold, three silver, and two bronze medals at the **World Championships**; and one each silver and bronze medals at the **Olympic Winter Games**. Their European and world titles were both won in 1993. Usova and Zhulin appeared for several years on **Champions on Ice** tours.

UZBEKISTAN. *See* MALININA, TATIANA.

V

VALÄR, HANS. *See* SWITZERLAND.

VALOVA, ELENA (1963–) AND VASILIEV, OLEG (1959–) (URS). Elena Valova and Oleg Vasiliev continued the unsurpassed tradition of Soviet and Russian pairs that began with the **Protopopovs** in the mid-1960s. From 1964 through 2006 Soviet and Russian pairs won every Olympic title, although duplicate gold medals were awarded to the Canadians, **Jamie Salé and David Pelletier** after the judging scandal at Salt Lake City in 2002. At the **World Championships** from 1965 through 2002, only six non-Soviet or Russian pairs won titles, and none of them more than once. Valova and Vasiliev compiled six silver and seven gold medals in 13 European, world, and Olympic competitions. They were the European champions for three consecutive years, 1984–1986, world champions in 1983, 1985, and 1988, and Olympic champions in 1984. Valova is currently a coach in the United States.

VANDERVELL, HENRY EUGENE (1824–1908). H. E. Vandervell, the "father of English style skating," joined the **London Skating Club** in 1855 and for the next 53 years was among its most active members. Even earlier, at age 16, he designed a new skate, actually a prototype of things to come because it was permanently fastened to the boot. At that time, blades were typically fastened to the boots with straps. As a skater, Vandervell was the inventor of a one-foot turn, the counter. As a writer, he collaborated with a younger colleague, Thomas Maxwell Witham, on an important book, *A System of Figure Skating*, which describes skating technique in mid-19th century England. Within six months after the **National Skating Association** (NSA) was formed in 1879 to regulate speed skating, figure skating was added, and Vandervell was named chair of the Ice Figure Committee, a position he held until his death in 1908. He also served on the committee established to include figure skating as the first winter Olympic sport at the London Games in 1908. His name is perpetuated by the Vandervell Trophy, which has been awarded annually since 1951 by the NSA for the best British performance of the year.

VANAGAS, POVILAS. *See* DROBIAZKO, MARGARITA AND VANAGAS, POVILAS.

VAN LAER, GERRIT WILLEM ADRIANN (1885–1945) (NED). Gerrit W. A. van Laer, a former speed skater, held offices in the **International Skating Union** from 1925 until his death in December 1945, as council member, 1927–1935; as a technical committee member for speed skating, 1931–1937; as vice president twice, 1925–1927 and 1935–1937; and as president, 1937–1945. He also served the Royal Dutch Skating Federation as its president from 1933 until 1937. *See also* NETHERLANDS.

VASILIEV, OLEG. *See* VALOVA, ELENA AND VASILIEV, OLEG.

VERNER, TOMÁŠ (1986–) (CZE). Thomáš Verner became the Czech national champion for the first of six times in 2002. He won two medals in six efforts at the **European Championships**, silver in 2007 and gold in 2008. Verner competed at seven **World Championships**, where his best results were fourth in 2007 and 2009, at two **Grand Prix Finals** where his best result was fourth in 2008, and at two **Olympic Winter Games**, placing 18th in 2006 and 19th in 2010.

VIENNA SKATING CLUB. The Wiener Eislaufverein (Vienna Skating Club), established in 1867, is the third oldest skating club in existence today. The **London Skating Club**, now the Royal Skating Club, dates from 1830; the **Philadelphia Skating Club and Humane Society** dates from 1849. The Vienna Skating Club was organized between the years of **Jackson Haines**'s two periods of residence there in 1865 and 1870, and he is credited with the inspiration for the Viennese style of skating that developed within the club over the next several years. Later referred to as the **international style**, it was adopted in the 1890s by the newly formed **International Skating Union** (ISU). The club oversees speed skating and ice hockey in addition to figure skating. From its early years, club activities have been extensive. Many **carnivals** were presented. In 1881, the first edition of *Spuren auf dem Eise* (Tracings on the Ice), a compendium of 413 figures, was published by three club members. In 1882, the first major international competition, the **Great International Skating Tournament**, was held in Vienna and sponsored by the club. Throughout the 20th century, many ISU championships have been held in Vienna.

VINSON, MARIBEL YERBA (1911–1961) (USA). Maribel Vinson was the U.S. ladies' champion for nine years, a record that stood for 68 years until

Michelle Kwan tied it in 2005. Competing in pairs, she was six times the champion, twice with Thornton Coolidge and four times with George Hill. At the **North American Championships**, she won the ladies' title in 1937 and with Hill the pairs' title in 1935. Competing at five **World Championships**, Vinson garnered two medals, silver in 1928 and bronze in 1930. Her Olympic effort in 1932 resulted in a bronze medal. After retiring from competition, she married the 1929 Canadian junior champion, Guy Owen (1913–1952). Vinson became a highly respected coach. Her most successful student was **Tenley Albright**, America's first lady world and Olympic champion. Other students include **Frank Carroll**, a longtime coach of many skaters including Michelle Kwan, and **Ronald Ludington**, a national champion and world bronze medalist in pairs with his sister Nancy who also became a longtime coach of many national and international competitors. Vinson coached her older daughter Maribel (1940–1961) and her pair partner Dudley Richards (1932–1961), and her younger daughter Laurence (1945–1961), a singles skater, to national titles in 1961. It was in a **plane crash** en route to the World Championships in Prague that year that Vinson, her two daughters, Richards, and the entire U.S. world team were lost. Vinson was also a sports writer for the *Boston Globe* and the *New York Times*. She was inducted into the **World Figure Skating Hall of Fame** in 2002. *See also* BELGIUM.

VIRTUE, TESSA (1989–) AND MOIR, SCOTT (1987–) (CAN). Tessa Virtue and Scott Moir were paired together as children in 1997. Seven years later in 2004, they won the Canadian junior **ice dancing** title. As seniors, they placed fourth, third, and second in consecutive years, 2005–2007, before becoming national champions three times, 2008–2010. At the **Four Continents Championships**, medals were won in each of four appearances, two bronze, one silver, and gold in 2008. Competing at four **World Championships**, they collected one medal of each color. Their world title in 2010 came by defeating **Meryl Davis and Charlie White** of the **United States** in a close competition decided by 1.4 points: 224.43 to 223.03. The result had been the same at the **Winter Olympic Games** one month earlier, although the scores were not as close: 221.57 to 215.74. Earlier that season, at the **Grand Prix Finals**, Virtue and Moir had placed second behind Davis and White, also in a close decision: 169.44 to 168.22. *See also* CANADA.

VISCONTI, GARY CHARLES (1945–) (USA). During the second half of the 1960s, **Scott Allen**, Gary Visconti, and **Tim Wood** won all of the gold medals at the national championships, while providing American fans with an exciting rivalry just four years after the **plane crash**. Visconti won medals every year, gold in 1965 and 1967, silver in 1966 and 1968, and bronze in 1969.

Competing at the **World Championships** each year, he won bronze medals in 1966 and 1967. Medals were also won at each of two **North American Championships**, gold in 1965 and bronze in 1967. His Olympic effort in 1968 resulted in a fifth-place finish.

VLASOV, ALEXANDR. *See* VOROBIEVA, IRINA AND LISOVSKI, IGOR.

VOLKOV, SERGEI (1949–1990) (URS). Sergei Volkov became in 1975 the **Soviet Union**'s first world champion in **singles** competition. No lady won the title until **Maria Butyrskaya** in 1999. It was Volkov's only European, world, or Olympic title, although he carried home silver medals from both the European and the **World Championships** in 1974. Volkov typically traced excellent **compulsory figures** but suffered from relatively weak **free skating**. In the year of his world title, he placed first in compulsory figures but sixth in the combined **short program** and **free skating**.

VOLPATO, RENÉE. *See* ITALY.

VOROBIEVA, IRINA (1958–) AND LISOVSKI, IGOR (1954–) (URS). Pair skaters Irina Vorobieva and Igor Lisovski of the Soviet Union had a relatively short international career. It began in 1979 with silver medals at the **European Championships** and fourth place at the **World Championships**. They did not compete in the Olympic year but returned in 1981, winning gold medals at both the European and **World Championships**. They slipped in the rankings during their next and final year, 1982, winning bronze medals at the European Championships and placing fifth at the World Championships. Upon turning professional Vorobieva and Lisovski skated in shows, including **Champions on Ice**. Before partnering with Lisovski, Vorobieva had a previous and longer competitive career with Alexandr Vlasov (1956–). They first appeared at the World Championships in 1974 and placed sixth. Competing every year through 1977, they improved consistently, placing fourth, third, and second. They also won medals in two European attempts, bronze in 1976 and silver in 1977. At the **Olympic Winter Games** in 1976, they placed fourth.

VRZÁŇOVÁ, ALENA "AJA" (1931–) (CZE). Aja Vrzáňová was one of several Czech skaters who distinguished themselves in the postwar years. She was coached in England by **Arnold Gerschwiler**. Vrzáňová arrived on the competitive scene immediately after the war and competed in every European, world, and Olympic competition for four years. From sixth place at the **European Championships** in 1947, she progressed in the next three years through medals of every color. Placing seventh at the **World Championships** that first year, she advanced to fifth a year later before becoming the lady world champion in 1949 and 1950. Her one Olympic appearance in 1948 at age 16 resulted in a fifth-place finish. After retiring from competitive skating, Vrzáňová moved to the United States and toured with **Ice Capades**. She was elected to the **World Figure Skating Hall of Fame** in 2009. *See also* CZECHOSLOVAKIA.

WAGNER, BARBARA (1938–) AND PAUL, ROBERT (1937–) (CAN). Barbara Wagner and Robert Paul were the Canadian junior pair champions in 1954 and the senior champions from 1956 through 1960. Sent to the **World Championships** in their first year as seniors in 1955, they placed fifth and repeated that placement in 1956. At the **Olympic Winter Games**, they placed sixth. During the next Olympic cycle, 1957–1960, Wagner and Paul were unbeatable, winning gold at two **North American Championships**, claiming all four world titles, and winning Olympic gold medals. Only one Canadian skater, **Barbara Ann Scott**, had won Olympic gold prior to Wagner and Paul, and not until 2002, when pair skaters **Jamie Salé and David Pelletier** were awarded duplicate gold medals, did Canadians win gold again. In 2010, **Tessa Virtue and Scott Moir** won Olympic gold medals in **ice dancing**. Wagner and Paul turned professional in 1960, skating with **Ice Capades**. Later they became coaches. Wagner and Paul were inducted into the **World Figure Skating Hall of Fame** in 1980. *See also* CANADA.

WAKEFIELD, LYMAN, JR. *See* AHRENS, JANETTE; FOURS.

WALKER, DAPHNE (1925–) (GBR). Daphne Walker was the third of three British ladies—**Cecilia Colledge**, **Megan Taylor**, and Walker—each of whom emerged on the national scene at age eleven. Collectively, they dominated ladies' skating internationally in the years immediately preceding World War II. In 1938 Walker entered the European and **World Championships** for the first time, placing 10th and seventh. A year later at the last holding of those competitions before the war, she claimed the bronze medals. Appearing after the war for one final year in 1947, Walker won bronze and silver medals. Turning professional, she appeared in skating shows in **Great Britain**, **South Africa**, **Canada**, and the **United States**.

WALLIS, DAPHNE. *See* WILKIE, REGINALD J. AND WALLIS, DAPHNE B.

WALLEY JUMP. The Walley is an edge jump from a backward inside edge to a backward outside edge on the same foot. The rotation of the jump is opposite to the approach edge. It is often employed in combination with other jumps. When toe assisted it is called a toe Walley. The jump is believed to have been first done in the 1930s by Nathaniel (Nate) Walley of the **United States**, a show skater who won the **Open Professional Championships** in 1934 and 1935. He was a member of the **Ice Capades** cast from 1944 through 1948. Walley taught skating in England, **Australia**, and the United States. *See also* JUMPS.

WALLEY, NATHANIEL. *See* WALLEY JUMP.

WALTER, HANNA (1939–) (AUT). Hanna Walter was the third of three remarkable Austrian ladies who competed in the late 1950s. **Hanna Eigel** was the national champion in 1955. Ingrid Wendl followed for three years, 1956–1958, and Walter became the champion for one year in 1959 after the others had retired. The results were similar at the **European Championships**. Eigel was the champion in 1955 and 1957, Wendl in 1956 and 1958, and Walter in 1959. At the **World Championships**, each of the three ladies claimed one silver medal, Eigel in 1957, Wendl in 1958, and Walter in 1959. All three competed at the 1956 **Olympic Winter Games**. Wendl won the bronze medal. Eigel placed fifth; Walter placed seventh.

WARING, LOIS AND BAINBRIDGE, WALTER H., JR. "RED" (USA). Lois Waring and Walter Bainbridge Jr. competed nationally in **ice dancing**, winning silver medals once, in 1946, and gold medals for the next three years, 1947–1949. They also won titles at the biennial **North American Championships** in 1947 and 1949, the ultimate achievement in ice dancing, which had not yet become a world discipline. In 1948, Waring and Bainbridge and two British couples demonstrated ice dancing at the St. Moritz **Olympic Winter Games** and while in Europe also demonstrated at an International Dance Conference, a major step toward making ice dancing a world discipline four years later. Bainbridge retired after the 1949 season and was for many years a coach, but Waring reappeared in 1950 with a new partner, Michael McGean (?–), who would later become her husband. They won the national title that year and again in 1952. For two years before ice dancing became a world discipline in 1952, the **International Skating Union** held "international dance competitions" at the World Championships. Waring and McGean won the first of them in 1950.

WATANABE, EMI CATHERINE (1959–) (JPN). Emi Watanabe was the first Japanese lady to win a medal at the **World Championships**. Competing every year from 1973 through 1980, she won the bronze medal in 1979. She competed also at two **Olympic Winter Games** with a best placement of sixth in 1980. **Minoru Sano** had won **Japan**'s first world medal, which was also bronze, in 1977. Although Japan had joined the **International Skating Union** in 1926, Japanese skaters appeared infrequently at the World Championships prior to 1962 but have since appeared every year, and Japan evolved into the first Asian powerhouse in figure skating.

WATSON, GILLIAM. *See* GILCHRIST, DONALD.

WATTS, GLYN. *See* MOISEEVA, IRINA AND MINENKOV, ANDREI.

WEIGHT, PAMELA AND THOMAS, PAUL (GBR). Runners up in **ice dancing** at the European and **World Championships** in 1954 were Paul Thomas and his first partner, Nesta Davies. Then in their second year of international competition, Thomas appeared in 1955 with a new partner, Pamela Weight, and they too were runners up at those championships. The following year, 1956, Weight and Thomas became European and world champions after which they retired. *See also* GREAT BRITAIN.

WEIR, JOHNNY (1984–) (USA). Johnny Weir won the U.S. title from 2004 through 2006, but for the next four years, his best success was winning the silver medal in 2008. In international competition, he has won **Grand Prix** events, including both Cup of China and Cup of Russia in 2008, but his best placement at the **Grand Prix Finals** was third in 2010. He competed just once at the **Four Continents Championships** in 2002 and placed fourth. Weir was sent to five **World Championships** where his best placement was third in 2008. His two Olympic efforts, 2006 and 2010, resulted in fifth- and sixth-place finishes.

WEISS, MICHAEL (1976–) (USA). Michael Weiss won the U.S. junior title in 1993 and the world junior title in 1994. He collected three national titles as a senior. Competing seven times at the **World Championships**, he won consecutive bronze medals in 1999 and 2000. His trips to the **Olympic Winter Games**, in 1998 and 2002, both resulted in seventh-place finishes. He won a gold medal at **Skate America** in 2003. Weiss employs a new design of skate blades of his own invention, called the "freedom blades," which are unique to him, having not been used by other major skaters. The blades are rounded at the back extending to the plate, which allows him to do a kind of heel to toe movement with the legs in a wide, inverted "V" while skating on the curved ends of the blades. Weiss has skated in many shows since turning professional in 2005.

WELD, THERESA. *See* BLANCHARD, THERESA WELD.

WENDL, INGRID (1940–) (AUT). Ingrid Wendl was a three-time national champion. Her five-year international career extended from 1954 through 1958. At her first **European Championship** she placed sixth. Skipping a year, she won one silver and two gold medals. In 1957, three Austrian ladies swept the medals: **Hanna Eigel**, gold; Wendl, silver; and **Hanna Walter**, bronze. At the **World Championships**, Wendl placed 12th in 1954 and fourth a year later. During her final three competitive years, she won one silver and two bronze medals. In one Olympic effort, in 1956, she won the bronze medal placing above her compatriots, Eigel and Walter.

WENDLAND, SCOTT. *See* MENO, JENNI AND SAND, TODD.

WESTWOOD, JEAN (1931–) AND DEMMY, LAWRENCE (1931–) (GBR). Ice dancing became a world discipline in 1952 but was not included at the **European Championships** until two years later. It did not become an Olympic discipline until 1976. Jean Westwood and Lawrence Demmy of **Great Britain** were the first world and European champions. They competed continually through 1955 and were never defeated. Following retirement from competition, they continued to leave their marks on the sport. Westwood crossed the Atlantic Ocean where she taught at major skating centers. Demmy remained in England. He served the **International Skating Union** for many years as a member of the ice dancing technical committee from 1967 until 1984, the last 15 years as its chair, as a member of the council from 1984 until 1993, and as vice president for figure skating from 1993 until 1998. He was elected an honorary vice president in 1998. Westwood and Demmy were honored in 1977 as the first ice dancers elected to the **World Figure Skating Hall of Fame**.

WEYDEN, ERIK VAN DER. *See* KEATS, EVA AND WEYDEN, ERIK VAN DER.

WHITE, CHARLIE. *See* DAVIS, MERYL AND WHITE, CHARLIE.

WILKES, DEBBI (1946–) AND REVELL, GUY (1941–1981) (CAN). Debbi Wilkes and Guy Revell were the Canadian junior pair champions in 1959 and the senior champions twice, 1963 and 1964. At the biennial **North American Championships** they won bronze medals in 1961 and gold medals in 1963. Competing just three times in alternate years at the **World Championships**, they placed 11th in 1960, fourth in 1962, and won the bronze medals in 1964. They also won bronze medals at the **Olympic Winter Games** that year in a close competition, narrowly defeating the Americans, **Vivian and Ronald Joseph**. Since retirement from competitive skating, Wilkes has remained actively involved in the sport, teaching skating, appearing in professional shows, serving as a television commentator, and writing two books.

WILKIE, REGINALD J. "REG" (1907–1962) AND WALLIS, DAPHNE B. (GBR). Reginald J. Wilkie and Daphne B. Wallis were British **ice dancing** champions from 1937 through 1939. They invented three dances, the Argentine tango, paso doble, and quickstep, all of which became international **compulsory dances**. In 1948, Wilkie was appointed by the **International Skating Union** (ISU) to serve on a committee charged with developing rules for competitions in ice dancing. Wilkie served subsequently on the first ISU ice dancing technical committee, 1949–1953. Wilkie and Wallis both became world dance judges. Wilkie was inducted into the **World Figure Skating Hall of Fame** in 1976.

WILLIAMS, BASIL. *See* JOHNSON, PHYLLIS WYATT AND JAMES HENRY.

WILSON, ATOY. *See* FAIRBANKS, MABEL.

WILSON, CONSTANCE. *See* SAMUEL, CONSTANCE WILSON.

WILSON, FLORENCE. *See* NORTH AMERICAN CHAMPIONSHIPS.

WILSON, MONTGOMERY S. "BUD" (1909–1964) (CAN). North American skaters did not compete at the **World Championships** prior to World War I, but between the world wars, Canadians competed at the World Championships four times, Americans 10 times. North Americans participated at all five of the **Olympic Winter Games**. Montgomery Wilson, the Canadian national champion nine times, won **Canada**'s first Olympic medal, bronze, at Lake Placid in 1932. He followed with a silver medal at the World Championships in Montreal two weeks later. Wilson had previously competed at the **St. Moritz** Games in 1928, placing 13th, and remained in Europe for the World Championships, placing seventh. He returned to Europe for his third Olympic and world efforts in 1936, placing fourth at the games and fifth at the World Championships. Wilson also competed in pairs with his sister, **Constance Wilson Samuel**. They claimed five national titles and competed twice at the World Championships, placing fourth in 1930 and sixth in 1932. The Wilson siblings dominated the biennial **North American Championships**. Beginning in 1929, Constance won four consecutive titles, Montgomery won six consecutive titles, and together they won three consecutive pair titles. Turning professional in 1939, Montgomery Wilson became a coach in the United States, first at St. Paul, Minnesota, and later in Boston. He was elected to the **World Figure Skating Hall of Fame** in 1976.

WILSON, VIRGINIA. *See* GILCHRIST, DONALD.

WIMBLEDON SKATING CLUB. *See* LONDON SKATING CLUB.

WIRTZ, ARTHUR. *See* HOLLYWOOD ICE REVIEW.

WITT, GUSTAVUS F. S. *See* NETHERLANDS.

WITT, KATARINA (1965–) (GDR). Katarina Witt is the only lady since World War II who has twice been an Olympic champion. **Dick Button** of the **United States** is the only man who has done so. Witt, who was coached by the legendary **Jutta Müller**, began her international career in 1979 at the age of 13, placing 14th at the **European Championships**. In 1980, she placed 13th and competed two months later at the **World Championships**, placing 10th. In 1981, she placed fifth at both competitions. Witt's strength was in **free skating**. Early in her career, she suffered from weak **compulsory figures**, but by 1984, they improved significantly. During the last seven years of her eligible career, Witt collected 12 gold and three silver medals. She placed lower only once, fourth at the World Championships in 1983, owing primarily to a placement of eighth in the compulsory figures. Witt amassed six consecutive European titles, 1982–1988, and faltered only once at the World Championships, placing second behind **Debra Thomas** of the United States in 1986. On that occasion, Witt presented an uncharacteristically weak short program. At the **Olympic Winter Games** in 1988, Witt and Thomas both skated to music from Georges Bizet's opera *Carmen*, which the media called the **Battle of the Carmens**. Witt demonstrated both the intensity that is associated with her often emotional routines and the strong nerves that made her a tough competitor. After the games, Witt turned professional, appearing in numerous shows, competing in competitions, and portraying Carmen in the film *Carmen on Ice*. She is one of several skaters who was reinstated and competed at the 1994 Olympics. She placed seventh, but her free-skating program is particularly memorable. She skated to the music "Where Have All the Flowers Gone?" in a tribute to war-torn Sarajevo, the city where she had won her first Olympic title 10 years earlier. Witt was inducted into the **World Figure Skating Hall of Fame** in 1995. *See also* GERMANY.

WOOD, TIMOTHY LYLE (1948–) (USA). Tim Wood was one of the most successful male skaters in the **United States** during the two decades after the 1961 **plane crash**. He was the novice champion in 1962, the junior champion in 1964, and the senior champion from 1968 through 1970. Wood first competed at the **World Championships** in 1965 and placed 13th. He did not compete the following year. In 1967 he placed ninth, but in a major leap forward, he won silver medals at both the World Championships and the **Olympic Winter Games** in 1968. Wood competed for two additional years, 1969 and 1970, and became a two-time world champion. Not since **David Jenkins** in 1959 had an American man held the title, and not until **Charlie Tickner** in 1978 did an American man hold it again. Wood's relatively short professional career included tours with **Ice Capades** and **Holiday on Ice**.

WORLD CHALLENGE OF CHAMPIONS. Following the success of the **World Professional Figure Skating Championships**, **Dick Button**, at the request of the American Broadcasting Corporation, created the World Challenge of Champions to be held outside the **United States** and at a different location each year. The format was a one-event competition with an exhibition following. The Challenge of Champions debuted in Paris in 1985. **Dorothy Hamill**, **Robin Cousins**, and pair skaters **Caitlin and Peter Carruthers** claimed the first titles. **Ice dancing** was not included until 1989. The competition was held annually for 14 years.

WORLD FIGURE SKATING CHAMPIONSHIPS. The **International Skating Union** (ISU) was established in 1892 to regulate speed skating and figure skating. The first figure skating championship under its auspices was the **European Championship** held in 1893. Championships had been held for the two previous years under the auspices of the German and Austrian Figure Skating Association. In 1896, the ISU held the first World Figure Skating Championship and discontinued the European Championships. It was held in St. Petersburg, **Russia**, on 9 February 1896, with four men competing in **compulsory figures** and **free skating**. **Gilbert Fuchs** of **Germany** became the first world champion. **Gustav Hügel**, who would become a three-time world champion, was second.

The World Championship was viewed as a competition specifically for men, but there was no rule preventing women from competing. In 1902, the championship was held in London, and **Madge Syers** stunned the skating world by entering the competition. She placed second to the reigning champion, **Ulrich Salchow**. Women skating competitively was a topic of discussion at the ISU's 1903 Congress, but no gender-specific legislation resulted because the subject had not been included on the agenda. In 1904 Syers entered the European Championships but withdrew after the compulsory figures. The subject was included on the agenda for the 1905 Congress, and a ladies' competition was approved. The first was held at **Davos, Switzerland**, in 1906. Madge Syers became the first champion. It was called initially a "championship of the ISU," but beginning in 1924 it was called a World Championship with the title becoming "lady world champion." The title "world champion" remained, as it does today, solely for men.

Two years after the establishment of the ladies' competition, the ISU implemented a competition for pair skaters, likewise referred to as a championship of the ISU. Anna Hübler and **Heinrich Burger** of Germany became the first pair champions in 1908. Second at the competition were **Phyllis and James Johnson** of **Great Britain** who later became two-time champions. In 1924, the title became world pair champions. **Ice dancing**, the fourth discipline, did not become a world championship sport until 1952. The first champions were **Jean Westwood and Lawrence Demmy** of Great Britain. The fifth and last discipline in world competition is **synchronized skating**. The first championship was held in 2000 at Minneapolis, Minnesota, and the winner was Team Surprise of **Sweden**.

The World Championships are the premier annual figure skating competitions open to skaters from all member federations and clubs of the ISU. They have been held continuously since 1896 missing only the war years, 1915–1921 and 1940–1946, and 1961, canceled because of the **plane crash** in Brussels, Belgium, which killed the entire **United States** team en route to the Championships in Prague, **Czechoslovakia**. The World Championships provide the culminating event of each skating season. The 100th holding of the World Figure Skating Championships was held in Torino, **Italy**, in 2010. For the ladies it was the 90th and for pairs the 88th. See Appendix C for a list of world medalists in all disciplines.

WORLD FIGURE SKATING HALL OF FAME. The World Figure Skating Hall of Fame was established in 1976 to recognize those persons who have contributed significantly to the sport as athletes, coaches, officials, and others making contributions in a noncompetitive manner. It is sponsored by U.S. Figure Skating but is recognized by the **International Skating Union** (ISU) as "representative of the sport as a whole." The Hall of Fame is located in Colorado Springs, Colorado, in the **World Figure Skating Museum**. Nominations are made to a committee which reviews them for consistency and specified requirements for election to the Hall of Fame and approves those who are included on a ballot sent to an international group of electors. A two-thirds vote by the electors is required for induction. The initial class of 20, inducted in 1976, included 11 world champions, all of whom were also

Olympic champions, as well as officials, coaches, and skaters who predate ISU competitions. There have been four years in which no one was inducted. Pairs and **ice dancing** couples can be inducted as such although in many cases just one member of a pair or couple have been inducted. Through 2010, Hall of Fame membership numbered 89 and represented 13 countries. See Appendix C for a complete list of Hall of Fame members.

WORLD FIGURE SKATING MUSEUM. The World Figure Skating Museum in its early days was primarily a small collection of trophies and miscellaneous skating memorabilia maintained in Boston, first at the **Skating Club of Boston** and later at the Central Office of the **United States Figure Skating Association** (USFSA). The collection was moved to the Broadmoor World Arena in Colorado Springs, Colorado, in 1965 but was not displayed. Seven years later, it was returned to Boston and was housed again at the Skating Club of Boston. When the USFSA moved its headquarters from Boston to Colorado Springs in 1979, the Museum was provided with its own space in the north end of the building, and that remains its location today. Although the collection is owned by USFSA, it has become a major repository for international skating materials, and large gifts have been made by many individuals. These include the collection of **Gillis Grafström** entitled "Skating in Art" placed on permanent loan by his widow. It contains prints, drawings, paintings, decorative arts, skates, and a costume worn by Grafström in competition. Many other gifts in kind have been made, including the complete archives of the British skating historian, **Dennis Bird**. The museum is open to the public and continually changes exhibits from its extensive collection of nearly 1,200 pairs of antiques skates, many costumes, including ones used in the **Ice Follies** and ones worn by major skaters such as **Janet Lynn** and **Torvill and Dean**, a photographic collection of some 20,000 images, a video and film collection of more than 3,500 items, a large collection of skating pins, medals, and trophies, and about 1,500 books. These as well as protocols, records, skating magazines, and other materials serve historians and writers who travel to the museum for research.

WORLD JUNIOR FIGURE SKATING CHAMPIONSHIPS. Junior championships had been held for many years in some countries before the **International Skating Union** (ISU) at its 1975 Congress adopted legislation establishing junior championships on a two-year trial basis with the proviso that if successful they would be permanently established as the World Junior Figure Skating Championships. The provisional championships were held at Megève, **France**, in 1976 and 1977. The quality of skating on both occasions was high, exceeding ISU expectations and justifying elevation to world status in 1978. The first World Junior Figure Skating Championships were also held at Megève where the champions were Jill Sawyer of the **United States**, Dennis Coi of **Canada**, pair skaters **Barbara Underhill and Paul Martini** of Canada, and ice dancers Tatiana Durasova and **Sergei Ponomarenko** of the **Soviet Union**. See Appendix F for a list of all medal winners at the World Junior Figure Skating Championships.

WORLD PROFESSIONAL CHAMPIONSHIPS. *See* OPEN PROFESSIONAL CHAMPIONSHIPS.

WORLD PROFESSIONAL FIGURE SKATING CHAMPIONSHIPS. Dick Button created the World Professional Figure Skating Championships, an invitational competition, usually referred to as the World Pros, in 1973. The championships were held that year in Tokyo, **Japan**. Prize money was awarded in three disciplines: ladies', men's, and **pairs**'. The champions were **Janet Lynn**, **Ronald Robertson**, and the **Protopopovs**. Seven years lapsed before the championships reappeared in Landover, Maryland, and became an annual event. In 1997 they were moved to Washington, D.C., and were held for four additional years. Button's management company, Candid Productions, was purchased by SFX Entertainment in 1999 and subsequently by Clear Channel Communications. The World Pros were last held in 2000.

WORLD SKATING FEDERATION. Following the judging controversy at the 2002 **Olympic Winter Games** in Salt Lake City in which the French judge admitted being pressured by her federation to favor the Russian pair, **Elena Berezhnaya and Anton Sikharulidze** over the Canadian pair **Jamie Salé and David Pelletier**, **International Skating Union** (ISU) president **Ottavio Cinquanta** began promoting an entirely new judging system for figure skating. Cinquanta, a former speed skater, wanted a more objective system. Movement in that direction occurred at the ISU Congress later that spring with the decision to test new ideas during the upcoming skating season. It led to increasing controversy over judging and credibility within the sport. A relatively large group of respected, well-known, and experienced officials, coaches, and skaters, reacting to the actions taken and experiments with a new scoring system tried in the fall of 2002, formed an organization called the World Skating Federation (WSF) which raised funds, adopted a constitution, and announced publicly its existence at the 2003 **World Figure Skating Championships** in Washington, D.C. Its stated purpose was to replace the ISU as the worldwide governing body for figure skating, although the organizers had not yet asked any national associations to join the WSF. A major problem was that the WSF had no established competitions for skaters to enter. Although the WFS's goals were laudable, the probability of success was low. In 2004, the ISU adopted the new **International Judging System**, which replaced the 6.0 and ordinal placement system, a long established tradition. Although some opposition to the new system remains today, the WSF as a corporation has been dissolved.

WÖTZEL, MANDY (1973–) AND STEUER, INGO (1966–) (GER). Pair skaters Mandy Wötzel and Ingo Steuer both competed with other partners before pairing together in 1993, Wötzel with Axel Rauschenbach and Steuer with Ines Müller. In their first year together, Wötzel and Steuer won silver medals at both the European and **World Championships**. The results of the next two years were uneven. In 1994 they placed fifth and fourth at those two competitions but withdrew from the **Olympics**. In 1995, they won gold medals at the **European Championships** but slipped to fifth at the World Championships. For their final three seasons before retirement, they medaled at all competitions entered. In 1996, medals at the European and World Championships were silver. In 1997, a silver medal at the European Championships preceded their world title. Earlier that season they won the title at the **Grand Prix Finals**. In 1998, their only effort was the Olympic Games, where they won the bronze medals. Wötzel and Steuer were featured on **Champions on Ice** tours for several years. *See also* GERMANY.

WREDE, LUDWIG (1894–1965) (AUT). Ludwig Wrede, a competitor for many years, was the Austrian champion once, in 1923, but never a European or world champion. He competed once before World War I, placing fifth at the **European Championships** in 1914. Appearing at four postwar European Championships, he collected two medals, silver in 1924 and bronze in 1929. At the **World Championships** he competed every year from 1923 through 1930, winning one bronze medal in 1929. He placed eighth at the 1928 **Olympic Winter Games**. Wrede was most successful as a pair skater, winning world and Olympic medals with two partners. Five-time Olympic champion **Herma Szabo** was his first partner. Twice the Austrian national champions, they competed at the World Championships three times, 1925–1927, claiming one bronze and two gold medals. Wrede's second partner, also for three years, was **Melitta Brunner**. They won a medal of each color at the Austrian championships, one bronze and two silver medals at the World Championships, and a bronze medal at the Olympic Winter Games in 1928.

WRIGHT, BENJAMIN TAPPAN (1922–) (USA). Benjamin T. Wright has been involved with figure skating since 1931. He is an honorary member and the historian for the **International Skating Union** (ISU), a former member and chair of the ISU figure skating technical committee, and an honorary world championship referee. He is also an honorary member, the historian, and the senior past president of the **United States Figure Skating Association** (USFSA). His two major books are *Skating Around the World, 1892–1992*, written for the centennial of the ISU, and *Skating in America*, written for the 75th anniversary of the USFSA. Numerous articles have appeared in ***Skating* magazine**, including a 10-article series in observance of the 85th anniversary of the magazine in 2008–2009. Wright served as a world judge for many years before becoming a referee and serving at the **World Championships** for 20 consecutive years, 1974–1993, and at the **Olympic Winter Games** for five consecutive holdings, 1976–1992. He was elected to the **World Figure Skating Hall of Fame** in 1997. Wright was married for more than 50 years to the late Mary Louise Premer, a 1941 **fours** champion and herself a championship judge who officiated at numerous national, North American, European, world, and Olympic championships.

WYLIE, PAUL STANTON (1964–) (USA). Paul Wylie became both the United States and the world junior champion in 1981. Eleven years later, he ended his amateur career as the Olympic silver medalist at the Albertville Games in 1992. Wylie never won a national or a world title at the senior level, but he developed into one of the most artistic skaters of his generation. He is also one of few elite level skaters who completed college while competing. As a professional he has competed in competitions and appeared in many shows. Wylie also worked as a commentator for NBC and now teaches skating.

YAGUDIN, ALEXEI (1980–) (RUS). Alexei Yagudin is considered one of the more artistic men to have competed in recent years. He began skating at age four and won the world junior title in 1996 at age 15. Yagudin proceeded to win European titles in 1998, 1999, and 2002 and world titles in 1998, 1999, 2000, and 2002, as well as an Olympic gold medal in 2002. He won all but one of the Grand Prix events at least once and the **Grand Prix Finals** in 1999 and 2002. During the later part of his competitive career, Yagudin was coached in the **United States** by **Tatiana Tarasova**. A strong rivalry existed between Yagudin and his countryman, **Evgeny Plushenko**. The two of them dominated men's skating at the turn of the century. Upon retirement, Yagudin joined the **Stars on Ice** tour. *See also* RUSSIA.

YAMAGUCHI, KRISTINE T. (1971–) (USA). Kristi Yamaguchi was one of the **United States**' most popular skaters during a relatively short eligible career, but her popularity soared even more as a professional. She won the world junior ladies' title in 1988. As a senior at the United States Championships, she placed second three times before winning the national title in 1992. In 1990, she won **Skate America**, and during her final two competitive years, 1991 and 1992, she won two world titles as well as the Olympic title in Albertville. Yamaguchi was one of three talented U.S. ladies who competed against each other in the early 1990s. At the national championships in 1991, **Tonya Harding** defeated Yamaguchi, the only time she did so, by skating a clean program which included the first triple **Axel Paulsen jump** done by an American lady. At the **World Championships**, their order was reversed. **Nancy Kerrigan** was the bronze medalist, and she completed a U.S. sweep of the medals, the only time that has been accomplished in ladies' competition. Early in her career, Yamaguchi competed in pairs with Rudy Galindo. They were the world junior champions in 1988 and the national senior champions in 1989 and 1990. Upon turning professional, Yamaguchi joined the **Stars on Ice** cast and skated in competitions as well. She was also a winner on the popular television program, "Dancing with the Stars." Yamaguchi was inducted into the **World Figure Skating Hall of Fame** in 1998.

YATES, ERNEST H. C. *See* DENCH, ROBERT.

Z

ZAGORODNIUK, VIACHESLAV (1972–) (UKR). Viacheslav Zagorodniuk competed first as a Soviet skater, then for one year, in 1992, under the banner of the **Commonwealth of Independent States** (CIS), and ended his career representing his native country, **Ukraine**. He won the world junior title in 1989 and the following year placed third at the **European Championships**. During his 10-year international career, 1989–1998, he collected four bronze, one silver, and in 1996 a gold medal at the European Championships. Zagorodniuk's only medal at the **World Championships** was bronze in 1994. His best Olympic result was eighth in 1992.

ZAITSEV, ALEXANDR. *See* RODNINA, IRINA.

ZAMBONI, FRANK J. (1901–1988). Frank Zamboni was an ice rink owner in southern California. He sought an efficient method to resurface the ice. At that time, ice was resurfaced by pulling a metal plane across the ice, spraying water on it, and finishing the process with a squeegee to remove excess water, a process typically taking about an hour. Beginning in 1942, Zamboni experimented with a motorized machine that seven years later replaced the crew of men required to resurface the ice. The process now done mechanically took fewer than 15 minutes and could be done multiple times daily. Zamboni then formed a company which manufactures and sells the machines. Although other manufacturers now produce similar machines, skaters and skating fans usually refer to all ice resurfacing machines as "Zambonis" regardless of the manufacturer. Frank Zamboni was honored with election to the **World Figure Skating Hall of Fame** in 2005.

ZAYAK, ELAINE KATHRYN (1965–) (USA). In 1979, at age 13, Elaine Zayak won gold medals at both the United States and the **World Junior Championships**. Her rise to the top ranks of skating was rapid. In 1981 she won the silver medal at the **World Championships** and a year later the world title, becoming the first lady to win both the junior and the senior title. She retired in 1984 at age 19 after a relatively short competitive career, but 10 years later for the Olympic year in 1994, the always tenacious Zayak reinstated and entered the United States Championships where she placed a remarkable fourth. Zayak is remembered for her athleticism. At a time when most ladies did no more than two triple **jumps**, Zayak included as many as six. She repeated jumps in her programs, which was allowed at that time, but it led the **International Skating Union** to adopt a rule that allows the repetition of jumps only in combination. The rule is often referred to as the "Zayak rule." Following her first retirement in 1984, Zayak joined the **Stars on Ice** tour.

ZAYAK RULE. *See* ZAYAK, ELAINE KATHRYN.

ZEEBROECK, ROBERT VAN. *See* BELGIUM.

ZENGER, KARL. *See* BROWNE, GEORGE HENRY.

ZHANG, DAN (1985–) AND ZHANG, HAO (1984–) (CHN). Dan Zhang and Hao Zhang share the same family name, but they are not related. They won the world junior pair title in 2003. Zhang and Zhang are the third of three Chinese pairs who have become dominant competitors internationally in the 21st century. **Xue Shen and Hongbo Zhao** first entered the **World Championships** in 1994 and were still competing in 2010. They won titles in 2002, 2003, and 2007. **Qing Pang and Jian Tong** first competed in 1999 and won the world title in 2010. Zhang and Zhang first competed in 2002. They won silver medals behind Pang and Tong in 2006 and behind **Aliona Savchenko and Robin Szolkowy** of **Germany** in 2008 and 2009. Zhang and Zhang won Four Continents titles in 2005 and 2010. Competing at three **Olympic Winter Games**, they placed 11th in 2002, second in 2006, and fifth in 2010. They have won several **Grand Prix** events and qualified for the **Grand Prix Finals** twice, 2008 and 2009, winning silver medals both times. *See also* CHINA.

ZHANG, HAO. *See* ZHANG, DAN AND ZHANG, HAO.

ZHAO, HONGBO. *See* SHEN, XUE AND ZHAO, HONGBO.

ZHARKOVA, ELENA. *See* LINICHUK, NATALIA AND KARPONOSOV, GENNADI.

ZHUK, NINA. *See* BAKUSHEVA, NINA AND ZHUK, STANISLAV.

ZHUK, STANISLAV. *See* BAKUSHEVA, NINA AND ZHUK, STANISLAV.

ZHUK, TATIANA (1946–) (URS). Tatiana Zhuk and her two partners, Alexandr Gavrilov (1943–) and Alexandr Gorelik (1945–) were coached by Tatiana's older brother, **Stanislav Zhuk**. In 1963, their first year on the international scene, Zhuk and Gavrilov won bronze medals at both the European and **World Championships**. In 1964, they again won bronze medals at the **European Championships** but slipped to sixth at the World Championships and placed fifth at the **Olympic Winter Games**. Zhuk then changed partners and with Gorelik repeated the results of two years earlier, winning bronze medals at the European and World Championships in 1965. A year later, the medals were silver. They did not compete internationally in 1967, but in the Olympic year, 1968, their two final efforts resulted in silver medals at the World Championships and the Olympic Winter Games.

ZHULIN, ALEXANDR. *See* USOVA, MAIA AND ZHULIN, ALEXANDR.

ZILLY, FRANZ. *See* GERMANY.

ZIMMERMAN, JOHN. *See* INA, KYOKO.

ZMIEVSKAYA, GALINA. *See* PETRENKO, VIKTOR.

ZÖLLER, GÜNTER. *See* MÜLLER, JUTTA.

ZWACK, KARL. *See* PAPEZ, IDI AND ZWACK, KARL.

Appendix A
ISU Members

Andorra	Federacio Andorrana Desports de Gel
Argentina	Federación Argentina de Patinaje Sobre Hielo
Armenia	Armenia Skating Federation
Australia	Ice Skating Australia Incorporated
Austria	Osterreichischer Eiskunstlauf Verband
Azerbaijan	The Skating Federation of Azerbaijan Republic
Belarus	Skating Federation of Belarus
Belgium	Federation Royale Belge de Patinage Artistique
Bosnia Herzegovina	Skating Federation of Bosnia and Herzegovina
Brazil	Brazilian Ice Sports Federation
Bulgaria	Bulgarian Skating Federation
Canada	Skate Canada
China	Chinese Skating Association
Chinese Taipei	Chinese Taipei Skating Union
Croatia	Croatian Skating Federation
Czech Republic	Czech Figure Skating Association
Denmark	Dansk Skøjte-Union
DPR Korea	Skating Association of the Democratic People's Republic of Korea
Estonia	The Estonian Skating Union
Finland	Suomen Taitoluistelulitto
France	Fédération Française des Sports de Glace
Georgia	Georgian Figure Skating Association
Germany	Deutsche Eislauf-Verband, e.V.
Great Britain	National Ice Skating Association of United Kingdom, Ltd.
Greece	Hellenic Ice Sports Federation
Hong Kong	Hong Kong Skating Union
Hungary	Hungarian National Skating Federation
Iceland	Icelandic Skating Association
India	Ice Skating Association of India
Ireland	Ice Skating Association of Ireland

Israel	Israel Ice Skating Federation
Italy	Federazione Italiana Sport del Ghiaccio
Japan	Japan Skating Federation
Kazakhstan	Kazakhstan Skating Federation
Latvia	The Latvian Skating Association
Lithuania	Lithuanian Skating Federation
Luxembourg	Union Luxembourgeoise de Patinage
Mexico	Federación Mexicana de Patinaje de Deportes de Invierno
Monaco	Federation Monegasque de Patinage
Mongolia	Skating Union of Mongolia
Montenegro	Skating Association of Montenegro
Netherlands	Koninklijke Nederlandsche Schaatsenrijders
New Zealand	New Zealand Ice Skating Association, Inc.
Norway	Norges Skøyteforbund
Philippines	Philippine Skating Union
Poland	Polish Figure Skating Association
Puerto Rico	Puerto Rico Skating Federation
Republic of Korea	Korea Skating Union
Romania	Romanian Skating Federation
Russia	The Figure Skating Federation of Russia
Singapore	Singapore Ice Skating Association
Serbia	Association of Skating Sports Serbia
Slovakia	Slovak Figure Skating Association
Slovenia	Slovene Skating Union
South Africa	South African Skating Federation
Spain	Federación Española de Deportes de Hielo
Sweden	Svenska Konstakningsförbundet
Sweden*	Stockholms Allmänna Skridskoklubb
Switzerland	Schweizer Eislauf-Verband
Switzerland*	Internationaler Shlittschuh-Club Davos
Thailand	Figure and Speed Skating Association of Thailand
Turkey	Turkish Ice Skating Federation
Ukraine	Ukranian Figure Skating Association
United States	U.S. Figure Skating
Uzbekistan	Figure Skating Federation of the Republic of Uzbekistan

*Club membership

Appendix B
ISU Officeholders

Entries for all presidents of the International Skating Union (ISU) are included in the dictionary section of this volume. Most of them served in other offices prior to becoming president. Former competitive skaters often remain active in their sport after their competitive years. A few of them have become ISU officeholders, and that service is noted in their dictionary entries. This appendix includes the most important elected offices. Owing to space limitations, elected and appointed secretaries, elected members of a few recently established committees and commissions, and appointed members to some elected committees have not been included. Officers whose exemplary service over many years have led the ISU to elect them after retirement to honorary positions are included. Prior to the ISU Congress in 1947, vice presidents served both sports regulated by the ISU, figure skating and speed skating. Beginning with the elections that year, separate vice presidents were elected for each sport. At the congress in 1949, the same procedure was implemented for council members. After those dates, only vice presidents and council members for figure skating are included in this appendix. The technical committees for singles and pair skating, ice dancing, and synchronized skating are permanent committees with the responsibility for recommending to the full council rules and procedures for their specific disciplines. Substitute committee members, a classification that no longer exists, are persons elected to those committees who vote only when full members are absent.

Presidents

Willem J. H. Mulier, NED	1892–1895
Viktor G. Balck, SWE	1895–1925
Ulrich Salchow, SWE	1925–1937
Gerrit W. A. van Laer, NED	1937–1945
Herbert J. Clarke, GBR	1945–1953
James Koch, SUI	1953–1967
Ernst Labin, AUT	1967
Jacques Favart, FRA	1967–1980

Olaf Poulsen, NOR	1980–1994
Ottavio Cinquanta, ITA	1994-

Vice Presidents

Emerich von Szent-Györgyi, HUN	1921–1925
Gerrit W. A. van Laer, NED	1925–1927, 1935–1937
Herbert J. Clarke, GBR	1927–1935, 1937–1945
Hans Valär, SUI	1945–1946
Ladislav Fürst, CZR	1946–1947

Vice Presidents for Figure Skating

Ladislav Fürst, CZR	1947–1949
Gustavus F. C. Witt, NED	1949–1953
James Koch, SUI	1953
Marcel Nicaise, BEL	1953–1957
Friedrich Kachler, AUT	1957–1959
Jacques Favart, FRA	1959–1967
John R. Shoemaker, USA	1967–1980
Hermann Schiechtl, FRG	1980–1984
Joseph Dědič, CZE	1984–1993
Lawrence Demmy, GBR	1993–1998
Katsuichiro Hisanaga, JPN	1998–2002
David M. Dore, CAN	2002–

Council Members

A. E. Barnaart, NED	1895–1900
Emerich von Szent-Györgyi, HUN	1895–1907, 1911–1921
Alfred Schulz, GER	1901–1903
Karl Fillunger, AUT	1903–1907
G. Herbert Fowler, GBR	1907–1913, 1921–1925
Otto Schwarz, GER	1907–1911
Hans Valär, SUI	1913–1921, 1925–1929, 1939–1945
Jan A. Schutter, NED	1921–1925
Herbert J. Clarke, GBR	1925–1927, 1935–1937
Yngvar Bryn, NOR	1925–1927
René Japiot, FRA	1927–1935
Gerrit W. A. van Laer, NED	1927–1931
Hermann Kleeberg, GER	1929–1939

Walter Jakobsson, FIN	1931–1937, 1939–1947
Hans Pfeiffer, AUT	1933–1935, 1937–1939
Gerhard Karlsen, NOR	1933–1939, 1946–1947
Ladislav Fürst, CZR	1935–1947
Jenö Minich, HUN	1937–1946
Max Hönicke, GER	1939–1946
August Anderberg, SWE	1946–1949
Walter S. Powell, USA	1947–1949
Cornelius P. Eecen, NED	1947–1949
Ossian Blomqvist, FIN	1947–1949
Walter S. Powell, USA	1949–1961
Marcel Nicaise, BEL	1949–1953, 1957–1959
Friedrich Kachler, AUT	1955–1957
Kenneth M. Beaumont, GBR	1959–1963
Henry M. Beatty, USA	1961–1967
Ernst Labin, AUT	1963–1967
Elemér Terták, HUN	1963–1988
John R. Shoemaker, USA	1967
Josef Dědič, CZE	1967–1984
Hermann Schiechtl, FRG	1967–1980
Donald H. Gilchrist, CAN	1980–1992
Lawrence Demmy, GBR	1984–1993
Sonia Bianchetti, ITA	1988–1992
Jürg Wilhelm, SUI	1992–1998
Charles A. DeMore, USA	1992–1994
Joyce Hisey, CAN	1992–2002
Katsuichiro Hisanaga, JAP	1994–1998
Claire W. Ferguson, USA	1994–2002
Didier Gaihaguet, FRA	1998–2002
Tjaša Andrée-Prosenc, SLO	1998–
Courtney J. L. Jones, GBR	2002–2010
Phyllis F. Howard, USA	2002–
Marie Lundmark, FIN	2002–
Junko Hiramatsu, JPN	2010–

Substitute Council Members

Hans D. A. Fabricius, NED	1895–1897
Ary Prims, GER/AUT	1895–1897
V. P. Sreznevsky, RUS	1897–1899, 1903–1905
Karl Fillunger, AUT	1897–1899, 1901–1903

William F. Adams, GBR	1899–1903
Alfred Schulz, GER	1899–1901
G. Herbert Fowler, GBR	1903–1907
Otto Schwarz, GER	1905–1907
F. J. Backer, NED	1907–1921
Hans Valär, SUI	1907–1913, 1921–1925, 1935–1939
Ludwig A. Thue, NOR	1913–1921
Andreas Claussen, NOR	1921–1925
René Japiot, FRA	1925–1927
Jenö Minich, HUN	1925–1927
Hans Pfeiffer, AUT	1927–1933, 1935–1937
Walter Jakobsson, FIN	1927–1929, 1937–1939
Bjarne Frang, NOR	1929–1931
Gerrit W. A. van Laer, NED	1931–1935
Ladislav Fürst, CZR	1933–1935
Gerhard Karlsen, NOR	1939–1946
August Anderberg, SWE	1939–1946
Alfred Winkler, SUI	1947–1949
Marcel Nicaise, BEL	1947–1949
Georges Torchon, FRA	1949–1955
Friedrich Kachler, AUT	1949–1955
Vladislav čáp, CZE	1955–1957
Kenneth M. Beaumont, GBR	1955–1959
Elemér Terták, HUN	1957–1959
Ernst Labin, AUT	1959–1963
Per Cock-Clausen, DEN	1959–1967
Hermann Schiechtl, FRG	1967
Leonard C. Seagrave, GBR	1969–1973
Oskar Madl, AUT	1973–1980
Charles A. De More, USA	1980–1992

Figure Skating Technical Committee Chairpersons

Herbert J. Clarke, GBR	1931–1937
Kurt Dannenberg, GER	1937–c.1945
Gustavus F. C. Witt, NED	1946–1949
Kenneth M. Beaumont, GBR	1949–1953
Werner Rittberger, FRG	1953–1955
Jakob Biedermann, SUI	1955–1956
Adolf Rosdol, AUT	1956–1957
Jacques Favart, FRA	1957–1959

Josef Dědič, CZE	1959–1967
Karl Enderlin, SUI	1967–1973
Sonia Bianchetti, ITA	1973–1988
Benjamin T. Wright, USA	1988–1992
Sally-Anne Stapleford, GBR	1992–2002
Alexander Lakernik, RUS	2002–

Figure Skating Technical Committee Members

Kurt Dannenberg, GER	1931–1937
Jenö Minich, HUN	1931–1937
Friedrich Kachler, AUT	1937–1939
Alois Sliva, CZR	1937–1947
August Anderberg, SWE	1939–1947
Walter Jakobsson, FIN	1947–1949
Vladimír Koudelka, CZR	1947–1949
Per Cock-Clausen, DEN	1949–1951
James Koch, SUI	1949–1963
Elemér Terták, HUN	1951–1953
Adolf Rosdol, AUT	1953–1956
Jakob Biedermann, SUI	1953–1955
Jacques Favart, FRA	1955–1957
Josef Dědič, CZE	1957–1959
Rudolf A. Marx, FRG	1957–1963
Karl Enderlin, SUI	1959–1967
Alexander D. C. Gordon, GBR	1963–1969
Sonia Bianchetti, ITA	1967–1973
Donald H. Gilchrist, CAN	1969–1971, 1973–1980
Oskar Madl, AUT	1971–1973
Benjamin T. Wright, USA	1973–1988
H. George Marsh, GBR	1975–1977
Valentin Piseev, URS	1977–1986
Martin Felsenreich, AUT	1980–1984
Jürg Wilhelm, SUI	1984–1992
Walburga Grimm, GDR	1984–2002
Tjaša Andrée Prosene, YUG	1986–1988
Britta Lindgren, SWE	1988–2002
Sally-Anne Stapleford, GBR	1988–1992
Katsuichiro Hisanaga, JAP	1992–1994
Hely Abbondati, FIN	1992–1994
Alexander Lakernik, RUS	1994–2002

Ronald T. Pfenning, USA	1994–2003
Junko Hiramatsu, JPN	2002–2010
Fabio Bianchetti, ITA	2002–
Vladislav Petukhov, UKR	2002–2006
Felicitas Babusikova, SVK	2004–2010
Rita Zonnekeyn, BEL	2006–
Susan Lynch, AUS	2010–

Figure Skating Technical Committee Substitute Members

Werner Rittberger, FRG	1955–1957
Mario Verdi, ITA	1957–1959
Alexander D. C. Gordon, GBR	1959–1963
Rudolf A. Marx, FRG	1963–1967
Donald H. Gilchrist, CAN	1953–1955, 1967–1969, 1971–1973
Oskar Madi, AUT	1969–1971
H. George Marsh, GBR	1973–1975

Ice Dancing Technical Committee Chairpersons

Marcel Nicaise, BEL	1949–1953
Reginald J. Wilkie, GBR	1953–1962
Henri Meudek, FRA	1962–1969
Lawrence Demmy, GBR	1969–1984
Hans Kutschera, AUT	1984–1996
Wolfgang Kunz, GER	1996–1998
Alexandr Gorshkov, RUS	1998–2010
Halina Gordon-Poltorak, POL	2010–

Ice Dancing Technical Committee Members

Reginald J. Wilkie, GBR	1949–1953
William O. Hickock, IV, USA	1949–1951, 1953–1957
Adolf Rosdol, AUT	1951–1953
Henri Meudec, FRA	1953–1962
F. Ritter Shumway, USA	1957–1959
Harold Hartshorne, USA	1959–1961
Hermann Schiechtl, FRG	1961–1967
H. Kendall Kelley, USA	1963–1967
Emil Skákala, CZE	1965–1980
Lawrence Demmy, GBR	1967–1969

Hans Kutschera, AUT	1969–1984
George J. Blundun, CAN	1975–1980
Wolfgang Kunz, FRG	1980–1996
Roland Wehinger, SUI	1980–1988
Alexandr Gorshkov, URS	1984–1998
Joyce Hisey, CAN	1984–1992
Pál Vásárhelyi, HUN	1988–1992
Courtney J. L. Jones, GBR	1992–1994, 1996–2002
Ann Shaw, CAN	1992–2006
Ludmila Mikhailovsklaya, UKR	1994–2006
Olga Gilardini, ITA	1998–2010
Halina Gordon-Poltorak, POL	2002–2010
Robert J. Horen, USA	2006–
Gilles Vandenbroeck, FRA	2010–
Alla Shekhovtseva, RUS	2010–

Ice Dancing Technical Committee Substitute Members

Elemér Terták, HUN	1955–1957
Hermann Schiechtl, FRG	1957–1961
H. Kendall Kelley, USA	1961–1963
Leonard C. Seagrave, GBR	1963–1965
Lawrence Demmy, GBR	1965–1967
Hans Kutschera, AUT	1967–1971
Henri Meudec, FRA	1969–1971
George J. Blundun, CAN	1971–1975

Synchronized Skating Technical Committee Chairpersons

Patricia S. French, USA	1994–1998
Marie Lundmark, FIN	1998–2002
Leon Lurje, SWE	2002–2006
Ulrich Linder, SUI	2006–2010
Christopher Buchanan, GBR	2010–

Synchronized Skating Technical Committee Members

Marie Lundmark, FIN	1994–1998
J. Douglas Steele, CAN	1994–1998
Monique Georgelin, FRA	1998–2002
Ulrich Linder, SUI	1998–2006

Patricia French, USA	1998–2002
Leon Lurje, SWE	1998–2002
Helen Volgusher, GBR	2002–2010
Joanne Shaw, CAN	2002–2010
Karen Wolanchuk, USA	2006–
Mika Saarelainen, FIN	2010–
Philippe Maitrot, FRA	2010–

Honorary Presidents

Viktor G. Balck, SWE	1925
Emerich von Szent-Györgyi, HUN	1933
Herbert J. Clarke, GBR	1955
James Koch, SUI	1967
Jacques Favart, FRA	1982
Olaf Poulsen, NOR	1994

Honorary Vice Presidents

Sven Laftman, SWE	1971
Hendrik Roos, NED	1977
John R. Shoemaker, USA	1980
Hermann Schiechtl, FRG	1984
Georg Petterson, SWE	1986
Jean Heckly, FRA	1992
Josef Dědič, CZE	1994
Lawrence Demmy, GBR	1998
Gerhard Zimmermann, GER	2010

Honorary Secretary

Georg Häsler, SUI	1975

Honorary Members

Hans Pfeiffer, AUT	1939
Gustavus F. C. Witt, NED	1953
Marcel Nicaise, BEL	1959
Friedrich Kachler, AUT	1959
Walter S. Powell, USA	1961
Reginald J. Wilkie, GBR	1963

Georg Krog, NOR	1969
Ernst Labin, AUT	1969
Harald Halvorsen, NOR	1969
Ernest J. G. Matthews, GBR	1977
Heinz Dragunsky, GDR	1980
Oskar Madl, AUT	1980
George J. Blundun, CAN	1980
Emil Skàkala, CZE	1980
Viktor Kapitonov, URS	1984
Arne Kvaalen, NOR	1984
Icilio Perucca, ITA	1988
Elemér Tertàk, HUN	1988
Donald H. Gilchrist, CAN	1992
Herman J. van Laer, NED	1992
Benjamin T. Wright, USA	1992
John Hurdis, CAN	1992
Charles A. DeMore, USA	1994
Hans Kutschera, AUT	1996
Jean Grenier, CAN	1996
Jürg-Christian Wilhelm, SUI	1998
Lars-Olof Eklund, SWE	1998
Jan W. P. Charisius, NED	1998
Wolfgang Kunz, GER	1998
Joyce Hisey, CAN	2002
Walburga Grimm, GER	2002
John Hall, GBR	2002
Maria Bialous-Zuchowicz, POL	2006
Claire Ferguson, USA	2006
Monique Georgelin, FRA	2006
Courtney J. L. Jones, GBR	2010
Myong-Hi Chang, KOR	2010
James L. Hawkins, USA	2010
Gerhardt Bubnik, CZE	2010
Ulf Linden, SWE	2010

Appendix C

Members: World Figure Skating Hall of Fame

1976

Tenley Albright USA
Andrée Joly and Pierre Brunet FRA
Richard Button USA
Peggy Fleming USA
Gillis Grafström SWE
Carol Heiss USA
Sonja Henie NOR
David Jenkins USA
Hayes Jenkins USA
Thomas Dow Richardson GBR
Jacques Gerschwiler SUI
Jackson Haines USA
Gustave Lussi SUI
Axel Paulsen NOR
Ulrich Salchow SWE
Karl Schäfer AUT
Reginald Wilkie GBR
Howard Nicholson USA
Edi Scholdan AUT
Montgomery Wilson CAN

1977

Wilhelm Böckl AUT
Jean Westwood and Lawrence Demmy GBR
Donald Jackson CAN

1978

Liudmila Belousova and Oleg Protopopov URS

1979

Maxi Herber and Ernst Baier GER
Barbara Ann Scott CAN

1980

Cecilia Colledge GBR
Barbara Wagner and Robert Paul CAN

1981

Madeleine Cave Syers GBR
Willie Frick GER
William Hickok IV USA

1982

Herma Szabo AUT

1983

None

1984

Louis Rubenstein CAN
Werner Groebli SUI
Frances Dafoe and Norris Bowden CAN

1985

Charlotte Oelschlagel GER
Arnold Gerschwiler SUI

1986

F. Ritter Shumway USA
Courtney J. L. Jones GBR

1987

None

1988

Liudmila Pakhomova and Alexandr Gorshkov URS

1989

Irina Rodnina URS
Jayne Torvill and Christopher Dean GBR

1990

Scott Hamilton USA

1991

John Curry GBR

1992

None

1993

Jeannette Altwegg GBR
Richard Dwyer USA
Ria Baran and Paul Falk GER
Jacques Favart FRA
Georg Häsler SUI
Ronald Robertson USA
Diane Towler and Bernard Ford GBR

1994

James Koch SUI

1995

Ekaterina Gordeeva and Sergei Grinkov URS
William Thayer Tutt USA
Katarina Witt GDR

1996

Brian Boitano USA

Herbert J. Clarke GBR
Sheldon Galbraith CAN

1997

Carlo Fassi ITA
Lily Kronberger HUN
Benjamin T. Wright USA

1998

Tom Collins CAN
Josef Dědič CZE
Felix Kaspar AUT
Kristi Yamaguchi USA

1999

Ronald Ludington USA
Gladys Hogg GBR

2000

Dorothy Hamill USA
Marina Klimova and Sergei Ponomarenko URS
John Nicks GBR

2001

Janet Lynn USA

2002

Maribel Vinson Owen USA

2003

Midori Ito JPN
Toller Cranston CAN
Jutta Müller GDR

2004

Tamara Moskvina URS

Donald Gilchrist CAN
Robin Cousins GBR

2005

Kurt Browning CAN
Frank Zamboni USA

2006

None

2007

Frank Carroll USA

2008

Tatiana Tarasova URS

2009

Alena Vrzáňová CZE
Brian Orser CAN
Barbara Underhill and Paul Martini CAN
Joyce Hisey CAN
Willy Bietak AUT
Nikolai Panin RUS

2010

Nobuo Sato JPN

Appendix D
Medalists at the World Figure Skating Championships

Ladies

Year	Location	Gold	Silver	Bronze
1906	Davos SUI	Madge Syers GBR	Jenny Herz AUT	Lily Kronberger HUN
1907	Vienna AUT	Madge Syers GBR	Jenny Herz AUT	Lily Kronberger HUN
1908	Troppau CZE	Lily Kronberger HUN	Elsa Rendschmidt GER	
1909	Budapest HUN	Lily Kronberger HUN		
1910	Berlin GER	Lily Kronberger HUN	Elsa Rendschmidt GER	
1911	Vienna AUT	Lily Kronberger HUN	Opika von Méray Horváth HUN	Ludowika Eilers GER
1912	Davos SUI	Opika von Méray Horváth HUN	Dorothy Greenhough-Smith GBR	Phyllis Johnson GBR
1913	Stockholm SWE	Opika von Méray Horváth HUN	Phyllis Johnson GBR	Svea Norén SWE
1914	St. Moritz SUI	Opika von Méray Horváth HUN	Angela Hanka AUT	Phyllis Johnson GBR
1915–1921	The World Championships were not held.			
1922	Stockholm, SWE	Herma Szabo AUT	Svea Norén SWE	Margot Moe NOR
1923	Vienna AUT	Herma Szabo AUT	Gisela Reichmann AUT	Svea Norén SWE
1924	Oslo NOR	Herma Szabo AUT	Ellen Brockhöfft GER	Beatrix Loughran USA
1925	Davos SUI	Herma Szabo AUT	Ellen Brockhöfft GER	Elisabeth Böckel GER
1926	Stockholm SWE	Herma Szabo AUT	Sonja Henie NOR	Kathleen Shaw GBR
1927	Oslo NOR	Sonja Henie NOR	Herma Szabo AUT	Karen Simensen NOR
1928	London GBR	Sonja Henie NOR	Maribel Vinson USA	Fritzi Burger AUT
1929	Budapest HUN	Sonja Henie NOR	Fritzi Burger AUT	Melitta Brunner AUT
1930	New York USA	Sonja Henie NOR	Cecil Smith CAN	Maribel Vinson USA
1931	Berlin GER	Sonja Henie NOR	Hilde Holovsky AUT	Fritzi Burger AUT
1932	Montreal CAN	Sonja Henie NOR	Fritzi Burger AUT	Constance Samuel CAN
1933	Stockholm SWE	Sonja Henie NOR	Vivi-Anne Hultén SWE	Hilde Holovsky AUT
1934	Oslo NOR	Sonja Henie NOR	Megan Taylor GBR	Liselotte Landbeck AUT

Year	Location	Gold	Silver	Bronze
1935	Vienna AUT	Sonja Henie NOR	Cecilia Colledge GBR	Vivi-Anne Hultén SWE
1936	Paris FRA	Sonja Henie NOR	Megan Taylor GBR	Vivi-Anne Hultén SWE
1937	London GBR	Cecilia Colledge GBR	Megan Taylor GBR	Vivi-Anne Hultén SWE
1938	Stockholm SWE	Megan Taylor GBR	Cecilia Colledge GBR	Hedy Stenuf USA
1939	Prague CZE	Megan Taylor GBR	Hedy Stenuf USA	Daphne Walker GBR
1940–1946	The World Championships were not held.			
1947	Stockholm SWE	Barbara Ann Scott CAN	Daphne Walker GBR	Gretchen Merrill USA
1948	Davos SW	Barbara Ann Scott CAN	Eva Pawlik AUT	Jirina Nekolová CZE
1949	Paris FRA	Alena Vrzáňová CZE	Yvonne Sherman USA	Jeannette Altwegg GBR
1950	London GBR	Alena Vrzáňová CZE	Jeannette Altwegg GBR	Yvonne Sherman USA
1951	Milan ITA	Jeannette Altwegg GBR	Jacqueline du Bief FRA	Sonya Klopfer USA
1952	Paris FRA	Jacqueline du Bief FRA	Sonya Klopfer USA	Virginia Baxter USA
1953	Davos, SUI	Tenley Albright USA	Gundi Busch GER	Valda Osborn GBR
1954	Oslo NOR	Gundi Busch GER	Tenley Albright USA	Erica Batchelor GBR
1955	Vienna AUT	Tenley Albright USA	Carol Heiss USA	Hanna Eigel AUT
1956	Garmisch-Partenkirchen FRG	Carol Heiss USA	Tenley Albright USA	Ingrid Wendl AUT
1957	Colorado Springs USA	Carol Heiss USA	Hanna Eigel AUT	Ingrid Wendl AUT
1958	Paris FRA	Carol Heiss USA	Ingrid Wendl AUT	Hanna Walter AUT
1959	Colorado Springs USA	Carol Heiss USA	Hanna Walter AUT	Sjoukje Dijkstra NED
1960	Vancouver CAN	Carol Heiss USA	Sjoukje Dijkstra NED	Barbara Roles USA
1961	The World Championships were not held.			
1962	Prague CZE	Sjoukje Dijkstra NED	Wendy Griner CAN	Regine Heitzer AUT
1963	Cortina ITA	Sjoukje Dijkstra NED	Regine Heitzer AUT	Nicole Hassler FRA

Year	Location	Gold	Silver	Bronze
1964	Dortmund FRG	Sjoukje Dijkstra NED	Regine Heitzer AUT	Petra Burka CAN
1965	Colorado Springs USA	Petra Burka CAN	Regine Heitzer AUT	Peggy Fleming USA
1966	Davos SUI	Peggy Fleming USA	Gabriele Seyfert GDR	Petra Burka CAN
1967	Vienna AUT	Peggy Fleming USA	Gabriele Seyfert GDR	Hana Mašková CZE
1968	Geneva SUI	Peggy Fleming USA	Gabriele Seyfert GDR	Hana Mašková CZE
1969	Colorado Springs USA	Gabriele Seyfert GDR	Beatrix Schuba AUT	Zsuzsa Almássy HUN
1970	Ljubljana YUG	Gabriele Seyfert GDR	Beatrix Schuba AUT	Julie Lynn Holmes USA
1971	Lyon FRA	Beatrix Schuba AUT	Julie Lynn Holmes USA	Karen Magnussen CAN
1972	Calgary, Alberta CAN	Beatrix Schuba AUT	Karen Magnussen CAN	Janet Lynn USA
1973	Bratislava CZE	Karen Magnussen CAN	Janet Lynn USA	Christine Errath GDR
1974	Munich FRG	Christine Errath GDR	Dorothy Hamill USA	Dianne de Leeuw NED
1975	Colorado Springs USA	Dianne de Leeuw NED	Dorothy Hamill USA	Christine Errath GDR
1976	Gothenburg SWE	Dorothy Hamill USA	Christine Errath GDR	Dianne de Leeuw NED
1977	Tokyo JPN	Linda Fratianne USA	Anett Pötzsch GDR	Dagmar Lurz FRG
1978	Ottawa CAN	Anett Pötzsch GDR	Linda Fratianne USA	Susanna Driano ITA
1979	Vienna AUT	Linda Fratianne USA	Anett Pötzsch GDR	Emi Watanabe JPN
1980	Dortmund FRG	Anett Pötzsch GDR	Dagmar Lurz FRG	Linda Fratianne USA
1981	Hartford USA	Denise Biellmann SUI	Elaine Zayak USA	Claudia Kristofics-Binder AUT
1982	Copenhagen DEN	Elaine Zayak USA	Katarina Witt GDR	Claudia Kristofics-Binder AUT
1983	Helsinki FIN	Rosalynn Sumners USA	Claudia Leistner FRG	Elena Vodorezova URS
1984	Ottawa CAN	Katarina Witt GDR	Anna Kondrashova URS	Elaine Zayak USA
1985	Tokyo JPN	Katarina Witt GDR	Kira Ivanova URS	Tiffany Chin USA
1986	Geneva SUI	Debra Thomas USA	Katarina Witt GDR	Tiffany Chin USA

Year	Location	Gold	Silver	Bronze
1987	Cincinnati USA	Katarina Witt GDR	Debra Thomas USA	Caryn Kadavy USA
1988	Budapest HUN	Katarina Witt GDR	Elizabeth Manley CAN	Debra Thomas USA
1989	Paris FRA	Midori Ito JPN	Claudia Leistner FRG	Jill Trenary USA
1990	Halifax CAN	Jill Trenary USA	Midori Ito JPN	Holly Cook USA
1991	Munich GER	Kristi Yamaguchi USA	Tonya Harding USA	Nancy Kerrigan USA
1992	Oakland USA	Kristi Yamaguchi USA	Nancy Kerrigan USA	Lu Chen CHN
1993	Prague CZE	Oksana Baiul UKR	Surya Bonaly FRA	Lu Chen CHN
1994	Chiba JPN	Yuka Sato JPN	Surya Bonaly FRA	Tanja Szewczenko GER
1995	Birmingham GBR	Lu Chen CHN	Surya Bonaly FRA	Nicole Bobek USA
1996	Edmonton CAN	Michelle Kwan USA	Lu Chen CHN	Irina Slutskaya RUS
1997	Lausanne SUI	Tara Lipinski USA	Michelle Kwan USA	Vanessa Gusmeroli FRA
1998	Minneapolis USA	Michelle Kwan USA	Irina Slutskaya RUS	Maria Butyrskaya RUS
1999	Helsinki FIN	Maria Butyrskaya RUS	Michelle Kwan USA	Julia Soldatova RUS
2000	Nice FRA	Michelle Kwan USA	Irina Slutskaya USA	Maria Butyrskaya RUS
2001	Vancouver CAN	Michelle Kwan USA	Irina Slutskaya RUS	Sarah Hughes USA
2002	Nagano JPN	Irina Slutskaya RUS	Michelle Kwan USA	Fumie Suguri JPN
2003	Washington USA	Michelle Kwan USA	Elena Sokolova RUS	Fumie Suguri JPN
2004	Dortmund GER	Shizuka Arakawa JPN	Sasha Cohen USA	Michelle Kwan USA
2005	Moscow RUS	Irina Slutskaya RUS	Sasha Cohen USA	Carolina Kostner ITA
2006	Calgary CAN	Kimmie Meissner USA	Fumie Suguri JPN	Sasha Cohen USA
2007	Tokyo JPN	Miki Ando JPN	Mao Asada JPN	Yu Na Kim KOR
2008	Gothenburg SWE	Mao Asada JPN	Carolina Kostner ITA	Yu Na Kim KOR
2009	Los Angeles USA	Yu Na Kim KOR	Joannie Rochette CAN	Miki Ando JPN
2010	Torino ITA	Mao Asada JPN	Yu Na Kim KOR	Laura Lepistö FIN

Men

Year	Location	Gold	Silver	Bronze
1896	St. Petersburg RUS	Gilbert Fuchs GER	Gustav Hügel AUT	Georg Sanders RUS
1897	Stockholm SWE	Gustav Hügel AUT	Ulrich Salchow SWE	Johan Lefstad NOR
1898	London GBR	Henning Grenander SWE	Gustav Hügel AUT	Gilbert Fuchs GER
1899	Davos SUI	Gustav Hügel AUT	Ulrich Salchow SWE	Edgar Syers GBR
1900	Davos SUI	Gustav Hügel AUT	Ulrich Salchow SWE	
1901	Stockholm SWE	Ulrich Salchow SWE	Gilbert Fuchs GER	
1902	London GBR	Ulrich Salchow SWE	Madge Syers GBR	Martin Gordan GER
1903	St. Petersburg RUS	Ulrich Salchow SWE	Nikolai Panin RUS	Max Bohatsch AUT
1904	Berlin GER	Ulrich Salchow SWE	Heinrich Burger AUT	Martin Gordan GER
1905	Stockholm SUI	Ulrich Salchow SWE	Max Bohatsch AUT	Per Thorén SWE
1906	Munich GER	Gilbert Fuchs GER	Heinrich Burger GER	Bror Meyer SWE
1907	Vienna AUT	Ulrich Salchow SWE	Max Bohatsch AUT	Gilbert Fuchs GER
1908	Troppau CZE	Ulrich Salchow SWE	Gilbert Fuchs GER	Heinrich Burger GER
1909	Stockholm SWE	Ulrich Salchow SWE	Per Thorén SWE	Ernst Herz AUT
1910	Davos SUI	Ulrich Salchow SWE	Werner Rittberger GER	Andor Szende HUN
1911	Berlin GER	Ulrich Salchow SWE	Werner Rittberger GER	Fritz Kachler AUT
1912	Manchester GBR	Fritz Kachler AUT	Werner Rittberger GER	Andor Szende HUN
1913	Vienna AUT	Fritz Kachler AUT	Wilhelm Böckl AUT	Andor Szende HUN
1914	Helsinki FIN	Gösta Sandahl SWE	Fritz Kachler AUT	Willy Böckl AUT
1915–1921	The World Championships were not held.			
1922	Stockholm, SWE	Gillis Grafström SWE	Fritz Kachler AUT	Willy Böckl AUT
1923	Vienna AUT	Fritz Kachler AUT	Wilhelm Böckl AUT	Gösta Sandahl SWE

Year	Location	Gold	Silver	Bronze
1924	Manchester GBR	Gillis Grafström SWE	Wilhelm Böckl AUT	Ernst Oppacher AUT
1925	Vienna AUT	Wilhelm Böckl AUT	Fritz Kachler AUT	Otto Preissecker AUT
1926	Berlin GER	Wilhelm Böckl AUT	Otto Preissecker AUT	John Page GBR
1927	Davos SUI	Wilhelm Böckl AUT	Otto Preissecker AUT	Karl Schäfer AUT
1928	Berlin GER	Wilhelm Böckl AUT	Karl Schäfer AUT	Hugo Distler AUT
1929	London GBR	Gillis Grafström SWE	Karl Schäfer AUT	Ludwig Wrede AUT
1930	New York USA	Karl Schäfer AUT	Roger Turner USA	Georg Gautschi SUI
1931	Berlin GER	Karl Schäfer AUT	Roger Turner USA	Ernst Baier GER
1932	Montreal CAN	Karl Schäfer AUT	Montgomery Wilson CAN	Ernst Baier GER
1933	Zurich SUI	Karl Schäfer AUT	Ernst Baier GER	Markus Nikkanen FIN
1934	Stockholm SWE	Karl Schäfer AUT	Ernst Baier GER	Erich Erdös AUT
1935	Budapest HUN	Karl Schäfer AUT	Jack Dunn GBR	Dénes Pataky HUN
1936	Paris FRA	Karl Schäfer AUT	Graham Sharp GBR	Felix Kaspar AUT
1937	Vienna AUT	Felix Kaspar AUT	Graham Sharp GBR	Elemér Terták HUN
1938	Berlin GER	Felix Kaspar AUT	Graham Sharp GBR	Herbert Alward AUT
1939	Budapest HUN	Graham Sharp GBR	Freddie Tomlins GBR	Horst Faber GER
1940–1946	The World Championships were not held.			
1947	Stockholm SWE	Hans Gerschwiler SUI	Richard Button USA	Arthur Apfel GBR
1948	Davos SUI	Richard Button USA	Hans Gerschwiler SUI	Ede Király HUN
1949	Paris FRA	Richard Button USA	Ede Király HUN	Edi Rada AUT
1950	London GBR	Richard Button USA	Ede Király HUN	Hayes Alan Jenkins USA
1951	Milan ITA	Richard Button USA	James Grogan USA	Helmut Seibt AUT
1952	Paris FRA	Richard Button USA	James Grogan USA	Hayes Alan Jenkins USA

Year	Location	Gold	Silver	Bronze
1953	Davos SUI	Hayes Alan Jenkins USA	James Grogan USA	Carlo Fassi ITA
1954	Oslo NOR	Hayes Alan Jenkins USA	James Grogan USA	Alain Giletti FRA
1955	Vienna AUT	Hayes Alan Jenkins USA	Ronald Robertson USA	David Jenkins USA
1956	Garmisch-Partenkirchen FRG	Hayes Alan Jenkins USA	Ronald Robertson USA	David Jenkins USA
1957	Colorado Springs USA	David Jenkins USA	Tim Brown USA	Charles Snelling CAN
1958	Paris FRA	David Jenkins USA	Tim Brown USA	Alain Giletti FRA
1959	Colorado Springs USA	David Jenkins USA	Donald Jackson CAN	Tim Brown USA
1960	Vancouver CAN	Alain Giletti FRA	Donald Jackson CAN	Alain Calmat FRA
1961	The World Championships were not held.			
1962	Prague CZE	Donald Jackson CAN	Karol Divin CZE	Alain Calmat FRA
1963	Cortina ITA	Donald McPherson CAN	Alain Calmat FRA	Manfred Schnelldorfer FRG
1964	Dortmund FRG	Manfred Schnelldorfer FRG	Alain Calmat FRA	Karol Divin CZE
1965	Colorado Springs USA	Alain Calmat FRA	Scott Allen USA	Donald Knight CAN
1966	Davos SUI	Emmerich Danzer AUT	Wolfgang Schwarz AUT	Gary Visconti USA
1967	Vienna AUT	Emmerich Danzer AUT	Wolfgang Schwarz AUT	Gary Visconti USA
1968	Geneva SUI	Emmerich Danzer AUT	Tim Wood USA	Patrick Pera FRA
1969	Colorado Springs USA	Tim Wood USA	Ondrej Nepela CZE	Patrick Pera FRA
1970	Ljubljana YUG	Tim Wood USA	Ondrej Nepela CZE	Günter Zöller GDR
1971	Lyon FRA	Ondrej Nepela CZE	Patrick Pera FRA	Sergei Chetverukhin URS
1972	Calgary CAN	Ondrej Nepela CZE	Sergei Chetverukhin URS	Vladimir Kovalev URS
1973	Bratislava CZE	Ondrej Nepela CZE	Sergei Chetverukhin URS	Jan Hoffmann GDR
1974	Munich FRG	Jan Hoffmann GDR	Sergei Volkov URS	Toller Cranston CAN
1975	Colorado Springs USA	Sergei Volkov URS	Vladimir Kovalev URS	John Curry GBR

Year	Location	Gold	Silver	Bronze
1976	Gothenburg SWE	John Curry GBR	Vladimir Kovalev URS	Jan Hoffmann GDR
1977	Tokyo JPN	Vladimir Kovalev URS	Jan Hoffmann GDR	Minoru Sano JPN
1978	Ottawa CAN	Charles Tickner USA	Jan Hoffmann GDR	Robin Cousins GBR
1979	Vienna AUT	Vladimir Kovalev URS	Robin Cousins GBR	Jan Hoffmann GDR
1980	Dortmund FRG	Jan Hoffmann GDR	Robin Cousins GBR	Charles Tickner USA
1981	Hartford USA	Scott Hamilton USA	David Santee USA	Igor Bobrin URS
1982	Copenhagen DEN	Scott Hamilton USA	Norbert Schramm FRG	Brian Pockar CAN
1983	Helsinki FIN	Scott Hamilton USA	Norbert Schramm FRG	Brian Orser CAN
1984	Ottawa CAN	Scott Hamilton USA	Brian Orser CAN	Alexandr Fadeev URS
1985	Tokyo JPN	Alexandr Fadeev URS	Brian Orser CAN	Brian Boitano USA
1986	Geneva SUI	Brian Boitano USA	Brian Orser CAN	Alexandr Fadeev URS
1987	Cincinnati USA	Brian Orser CAN	Brian Boitano USA	Alexandr Fadeev URS
1988	Budapest HUN	Brian Boitano USA	Brian Orser CAN	Viktor Petrenko URS
1989	Paris FRA	Kurt Browning CAN	Christopher Bowman USA	Grzegorz Filipowski POL
1990	Halifax CAN	Kurt Browning CAN	Viktor Petrenko URS	Christopher Bowman USA
1991	Munich GER	Kurt Browning CAN	Viktor Petrenko URS	Todd Eldredge USA
1992	Oakland USA	Viktor Petrenko CIS	Kurt Browning CAN	Elvis Stojko CAN
1993	Prague CZE	Kurt Browning CAN	Elvis Stojko CAN	Alexei Urmanov RUS
1994	Chiba JPN	Elvis Stojko CAN	Philippe Candeloro FRA	Viacheslav Zagorodniuk UKR
1995	Birmingham GBR	Elvis Stojko CAN	Todd Eldredge USA	Philippe Candeloro FRA
1996	Edmonton CAN	Todd Eldredge USA	Ilia Kulik RUS	Rudy Galindo USA
1997	Lausanne SUI	Elvis Stojko CAN	Todd Eldredge USA	Alexei Yagudin RUS
1998	Minneapolis USA	Alexei Yagudin RUS	Todd Eldredge USA	Evgeny Plushenko RUS

Year	Location	Gold	Silver	Bronze
1999	Helsinki FIN	Alexei Yagudin RUS	Evgeny Plushenko RUS	Michael Weiss USA
2000	Nice FRA	Alexei Yagudin RUS	Elvis Stojko CAN	Michael Weiss USA
2001	Vancouver CAN	Evgeny Plushenko RUS	Alexei Yagudin RUS	Todd Eldredge USA
2002	Nagano JPN	Alexei Yagudin RUS	Timothy Goebel USA	Takeshi Honda JPN
2003	Washington USA	Evgeny Plushenko RUS	Timothy Goebel USA	Takeshi Honda JPN
2004	Dortmund GER	Evgeny Plushenko RUS	Brian Joubert FRA	Stefan Lindemann GER
2005	Moscow RUS	Stéphane Lambiel SUI	Jeffrey Buttle CAN	Evan Lysacek USA
2006	Calgary CAN	Stéphane Lambiel SUI	Brian Joubert FRA	Evan Lysacek USA
2007	Tokyo JPN	Brian Joubert FRA	Daisuke Takahashi JPN	Stéphane Lambiel SUI
2008	Gothenburg SWE	Jeffrey Buttle CAN	Brian Joubert FRA	Johnny Weir USA
2009	Los Angeles USA	Evan Lysacek USA	Patrick Chan CAN	Brian Joubert FRA
2010	Torino ITA	Daisuke Takahashi JPN	Patrick Chan CAN	Brian Joubert FRA

Pairs

Year	Location	Gold	Silver	Bronze
1908	St. Petersburg RUS	Anna Hübler & Heinrich Burger GER	Phyllis Johnson & James Johnson GBR	A. L. Fischer & L. P. Popowa RUS
1909	Stockholm SWE	Phyllis Johnson & James Johnson GBR	Valborg Lindahl & Nils Rosenius SWE	Gertrud Ström & Richard Johansson SWE
1910	Berlin GER	Anna Hübler & Heinrich Burger GER	Ludowika Eilers & Walter Jakobsson FIN	Phyllis Johnson & James Johnson GBR
1911	Vienna AUT	Ludowika Eilers & Walter Jakobsson FIN		
1912	Manchester GBR	Phyllis Johnson & James Johnson GBR	Ludowika Jakobsson & Walter Jakobsson FIN	Alexia Bryn & Yngvar Bryn NOR
1913	Stockholm SWE	Helene Engelmann & Karl Mejstrik AUT	Ludowika Jakobsson & Walter Jakobsson FIN	Christa von Szabo & Leo Horwitz AUT
1914	St. Moritz SUI	Ludowika Jakobsson & Walter Jakobsson FIN	Helene Engelmann & Karl Mejstrik AUT	Christa von Szabo & Leo Horwitz AUT
1915–1921	The World Championships were not held.			
1922	Davos SUI	Helene Engelmann & Alfred Berger AUT	Ludowika Jakobsson & Walter Jakobsson FIN	Margaret Metzner & Paul Metzner GER
1923	Oslo NOR	Ludowika Jakobsson & Walter Jakobsson FIN	Alexia Bryn & Yngvar Bryn NOR	Elna Henrikson & Kaj af Ekström SWE
1924	Manchester GBR	Helene Engelmann & Alfred Berger AUT	Ethel Muckelt & John Page GBR	Elna Henrikson & Kaj af Ekström SWE
1925	Vienna AUT	Herma Szabo & Ludwig Wrede AUT	Andrée Joly & Pierre Brunet FRA	Lilly Scholz & Otto Kaiser AUT
1926	Berlin GER	Andrée Joly & Pierre Brunet FRA	Lilly Scholz & Otto Kaiser AUT	Herma Szabo & Ludwig Wrede AUT
1927	Vienna AUT	Herma Szabo & Ludwig Wrede AUT	Lilly Scholz & Otto Kaiser AUT	Else Hoppe & Oscar Hoppe CZE

Year	Location	Gold	Silver	Bronze
1928	London GBR	Andrée Brunet & Pierre Brunet FRA	Lilly Scholz & Otto Kaiser AUT	Melitta Brunner & Ludwig Wrede AUT
1929	Budapest HUN	Lilly Scholz & Otto Kaiser AUT	Melitta Brunner & Ludwig Wrede AUT	Olga Orgonista & Sándor Szalay HUN
1930	New York USA	Andrée Brunet & Pierre Brunet FRA	Melitta Brunner & Ludwig Wrede AUT	Beatrix Loughran & Sherwin Badger USA
1931	Berlin GER	Emília Rotter & László Szollás HUN	Olga Orgonista & Sándor Szalay HUN	Idi Papez & Karl Zwack AUT
1932	Montreal CAN	Andrée Brunet & Pierre Brunet FRA	Emília Rotter & László Szollás HUN	Beatrix Loughran & Sherwin Badger USA
1933	Stockholm SWE	Emília Rotter & László Szollás HUN	Idi Papez & Karl Zwack AUT	Randi Bakke & Christen Christensen NOR
1934	Helsinki FIN	Emília Rotter & László Szollás HUN	Idi Papez & Karl Zwack AUT	Maxi Herber & Ernst Baier GER
1935	Budapest HUN	Emília Rotter & László Szollás HUN	Ilse Pausin & Erich Pausin AUT	Lucy Galló & Rezsö Dillinger HUN
1936	Paris FRA	Maxi Herber & Ernst Baier GER	Ilse Pausin & Erich Pausin AUT	Violet Cliff & Leslie Cliff GBR
1937	London GBR	Maxi Herber & Ernst Baier GER	Ilse Pausin & Erich Pausin AUT	Violet Cliff & Leslie Cliff GBR
1938	Berlin GER	Maxi Herber & Ernst Baier GER	Ilse Pausin & Erich Pausin AUT	Inge Koch & Günther Noack GER
1939	Budapest HUN	Maxi Herber & Ernst Baier GER	Ilse Pausin & Erich Pausin AUT	Inge Koch & Günther Noack GER
1940–1946	The World Championships were not held.			
1947	Stockholm SWE	Micheline Lannoy & Pierre Baugniet BEL	Karol Kennedy & Peter Kennedy USA	Suzanne Diskeuve & Edmond Verbustel BEL
1948	Davos SUI	Micheline Lannoy & Pierre Baugniet BEL	Andrea Kekéssy & Ede Király HUN	Suzanne Morrow & Wallace Diestelmeyer CAN

Year	Location	Gold	Silver	Bronze
1949	Paris FRA	Andrea Kekéssy & Ede Király HUN	Karol Kennedy & Peter Kennedy USA	Anne Davies & Carleton Hoffner Jr. USA
1950	London GBR	Karol Kennedy & Peter Kennedy USA	Jennifer Nicks & John Nicks GBR	Marianna Nagy & László Nagy HUN
1951	Milan ITA	Ria Baran & Paul Falk GER	Karol Kennedy & Peter Kennedy USA	Jennifer Nicks & John Nicks GBR
1952	Paris FRA	Ria Falk & Paul Falk GER	Karol Kennedy & Peter Kennedy USA	Jennifer Nicks & John Nicks GBR
1953	Davos SUI	Jennifer Nicks & John Nicks GBR	Frances Dafoe & Norris Bowden CAN	Marianna Nagy & László Nagy HUN
1954	Oslo NOR	Frances Dafoe & Norris Bowden CAN	Silvia Grandjean & Michel Grandjean SUI	Elisabeth Schwarz & Kurt Oppelt AUT
1955	Vienna AUT	Frances Dafoe & Norris Bowden CAN	Elisabeth Schwarz & Kurt Oppelt AUT	Marianna Nagy & László Nagy HUN
1956	Garmisch-Partenkirchen FRG	Elisabeth Schwarz & Kurt Oppelt AUT	Frances Dafoe & Norris Bowden CAN	Marika Kilius & Franz Ningel FRG
1957	Colorado Springs USA	Barbara Wagner & Robert Paul CAN	Marika Kilius & Franz Ningel FRG	Maria Jelinek & Otto Jelinek CAN
1958	Paris FRA	Barbara Wagner & Robert Paul CAN	Věra Suchánková & Zdeněk Doležal CZE	Maria Jelinek & Otto Jelinek CAN
1959	Colorado Springs USA	Barbara Wagner & Robert Paul CAN	Marika Kilius & Hans-Jürgen Bäumler FRG	Nancy Ludington & Ronald Ludington USA
1960	Vancouver CAN	Barbara Wagner & Robert Paul CAN	Maria Jelinek & Otto Jelinek CAN	Marika Kilius & Hans-Jürgen Bäumler FRG
1961	The World Championships were not held.			

Year	Location	Gold	Silver	Bronze
1962	Prague CZE	Maria Jelinek & Otto Jelinek CAN	Liudmila Belousova & Oleg Protopopov URS	Margret Göbl & Franz Ningel FRG
1963	Cortina ITA	Marika Kilius & Hans-Jürgen Bäumler FRG	Liudmila Belousova & Oleg Protopopov URS	Tatiana Zhuk & Alexandr Gavrilov URS
1964	Dortmund FRG	Marika Kilius & Hans-Jürgen Bäumler FRG	Liudmila Belousova & Oleg Protopopov URS	Debbi Wilkes & Guy Revell CAN
1965	Colorado Springs USA	Liudmila Belousova & Oleg Protopopov URS	Vivian Joseph & Ronald Joseph USA	Tatiana Zhuk & Alexandr Gorelik URS
1966	Davos SUI	Liudmila Belousova & Oleg Protopopov URS	Tatiana Zhuk & Alexandr Gorelik URS	Cynthia Kauffmann & Ronald Kauffmann USA
1967	Vienna AUT	Liudmila Belousova & Oleg Protopopov URS	Margot Glockshuber & Wolfgang Danne FRG	Cynthia Kauffmann & Ronald Kauffmann USA
1968	Geneva SUI	Liudmila Belousova & Oleg Protopopov URS	Tatiana Zhuk & Alexandr Gorelik URS	Cynthia Kauffmann & Ronald Kauffmann USA
1969	Colorado Springs USA	Irina Rodnina & Alexei Ulanov URS	Tamara Moskvina & Alexei Mishin URS	Liudmila Belousova & Oleg Protopopov URS
1970	Ljubljana YUG	Irina Rodnina & Alexei Ulanov URS	Liudmila Smirnova & Andrei Suraikin URS	Heidemarie Steiner & Heinz-Ulrich Walther GDR
1971	Lyon FRA	Irina Rodnina & Alexei Ulanov URS	Liudmila Smirnova & Andrei Suraikin URS	Alicia Jo Starbuck & Kenneth Shelley USA
1972	Calgary CAN	Irina Rodnina & Alexei Ulanov URS	Liudmila Smirnova & Andrei Suraikin URS	Alicia Jo Starbuck & Kenneth Shelley USA
1973	Bratislava CZE	Irina Rodnina & Alexandr Zaitsev URS	Liudmila Smirnova & Alexei Ulanov URS	Manuela Gross & Uwe Kagelmann GDR
1974	Munich FRG	Irina Rodnina & Alexandr Zaitsev URS	Liudmila Smirnova & Alexei Ulanov URS	Romy Kermer & Rolf Österreich GDR

Year	Location	Gold	Silver	Bronze
1975	Colorado Springs USA	Irina Rodnina & Alexandr Zaitsev URS	Romy Kermer & Rolf Österreich GDR	Manuela Gross & Uwe Kagelmann GDR
1976	Gothenburg SWE	Irina Rodnina & Alexandr Zaitsev URS	Romy Kermer & Rolf Österreich GDR	Irina Vorobieva & Alexandr Vlasov URS
1977	Tokyo JPN	Irina Rodnina & Alexandr Zaitsev URS	Irina Vorobieva & Alexandr Vlasov URS	Tai Babilonia & Randy Gardner USA
1978	Ottawa CAN	Irina Rodnina & Alexandr Zaitsev URS	Manuela Gross & Uwe Kagelmann GDR	Tai Babilonia & Randy Gardner USA
1979	Vienna AUT	Tai Babilonia & Randy Gardner USA	Marina Cherkasova & Sergei Shakhrai URS	Sabine Baess & Tassilo Thierbach GDR
1980	Dortmund FRG	Marina Cherkasova & Sergei Shakhrai URS	Manuela Gross & Uwe Kagelmann GDR	Marina Pestova & Stanislav Leonovich URS
1981	Hartford USA	Irina Vorobieva & Igor Lisovski URS	Sabine Baess & Tassilo Thierbach GDR	Christina Riegel & Andreas Nischwitz FRG
1982	Copenhagen DEN	Sabine Baess & Tassilo Thierbach GDR	Marina Pestova & Stanislav Leonovich URS	Caitlin Carruthers & Peter Carruthers USA
1983	Helsinki FIN	Elena Valova & Oleg Vasiliev URS	Sabine Baess & Tassilo Thierbach GDR	Barbara Underhill & Paul Martini CAN
1984	Ottawa CAN	Barbara Underhill & Paul Martini CAN	Elena Valova & Oleg Vasiliev URS	Sabine Baess & Tassilo Thierbach GDR
1985	Tokyo JPN	Elena Valova & Oleg Vasiliev URS	Larisa Selezneva & Oleg Makarov URS	Katherina Matousek & Lloyd Eisler CAN
1986	Geneva SUI	Ekaterina Gordeeva & Sergei Grinkov URS	Elena Valova & Oleg Vasiliev URS	Cynthia Coull & Mark Rowsom CAN
1987	Cincinnati USA	Ekaterina Gordeeva & Sergei Grinkov URS	Elena Valova & Oleg Vasiliev URS	Jill Watson & Peter Oppegard USA

Year	Location	Gold	Silver	Bronze
1988	Budapest HUN	Elena Valova & Oleg Vasiliev URS	Ekaterina Gordeeva & Sergei Grinkov URS	Larisa Selezneva & Oleg Makarov URS
1989	Paris FRA	Ekaterina Gordeeva & Sergei Grinkov URS	Cindy Landry & Lyndon Johnston CAN	Elena Bechke & Denis Petrov URS
1990	Halifax CAN	Ekaterina Gordeeva & Sergei Grinkov URS	Isabelle Brasseur & Lloyd Eisler CAN	Natalia Mishkutenok & Artur Dmitriev URS
1991	Munich GER	Natalia Mishkutenok & Artur Dmitriev URS	Isabelle Brasseur & Lloyd Eisler CAN	Natasha Kuchiki & Todd Sand USA
1992	Oakland USA	Natalia Mishkutenok & Artur Dmitriev URS	Radka Kovaříková & René Novotný CZE	Isabelle Brasseur & Lloyd Eisler CAN
1993	Prague CZE	Isabelle Brasseur & Lloyd Eisler CAN	Mandy Wötzel & Ingo Steuer GER	Evgenia Shishkova & Vadim Naumov RUS
1994	Chiba JPN	Evgenia Shishkova & Vadim Naumov RUS	Isabelle Brasseur & Lloyd Eisler CAN	Marina Eltsova & Andrei Bushkov RUS
1995	Birmingham GBR	Radka Kovaříková & René Novotný CZE	Evgenia Shishkova & Vadim Naumov RUS	Jenni Meno & Todd Sand USA
1996	Edmonton CAN	Marina Eltsova & Andrei Bushkov RUS	Mandy Wötzel & Ingo Steuer GER	Jenni Meno & Todd Sand USA
1997	Lausanne SUI	Mandy Wötzel & Ingo Steuer GER	Marina Eltsova & Andrei Bushkov RUS	Oksana Kazakova & Artur Dmitriev RUS
1998	Minneapolis USA	Elena Berezhnaya & Anton Sikharulidze RUS	Jenni Meno & Todd Sand USA	Peggy Schwarz & Mirko Müller GER
1999	Helsinki FIN	Elena Berezhnaya & Anton Sikharulidze RUS	Xue Shen & Hongbo Zhao CHN	Dorota Zagorska & Mariusz Siudek POL
2000	Nice FRA	Maria Petrova & Alexei Tikhonov RUS	Xue Shen & Hongbo Zhao CHN	Sarah Abitbol & Stephane Bernadis FRA

Year	Location	Gold	Silver	Bronze
2001	Vancouver CAN	Jamie Salé & David Pelletier CAN	Elena Berezhnaya & Anton Sikharulidze RUS	Xue Shen & Hongbo Zhao CHN
2002	Nagano JPN	Xue Shen & Hongbo Zhao CHN	Tatiana Totmianina & Maxim Marinin RUS	Kyoko Ina & John Zimmerman USA
2003	Washington USA	Xue Shen & Hongbo Zhao CHN	Tatiana Totmianina & Maxim Marinin RUS	Maria Petrova & Alexei Tikhonov RUS
2004	Dortmund GER	Tatiana Totmianina & Maxim Marinin RUS	Xue Shen & Hongbo Zhao CHN	Qing Pang & Jian Tong CHN
2005	Moscow RUS	Tatiana Totmianina & Maxim Marinin RUS	Maria Petrova & Alexei Tikhonov RUS	Dan Zhang & Hao Zhang CHN
2006	Calgary CAN	Qing Pang & Jian Tong CHN	Dan Zhang & Hao Zhang CHN	Maria Petrova & Alexei Tikhonov RUS
2007	Tokyo JPN	Xue Shen & Hongbo Zhao CHN	Qing Pang & Jian Tong CHN	Aliona Savchenko & Robin Szolkowy GER
2008	Gothenburg SWE	Aliona Savchenko & Robin Szolkowy GER	Dan Zhang & Hao Zhang CHN	Jessica Dube & Bryce Davison CAN
2009	Los Angeles USA	Aliona Savchenko & Robin Szolkowy GER	Dan Zhang & Hao Zhang CHN	Yuko Kavaguti & Alexandr Smirnov RUS
2010	Torino ITA	Qing Pang & Jian Tong CHN	Aliona Savchenko & Robin Szolkowy GER	Yuko Kavaguti & Alexandr Smirnov RUS

Ice Dancing

Year	Location	Gold	Silver	Bronze
1952	Paris FRA	Jean Westwood & Lawrence Demmy GBR	Joan Dewhirst & John Slater GBR	Carol Peters & Daniel Ryan USA
1953	Davos SUI	Jean Westwood & Lawrence Demmy GBR	Joan Dewhirst & John Slater GBR	Carol Peters & Daniel Ryan USA
1954	Oslo NOR	Jean Westwood & Lawrence Demmy GBR	Nesta Davies & Paul Thomas GBR	Carmel Bodel & Edward Bodel USA
1955	Vienna AUT	Jean Westwood & Lawrence Demmy GBR	Pamela Weight & Paul Thomas GBR	Barbara Radford & Raymond Lockwood GBR
1956	Garmisch-Partenkirchen FRG	Pamela Weight & Paul Thomas GBR	June Markham & Courtney Jones GBR	Barbara Thompson & Gerard Rigby GBR
1957	Colorado Springs USA	June Markham & Courtney Jones GBR	Geraldine Fenton & William McLachlan CAN	Sharon McKenzie & Bert Wright USA
1958	Paris FRA	June Markham & Courtney Jones GBR	Geraldine Fenton & William McLachlan CAN	Andrée Anderson & Donald Jacoby USA
1959	Colorado Springs USA	Doreen Denny & Courtney Jones GBR	Andrée Anderson & Donald Jacoby USA	Geraldine Fenton & William McLachlan CAN
1960	Vancouver CAN	Doreen Denny & Courtney Jones GBR	Virginia Thompson & William McLachlan CAN	Christiane Guhel & Jean Paul Guhel FRA
1961	The World Championships were not held.			
1962	Prague CZE	Eva Romanová & Pavel Roman CZE	Christiane Guhel & Jean Paul Guhel FRA	Virginia Thompson & William McLachlan CAN
1963	Cortina ITA	Eva Romanová & Pavel Roman CZE	Linda Shearman & Michael Phillips GBR	Paulette Doan & Kenneth Ormsby CAN
1964	Dortmund FRG	Eva Romanová & Pavel Roman CZE	Paulette Doan & Kenneth Ormsby CAN	Janet Sawbridge & David Hickinbottom GBR

Year	Location	Gold	Silver	Bronze
1965	Colorado Springs USA	Eva Romanová & Pavel Roman CZE	Janet Sawbridge & David Hickinbottom GBR	Lorna Dyer & John Carrell USA
1966	Davos SUI	Diane Towler & Bernard Ford GBR	Kristin Fortune & Dennis Sveum USA	Lorna Dyer & John Carrell USA
1967	Vienna AUT	Diane Towler & Bernard Ford GBR	Lorna Dyer & John Carrell USA	Yvonne Suddick & Malcolm Cannon GBR
1968	Geneva SUI	Diane Towler & Bernard Ford GBR	Yvonne Suddick & Malcolm Cannon GBR	Janet Sawbridge & Jon Lane GBR
1969	Colorado Springs USA	Diane Towler & Bernard Ford GBR	Liudmila Pakhomova & Alexandr Gorshkov URS	Judy Schwomeyer & James Sladky USA
1970	Ljubljana YUG	Liudmila Pakhomova & Alexandr Gorshkov URS	Judy Schwomeyer & James Sladky USA	Angelika Buck & Erich Buck FRG
1971	Lyon FRA	Liudmila Pakhomova & Alexandr Gorshkov URS	Angelika Buck & Erich Buck FRG	Judy Schwomeyer & James Sladky USA
1972	Calgary CAN	Liudmila Pakhomova & Alexandr Gorshkov URS	Angelika Buck & Erich Buck FRG	Judy Schwomeyer & James Sladky USA
1973	Bratislava CZE	Liudmila Pakhomova & Alexandr Gorshkov URS	Angelika Buck & Erich Buck FRG	Hilary Green & Glyn Watts GBR
1974	Munich FRG	Liudmila Pakhomova & Alexandr Gorshkov URS	Hilary Green & Glyn Watts GBR	Natalia Linichuk & Gennadi Karponosov URS
1975	Colorado Springs USA	Irina Moiseeva & Andrei Minenkov URS	Colleen O'Connor & Jim Millns USA	Hilary Green & Glyn Watts GBR
1976	Gothenburg SWE	Liudmila Pakhomova & Alexandr Gorshkov URS	Irina Moiseeva & Andrei Minenkov URS	Colleen O'Connor & Jim Millns USA
1977	Tokyo JPN	Irina Moiseeva & Andrei Minenkov URS	Janet Thompson & Warren Maxwell GBR	Natalia Linichuk & Gennadi Karponosov URS

Year	Location	Gold	Silver	Bronze
1978	Ottawa CAN	Natalia Linichuk & Gennadi Karponosov URS	Irina Moiseeva & Andrei Minenkov URS	Krisztina Regöczy & András Sallay HUN
1979	Vienna AUT	Natalia Linichuk & Gennadi Karponosov URS	Krisztina Regöczy & András Sallay HUN	Irina Moiseeva & Andrei Minenkov URS
1980	Dortmund FRG	Krisztina Regöczy & András Sallay HUN	Natalia Linichuk & Gennadi Karponosov URS	Irina Moiseeva & Andrei Minenkov URS
1981	Hartford USA	Jayne Torvill & Christopher Dean GBR	Irina Moiseeva & Andrei Minenkov URS	Natalia Bestemianova & Andrei Bukin URS
1982	Copenhagen DEN	Jayne Torvill & Christopher Dean GBR	Natalia Bestemianova & Andrei Bukin URS	Irina Moiseeva & Andrei Minenkov URS
1983	Helsinki FIN	Jayne Torvill & Christopher Dean GBR	Natalia Bestemianova & Andrei Bukin URS	Judy Blumberg & Michael Seibert USA
1984	Ottawa CAN	Jayne Torvill & Christopher Dean GBR	Natalia Bestemianova & Andrei Bukin URS	Judy Blumberg & Michael Seibert USA
1985	Tokyo JPN	Natalia Bestemianova & Andrei Bukin URS	Marina Klimova & Sergei Ponomarenko URS	Judy Blumberg & Michael Seibert USA
1986	Geneva SUI	Natalia Bestemianova & Andrei Bukin URS	Marina Klimova & Sergei Ponomarenko URS	Tracy Wilson & Robert McCall CAN
1987	Cincinnati USA	Natalia Bestemianova & Andrei Bukin URS	Marina Klimova & Sergei Ponomarenko URS	Tracy Wilson & Robert McCall CAN
1988	Budapest HUN	Natalia Bestemianova & Andrei Bukin URS	Marina Klimova & Sergei Ponomarenko URS	Tracy Wilson & Robert McCall CAN
1989	Paris FRA	Marina Klimova & Sergei Ponomarenko URS	Maia Usova & Alexandr Zhulin URS	Isabelle Duchesnay & Paul Duchesnay FRA
1990	Halifax CAN	Marina Klimova & Sergei Ponomarenko URS	Isabelle Duchesnay & Paul Duchesnay FRA	Maia Usova & Alexandr Zhulin URS

Year	Location	Gold	Silver	Bronze
1991	Munich GER	Isabelle Duchesnay & Paul Duchesnay FRA	Marina Klimova & Sergei Ponomarenko URS	Maia Usova & Alexandr Zhulin URS
1992	Oakland USA	Maia Usova & Alexandr Zhulin CIS	Maia Usova & Alexandr Zhulin CIS	Oksana Grishchuk & Evgeny Platov CIS
1993	Prague CZE	Maia Usova & Alexandr Zhulin RUS	Oksana Grishchuk & Evgeny Platov RUS	Anjelika Krylova & Vladimir Fedorov RUS
1994	Chiba JPN	Anjelika Krylova & Vladimir Fedorov RUS	Sophie Moniotte & Pascal Lavanchy FRA	Susanna Rahkamo & Petri Kokko FIN
1995	Birmingham GBR	Oksana Grishchuk & Evgeny Platov RUS	Susanna Rahkamo & Petri Kokko FIN	Sophie Moniotte & Pascal Lavanchy FRA
1996	Edmonton CAN	Oksana Grishchuk & Evgeny Platov RUS	Anjelika Krylova & Oleg Ovsiannikov RUS	Shae-Lynn Bourne & Victor Kraatz CAN
1997	Lausanne SUI	Oksana Grishchuk & Evgeny Platov RUS	Anjelika Krylova & Oleg Ovsiannikov RUS	Shae-Lynn Bourne & Victor Kraatz CAN
1998	Minneapolis USA	Anjelika Krylova & Oleg Ovsiannikov RUS	Marina Anissina & Gwendal Peizerat FRA	Shae-Lynn Bourne & Victor Kraatz CAN
1999	Helsinki FIN	Anjelika Krylova & Oleg Ovsiannikov RUS	Marina Anissina & Gwendal Peizerat FRA	Shae-Lynn Bourne & Victor Kraatz CAN
2000	Nice FRA	Marina Anissina & Gwendal Peizerat FRA	Barbara Fusar-Poli & Maurizio Margaglio ITA	Margarita Drobiazko & Povilas Vanagas LTU
2001	Vancouver CAN	Barbara Fusar-Poli & Maurizio Margaglio ITA	Marina Anissina & Gwendal Peizerat FRA	Irina Lobacheva & Ilia Averbukh RUS
2002	Nagano JPN	Irina Lobacheva & Ilia Averbukh RUS	Shae-Lynn Bourne & Victor Kraatz CAN	Galit Chait & Sergei Sakhnovski ISR
2003	Washington USA	Shae-Lynn Bourne & Victor Kraatz CAN	Irina Lobacheva & Ilia Averbukh RUS	Albena Denkova & Maxim Staviyski BUL

Year	Location	Gold	Silver	Bronze
2004	Dortmund GER	Tatiana Navka & Roman Kostomarov RUS	Albena Denkova & Maxim Staviyski BUL	Kati Winkler & Rene Lohse GER
2005	Moscow RUS	Tatiana Navka & Roman Kostomarov RUS	Tanith Belbin & Benjamin Agosto USA	Elena Grushina & Ruslan Goncharov UKR
2006	Calgary CAN	Albena Denkova & Maxim Staviyski BUL	Marie-France Dubreuil & Patrice Lauzon CAN	Tanith Belbin & Benjamin Agosto USA
2007	Tokyo JPN	Albena Denkova & Maxim Staviyski BUL	Marie-France Dubreuil & Patrice Lauzon CAN	Tanith Belbin & Benjamin Agosto USA
2008	Gothenburg SWE	Isabelle Delobel & Olivier Schoenfelder FRA	Tessa Virtue & Scott Moir CAN	Jana Khokhlova & Sergei Novitski RUS
2009	Los Angeles USA	Oksana Domnina & Maxim Shabalin RUS	Tanith Belbin & Benjamin Agosto USA	Tessa Virtue & Scott Moir CAN
2010	Torino ITA	Tessa Virtue & Scott Moir CAN	Meryl Davis & Charlie White USA	Federica Faiella & Massimo Scali ITA

Synchronized Skating

Year	Location	Gold	Silver	Bronze
2000	Minneapolis USA	Team Surprise SWE	black ice CAN	Marigold Ice Unity FIN
2001	Helsinki FIN	Team Surprise SWE	Rockettes FIN	black ice CAN
2002	Rouen FRA	Marigold Ice Unity FIN	Team Surprise SWE	black ice CAN
2003	Ottawa, Ontario CAN	Team Surprise SWE	Marigold Ice Unity FIN	Les Supremes CAN
2004	Zagreb CRO	Marigold Ice Unity FIN	Team Surprise SWE	Rockettes FIN
2005	Gothenburg SWE	Team Surprise SWE	black ice CAN	Marigold Ice Unity FIN
2006	Prague CZE	Marigold Ice Unity FIN	Team Surprise SWE	Rockettes FIN
2007	London CAN	Team Surprise SWE	Miami University USA	Nexxice CAN
2008	Budapest HUN	Rockettes FIN	Team Surprise SWE	Nexxice CAN
2009	Zagreb CRO	Nexxice CAN	Team Unique FIN	Team Surprise SWE
2010	Colorado Springs USA	Rockettes FIN	Marigold Ice Unity FIN	Haydenettes USA

Appendix E
Medalists at the European Figure Skating Championships

Ladies

Year	Location	Gold	Silver	Bronze
1930	Vienna AUT	Fritzi Burger AUT	Ilse Hornung AUT	Vivi-Anne Hultén SWE
1931	St. Moritz SUI	Sonja Henie NOR	Fritzi Burger AUT	Hilde Holovsky AUT
1932	Paris FRA	Sonja Henie NOR	Fritzi Burger AUT	Vivi-Anne Hultén SWE
1933	London GBR	Sonja Henie NOR	Cecilia Colledge GBR	Fritzi Burger AUT
1934	Prague CZE	Sonja Henie NOR	Liselotte Landbeck AUT	Maribel Vinson USA
1935	St. Moritz SUI	Sonja Henie NOR	Liselotte Landbeck AUT	Cecilia Colledge GBR
1936	Berlin GER	Sonja Henie NOR	Cecilia Colledge GBR	Megan Taylor GBR
1937	Prague CZE	Cecilia Colledge GBR	Megan Taylor GBR	Emmy Putzinger AUT
1938	St. Moritz SUI	Cecilia Colledge GBR	Megan Taylor GBR	Emmy Putzinger AUT
1939	London GBR	Cecilia Colledge GBR	Megan Taylor GBR	Daphne Walker GBR
1940–1946	The European Championships were not held.			
1947	Davos SUI	Barbara Ann Scott CAN	Gretchen Merrill USA	Daphne Walker GBR
1948	Prague CZE	Barbara Ann Scott CAN	Eva Pawlik AUT	Alena Vrzáňová CZE
1949	Milan ITA	Eva Pawlik AUT	Alena Vrzáňová CZE	Jeannette Altwegg GBR
1950	Oslo NOR	Alena Vrzáňová CZE	Jeannette Altwegg GBR	Jacqueline du Bief FRA
1951	Zurich SUI	Jeannette Altwegg GBR	Jacqueline du Bief FRA	Barbara Wyatt GBR
1952	Vienna AUT	Jeannette Altwegg GBR	Jacqueline du Bief FRA	Barbara Wyatt GBR
1953	Dortmund FRG	Valda Osborn GBR	Gundi Busch GER	Erica Batchelor GBR
1954	Bolzano ITA	Gundi Busch GER	Erica Batchelor GBR	Yvonne Sugden GBR
1955	Budapest HUN	Hanna Eigel AUT	Yvonne Sugden GBR	Erica Batchelor GBR
1956	Paris FRA	Ingrid Wendl AUT	Yvonne Sugden GBR	Erica Batchelor GBR
1957	Vienna AUT	Hanna Eigel AUT	Ingrid Wendl AUT	Hanna Walter AUT
1958	Bratislava CZE	Ingrid Wendl AUT	Hanna Walter AUT	Joan Haanappel NED
1959	Davos SUI	Hanna Walter AUT	Sjoukje Dijkstra NED	Joan Haanappel NED

Year	Location	Gold	Silver	Bronze
1960	Garmisch-Partenkirchen GER	Sjoukje Dijkstra NED	Regine Heitzer AUT	Joan Haanappel NED
1961	Berlin GER	Sjoukje Dijkstra NED	Regine Heitzer AUT	Jana Mrázková CZE
1962	Geneva SUI	Sjoukje Dijkstra NED	Regine Heitzer AUT	Karin Frohner AUT
1963	Budapest HUN	Sjoukje Dijkstra NED	Nicole Hassler FRA	Regine Heitzer AUT
1964	Grenoble FRA	Sjoukje Dijkstra NED	Regine Heitzer AUT	Nicole Hassler FRA
1965	Moscow URS	Regine Heitzer AUT	Sally-Anne Stapleford GBR	Nicole Hassler FRA
1966	Bratislava CZE	Regine Heitzer AUT	Gabriele Seyfert GDR	Nicole Hassler FRA
1967	Ljubljana YUG	Gabriele Seyfert GDR	Hana Mašková CZE	Zsuzsa Almássy HUN
1968	Västerås SWE	Hana Mašková CZE	Gabriele Seyfert GDR	Beatrix Schuba AUT
1969	Garmish-Partenkirchen GER	Gabriele Seyfert GDR	Hana Mašková CZE	Beatrix Schuba AUT
1970	Leningrad URS	Gabriele Seyfert GDR	Beatrix Schuba AUT	Zsuzsa Almássy HUN
1971	Zurich SUI	Beatrix Schuba AUT	Zsuzsa Almássy HUN	Rita Trapanese ITA
1972	Gothenburg SWE	Beatrix Schuba AUT	Rita Trapanese ITA	Sonja Morgenstern GDR
1973	Cologne FRG	Christine Errath GDR	Jean Scott GBR	Karin Iten SUI
1974	Zagreb YUG	Christine Errath GDR	Dianne de Leeuw NED	Liana Drahová CZE
1975	Copenhagen DEN	Christine Errath GDR	Dianne de Leeuw NED	Anett Pötzsch GDR
1976	Geneva SUI	Dianne de Leeuw NED	Anett Pötzsch GDR	Christine Errath GDR
1977	Helsinki FIN	Anett Pötzsch GDR	Dagmar Lurz FRG	Susanna Driano ITA
1978	Strasbourg FRA	Anett Pötzsch GDR	Dagmar Lurz FRG	Elena Vodorezova URS
1979	Zagreb YUG	Anett Pötzsch GDR	Dagmar Lurz FRG	Denise Biellmann SUI
1980	Gothenburg SWE	Anett Pötzsch GDR	Dagmar Lurz FRG	Susanna Driano ITA
1981	Innsbruck AUT	Denise Biellmann SUI	Sanda Dubravčić YUG	Claudia Kristofics-Binder AUT
1982	Lyon FRA	Claudia Kristofics-Binder AUT	Katarina Witt GDR	Elena Vodorezova URS
1983	Dortmund FRG	Katarina Witt GDR	Elena Vodorezova URS	Claudia Leistner FRG
1984	Budapest HUN	Katarina Witt GDR	Manuela Ruben FRG	Anna Kondrashova URS

Year	Location	Gold	Silver	Bronze
1985	Gothenburg SWE	Katarina Witt GDR	Kira Ivanova URS	Claudia Leistner FRG
1986	Copenhagen DEN	Katarina Witt GDR	Kira Ivanova URS	Anna Kondrashova URS
1987	Sarajevo YUG	Katarina Witt GDR	Kira Ivanova URS	Anna Kondrashova URS
1988	Prague CZE	Katarina Witt GDR	Kira Ivanova URS	Anna Kondrashova URS
1989	Birmingham GBR	Claudia Leistner FRG	Natalia Lebedeva URS	Patricia Neske FRG
1990	Leningrad URS	Evelyn Grossmann GDR	Natalia Lebedeva URS	Marina Kielmann FRG
1991	Sofia BUL	Surya Bonaly FRA	Evelyn Grossmann GDR	Marina Kielmann FRG
1992	Lausanne SUI	Surya Bonaly FRA	Marina Kielmann FRG	Patricia Neske FRG
1993	Helsinki FIN	Surya Bonaly FRA	Oksana Baiul UKR	Marina Kielmann FRG
1994	Copenhagen DEN	Surya Bonaly FRA	Oksana Baiul UKR	Olga Markova RUS
1995	Dortmund GER	Surya Bonaly FRA	Olga Markova RUS	Elena Liashenko UKR
1996	Sofia BUL	Irina Slutskaya RUS	Surya Bonaly FRA	Maria Butyrskaya RUS
1997	Paris FRA	Irina Slutskaya RUS	Krisztina Czako HUN	Yulia Lavrenchuk UKR
1998	Milan ITA	Maria Butyrskaya RUS	Irina Slutskaya RUS	Tanja Szewczenko GER
1999	Prague CZE	Maria Butyrskaya RUS	Julia Soldatova RUS	Viktoria Volchkova RUS
2000	Vienna AUT	Irina Slutskaya RUS	Maria Butyrskaya RUS	Viktoria Volchkova RUS
2001	Bratislava, CZE	Irina Slutskaya RUS	Maria Butyrskaya RUS	Viktoria Volchkova RUS
2002	Lausanne SUI	Maria Butyrskaya RUS	Irina Slutskaya RUS	Viktoria Volchkova RUS
2003	Malmö SWE	Irina Slutskaya RUS	Elena Sokolova RUS	Julia Sebestyen HUN
2004	Budapest HUN	Julia Sebestyen HUN	Elena Liashenko UKR	Elena Sokolova RUS
2005	Torino ITA	Irina Slutskaya RUS	Susanna Pöykiö FIN	Elena Liashenko UKR
2006	Lyon FRA	Irina Slutskaya RUS	Elena Sokolova RUS	Carolina Kostner ITA
2007	Warsaw POL	Carolina Kostner ITA	Sarah Meier SUI	Kiira Korpi FIN
2008	Zagreb CRO	Carolina Kostner ITA	Sarah Meier SUI	Laura Lepistö FIN
2009	Helsinki FIN	Laura Lepistö FIN	Carolina Kostner ITA	Susanna Pöykiö FIN
2010	Tallinn EST	Carolina Kostner ITA	Laura Lepistö FIN	Elene Gedevanishvili GEO

Men

Year	Location	Gold	Silver	Bronze
1891	Hamburg GER	Oskar Uhlig GER	A. Schmitson GER	Franz Zilly GER
1892	Vienna AUT	Eduard Engelmann, Jr. AUT	Tibor von Földváry HUN	Georg Zachariades AUT
1893	Berlin GER	Eduard Engelmann, Jr. AUT	Henning Grenander AUT	Georg Zachariades AUT
1894	Vienna AUT	Eduard Engelmann, Jr. AUT	Gustav Hügel AUT	Tibor von Földváry HUN
1895	Budapest HUN	Tibor von Földváry HUN	Gustav Hügel AUT	Gilbert Fuchs GER
1896–1897	The European Championships were not held.			
1898	Trondheim NOR	Ulrich Salchow SWE	Johan Lefstad NOR	Oscar Holthe NOR
1899	Davos SWI	Ulrich Salchow SWE	Gustav Hügel AUT	Ernst Fellner AUT
1900	Berlin GER	Ulrich Salchow SWE	Gustav Hügel AUT	Oscar Holthe NOR
1901	Vienna AUT	Gustav Hügel AUT	Gilbert Fuchs GER	Ulrich Salchow SWE
1902–1903	The European Championships were not held.			
1904	Davos SWI	Ulrich Salchow SWE	Max Bohatsch AUT	Nikolai Panin RUS
1905	Bonn GER	Max Bohatsch AUT	Heinrich Burger GER	Karl Zenger GER
1906	Davos SWI	Ulrich Salchow SWE	Ernst Herz AUT	Per Thorén SWE
1907	Berlin GER	Ulrich Salchow SWE	Gilbert Fuchs GER	Ernst Herz AUT
1908	Warsaw POL	Ernst Herz AUT	Nikolai Panin RUS	S. Predrzymirski AUT
1909	Budapest HUN	Ulrich Salchow SWE	Gilbert Fuchs GER	Per Thorén SWE
1910	Berlin GER	Ulrich Salchow SWE	Werner Rittberger GER	Per Thorén SWE
1911	Leningrad RUS	Per Thorén SWE	Karl Ollow RUS	Werner Rittberger GER
1912	Stockholm SWE	Gösta Sandahl SWE	Ivan Malinin RUS	Martin Stixrud NOR
1913	Oslo NOR	Ulrich Salchow SWE	Andor Szende HUN	Willy Böckl AUT
1914	Vienna AUT	Fritz Kachler AUT	Alexander Krogh NOR	Willy Böckl AUT

Year	Location	Gold	Silver	Bronze
1915–1921	The European Championships were not held.			
1922	Davos SWI	Wilhelm Böckl AUT	Fritz Kachler AUT	Ernst Oppacher AUT
1923	Oslo NOR	Wilhelm Böckl AUT	Martin Stixrud NOR	Gunnar Jakobsson FIN
1924	Davos SWI	Fritz Kachler AUT	Ludwig Wrede AUT	Werner Rittberger GER
1925	Triberg GER	Wilhelm Böckl AUT	Werner Rittberger GER	Otto Preissecker AUT
1926	Davos SWI	Wilhelm Böckl AUT	Otto Preissecker AUT	Georg Gautschi SWI
1927	Vienna AUT	Wilhelm Böckl AUT	Hugo Distler AUT	Karl Schäfer AUT
1928	Troppau CSR	Wilhelm Böckl AUT	Karl Schäfer AUT	Otto Preissecker AUT
1929	Davos SWI	Karl Schäfer AUT	Georg Gautschi SWI	Ludwig Wrede AUT
1930	Berlin GER	Karl Schäfer AUT	Otto Gold CSR	Markus Nikkanen FIN
1931	Vienna AUT	Karl Schäfer AUT	Ernst Baier GER	Hugo Distler AUT
1932	Paris FRA	Karl Schäfer AUT	Ernst Baier GER	Erich Erdös AUT
1933	London GRB	Karl Schäfer AUT	Ernst Baier GER	Erich Erdös AUT
1934	Seefeld GER	Karl Schäfer AUT	Dénes Pataky HUN	Elemér Terták HUN
1935	St. Moritz SWI	Karl Schäfer AUT	Felix Kaspar AUT	Ernst Baier GER
1936	Berlin GER	Karl Schäfer AUT	Graham Sharp GBR	Ernst Baier GER
1937	Prague CZE	Felix Kaspar AUT	Graham Sharp GBR	Elemér Terták HUN
1938	St. Moritz SWI	Felix Kaspar AUT	Graham Sharp GBR	Herbert Alward AUT
1939	London GRB	Graham Sharp GBR	Freddie Tomlins GBR	Horst Faber GER
1940–1946	The European Championships were not held.			
1947	Davos SWI	Hans Gerschwiler SWI	Vladislav Čáp CSR	Fernand Leemans BEL
1948	Prague CSR	Richard Button USA	Hans Gerschwiler SWI	Edi Rada AUT
1949	Milan ITA	Edi Rada AUT	Ede Király HUN	Helmut Seibt AUT

Year	Location	Gold	Silver	Bronze
1950	Oslo NOR	Ede Király HUN	Helmut Seibt AUT	Carlo Fassi ITA
1951	Zurich SWI	Helmut Seibt AUT	Horst Faber GER	Carlo Fassi ITA
1952	Vienna AUT	Helmut Seibt AUT	Carlo Fassi ITA	Michael Carrington GRB
1953	Dortmund FRG	Carlo Fassi ITA	Alain Giletti FRA	Freimut Stein GER
1954	Bolzano ITA	Carlo Fassi ITA	Alain Giletti FRA	Karol Divin CZE
1955	Budapest HUN	Alain Giletti FRA	Michael Booker GRB	Karol Divin CZE
1956	Paris FRA	Alain Giletti FRA	Michael Booker GRB	Karol Divin CZE
1957	Vienna AUT	Alain Giletti FRA	Karol Divin CZE	Michael Booker GRB
1958	Bratislava CZE	Karol Divin CZE	Alain Giletti FRA	Alain Calmat FRA
1959	Davos SWI	Karol Divin CZE	Alain Giletti FRA	Norbert Felsinger AUT
1960	Garmisch-Partenkirchen GER	Alain Giletti FRA	Norbert Felsinger AUT	Manfred Schnelldorfer FRG
1961	Berlin FRG	Alain Giletti FRA	Alain Calmat FRA	Manfred Schnelldorfer FRG
1962	Geneva SWI	Alain Giletti FRA	Karol Divin CZE	Manfred Schnelldorfer FRG
1963	Budapest HUN	Alain Calmat FRA	Manfred Schnelldorfer FRG	Emmerich Danzer AUT
1964	Grenoble FRA	Alain Calmat FRA	Manfred Schnelldorfer FRG	Karol Divin CZE
1965	Moscow URS	Emmerich Danzer AUT	Alain Calmat FRA	Peter Jonas AUT
1966	Bratislava CZE	Emmerich Danzer AUT	Wolfgang Schwarz AUT	Ondrej Nepela CZE
1967	Ljubljana YUG	Emmerich Danzer AUT	Wolfgang Schwarz AUT	Ondrej Nepela CZE
1968	Västerås SWE	Emmerich Danzer AUT	Wolfgang Schwarz AUT	Ondrej Nepela CZE
1969	Garmish-Partenkirchen FRG	Ondrej Nepela CZE	Patrick Pera FRA	Sergei Chetverukhin URS
1970	Leningrad URS	Ondrej Nepela CZE	Patrick Pera FRA	Günter Zöller GDR
1971	Zurich SWI	Ondrej Nepela CZE	Sergei Chetverukhin URS	Haig Oundjian GRB
1972	Gothenburg SWE	Ondrej Nepela CZE	Sergei Chetverukhin URS	Patrick Pera FRA
1973	Cologne FRG	Ondrej Nepela CZE	Sergei Chetverukhin URS	Jan Hoffmann GDR
1974	Zagreb YUG	Jan Hoffmann GDR	Sergei Volkov URS	John Curry GRB

Year	Location	Gold	Silver	Bronze
1975	Copenhagen DEN	Vladimir Kovalev URS	John Curry GRB	Yuri Ovchinnikov URS
1976	Geneva SWI	John Curry GRB	Vladimir Kovalev URS	Jan Hoffmann GDR
1977	Helsinki FIN	Jan Hoffmann GDR	Vladimir Kovalev URS	Robin Cousins GRB
1978	Strasbourg FRA	Jan Hoffmann GDR	Vladimir Kovalev URS	Robin Cousins GRB
1979	Zagreb YUG	Jan Hoffmann GDR	Vladimir Kovalev URS	Robin Cousins GRB
1980	Gothenburg SWE	Robin Cousins GRB	Jan Hoffmann GDR	Vladimir Kovalev URS
1981	Innsbruck AUT	Igor Bobrin URS	Jean-Christophe Simond FRA	Norbert Schramm FRG
1982	Lyon FRA	Norbert Schramm FRG	Jean-Christophe Simond FRA	Igor Bobrin URS
1983	Dortmund FRG	Norbert Schramm FRG	Jozef Sabovčík CZE	Alexandr Fadeev URS
1984	Budapest HUN	Alexandr Fadeev URS	Rudi Cerne FRG	Norbert Schramm FRG
1985	Gothenburg SWE	Jozef Sabovčík CZE	Vladimir Kotin URS	Grzegorz Filpowski POL
1986	Copenhagen DEN	Jozef Sabovčík CZE	Vladimir Kotin URS	Alexandr Fadeev URS
1987	Sarajevo YUG	Alexandr Fadeev URS	Vladimir Kotin URS	Viktor Petrenko URS
1988	Prague CZE	Alexandr Fadeev URS	Vladimir Kotin URS	Viktor Petrenko URS
1989	Birmingham GRB	Alexandr Fadeev URS	Grzegorz Filpowski POL	Petr Barna CZE
1990	Leningrad URS	Viktor Petrenko URS	Petr Barna CZE	Viacheslav Zegorodniuk URS
1991	Sofia BUL	Viktor Petrenko URS	Petr Barna CZE	Viacheslav Zegorodniuk URS
1992	Lausanne SWI	Petr Barna CZE	Viktor Petrenko EUN	Alexei Urmanov EUN
1993	Helsinki FIN	Dmitri Dmitrenko UKR	Philippe Candeloro FRA	Eric Millot FRA
1994	Copenhagen DEN	Viktor Petrenko UKR	Viacheslav Zagorodniuk UKR	Alexei Urmanov RUS
1995	Dortmund GER	Ilia Kulik RUS	Alexei Urmanov RUS	Viacheslav Zagorodniuk UKR
1996	Sofia BUL	Viacheslav Zagorodniuk UKR	Igor Pashkevich RUS	Ilia Kulik RUS
1997	Paris FRA	Alexei Urmanov RUS	Philippe Candeloro FRA	Viacheslav Zagorodniuk UKR
1998	Milan ITA	Alexei Yagudin RUS	Evgeny Plushenko RUS	Alexandr Abt RUS
1999	Prague CZE	Alexei Yagudin RUS	Evgeny Plushenko RUS	Alexei Urmanov RUS

Year	Location	Gold	Silver	Bronze
2000	Vienna AUT	Evgeny Plushenko RUS	Alexei Yagudin RUS	Dmitri Dmitrenko UKR
2001	Bratislava, CZE	Evgeny Plushenko RUS	Alexei Yagudin RUS	Stanick Jeannette FRA
2002	Lausanne SUI	Alexei Yagudin RUS	Alexandr Abt RUS	Brian Joubert FRA
2003	Malmö SWE	Evgeny Plushenko RUS	Brian Joubert FRA	Stanick Jeannette FRA
2004	Budapest HUN	Brian Joubert FRA	Evgeny Plushenko RUS	Ilia Klimkin RUS
2005	Torino ITA	Evgeny Plushenko RUS	Brian Joubert FRA	Stefan Lindemann GER
2006	Lyon FRA	Evgeny Plushenko RUS	Stéphane Lambiel SUI	Brian Joubert FRA
2007	Warsaw POL	Brian Joubert FRA	Tomáš Verner CZE	Kevin van der Perren BEL
2008	Zagreb CRO	Tomáš Verner CZE	Stéphane Lambiel SUI	Brian Joubert FRA
2009	Helsinki FIN	Brian Joubert FRA	Samuel Contesti ITA	Kevin van der Perren BEL
2010	Tallinn EST	Evgeny Plushenko RUS	Stéphane Lambiel SUI	Brian Joubert FRA

Pairs

Year	Location	Gold	Silver	Bronze
1930	Vienna AUT	Olga Orgonista & Sándor Szalay HUN	Emilia Rotter & László Szollás HUN	Gisela Hochhaltinger & Otto Preissecker AUT
1931	St. Moritz SWI	Olga Orgonista & Sándor Szalay HUN	Emilia Rotter & László Szollás HUN	Lilly Gaillard & Willy Petter AUT
1932	Paris FRA	Andrée Brunet & Pierre Brunet FRA	Lilly Gaillard & Willy Petter AUT	Idi Papez & Karl Zwack AUT
1933	London GRB	Idi Papez & Karl Zwack AUT	Lilly Scholz-Gaillard & Willy Petter AUT	Mollie Phillips & Rodney Murdoch GRB
1934	Prague CSR	Emilia Rotter & László Szollás HUN	Idi Papez & Karl Zwack AUT	Zofja Bilorowna & Tadeusz Kowalski POL
1935	St. Moritz SWI	Maxi Herber & Ernst Baier GER	Idi Papez & Karl Zwack AUT	Lucy Galló & Rezsö Dillinger HUN
1936	Berlin GER	Maxi Herber & Ernst Baier GER	Violet Cliff & Leslie Cliff GRB	Piroska Szekrényessy & Attila Szekrényessy HUN
1937	Prague CZE	Maxi Herber & Ernst Baier GER	Ilse Pausin & Erich Pausin AUT	Piroska Szekrényessy & Attila Szekrényessy HUN
1938	Troppau CZE	Maxi Herber & Ernst Baier GER	Ilse Pausin & Erich Pausin AUT	Inge Koch & Günther Noack GER
1939	Zakopane POL	Maxi Herber & Ernst Baier GER	Ilse Pausin & Erich Pausin AUT	Inge Koch & Günther Noack GER
1940–1946	The European Championships were not held.			
1947	Davos SWI	Micheline Lannoy & Pierre Baugniet BEL	Winifred Silverthorne & Dennis Silverthorne GBR	Suzanne Diskeuve & Edmond Verbustel BEL
1948	Prague CSR	Andrea Kekéssy & Ede Király HUN	Blazena Knittlová & Karel Vosatka CZE	Herta Ratzenhofer & Emil Ratzenhofer AUT
1949	Milan ITA	Andrea Kekéssy & Ede Király HUN	Marianna Nagy & László Nagy HUN	Herta Ratzenhofer & Emil Ratzenhofer AUT

Year	Location	Gold	Silver	Bronze
1950	Oslo NOR	Marianna Nagy & László Nagy HUN	Eliane Steinemann & André Calame SWI	Jennifer Nicks & John Nicks GRB
1951	Zurich SWI	Ria Baran & Paul Falk GER	Eliane Steinemann & André Calame SWI	Silvia Grandjean & Michel Grandjean SWI
1952	Vienna AUT	Ria Falk & Paul Falk GER	Jennifer Nicks & John Nicks GRB	Marianna Nagy & László Nagy HUN
1953	Dortmund FRG	Jennifer Nicks & John Nicks GRB	Marianna Nagy & László Nagy HUN	Elisabeth Schwarz & Kurt Oppelt AUT
1954	Bolzano ITA	Silvia Grandjean & Michel Grandjean SWI	Elisabeth Schwarz & Kurt Oppelt AUT	Sonja Balunová & Miroslav Balun CZE
1955	Budapest HUN	Marianna Nagy & László Nagy HUN	Věra Suchánková & Zdeněk Doležal CZE	Marika Kilius & Franz Ningel GER
1956	Paris FRA	Elisabeth Schwarz & Kurt Oppelt AUT	Marianna Nagy & László Nagy HUN	Marika Kilius & Franz Ningel FRG
1957	Vienna AUT	Věra Suchánková & Zdeněk Doležal CZE	Marianna Nagy & László Nagy HUN	Marika Kilius & Franz Ningel FRG
1958	Bratislava CZE	Věra Suchánková & Zdeněk Doležal CZE	Nina Zhuk & Stanislav Zhuk URS	Joyce Coates & Anthony Holles GBR
1959	Davos SWI	Marika Kilius & Hans-Jürgen Bäumler FRG	Nina Zhuk & Stanislav Zhuk URS	Joyce Coates & Anthony Holles GBR
1960	Garmisch-Partenkirchen GER	Marika Kilius & Hans-Jürgen Bäumler FRG	Nina Zhuk & Stanislav Zhuk URS	Margret Göbl & Franz Ningel FRG
1961	Berlin GER	Marika Kilius & Hans-Jürgen Bäumler FRG	Margret Göbl & Franz Ningel FRG	Margrit Senf & Peter Göbel GDR
1962	Geneva SWI	Marika Kilius & Hans-Jürgen Bäumler FRG	Liudmila Belousova & Oleg Protopopov URS	Margret Göbl & Franz Ningel FRG

Year	Location	Gold	Silver	Bronze
1963	Budapest HUN	Marika Kilius & Hans-Jürgen Bäumler FRG	Liudmila Belousova & Oleg Protopopov URS	Tatiana Zhuk & Alexandr Gavrilov URS
1964	Grenoble FRA	Marika Kilius & Hans-Jürgen Bäumler FRG	Liudmila Belousova & Oleg Protopopov URS	Tatiana Zhuk & Alexandr Gavrilov URS
1965	Moscow URS	Liudmila Belousova & Oleg Protopopov URS	Gerda Johner & Ruedi Johner SWI	Tatiana Zhuk & Alexandr Gavrilov URS
1966	Bratislava CZE	Liudmila Belousova & Oleg Protopopov URS	Tatiana Zhuk & Alexandr Gavrilov URS	Margot Glockshuber & Wolfgang Danne FRG
1967	Ljubljana YUG	Liudmila Belousova & Oleg Protopopov URS	Margot Glockshuber & Wolfgang Danne FRG	Heidemarie Steiner & Heinz-Ulrich Walther GDR
1968	Västerås SWE	Liudmila Belousova & Oleg Protopopov URS	Tamara Moskvina & Alexei Mishin URS	Heidemarie Steiner & Heinz-Ulrich Walther GDR
1969	Garmish-Partenkirchen FRG	Irina Rodnina & Alexei Ulanov URS	Liudmila Belousova & Oleg Protopopov URS	Tamara Moskvina & Alexei Mishin URS
1970	Leningrad URS	Irina Rodnina & Alexei Ulanov URS	Liudmila Smirnova & Andrei Suraikin URS	Heidemarie Steiner & Heinz-Ulrich Walther GDR
1971	Zurich SWI	Irina Rodnina & Alexei Ulanov URS	Liudmila Smirnova & Andrei Suraikin URS	Galina Karelina & Georgi Proskurin URS
1972	Gothenburg SWE	Irina Rodnina & Alexei Ulanov URS	Liudmila Smirnova & Andrei Suraikin URS	Manuela Gross & Uwe Kagelmann GDR
1973	Cologne FRG	Irina Rodnina & Alexei Ulanov URS	Liudmila Smirnova & Andrei Suraikin URS	Almut Lehmann & Herbert Wiesinger FRG
1974	Zagreb YUG	Irina Rodnina & Alexandr Zaitsev URS	Romy Kermer & Rolf Österreich GDR	Liudmila Smirnova & Alexei Ulanov URS
1975	Copenhagen DEN	Irina Rodnina & Alexandr Zaitsev URS	Romy Kermer & Rolf Österreich GDR	Manuela Gross & Uwe Kagelmann GDR

Year	Location	Gold	Silver	Bronze
1976	Geneva SWI	Irina Rodnina & Alexandr Zaitsev URS	Romy Kermer & Rolf Österreich GDR	Irina Vorobieva & Alexandr Vlasov URS
1977	Helsinki FIN	Irina Rodnina & Alexandr Zaitsev URS	Irina Vorobieva & Alexandr Vlasov URS	Marina Cherkasova & Sergei Shakhrai URS
1978	Strasbourg FRA	Irina Rodnina & Alexandr Zaitsev URS	Marina Cherkasova & Sergei Shakhrai URS	Manuela Mager & Uwe Bewersdorff GDR
1979	Zagreb YUG	Marina Cherkasova & Sergei Shakhrai URS	Irina Vorobieva & Igor Lisovski URS	Sabine Baess & Tassilo Thierbach GDR
1980	Gothenburg SWE	Irina Rodnina & Alexandr Zaitsev URS	Marina Cherkasova & Sergei Shakhrai URS	Marina Pestova & Stanislav Leonovich URS
1981	Innsbruck AUT	Irina Vorobieva & Igor Lisovski URS	Christina Riegel & Andreas Nischwitz FRG	Marina Cherkasova & Sergei Shakhrai URS
1982	Lyon FRA	Sabine Baess & Tassilo Thierbach GDR	Marina Pestova & Stanislav Leonovich URS	Irina Vorobieva & Igor Lisovski URS
1983	Dortmund FRG	Sabine Baess & Tassilo Thierbach GDR	Elena Valova & Oleg Vasiliev URS	Birgit Lorenz & Knut Schubert GDR
1984	Budapest HUN	Elena Valova & Oleg Vasiliev URS	Sabine Baess & Tassilo Thierbach GDR	Birgit Lorenz & Knut Schubert GDR
1985	Gothenburg SWE	Elena Valova & Oleg Vasiliev URS	Larisa Selezneva & Oleg Makarov URS	Veronika Pershina & Marat Akbarov URS
1986	Copenhagen DEN	Elena Valova & Oleg Vasiliev URS	Ekaterina Gordeeva & Sergei Grinkov URS	Elena Bechke & Valeri Kornienko URS
1987	Sarajevo YUG	Larisa Selezneva & Oleg Makarov URS	Elena Valova & Oleg Vasiliev URS	Katrin Kanitz & Tobias Schröter GDR
1988	Prague CZE	Ekaterina Gordeeva & Sergei Grinkov URS	Larisa Selezneva & Oleg Makarov URS	Peggy Schwarz & Alexander König GDR

Year	Location	Gold	Silver	Bronze
1989	Birmingham GRB	Larisa Selezneva & Oleg Makarov URS	Mandy Wötzel & Axel Rauschenbach GDR	Natalia Mishkutenok & Artur Dmitriev URS
1990	Leningrad URS	Ekaterina Gordeeva & Sergei Grinkov URS	Larisa Selezneva & Oleg Makarov URS	Natalia Mishkutenok & Artur Dmitriev URS
1991	Sofia BUL	Natalia Mishkutenok & Artur Dmitriev URS	Elena Bechke & Denis Petrov URS	Evgenia Shishkova & Vadim Naumov URS
1992	Lausanne SWI	Natalia Mishkutenok & Artur Dmitriev URS	Elena Bechke & Denis Petrov URS	Evgenia Shishkova & Vadim Naumov CIS
1993	Helsinki FIN	Marina Eltsova & Andrei Bushkov RUS	Mandy Wötzel & Ingo Steuer GER	Evgenia Shishkova & Vadim Naumov RUS
1994	Copenhagen DEN	Ekaterina Gordeeva & Sergei Grinkov URS	Evgenia Shishkova & Vadim Naumov RUS	Natalia Mishkutenok & Artur Dmitriev RUS
1995	Dortmund GER	Mandy Wötzel & Ingo Steuer GER	Radka Kovaříková & René Novotný CZE	Evgenia Shishkova & Vadim Naumov RUS
1996	Sofia BUL	Oksana Kazakova & Artur Dmitriev RUS	Mandy Wötzel & Ingo Steuer GER	Sarah Abitbol & Stephane Bernadis FRA
1997	Paris FRA	Marina Eltsova & Andrei Bushkov RUS	Mandy Wötzel & Ingo Steuer GER	Elena Berezhnaya & Anton Sikharulidze RUS
1998	Milan ITA	Elena Berezhnaya & Anton Sikharulidze RUS	Oksana Kazakova & Artur Dmitriev RUS	Sarah Abitbol & Stephane Bernadis FRA
1999	Prague CZE	Maria Petrova & Alexei Tikhonov RUS	Dorota Zagorska & Mariusz Siudek POL	Sarah Abitbol & Stephane Bernadis FRA
2000	Vienna AUT	Elena Berezhnaya & Anton Sikharulidze RUS	Maria Petrova & Alexei Tikhonov RUS	Dorota Zagorska & Mariusz Siudek POL
2001	Bratislava, CZE	Elena Berezhnaya & Anton Sikharulidze RUS	Tatiana Totmianina & Maxim Marinin RUS	Sarah Abitbol & Stephane Bernadis FRA

Year	Location	Gold	Silver	Bronze
2002	Lausanne SUI	Tatiana Totmianina & Maxim Marinin RUS	Sarah Abitbol & Stephane Bernadis FRA	Maria Petrova & Alexei Tikhonov RUS
2003	Malmö SWE	Tatiana Totmianina & Maxim Marinin RUS	Sarah Abitbol & Stephane Bernadis FRA	Maria Petrova & Alexei Tikhonov RUS
2004	Budapest HUN	Tatiana Totmianina & Maxim Marinin RUS	Maria Petrova & Alexei Tikhonov RUS	Dorota Zagorska & Mariusz Siudek POL
2005	Torino ITA	Tatiana Totmianina & Maxim Marinin RUS	Julia Obertas & Sergei Slavnov RUS	Maria Petrova & Alexei Tikhonov RUS
2006	Lyon FRA	Tatiana Totmianina & Maxim Marinin RUS	Aliona Savchenko & Robin Szolkowy GER	Maria Petrova & Alexei Tikhonov RUS
2007	Warsaw POL	Aliona Savchenko & Robin Szolkowy GER	Maria Petrova & Alexei Tikhonov RUS	Dorota Siudek & Mariusz Siudek POL
2008	Zagreb CRO	Aliona Savchenko & Robin Szolkowy GER	Maria Mukhortova & Maxim Trankov RUS	Yuko Kawaguti & Alexandr Smirnov RUS
2009	Helsinki FIN	Aliona Savchenko & Robin Szolkowy GER	Yuko Kawaguti & Alexandr Smirnov RUS	Maria Mukhortova & Maxim Trankov RUS
2010	Tallinn EST	Yuko Kawaguti & Alexandr Smirnov RUS	Aliona Savchenko & Robin Szolkowy GER	Maria Mukhortova & Maxim Trankov RUS

Ice Dancing

Year	Location	Gold	Silver	Bronze
1954	Bolzano ITA	Jean Westwood & Lawrence Demmy GRB	Nesta Davies & Paul Thomas GRB	Barbara Radford & Raymond Lockwood GRB
1955	Budapest HUN	Jean Westwood & Lawrence Demmy GRB	Pamela Weight & Paul Thomas GRB	Barbara Radford & Raymond Lockwood GRB
1956	Paris FRA	Pamela Weight & Paul Thomas GRB	June Markham & Courtney Jones GRB	Barbara Thompson & Gerard Rigby GRB
1957	Vienna AUT	June Markham & Courtney Jones GRB	Barbara Thompson & Gerard Rigby GRB	Catherine Morris & Michael Robinson GRB
1958	Bratislava CZE	June Markham & Courtney Jones GRB	Catherine Morris & Michael Robinson GRB	Barbara Thompson & Gerard Rigby GRB
1959	Davos SWI	Doreen Denny & Courtney Jones GRB	Catherine Morris & Michael Robinson GRB	Christiane Guhel & Jean Paul Guhel FRA
1960	Garmisch-Partenkirchen FGR	Doreen Denny & Courtney Jones GRB	Christiane Guhel & Jean Paul Guhel FRA	Mary Parry & Roy Mason GRB
1961	Berlin FRG	Doreen Denny & Courtney Jones GRB	Christiane Guhel & Jean Paul Guhel FRA	Linda Shearman & Michael Phillips GRB
1962	Geneva SWI	Christiane Guhel & Jean Paul Guhel FRA	Linda Shearman & Michael Phillips GRB	Eva Romanová & Pavel Roman CZE
1963	Budapest HUN	Linda Shearman & Michael Phillips GRB	Eva Romanová & Pavel Roman CZE	Janet Sawbridge & David Hickinbottom GRB
1964	Grenoble FRA	Eva Romanová & Pavel Roman CZE	Janet Sawbridge & David Hickinbottom GRB	Yvonne Suddick & Roger Kennerson GRB
1965	Moscow URS	Eva Romanová & Pavel Roman CZE	Janet Sawbridge & David Hickinbottom GRB	Yvonne Suddick & Roger Kennerson GRB
1966	Bratislava CZE	Diane Towler & Bernard Ford GRB	Yvonne Suddick & Roger Kennerson GRB	Jitka Babická & Jaromir Holan CZE
1967	Ljubljana YUG	Diane Towler & Bernard Ford GRB	Yvonne Suddick & Malcolm Cannon GRB	Brigitte Martin & Francis Gamichon FRA
1968	Västerås SWE	Diane Towler & Bernard Ford GRB	Yvonne Suddick & Malcolm Cannon GRB	Janet Sawbridge & Jon Lane GRB

Year	Location	Gold	Silver	Bronze
1969	Garmisch-Partenkirchen GER	Diane Towler & Bernard Ford GRB	Janet Sawbridge & Jon Lane GRB	Liudmila Pakhomova & Alexandr Gorshkov URS
1970	Leningrad URS	Liudmila Pakhomova & Alexandr Gorshkov URS	Angelika Buck & Erich Buck FRG	Tatiana Voitiuk & Viacheslav Zhigalin URS
1971	Zurich SWI	Liudmila Pakhomova & Alexandr Gorshkov URS	Angelika Buck & Erich Buck FRG	Susan Getty & Roy Bradshaw GRB
1972	Gothenburg SWE	Angelika Buck & Erich Buck FRG	Liudmila Pakhomova & Alexandr Gorshkov URS	Janet Sawbridge & Peter Dalby GRB
1973	Cologne FRG	Liudmila Pakhomova & Alexandr Gorshkov URS	Angelika Buck & Erich Buck FRG	Hilary Green & Glyn Watts GRB
1974	Zagreb YUG	Liudmila Pakhomova & Alexandr Gorshkov URS	Hilary Green & Glyn Watts GRB	Natalia Linichuk & Gennadi Karponosov URS
1975	Copenhagen DEN	Liudmila Pakhomova & Alexandr Gorshkov URS	Hilary Green & Glyn Watts GRB	Natalia Linichuk & Gennadi Karponosov URS
1976	Geneva SWI	Liudmila Pakhomova & Alexandr Gorshkov URS	Irina Moiseeva & Andrei Minenkov URS	Natalia Linichuk & Gennadi Karponosov URS
1977	Helsinki FIN	Irina Moiseeva & Andrei Minenkov URS	Krisztina Regöczy & András Sallay HUN	Natalia Linichuk & Gennadi Karponosov URS
1978	Strasbourg FRA	Irina Moiseeva & Andrei Minenkov URS	Natalia Linichuk & Gennadi Karponosov URS	Krisztina Regöczy & András Sallay HUN
1979	Zagreb YUG	Natalia Linichuk & Gennadi Karponosov URS	Irina Moiseeva & Andrei Minenkov URS	Krisztina Regöczy & András Sallay HUN
1980	Gothenburg SWE	Natalia Linichuk & Gennadi Karponosov URS	Krisztina Regöczy & András Sallay HUN	Irina Moiseeva & Andrei Minenkov URS
1981	Innsbruck AUT	Jayne Torvill & Christopher Dean GRB	Irina Moiseeva & Andrei Minenkov URS	Natalia Linichuk & Gennadi Karponosov URS
1982	Lyon FRA	Jayne Torvill & Christopher Dean GRB	Natalia Bestemianova & Andrei Bukin URS	Irina Moiseeva & Andrei Minenkov URS

Year	Location	Gold	Silver	Bronze
1983	Dortmund FRG	Natalia Bestemianova & Andrei Bukin URS	Olga Volozhinskaia & Alexandr Svinin URS	Karen Barber & Nicholas Slater GBR
1984	Budapest HUN	Jayne Torvill & Christopher Dean GRB	Natalia Bestemianova & Andrei Bukin URS	Marina Klimova & Sergei Ponomarenko URS
1985	Gothenburg SWE	Natalia Bestemianova & Andrei Bukin URS	Marina Klimova & Sergei Ponomarenko URS	Petra Born & Rainer Schönborn FRG
1986	Copenhagen DEN	Natalia Bestemianova & Andrei Bukin URS	Marina Klimova & Sergei Ponomarenko URS	Natalia Annenko & Genrikh Sretenski URS
1987	Sarajevo YUG	Natalia Bestemianova & Andrei Bukin URS	Marina Klimova & Sergei Ponomarenko URS	Natalia Annenko & Genrikh Sretenski URS
1988	Prague CZE	Natalia Bestemianova & Andrei Bukin URS	Natalia Annenko & Genrikh Sretenski URS	Isabelle Duchesnay & Paul Duchesnay FRA
1989	Birmingham GRB	Marina Klimova & Sergei Ponomarenko URS	Maia Usova & Alexandr Zhulin URS	Natalia Annenko & Genrikh Sretenski URS
1990	Leningrad URS	Marina Klimova & Sergei Ponomarenko URS	Maia Usova & Alexandr Zhulin URS	Isabelle Duchesnay & Paul Duchesnay FRA
1991	Sofia BUL	Marina Klimova & Sergei Ponomarenko URS	Isabelle Duchesnay & Paul Duchesnay FRA	Maia Usova & Alexandr Zhulin URS
1992	Lausanne SWI	Marina Klimova & Sergei Ponomarenko URS	Maia Usova & Alexandr Zhulin URS	Oksana Grishchuk & Evgeny Platov CIS
1993	Helsinki FIN	Maia Usova & Alexandr Zhulin URS	Oksana Grishchuk & Evgeny Platov RUS	Susanna Rahkamo & Petri Kokko FIN
1994	Copenhagen DEN	Jayne Torvill & Christopher Dean GRB	Oksana Grishchuk & Evgeny Platov RUS	Maia Usova & Alexandr Zhulin RUS
1995	Dortmund GER	Susanna Rahkamo & Petri Kokko FIN	Sophie Moniotte & Pascal Lavanchy FRA	Anjelika Krylova & Oleg Ovsiannikov RUS
1996	Sofia BUL	Oksana Grishchuk & Evgeny Platov RUS	Anjelika Krylova & Oleg Ovsiannikov RUS	Irina Romanova & Igor Yaroshenko UKR

Year	Location	Gold	Silver	Bronze
1997	Paris FRA	Oksana Grishchuk & Evgeny Platov RUS	Anjelika Krylova & Oleg Ovsiannikov RUS	Sophie Moniotte & Pascal Lavanchy FRA
1998	Milan ITA	Oksana Grishchuk & Evgeny Platov RUS	Anjelika Krylova & Oleg Ovsiannikov RUS	Marina Anissina & Gwendal Peizerat FRA
1999	Prague CZE	Anjelika Krylova & Oleg Ovsiannikov RUS	Marina Anissina & Gwendal Peizerat FRA	Irina Lobacheva & Ilia Averbukh RUS
2000	Vienna AUT	Marina Anissina & Gwendal Peizerat FRA	Barbara Fusar-Poli & Maurizio Margaglio ITA	Margarita Drobiazko & Povilas Vanagas LTU
2001	Bratislava, CZE	Barbara Fusar-Poli & Maurizio Margaglio ITA	Marina Anissina & Gwendal Peizerat FRA	Irina Lobacheva & Ilia Averbukh RUS
2002	Lausanne SUI	Marina Anissina & Gwendal Peizerat FRA	Barbara Fusar-Poli & Maurizio Margaglio ITA	Irina Lobacheva & Ilia Averbukh RUS
2003	Malmö SWE	Irina Lobacheva & Ilia Averbukh RUS	Albena Denkova & Maxim Staviski BUL	Tatiana Navka & Roman Kostomarov RUS
2004	Budapest HUN	Tatiana Navka & Roman Kostomarov RUS	Albena Denkova & Maxim Staviski BUL	Elena Grushina & Ruslan Goncharov UKR
2005	Torino ITA	Tatiana Navka & Roman Kostomarov RUS	Elena Grushina & Ruslan Goncharov UKR	Isabelle Delobel & Olivier Schoenfelder FRA
2006	Lyon FRA	Tatiana Navka & Roman Kostomarov RUS	Elena Grushina & Ruslan Goncharov UKR	Margarita Drobiazko & Povilas Vanagas LTU
2007	Warsaw POL	Isabelle Delobel & Olivier Schoenfelder FRA	Oksana Domnina & Maxim Shabalin RUS	Albena Denkova & Maxim Staviski BUL
2008	Zagreb CRO	Oksana Domnina & Maxim Shabalin RUS	Isabelle Delobel & Olivier Schoenfelder FRA	Jana Khokhlova & Sergei Novitski RUS
2009	Helsinki FIN	Jana Khokhlova & Sergei Novitski RUS	Federica Faiella & Massimo Scali ITA	Sinead Kerr & John Kerr GBR
2010	Tallinn EST	Oksana Domnina & Maxim Shabalin RUS	Federica Faiella & Massimo Scali ITA	Jana Khokhlova & Sergei Novitski RUS

Appendix F

Medalists at the Four Continents Figure Skating Championships

Ladies

Year	Location	Gold	Silver	Bronze
1999	Halifax CAN	Tatiana Malinina UZB	Amber Corwin USA	Angela Nikodinov USA
2000	Osaka JPN	Angela Nikodinov USA	Stacey Pensgen USA	Annie Bellemare CAN
2001	Salt Lake City USA	Fumie Suguri JPN	Angela Nikodinov USA	Yoshie Onda JPN
2002	Jeonju KOR	Jennifer Kirk USA	Shizuka Arakawa JPN	Yoshie Onda JPN
2003	Beijing CHN	Fumie Suguri JPN	Shizuka Arakawa JPN	Yukari Nakano JPN
2004	Hamilton CAN	Yukina Ota JPN	Cynthia Phaneuf CAN	Amber Corwin USA
2005	Gangreung KOR	Fumie Suguri JPN	Yoshi Onda JPN	Jennifer Kirk USA
2006	Colorado Springs USA	Katy Taylor USA	Yukari Nakano JPN	Beatrisa Liang USA
2007	Colorado Springs USA	Kimmie Meissner USA	Emily Hughes USA	Joannie Rochette CAN
2008	Coyang City KOR	Mao Asada JPN	Joannie Rochette CAN	Miki Ando JPN
2009	Vancouver CAN	Yu Na Kim KOR	Joannie Rochette CAN	Mao Asada JPN
2010	Jeonju City KOR	Mao Asada JPN	Akiko Suzuki JPN	Caroline Zhang USA

Men

Year	Location	Gold	Silver	Bronze
1999	Halifax CAN	Takeshi Honda JPN	Chengjiang Li CHN	Elvis Stojko CAN
2000	Osaka JPN	Elvis Stojko CAN	Chengjiang Li CHN	Min Zhang CHN
2001	Salt Lake City USA	Chengjiang Li CHN	Takeshi Honda JPN	Michael Weiss USA
2002	Jeonju KOR	Jeffrey Buttle CAN	Takeshi Honda JPN	Song Gao CHN
2003	Beijing CHN	Takeshi Honda JPN	Min Zhang CHN	Chengjiang Li CHN
2004	Hamilton CAN	Jeffrey Buttle CAN	Emanuel Sandhu CAN	Evan Lysacek USA
2005	Gangreung KOR	Evan Lysacek USA	Chengjiang Li CHN	Daisuka Takahashi JPN
2006	Colorado Springs USA	Nobunari Oda JPN	Christopher Mabee CAN	Matthew Savoie USA
2007	Colorado Springs USA	Evan Lysacek USA	Jeffrey Buttle CAN	Jeremy Abbott USA
2008	Coyang City KOR	Daisuke Takahashi JPN	Jeffrey Buttle CAN	Evan Lysacek USA
2009	Vancouver CAN	Patrick Chan CAN	Evan Lysacek USA	Takahiko Kozuka JPN
2010	Jeonju City KOR	Adam Rippon USA	Tatsuki Machida JPN	Kevin Reynolds CAN

Pairs

Year	Location	Gold	Silver	Bronze
1999	Halifax CAN	Xue Shen & Hongbo Zhao CHN	Kristy Sargeant & Kris Wirtz CAN	Danielle Hartsell & Steve Hartsell USA
2000	Osaka JPN	Jamie Salé & David Pelletier CAN	Kyoko Ina & John Zimmerman USA	Tiffany Scott & Philip Dulebohn USA
2001	Salt Lake City USA	Jamie Salé & David Pelletier CAN	Xue Shen & Hongbo Zhao CHN	Kyoko Ina & John Zimmerman USA
2002	Jeonju KOR	Qing Pang & Jian Tong CHN	Anabelle Langlois & Patrice Archetto CAN	Dan Zhang & Hao Zhang CHN
2003	Beijing CHN	Xue Shen & Hongbo Zhao CHN	Qing Pang & Jian Tong CHN	Dan Zhang & Hao Zhang CHN
2004	Hamilton CAN	Qing Pang & Jian Tong CHN	Dan Zhang & Hao Zhang CHN	Valerie Marcoux & Craig Buntin CAN
2005	Gangreung KOR	Dan Zhang & Hao Zhang CHN	Qing Pang & Jian Tong CHN	Katheryn Orscher & Garrett Lucash USA
2006	Colorado Springs USA	Rena Inoue & John Baldwin USA	Utako Wakamatsu & Jean-Sebastien Fecteau CAN	Elizabeth Putnam & Sean Wirtz CAN
2007	Colorado Springs USA	Xue Shen & Hongbo Zhao CHN	Qing Pang & Jian Tong CHN	Rena Inoue & John Baldwin USA
2008	Coyang City KOR	Qing Pang & Jian Tong CHN	Dan Zhang & Hao Zhang CHN	Brooke Castile & Benjamin Okolski USA
2009	Vancouver CAN	Qing Pang & Jian Tong CHN	Jessica Dube & Bryce Davison CAN	Dan Zhang & Hao Zhang CHN
2010	Jeonju City KOR	Dan Zhang & Hao Zhang CHN	Keauna McLaughlin & Rockne Brubaker USA	Meagan Duhamel & Craig Buntin CAN

Ice Dancing

Year	Location	Gold	Silver	Bronze
1999	Halifax CAN	Shae-Lynn Bourne & Victor Kraatz CAN	Chantal Lefebvre & Michel Brunet CAN	Naomi Lang & Peter Tchernyshev USA
2000	Osaka JPN	Naomi Lang & Peter Tchernyshev USA	Marie-France Dubreuil & Patrice Lauzon CAN	Jamie Silverstein & Justin Pekarek USA
2001	Salt Lake City USA	Shae-Lynn Bourne & Victor Kraatz CAN	Naomi Lang & Peter Tchernyshev USA	Marie-France Dubreuil & Patrice Lauzon CAN
2002	Jeonju KOR	Naomi Lang & Peter Tchernyshev USA	Tanith Belbin & Benjamin Agosto USA	Megan Wing & Aaron Lowe CAN
2003	Beijing CHN	Shae-Lynn Bourne & Victor Kraatz CAN	Tanith Belbin & Benjamin Agosto USA	Naomi Lang & Peter Tchernyshev USA
2004	Hamilton CAN	Tanith Belbin & Benjamin Agosto USA	Marie-France Dubreuil & Patrice Lauzon CAN	Megan Wing & Aaron Lowe CAN
2005	Gangreung KOR	Tanith Belbin & Benjamin Agosto USA	Melissa Gregory & Denis Petukhov USA	Lydia Manon & Ryan O'Meara USA
2006	Colorado Springs USA	Tanith Belbin & Benjamin Agosto USA	Morgan Matthews & Maxim Zavozin USA	Tessa Virtue & Scott Moir CAN
2007	Colorado Springs USA	Marie-France Dubreuil & Patrice Lauzon CAN	Tanith Belbin & Benjamin Agosto USA	Tessa Virtue & Scott Moir CAN
2008	Coyang City KOR	Tessa Virtue & Scott Moir CAN	Meryl Davis & Charlie White USA	Kimberly Navarro & Brent Bommentre USA
2009	Vancouver CAN	Meryl Davis & Charlie White USA	Tessa Virtue & Scott Moir CAN	Emily Samuelson & Evan Bates USA
2010	Jeonju City KOR	Kaitlyn Weaver & Andrew Poje CAN	Allie Hann-McCurdy & Michael Coreno CAN	Madison Hubbell & Keiffer Hubbell USA

Appendix G
Medalists at the North American Figure Skating Championships

Ladies

Year	Location	Gold	Silver	Bronze
1923	Otawa, Ontario	Theresa Blanchard USA	Beatrix Loughran USA	Dorothy Jenkins CAN
1925	Boston, Massachusetts	Beatrix Loughran USA	Cecil Smith CAN	Theresa Blanchard USA
1927	Toronto, Ontario	Beatrix Loughran USA	Constance Wilson CAN	Cecil Smith CAN
1929	Boston, Massachusetts	Constance Wilson CAN	Maribel Vinson USA	Suzanne Davis USA
1931	Ottawa, Ontario	Constance Wilson CAN	Elizabeth Fisher CAN	Edith Secord USA
1933	New York, New York	Constance W. Samuel CAN	Cecil S. Gooderham CAN	Suzanne Davis USA
1935	Montreal, Quebec	Constance W. Samuel CAN	Maribel Vinson USA	Suzanne Davis USA
1937	Boston, Massachusetts	Maribel Vinson USA	Veronica Clarke CAN	Eleanor O'Meara CAN
1939	Toronto, Ontario	Mary Rose Thacker CAN	Joan Tozzer USA	Norah McCarthy CAN
1941	Ardmore, Pennsylvania	Mary Rose Thacker CAN	Eleanor O'Meara CAN	Norah McCarthy CAN
1943	The North American Championships were not held.			
1945	New York, New York	Barbara Ann Scott CAN	Gretchen Merrill USA	Janette Ahrens USA
1947	Ottawa, Ontario	Barbara Ann Scott CAN	Janette Ahrens USA	Yvonne Sherman USA
1949	Ardmore, Pennsylvania	Yvonne Sherman USA	Marlene Smith CAN	Virginia Baxter USA
1951	Calgary, Alberta	Sonya Klopfer USA	Suzanne Morrow CAN	Tenley Albright USA
1953	Cleveland, Ohio	Tenley Albright USA	Carol Heiss USA	Barbara Gratton CAN
1955	Regina, Saskatchewan	Tenley Albright USA	Carol Heiss USA	Patricia Firth USA
1957	Rochester, New York	Carol Heiss USA	Carole Jane Pachl CAN	Joan Schenke USA
1959	Toronto, Ontario	Carol Heiss USA	Lynn Finnegan USA	Nancy Heiss USA
1961	Philadelphia, Pennsylvania	Laurence Owen USA	Wendy Griner CAN	Sonia Snelling CAN
1963	Vancouver, British Columbia	Wendy Griner CAN	Petra Burka CAN	Shirra Kenworthy CAN
1965	Rochester, New York	Petra Burka CAN	Peggy Fleming USA	Valerie Jones CAN
1967	Montreal, Quebec	Peggy Fleming USA	Valerie Jones CAN	Albertina Noyes USA
1969	Oakland, California	Janet Lynn USA	Karen Magnussen CAN	Linda Carbonetto CAN
1971	Peterborough, Ontario	Karen Magnussen CAN	Janet Lynn USA	Suna Murray USA

Men

Year	Location	Gold	Silver	Bronze
1923	Otawa, Ontario	Sherwin Badger USA	Melville Rogers CAN	
1925	Boston, Massachusetts	Melville Rogers CAN	Nathaniel Niles USA	
1927	Toronto, Ontario	Melville Rogers CAN	Sherwin Badger USA	Roger Turner USA
1929	Boston, Massachusetts	Montgomery Wilson CAN	Roger Turner USA	Frederick Goodridge USA
1931	Ottawa, Ontario	Montgomery Wilson CAN	James Madden USA	Gail Borden, II USA
1933	New York, New York	Montgomery Wilson CAN	James Madden USA	Robin Lee USA
1935	Montreal, Quebec	Montgomery Wilson CAN	Robin Lee USA	James Madden USA
1937	Boston, Massachusetts	Montgomery Wilson CAN	Robin Lee USA	Ralph McCreath CAN
1939	Toronto, Ontario	Montgomery Wilson CAN	Robin Lee USA	Ralph McCreath CAN
1941	Ardmore, Pennsylvania	Ralph McCreath CAN	Eugene Turner USA	William Grimditch, Jr. USA
1943	The North American Championships were not held.			
1945	Men's events were not held.			
1947	Ottawa, Ontario	Richard Button USA	James Grogan USA	Wallace Diestelmeyer CAN
1949	Ardmore, Pennsylvania	Richard Button USA	James Grogan USA	Hayes Jenkins USA
1951	Calgary, Alberta	Richard Button USA	James Grogan USA	Hayes Jenkins USA
1953	Cleveland, Ohio	Hayes Jenkins USA	Peter Firstbrook CAN	Ronald Robertson USA
1955	Regina, Saskatchewan	Hayes Jenkins USA	David Jenkins USA	Charles Snelling CAN
1957	Rochester, New York	David Jenkins USA	Charles Snelling CAN	Tim Brown USA
1959	Toronto, Ontario	Donald Jackson CAN	Tim Brown USA	Robert Brewer USA
1961	Philadelphia, Pennsylvania	Donald Jackson CAN	Bradley Lord USA	Gregory Kelley USA
1963	Vancouver, British Columbia	Donald McPherson CAN	Tommy Litz USA	Scott Allen USA
1965	Rochester, New York	Gary Visconti USA	Scott Allen USA	Donald Knight CAN
1967	Montreal, Quebec	Donald Knight CAN	Scott Allen USA	Gary Visconti USA
1969	Oakland, California	Tim Wood USA	Jay Humphry CAN	John Petkevich USA
1971	Peterborough, Ontario	John Petkevich USA	Toller Cranston CAN	Kenneth Shelley USA

Pairs

Year	Location	Gold	Silver	Bronze
1923	Otawa, Ontario	Dorothy Jenkins & Gordon McLennan CAN	Theresa Blanchard & Nathaniel Niles USA	Clara Frothingham & Charles Rotch USA
1925	Boston, Massachusetts	Theresa Blanchard & Nathaniel Niles USA	Gladys Rogers & Melville Rogers CAN	
1927	Toronto, Ontario	Marion McDougall & Chauncey Bangs CAN	Theresa Blanchard & Nathaniel Niles USA	Constance Wilson & Montgomery Wilson CAN
1929	Boston, Massachusetts	Constance Wilson & Montgomery Wilson CAN	Theresa Blanchard & Nathaniel Niles USA	Maribel Vinson & Thornton Coolidge USA
1931	Ottawa, Ontario	Constance Wilson & Montgomery Wilson CAN	Frances Claudet & Chauncey Bangs CAN	Beatrix Loughran & Sherwin Badger USA
1933	New York, New York	Constance Wilson & Montgomery Wilson CAN	Maud E. Smith & Jack Eastwood CAN	Kathleen Lopdell & Donald Cruikshank CAN
1935	Montreal, Quebec	Maribel Vinson & George Hill USA	Constance Wilson & Montgomery Wilson CAN	Louise Bertram & Stewart Reburn CAN
1937	Boston, Massachusetts	Veronica Clarke & Ralph McCreath CAN	Maribel Vinson & George Hill USA	Grace Madden & James Madden USA
1939	Toronto, Ontario	Joan Tozzer & Bernard Fox USA	Veronica Clarke & Ralph McCreath CAN	Aidrie Cruikshank & Donald Cruikshank CAN
1941	Ardmore, Pennsylvania	Eleanor O'Meara & Ralph McCreath CAN	Donna Atwood & Eugene Turner USA	Patricia Vaeth & Jack Might USA
1943	The North American Championships were not held.			
1945	The pairs event was not held.			

Year	Location	Gold	Silver	Bronze
1947	Ottawa, Ontario	Suzanne Morrow & Wallace Diestelmeyer CAN	Yvonne Sherman & Robert Swenning USA	Karol Kennedy & Peter Kennedy USA
1949	Ardmore, Pennsylvania	Karol Kennedy & Peter Kennedy USA	Marlene Smith & Donald Gilchrist CAN	Irine Maguire & Walter Muehlbronner USA
1951	Calgary, Alberta	Karol Kennedy & Peter Kennedy USA	Janet Gerhauser & John Nightingale USA	Jane Kirby & Donald Tobin CAN
1953	Cleveland, Ohio	Frances Dafoe & Norris Bowden CAN	Carole Ormaca & Robin Greiner USA	Margaret Graham & Hugh Graham, Jr. USA
1955	Regina, Saskatchewan	Frances Dafoe & Norris Bowden CAN	Carole Ormaca & Robin Greiner USA	Barbara Wagner & Robert Paul CAN
1957	Rochester, New York	Barbara Wagner & Robert Paul CAN	Maria Jelinek & Otto Jelinek CAN	Nancy Rouillard & Ronald Ludington USA
1959	Toronto, Ontario	Barbara Wagner & Robert Paul CAN	Nancy Ludington & Ronald Ludington USA	Maribel Owen & Dudley Richards USA
1961	Philadelphia, Pennsylvania	Maria Jelinek & Otto Jelinek CAN	Maribel Owen & Dudley Richards USA	Debbi Wilkes & Guy Revell CAN
1963	Vancouver, British Columbia	Debbi Wilkes & Guy Revell CAN	Gertrude Desjardins & Maurice Lafrance CAN	Vivian Joseph & Ronald Joseph USA
1965	Rochester, New York	Vivian Joseph & Ronald Joseph USA	Cynthia Kauffman & Ronald Kauffman USA	Susan Huehnergard & Paul Huehnergard CAN
1967	Montreal, Quebec	Cynthia Kauffman & Ronald Kauffman USA	Susan Berens & Roy Wagelein USA	Betty Lewis & Richard Gilbert USA
1969	Oakland, California	Cynthia Kauffman & Ronald Kauffman USA	Alicia Jo Starbuck & Kenneth Shelley USA	Mary Petrie & Robert McAvoy CAN
1971	Peterborough, Ontario	Alicia Jo Starbuck & Kenneth Shelley USA	Melissa Militano & Mark Militano USA	Sandra Bezic & Val Bezic CAN

Ice Dancing

Year	Location	Gold	Silver	Bronze
1947	Ottawa, Ontario	Lois Waring & Walter Bainbridge, Jr. USA	Anne Davies & Carleton Hoffner, Jr. USA	Marcella Willis & Frank Davenport USA
1949	Ardmore, Pennsylvania	Lois Waring & Walter Bainbridge, Jr. USA	Irene Maguire & Walter Muehlbronner USA	Anne Davies & Carleton Hoffner, Jr. USA
1951	Calgary, Alberta	Carmel Bodel & Edward Bodel USA	Carol Peters & Daniel Ryan USA	Pierrette Paquin & Donald Tobin CAN
1953	Cleveland, Ohio	Carol Peters & Daniel Ryan USA	Virginia Hoyns & Donald Jacoby USA	Carmel Bodel & Edward Bodel USA
1955	Regina, Saskatchewan	Carmel Bodel & Edward Bodel USA	Joan Zamboni & Roland Junso USA	Virginia Hoyns & William Kipp USA
1957	Rochester, New York	Geraldine Fenton & William McLachlan CAN	Joan Zamboni & Roland Junso USA	Sharon McKenzie & Bert Wright USA
1959	Toronto, Ontario	Geraldine Fenton & William McLachlan CAN	Andrée Jacoby & Donald Jacoby USA	Anne Martin & Edward Collins CAN
1961	Philadelphia, Pennsylvania	Virginia Thompson & William McLachlan CAN	Donna Carrier & Roger Campbell USA	Paulette Doan & Kenneth Ormsby CAN
1963	Vancouver, British Columbia	Paulette Doan & Kenneth Ormsby CAN	Donna Lee Mitchell & John Mitchell CAN	Sally Schantz & Stanley Urban USA
1965	Rochester, New York	Lorna Dyer & John Carrell USA	Kristin Fortune & Dennis Sveum USA	Carole Forrest & Kevin Lethbridge CAN
1967	Montreal, Quebec	Lorna Dyer & John Carrell USA	Joni Graham & Donald Phillips CAN	Judy Schwomeyer & James Sladky USA
1969	Oakland, California	Donna Taylor & Bruce Lennie CAN	Judy Schwomeyer & James Sladky USA	Debbie Gerken & Raymond Tiedemann USA
1971	Peterborough, Ontario	Judy Schwomeyer & James Sladky USA	Ann Millier & Harvey Millier USA	Mary Campbell & Johnny Johns USA

Note: Ice dancing was not part of the formal competition until 1947.

Fours

Year	Location	Gold	Silver	Bronze
1923	Ottawa, Ontario	Elizabeth Blair	Clara Hartmann	Clara Frothingham
		Florence Wilson	Grace Munstock	Theresa Blanchard
		Philip Chrysler	Paul Armitage	Charles Rotch
		C. R. Morphy CAN	Joel Liberman USA	Sherwin Badger USA
1925–1931	Fours events were not held.			
1933	New York, New York	Margaret Davis	Constance Samuel	Theresa Blanchard
		Prudence Holbrook	Elizabeth Fisher	Suzanne Davis
		Melville Rogers	Montgomery Wilson	Richard Hapgood
		Guy Owen CAN	Hubert Sprott	Fred Parmenter USA
1935	Montreal, Quebec	Margaret Davis	Nettie Prantel	Suzanne Davis
		Prudence Holbrook	Ardelle Kloss	Grace Madden
		Melville Rogers	Joseph Savage	Frederick Goodridge
		Guy Owen CAN	Roy Hunt USA	George Hill USA
1937	Boston, Massachusetts	Margaret Davis	Naomi Slater	Nettie Prantel
		Prudence Holbook	Aidrie Cruikshank	Ardelle Kloss
		Melville Rogers	Jack Hose	Joseph Savage
		Guy Owen CAN	Donald Cruikshank CAN	George Boltres
1939	Toronto, Ontario	Hazel Caley	Ruth Hall	Marjorie Parker
		Dorothy Caley	Gillian Watson	Nettie Prantel
		Montgomery Wilson	Donald Gilchrist	Joseph Savage
		Ralph McCreath CAN	Sandy McKechnie CAN	George Boltres USA

Year	Location	Gold	Silver	Bronze
1941	Armore, Pennsylvania	Janette Ahrens	Therese McCarthy	
		Mary Louise Premer	Virginia Wilson	
		Lyman Wakefield	Donald Gilchrist	
		Robert Uppgren USA	Michael Kirby CAN	
1943	The North American Championships were not held.			
1945–1947	Fours events were not held.			
1949	Ardmore, Pennsylvania	Marilyn Thomsen	Mary Kenner	Jean Matze
		Janet Gerhauser	Vera Smith	Elizabeth Royer
		Marlyn Thomsen	Peter Dunfield	Henry Mayer, IV
		John Nightingale USA	Peter Firstbrook CAN	Newbold Black, IV USA
1951–1971	Fours events were not held.			

Appendix H

Medalists in Figure Skating at the Olympic Winter Games

Note: The Olympic Winter Games date from 1924.
Figure skating events prior to that were part of the Olympic Games.

Ladies

Year	Location	Gold	Silver	Bronze
1908	London GBR	Madge Syers GBR	Elsa Rendschmidt GER	Dorothy Greenhough-Smith GBR
1912	Figure skating events were not held.			
1916	The Olympic Games were not held.			
1920	Antwerp BEL	Magda Mauroy-Julin SWE	Svea Norén SWE	Theresa Weld USA
1924	Charmonix FRA	Herma Szabo AUT	Beatrix Loughran USA	Ethel Muckelt GBR
1928	St. Moritz SWI	Sonja Henie NOR	Fritzi Burger AUT	Beatrix Loughran USA
1932	Lake Placid USA	Sonja Henie NOR	Fritzi Burger AUT	Maribel Vinson USA
1936	Garmisch-Partenkirchen GER	Sonja Henie NOR	Cecilia Colledge GBR	Vivi-Anne Hultén SWE
1940	The Olympic Winter Games were not held.			
1944	The Olympic Winter Games were not held.			
1948	St. Moritz SWI	Barbara Ann Scott CAN	Eva Pawlik AUT	Jeannette Altwegg GBR
1952	Oslo NOR	Jeannette Altwegg GBR	Tenley Albright USA	Jacqueline du Bief FRA
1956	Cortina ITA	Tenley Albright USA	Carol Heiss USA	Ingrid Wendl AUT
1960	Squaw Valley USA	Carol Heiss USA	Sjoukje Dijkstra NED	Barbara Roles USA
1964	Innsbruck AUT	Sjoukje Dijkstra NED	Regine Heitzer AUT	Petra Burka CAN
1968	Grenoble FRA	Peggy Fleming USA	Gabriele Seyfert GDR	Hana Mašková CZE
1972	Sapporo JPN	Beatrix Schuba AUT	Karen Magnussen CAN	Janet Lynn USA
1976	Innsbruck AUT	Dorothy Hamill USA	Dianne de Leeuw NED	Christine Errath GDR
1980	Lake Placid USA	Anett Pötzsch GDR	Linda Fratianne USA	Dagmar Lurz FRG
1984	Sarajevo YUG	Katarina Witt GDR	Rosalynn Sumners USA	Kira Ivanova URS

Year	Location	Gold	Silver	Bronze
1988	Calgary, Alberta CAN	Katarina Witt GDR	Elizabeth Manley CAN	Debra Thomas USA
1992	Albertville FRA	Kristi Yamaguchi USA	Midori Ito JPN	Nancy Kerrigan USA
1994	Hamar NOR	Oksana Baiul UKR	Nancy Kerrigan USA	Lu Chen CHN
1998	Nagano JPN	Tara Lipiniski USA	Michelle Kwan USA	Lu Chen CHN
2002	Salt Lake City USA	Sarah Hughes USA	Irina Slutskaya RUS	Michelle Kwan USA
2006	Torino ITA	Shizuka Arakawa JPN	Sasha Cohen USA	Irina Slutskaya RUS
2010	Vancouver CAN	Yu Na Kim KOR	Mao Asada JPN	Joannie Rochette CAN

Men

Year	Location	Gold	Silver	Bronze
1908	London GBR	Ulrich Salchow SWE	Richard Johansson SWE	Per Thorén SWE
1912	Figure skating events were not held.			
1916	The Olympic Games were not held.			
1920	Antwerp BEL	Gillis Grafström SWE	Andreas Krogh NOR	Martin Stixrud NOR
1924	Charmonix FRA	Gillis Grafström SWE	Wilhelm Böckl AUT	Georg Gautschi SWI
1928	St. Moritz SWI	Gillis Grafström SWE	Wilhelm Böckl AUT	Robert van Zeebroeck BEL
1932	Lake Placid USA	Karl Schäfer AUT	Gillis Grafström SWE	Montgomery Wilson CAN
1936	Garmisch-Partenkirchen GER	Karl Schäfer AUT	Ernst Baier GER	Felix Kaspar AUT
1940	The Olympic Winter Games were not held.			
1944	The Olympic Winter Games were not held.			
1948	St. Moritz SWI	Richard Button USA	Hans Gerschwiler SWI	Edi Rada AUT
1952	Oslo NOR	Richard Button USA	Helmut Seibt AUT	James Grogan USA
1956	Cortina ITA	Hayes Jenkins USA	Ronald Robertson USA	David Jenkins USA
1960	Squaw Valley USA	David Jenkins USA	Karol Divin CZE	Donald Jackson CAN
1964	Innsbruck AUT	Manfred Schnelldorfer FRG	Alain Calmat FRA	Scott Allen USA
1968	Grenoble FRA	Wolfgang Schwarz AUT	Tim Wood USA	Patrick Pera FRA
1972	Sapporo JPN	Ondrej Nepela CZE	Sergei Chetverukhin URS	Patrick Pera FRA
1976	Innsbruck AUT	John Curry GBR	Vladimir Kovalev URS	Toller Cranston CAN
1980	Lake Placid USA	Robin Cousins GBR	Jan Hoffmann GDR	Charles Tickner USA
1984	Sarajevo YUG	Scott Hamilton USA	Brian Orser CAN	Jozef Sabovčík CZE

Year	Location	Gold	Silver	Bronze
1988	Calgary, Alberta CAN	Brian Boitano USA	Brian Orser CAN	Viktor Petrenko URS
1992	Albertville FRA	Viktor Petrenko CIS	Paul Wylie USA	Christopher Bowman USA
1994	Hamar NOR	Alexei Urmanov RUS	Elvis Stojko CAN	Philippe Candeloro FRA
1998	Nagano JPN	Ilia Kulik RUS	Elvis Stojko CAN	Philippe Candeloro FRA
2002	Salt Lake City USA	Alexei Yagudin RUS	Evgeny Plushenko RUS	Timothy Goebel USA
2006	Torino ITA	Evgeny Plushenko RUS	Stéphane Lambiel SUI	Jeffrey Buttle CAN
2010	Vancouver CAN	Evan Lysacek USA	Evgeny Plushenko RUS	Daisuke Takahashi JPN

Pairs

Year	Location	Gold	Silver	Bronze
1908	London GBR	Anna Hübler & Heinrich Burger GER	Phyllis Johnson & James Johnson GBR	Madge Syers & Edgar Syers GBR
1912	Figure skating events were not held.			
1916	The Olympic Games were not held.			
1920	Antwerp BEL	Ludowika Jakobsson & Walter Jakobsson FIN	Alexia Bryn & Yngvar Bryn NOR	Phyllis Johnson & James Johnson GBR
1924	Charmonix FRA	Helene Engelmann & Alfred Berger AUT	Ludowika Jakobsson & Walter Jakobsson FIN	Andrée Joly & Pierre Brunet FRA
1928	St. Moritz SWI	Andrée Joly & Pierre Brunet FRA	Lilly Scholz & Otto Kaiser AUT	Melitta Brunner & Ludwig Wrede AUT
1932	Lake Placid USA	Andrée Brunet & Pierre Brunet FRA	Beatrix Loughran & Sherwin Badger USA	Emilia Rotter & László Szollás HUN
1936	Garmisch-Partenkirchen GER	Maxi Herber & Ernst Baier GER	Ilse Pausin & Erich Pausin AUT	Emilia Rotter & László Szollás HUN
1940	The Olympic Winter Games were not held.			
1944	The Olympic Winter Games were not held.			
1948	St. Moritz SWI	Micheline Lannoy & Pierre Baugniet BEL	Andrea Kekéssy & Ede Király HUN	Suzanne Morrow & Wallace Diestelmeyer CAN
1952	Oslo NOR	Ria Falk & Paul Falk GER	Karol Kennedy & Peter Kennedy USA	Marianna Nagy & László Nagy HUN
1956	Cortina ITA	Elisabeth Schwarz & Kurt Oppelt AUT	Frances Dafoe & Norris Bowden CAN	Marianna Nagy & László Nagy HUN
1960	Squaw Valley USA	Barbara Wagner & Robert Paul CAN	Marika Kilius & Hans-Jürgen Bäumler GER	Nancy Ludington & Ronald Ludington USA

Year	Location	Gold	Silver	Bronze
1964	Innsbruck AUT	Liudmila Belousova & Oleg Protopopov URS	Marika Kilius & Hans-Jürgen Bäumler GER	Debbi Wilkes & Guy Revell CAN
1968	Grenoble FRA	Liudmila Belousova & Oleg Protopopov URS	Tatiana Zhuk & Alexandr Gorelik URS	Margot Glockshuber & Wolfgang Danne FRG
1972	Sapporo JPN	Irina Rodnina & Alexei Ulanov URS	Liudmila Smirnova & Andrei Suraikin URS	Manuela Gross & Uwe Kagelmann GDR
1976	Innsbruck AUT	Irina Rodnina & Alexei Ulanov URS	Romy Kermer & Rolf Österreich GDR	Manuela Gross & Uwe Kagelmann GDR
1980	Lake Placid USA	Irina Rodnina & Alexandr Zaitsev URS	Marina Cherkasova & Sergei Shakhrai URS	Manuela Mager & Uwe Bewersdorff GDR
1984	Sarajevo YUG	Elena Valova & Oleg Vasiliev URS	Caitlin Carruthers & Peter Carruthers USA	Larisa Selezneva & Oleg Makarov URS
1988	Calgary, Alberta CAN	Ekaterina Gordeeva & Sergei Grinkov URS	Elena Valova & Oleg Vasiliev URS	Jill Watson & Peter Oppegard USA
1992	Albertville FRA	Natalia Mishkutenok & Artur Dmitriev CIS	Elena Bechke & Denis Petrov CIS	Isabelle Brasseur & Lloyd Eisler CAN
1994	Hamar NOR	Ekaterina Gordeeva & Sergei Grinkov RUS	Natalia Mishkutenok & Artur Dmitriev RUS	Isabelle Brasseur & Lloyd Eisler CAN
1998	Nagano JPN	Oksana Kazakova & Artur Dmitriev RUS	Elena Berezhnaya & Anton Sikharulidze RUS	Mandy Wötzel & Ingo Steuer GER
2002	Salt Lake City USA	Elena Berezhnaya & Anton Sikharulidze RUS	* Jamie Salé & David Pelletier CAN	Xue Shen & Hongbo Zhao CHN
2006	Torino ITA	Tatiana Totmianina & Maxim Marinin RUS	Dan Zhang & Hao Zhang CHN	Xue Shen & Hongbo Zhao CHN
2010	Vancouver CAN	Xue Shen & Hongbo Zhao CHN	Qing Pang & Jian Tong CHN	Aliona Savchenko & Robin Szolkowy GER

* Salé and Pelletier were subsequently awarded duplicate gold medals by the IOC at the request of the ISU.

Ice Dancing

Year	Location	Gold	Silver	Bronze
1976	Innsbruck AUT	Liudmila Pakhomova & Alexandr Gorshkov URS	Irina Moiseeva & Andrei Minenkov URS	Colleen O'Connor & Jim Millns USA
1980	Lake Placid USA	Natalia Linichuk & Gennadi Karponosov URS	Krisztina Regöczy & András Sallay HUN	Irina Moiseeva & Andrei Minenkov URS
1984	Sarajevo YUG	Jayne Torvill & Christopher Dean GBR	Natalia Bestemianova & Andrei Bukin URS	Marina Klimova & Sergei Ponomarenko URS
1988	Calgary CAN	Natalia Bestemianova & Andrei Bukin URS	Marina Klimova & Sergei Ponomarenko URS	Tracy Wilson & Robert McCall CAN
1992	Albertville FRA	Marina Klimova & Sergei Ponomarenko CIS	Isabelle Duchesnay & Paul Duchesnay FRA	Maia Usova & Alexandr Zhulin CIS
1994	Hamar NOR	Oksana Grishchuk & Evgeny Platov RUS	Maia Usova & Alexandr Zhulin RUS	Jayne Torvill & Christopher Dean GBR
1998	Nagano JPN	Oksana Grishchuk & Evgeny Platov RUS	Anjelika Krylova & Oleg Ovsiannikov RUS	Marina Anissina & Gwendal Peizerat FRA
2002	Salt Lake City USA	Marina Anissina & Gwendal Peizerat FRA	Irina Lobacheva & Ilia Averbukh RUS	Barbara Fusar-Poli & Maurizio Margaglio ITA
2006	Torino ITA	Tatiana Navka & Roman Kostomarov RUS	Tanith Belbin & Benjamin Agosto USA	Elena Grushina & Ruslan Goncharov BUL
2010	Vancouver CAN	Tessa Virtue & Scott Moir CAN	Meryl Davis & Charlie White USA	Oksana Domnina & Maxim Shabalin RUS

Special Figures

Year	Location	Gold	Silver	Bronze
1908	London GBR	Nikolai Panin RUS	Arthur Cumming GBR	George Hall-Say GBR

Appendix I
Medalists at the Grand Prix Finals in Figure Skating

Ladies

Year	Location	Gold	Silver	Bronze
1996	Paris FRA	Michelle Kwan USA	Irina Slutskaya RUS	Josée Chouniard CAN
1997	Hamilton CAN	Tara Lipinski USA	Michelle Kwan USA	Irina Slutskaya RUS
1998	Munich GER	Tara Lipinski USA	Tanja Szewczenko GER	Maria Butyrskaya RUS
1999	St. Petersburg RUS	Tatiana Malinina UZB	Maria Butyrskaya RUS	Irina Slutskaya RUS
2000	Lyon FRA	Irina Slutskaya RUS	Michelle Kwan USA	Maria Butyrskaya RUS
2001	Tokyo JPN	Irina Slutskaya RUS	Michelle Kwan USA	Sarah Hughes USA
2002	Kitchener CAN	Irina Slutskaya RUS	Michelle Kwan USA	Sarah Hughes USA
2003	St. Petersburg RUS	Sasha Cohen USA	Irina Slutskaya RUS	Viktoria Volchkova RUS
2004	Colorado Springs USA	Fumie Suguri JPN	Sasha Cohen USA	Shizuka Arakawa JPN
2005	Beijing CHN	Irina Slutskaya RUS	Shizuka Arakawa JPN	Joannie Rochette CAN
2006	Tokyo JPN	Mao Asada JPN	Irina Slutskaya RUS	Yukari Nakano JPN
2007	St. Petersburg RUS	Yu Na Kim KOR	Mao Asada JPN	Sarah Meier SUI
2008	Torino ITA	Yu Na Kim KOR	Mao Asada JPN	Carolina Kostner ITA
2009	Goyang City KOR	Mao Asada JPN	Yu Na Kim KOR	Carolina Kostner ITA
2010	Tokyo JPN	Yu Na Kim KOR	Miki Ando JPN	Akiko Suzuki JPN

Men

Year	Location	Gold	Silver	Bronze
1996	Paris FRA	Alexei Urmanov RUS	Elvis Stojko CAN	Eric Millo FRA
1997	Hamilton CAN	Elvis Stojko CAN	Todd Eldredge USA	Alexei Urmanov RUS
1998	Munich GER	Ilia Kulik RUS	Elvis Stojko CAN	Todd Eldredge USA
1999	St. Petersburg RUS	Alexei Yagudin RUS	Alexei Urmanov RUS	Evgeny Plushenko RUS
2000	Lyon FRA	Evgeny Plushenko RUS	Elvis Stojko CAN	Timothy Goebel USA
2001	Tokyo JPN	Evgeny Plushenko RUS	Alexei Yagudin RUS	Matthew Savoie USA
2002	Kitchener CAN	Alexei Yagudin RUS	Evgeny Plushenko RUS	Timothy Goebel USA
2003	St. Petersburg RUS	Evgeny Plushenko RUS	Ilia Kimkin RUS	Brian Joubert FRA
2004	Colorado Springs USA	Emanuel Sandhu CAN	Evgeny Plushenko RUS	Michael Weiss USA
2005	Beijing CHN	Evgeny Plushenko RUS	Jeffrey Buttle CAN	Chengjiang Li CHN
2006	Tokyo JPN	Stéphane Lambiel SUI	Jeffrey Buttle CAN	Daisuke Takahashi JPN
2007	St. Petersburg RUS	Brian Joubert FRA	Daisuke Takahashi JPN	Nobunari Oda JPN
2008	Torino ITA	Stéphane Lambiel SUI	Daisuke Takahashi JPN	Evan Lysacek USA
2009	Goyang City KOR	Jeremy Abbott USA	Takahiko Kozuka JPN	Johnny Weir USA
2010	Tokyo JPN	Evan Lysacek USA	Nobunari Oda JPN	Johnny Weir USA

Pairs

Year	Location	Gold	Silver	Bronze
1996	Paris FRA	Evgenia Shishkova & Vadim Naumov RUS	Marina Eltsova & Andrei Bushkov RUS	Mandy Wötzel & Ingo Steuer GER
1997	Hamilton CAN	Mandy Wötzel & Ingo Steuer GER	Oksana Kazakova & Artur Dmitriev RUS	Marina Eltsova & Andrei Bushkov RUS
1998	Munich GER	Elena Berezhnaya & Anton Sikharulidze RUS	Mandy Wötzel & Ingo Steuer GER	Oksana Kazakova & Artur Dmitriev RUS
1999	St. Petersburg RUS	Xue Shen & Hongbo Zhao CHN	Elena Berezhnaya & Anton Sikharulidze RUS	Maria Petrova & Alexei Tikhonov RUS
2000	Lyon FRA	Xue Shen & Hongbo Zhao CHN	Sarah Abitol & Stephane Bernadis FRA	Elena Berezhnaya & Anton Sikharulidze RUS
2001	Tokyo JPN	Jamie Salé & David Pelletier CAN	Elena Berezhnaya & Anton Sikharulidze RUS	Xue Shen & Hongbo Zhao CHN
2002	Kitchener CAN	Jamie Salé & David Pelletier CAN	Elena Berezhnaya & Anton Sikharulidze RUS	Xue Shen & Hongbo Zhao CHN
2003	St. Petersburg RUS	Tatiana Totmianina & Maxim Marinin RUS	Xue Shen & Hongbo Zhao CHN	Maria Petrova & Alexei Tikhonov RUS
2004	Colorado Springs USA	Xue Shen & Hongbo Zhao CHN	Tatiana Totmianina & Maxim Marinin RUS	Maria Petrova & Alexei Tikhonov RUS
2005	Beijing CHN	Xue Shen & Hongbo Zhao CHN	Maria Petrova & Alexei Tikhonov RUS	Qing Pang & Jian Tong CHN
2006	Tokyo JPN	Tatiana Totmianina & Maxim Marinin RUS	Dan Zhang & Hao Zhang CHN	Aliona Savchenko & Robin Szolkowy GER
2007	St. Petersburg RUS	Xue Shen & Hongbo Zhao CHN	Aliona Savchenko & Robin Szolkowy GER	Dan Zhang & Hao Zhang CHN
2008	Torino ITA	Aliona Savchenko & Robin Szolkowy GER	Dan Zhang & Hao Zhang CHN	Qing Pang & Jian Tong CHN
2009	Goyang City KOR	Qing Pang & Jian Tong CHN	Dan Zhang & Hao Zhang CHN	Aliona Savchenko & Robin Szolkowy GER
2010	Tokyo JPN	Xue Shen & Hongbo Zhao CHN	Qing Pang & Jian Tong CHN	Aliona Savchenko & Robin Szolkowy GER

Ice Dancing

Year	Location	Gold	Silver	Bronze
1996	Paris FRA	Oksana Grishchuk & Evgeny Platov RUS	Angelika Krylova & Oleg Ovsiannikov RUS	Marina Anissina & Gwendal Peizerat FRA
1997	Hamilton CAN	Shae-Lynn Bourne & Victor Kraatz CAN	Angelika Krylova & Oleg Ovsiannikov RUS	Marina Anissina & Gwendal Peizerat FRA
1998	Munich GER	Oksana Grishchuk & Evgeny Platov RUS	Shae-Lynn Bourne & Victor Kraatz CAN	Marina Anissina & Gwendal Peizerat FRA
1999	St. Petersburg RUS	Angelika Krylova & Oleg Ovsiannikov RUS	Marina Anissina & Gwendal Peizerat FRA	Irina Lobacheva & Ilia Averbukh RUS
2000	Lyon FRA	Marina Anissina & Gwendal Peizerat FRA	Barbara Fusar-Poli & Maurizio Margaglio ITA	Margarita Drobiazko & Povilas Vanagas LTU
2001	Tokyo JPN	Barbara Fusar-Poli & Maurizio Margaglio ITA	Irina Lobacheva & Ilia Averbukh RUS	Margarita Drobiazko & Povilas Vanagas LTU
2002	Kitchener CAN	Shae-Lynn Bourne & Victor Kraatz CAN	Marina Anissina & Gwendal Peizerat FRA	Margarita Drobiazko & Povilas Vanagas LTU
2003	St. Petersburg RUS	Irina Lobacheva & Ilia Averbukh RUS	Tatiana Navka & Roman Kostomarov RUS	Albena Denkova & Maxim Staviyski BUL
2004	Colorado Springs USA	Tatiana Navka & Roman Kostomarov RUS	Albena Denkova & Maxim Staviyski BUL	Tanith Belbin & Benjamin Agosto USA
2005	Beijing CHN	Tatiana Navka & Roman Kostomarov RUS	Tanith Belbin & Benjamin Agosto USA	Albena Denkova & Maxim Staviyski BUL
2006	Tokyo JPN	Tatiana Navka & Roman Kostomarov RUS	Elena Grushina & Ruslan Goncharov UKR	Marie-France Dubreuil & Patrice Lauzon CAN
2007	St. Petersburg RUS	Albena Denkova & Maxim Staviyski BUL	Marie-France Dubreuil & Patrice Lauzon CAN	Oksana Domnina & Maxim Shabalin RUS
2008	Torino ITA	Oksana Domnina & Maxim Shabalin RUS	Tanith Belbin & Benjamin Agosto USA	Isabelle Delobel & Olivier Schoenfelder FRA
2009	Goyang City KOR	Isabelle Delobel & Olivier Schoenfelder FRA	Oksana Domnina & Maxim Shabalin RUS	Meryl Davis & Charlie White USA
2010	Tokyo JPN	Meryl Davis & Charlie White USA	Tessa Virtue & Scott Moir CAN	Nathalie Pechalat & Fabian Bourzat FRA

Appendix J

Medalists at the World Junior Figure Skating Championships

Ladies

Year	Location	Gold	Silver	Bronze
1978	Megève FRA	Jill Sawyer USA	Kira Ivanova URS	Petra Ernert FRG
1979	Augsburg FRG	Elaine Zayak USA	Manuela Ruben FRG	Jacki Farrell USA
1980	Megève FRA	Rosalynn Sumners USA	Kay Thomson CAN	Carola Paul GDR
1981	London CAN	Tiffany Chin USA	Marina Serova URS	Anna Antonova URS
1982	Oberstdorf FRG	Janina Wirth GDR	Cornelia Tesch FRG	Elizabeth Manley CAN
1983	Sarajevo YUG	Simone Koch GDR	Karin Hendschke GDR	Parthena Sarafidis AUT
1984	Sapporo JPN	Karin Hendschke GDR	Simone Koch GDR	Midori Ito JAP
1985	Colorado Springs USA	Tatiana Andreeva URS	Susanne Becher GDR	Natalia Gorbenko URS
1986	Sarajevo YUG	Natalia Gorbenko URS	Susanne Becher FRG	Linda Florkevich CAN
1987	Kitchener CAN	Cindy Bortz USA	Susanne Becher FRG	Shannon Allison CAN
1988	Brisbane AUS	Kristi Yamaguchi USA	Junko Yaginuma JAP	Yukiko Kashihara JPN
1989	Sarajevo YUG	Jessica Mills USA	Junko Yaginuma JPN	Surya Bonaly FRA
1990	Colorado Springs USA	Yuka Sato JPN	Surya Bonaly FRA	Tanja Krienke GDR
1991	Budapest HUN	Surya Bonaly FRA	Lisa Ervin USA	Lu Chen CHN
1992	Hull CAN	Laetitia Hubert FRA	Lisa Ervin USA	Lu Chen CHN
1993	Seoul KOR	Kumiko Koiwai JPN	Lisa Ervin USA	Tonia Szewczenko GER
1994	Colorado Springs USA	Michelle Kwan USA	Kristina Czako HUN	Irina Slutskaya RUS
1995	Budapest HUN	Irina Slutskaya RUS	Elena Ivanova RUS	Kristina Czako HUN
1996	Brisbane AUS	Elena Ivanova RUS	Elena Pingacheva RUS	Nadejda Kanaeva RUS
1997	Seoul KOR	Sydney Vogel USA	Elena Sokolova RUS	Elena Ivanova RUS

Year	Location	Gold	Silver	Bronze
1998	Saint John CAN	Julia Soldatova RUS	Elena Ivanova RUS	Viktoria Volchkova RUS
1999	Zagreb CRO	DariaTimoshenko RUS	Sarah Hughes USA	Viktoria Volchkova RUS
2000	Oberstdorf GER	Jennifer Kirk USA	Donna Stellato USA	Sarah Meier SUI
2001	Sofia BUL	Kristina Oblasova RUS	Ann Patrice McDonough USA	Susanne Poykio FIN
2002	Hamar NOR	Ann Patrice McDonough USA	Yukari Nakano JPN	Miki Ando JPN
2003	Ostrava CZE	Yukina Ota JPN	Miki Ando JPN	Carolina Kostner ITA
2004	The Hague NED	Miki Ando JPN	Kimmie Meissner USA	Katy Taylor USA
2005	Kitchener CAN	Mao Asada JPN	Yu Na Kim KOR	Emily Hughes USA
2006	Ljubljana SLO	Yu Na Kim KOR	Mao Asada JPN	Christine Zukowski USA
2007	Oberstdorf GER	Caroline Zhang USA	Mirai Nagasu USA	Ashley Wagner USA
2008	Sofia BUL	Rachael Flatt USA	Caroline Zhang USA	Mirai Nagasu USA
2009	Sofia BUL	Alena Leonova RUS	Caroline Zhang USA	Ashley Wagner USA
2010	The Hague NED	Kanako Murakami JPN	Agnes Zawadzki USA	Polina Agafonova RUS

Men

Year	Location	Gold	Silver	Bronze
1978	Megève FRA	Dennis Coi CAN	Vladimir Kotin URS	Brian Boitano USA
1979	Augsburg FRG	Vitali Egorov URS	Bobby Beauchamp USA	Alexandr Fadeev URS
1980	Megève FRA	Alexandr Fadeev URS	Vitali Egorov URS	Falko Kirsten GDR
1981	London CAN	Paul Wylie USA	Juri Bureiko URS	Scott Williams USA
1982	Oberstdorf FRG	Scott Williams USA	Paul Guerrero USA	Alexander König GDR
1983	Sarajevo YUG	Christopher Bowman USA	Philippe Roncoli FRA	Nils Köpp GDR
1984	Sapporo JPN	Viktor Petrenko URS	Marc Ferland CAN	Tom Cierniak USA
1985	Colorado Springs USA	Erik Larson USA	Viktor Petrenko URS	Rudy Galindo USA
1986	Sarajevo YUG	Vladimir Petrenko URS	Rudy Galindo USA	Yuri Tsimbaliuk URS
1987	Kitchener CAN	Rudy Galindo USA	Todd Eldredge USA	Yuri Tsimbaliuk URS
1988	Brisbane AUS	Todd Eldredge USA	Viacheslav Zagorodniuk URS	Yuri Tsimbaliuk URS
1989	Sarajevo YUG	Viacheslav Zagorodniuk URS	Shepherd Clark USA	Masakazu Kagiyama JPN
1990	Colorado Springs USA	Igor Pashkevich URS	Alexei Urmanov URS	John Baldwin, Jr. USA
1991	Budapest HUN	Vasili Eremenko URS	Alexandr Abt URS	Nicolas Petorin FRA
1992	Hull CAN	Dmitri Dmitrenko CIS	Konstantin Kostin CIS	Damon Allen USA
1993	Seoul KOR	Evgeny Pliuta UKR	Michael Weiss USA	Ilia Kulik RUS
1994	Colorado Springs USA	Michael Weiss USA	Naoki Shigematsu JPN	Jere Michael USA
1995	Budapest HUN	Ilia Kulik RUS	Thierry Cerez FRA	Seiichi Suzuki JPN
1996	Brisbane AUS	Alexei Yagudin RUS	Takeshi Honda JPN	Zhengxin Guo CHN
1997	Seoul KOR	Evgeny Plushenko RUS	Timothy Goebel USA	Zhengxin Guo CHN

Year	Location	Gold	Silver	Bronze
1998	Saint John CAN	Derrick Delmore USA	Sergei Davydov RUS	Li Yunfei CHN
1999	Zagreb CRO	Ilia Klimkin RUS	Vincent Restencourt FRA	Yosuke Takeuchi JPN
2000	Oberstdorf GER	Stefan Lindemann GER	Vincent Restencourt FRA	Matthew Savoie USA
2001	Sofia BUL	Johnny Weir USA	Evan Lysacek USA	Vincent Restencourt FRA
2002	Hamar NOR	Daisuke Takahashi JPN	Kevin van der Perren BEL	Stanislav Timchenko RUS
2003	Ostrava CZE	Alexandr Shubin RUS	Evan Lysacek USA	Alban Preaubert FRA
2004	The Hague NED	Andrei Griazev RUS	Evan Lysacek USA	Jordan Brauninger USA
2005	Kitchener CAN	Nobunari Oda JPN	Yannick Ponsero FRA	Sergei Dobrin RUS
2006	Ljubljana SLO	Takahiko Kozuka JPN	Sergei Voronov RUS	Yannick Ponsero FRA
2007	Oberstdorf GER	Stephen Carriere USA	Patrick Chan CAN	Sergei Voronov RUS
2008	Sofia BUL	Adam Rippon USA	Artem Borodulin RUS	Jinlin Guan CHN
2009	Sofia BUL	Adam Rippon USA	Michal Brezina CZE	Artem Grigoriev RUS
2010	The Hague NED	Yuzuru Hanyu JPN	Nan Song CHN	Artur Gachinski RUS

Pairs

Year	Location	Gold	Silver	Bronze
1978	Megève FRA	Barbara Underhill & Paul Martini CAN	Jana Blahová & Ludek Fěno CZE	Beth Flora & Ken Flora USA
1979	Augsburg CAN	Veronika Pershina & Marat Akbarov URS	Larisa Selezneva & Oleg Makarov URS	Lorri Baier & Lloyd Eisler CAN
1980	Megève FRA	Larisa Selezneva & Oleg Makarov URS	Marina Nikitiuk & Rashid Kadyrkaev URS	Kathia Dubec & Xavier Douillard FRA
1981	London CAN	Larisa Selezneva & Oleg Makarov URS	Lorri Baier & Lloyd Eisler CAN	Marina Nikitiuk & Rashid Kadyrkaev URS
1982	Oberstdorf FRG	Marina Avstiskaia & Yuri Kvashnin URS	Inna Bekker & Sergei Likhanski URS	Babette Preussler & Torsten Ohlov GDR
1983	Sarajevo YUG	Marina Avstiskaia & Yuri Kvashnin URS	Peggy Seidel & Ralf Seifert GDR	Inna Bekker & Sergei Likhanski URS
1984	Sapparo JPN	Manuela Landgraf & Ingo Steuer GDR	Susan Dungjen & Jason Dungjen USA	Olga Neizvestnaia & Sergei Hudiakov URS
1985	Colorado Springs USA	Ekaterina Gordeeva & Sergei Grinkov URS	Irina Mironenko & Dmitri Shkidchenko URS	Elena Gud & Evgeny Koltun URS
1986	Sarajevo YUG	Elena Leonova & Gennadi Krasnitski URS	Irina Mironenko & Dmitri Shkidchenko URS	Ekaterina Murugova & Artem Torgashev URS
1987	Kitchener CAN	Elena Leonova & Gennadi Krasnitski URS	Ekaterina Murugova & Artem Torgashev URS	Kristi Yamaguchi & Rudy Galindo USA
1988	Brisbane AUS	Kristi Yamaguchi & Rudy Galindo USA	Evgenia Cherisheva & Dmitri Sukhanov URS	Yulia Liashenko & Andrei Bushkov URS
1989	Sarajevo YUG	Evgenia Cherisheva & Dmitri Sukhanov URS	Angela Caspari & Marno Kreft GDR	Irina Saifutdinova & Alexei Tikhonov URS

Year	Location	Gold	Silver	Bronze
1990	Colorado Springs USA	Natalia Krestianinova & Alexei Torchinski URS	Svetlana Pristav & Vladislav Tkachenko URS	Jennifer Heurlin & John Frederiksen USA
1991	Budapest HUN	Natalia Krestianinova & Alexei Torchinski URS	Svetlana Pristav & Vladislav Tkachenko URS	Jennifer Heurlin & John Frederiksen USA
1992	Hull CAN	Natalia Krestianinova & Alexei Torchinski URS	Caroline Haddad & Jean-Sebastien Fectau CAN	Svetlana Pristav & Vladislav Tkachenko CIS
1993	Seoul KOR	Inga Korshunova & Dmitry Saveliev RUS	Maria Petrova & Anton Sikharulidze RUS	Isabelle Coulombe & Bruno Marcotte CAN
1994	Colorado Springs USA	Maria Petrova & Anton Sikharulidze RUS	Caroline Haddad & Jean-Sebastien Fectau CAN	Galina Maniachenko & Evgeny Gigursky UKR
1995	Budapest HUN	Maria Petrova & Anton Sikharulidze RUS	Danielle Hartsel & Steve Hartsell USA	Evgenia Filonenko & Igor Marchenko UKR
1996	Brisbane AUS	Viktoria Makisuta & Vladislav Zhovnirsky RUS	Evgenia Filonenko & Igor Marchenko UKR	Danielle Hartsel & Steve Hartsell USA
1997	Seoul KOR	Danielle Hartsell & Steve Hartsell USA	Maria Petrova & Teimuraz Pouline RUS	Viktoria Makisuta & Vladislav Zhovnirsky RUS
1998	Saint John CAN	Julia Obertas & Dmitry Palamarchuk UKR	Svetlana Nikolaeva & Alexei Sokolov RUS	Viktoria Makisuta & Vladislav Zhovnirsky RUS
1999	Zagreb CRO	Julia Obertas & Dmitry Palamarchuk UKR	Laura Handy & Paul Binnebose USA	Viktoria Makisuta & Vladislav Zhovnirsky RUS
2000	Oberstdorf GER	Aljona Savchenko & Stanislav Morozov GER	Julia Obertas & Dmitry Palamarchuk UKR	Julia Shapiro & Alexei Sokolov RUS
2001	Sofia BUL	Dan Zhang & Hao Zhang CHN	Yuko Kawaguchi & Alexander Markuntsov JPN	Kristen Roth & Michael McPherson USA

Year	Location	Gold	Silver	Bronze
2002	Hamar NOR	Elena Riabchuck & Stanislav Zakharov RUS	Julia Karbovskaya & Sergei Slavnov RUS	Yang Ding & Zhongfei Ren CHN
2003	Ostrava CZE	Dan Zhang & Hao Zhang CHN	Yang Ding & Zhongfei Ren CHN	Jennifer Don & Jonathan Hunt USA
2004	The Hague NED	Natalian Shestakova & Pavel Lebedev RUS	Jessica Dubé & Bryce Davison CAN	Maria Mukhortova & MaximTrankov RUS
2005	Kitchener CAN	Maria Mukhortova & Maxim Trankov RUS	Jessica Dubé & Bryce Davison CAN	Tatiana Kokoreva & Egor Golovkin RUS
2006	Ljubljana SLO	Julia Vlassov & Drew Meekins USA	Kendra Moyle & Andy Seitz USA	Ksenia Krasilnokova & Konstantin Bezaternikh RUS
2007	Oberstdorf GER	Keauna McLaughlin & Rockne Brubaker USA	Vera Basarova & Yuri Larionov RUS	Ksenia Krasilnokova & Konstantin Bezaternikh RUS
2008	Sofia BUL	Ksenia Krasilnokova & Konstantin Bezaternikh RUS	Lubov Iliushechkina & Nodari Maisuradze RUS	Huibo Dong & Yiming Wu CHN
2009	Sofia BUL	Lubov Iliushechkina & Nodari Maisuradze RUS	Anastasia Martiusheva & Alexei Rogonov RUS	Marissa Castelli & Simon Shnapir USA
2010	The Hague NED	Wenjing Sui & Cong Han CHN	Narumi Takahashi & Mervin Tran JPN	Ksenia Stolbova & Fedor Klimov RUS

Ice Dancing

Year	Location	Gold	Silver	Bronze
1978	Megève FRA	Tatiana Durasova & Sergei Ponomarenko URS	Kelly Johnson & Kris Barber CAN	Natalie Herve & Pierre Husarek FRA
1979	Augsburg FRG	Tatiana Durasova & Sergei Ponomarenko URS	Elena Batanova & Andrei Antonov URS	Kelly Johnson & Kris Barber CAN
1980	Megève FRA	Elena Batanova & Alexei Soloviev URS	Judit Péterfy & Csaba Bálint HUN	Renée Roca & Andrew Quellette USA
1981	London CAN	Elena Batanova & Alexei Soloviev URS	Natalia Annenko & Vadim Karkachev URS	Karyn Garossino & Rodney Garossino CAN
1982	Oberstdorf GER	Natalia Annenko & Vadim Karkachev URS	Tatiana Gladkova & Igor Shpilband URS	Lynda Malek & Alexander Miller USA
1983	Sarajevo YUG	Tatiana Gladkova & Igor Shpilband URS	Elena Novikova & Oleg Bliakhman URS	Chistine Chiniard & Martial Mette FRA
1984	Sapporo JPN	Elena Krikanova & Evgeny Platov URS	Christina Yatsuhashi & Keith Yatsuhashi USA	Svetiana Liapina & Georgi Sur URS
1985	Colorado Springs USA	Elena Krikanova & Evgeny Platov URS	Svetiana Liapina & Georgi Sur URS	Doriane Bontemps & Charles Paliard FRA
1986	Sarajevo YUG	Elena Krikanova & Evgeny Platov URS	Svetlana Serkeli & Andrei Zharkov URS	Corinne Paliard & Didier Courtois FRA
1987	Kitchener CAN	Ilona Melnichenko & Gennadi Kaskov URS	Oksana Grishchuk & Alexandr Chichkov URS	Catherine Pal & Donald Godfrey CAN
1988	Brisbane AUS	Oksana Grishchuk & Alexandr Chichkov URS	Irina Antsiferova & Maxim Sevastianov URS	Maria Orlova & Oleg Ovsiannikov URS
1989	Sarajevo YUG	Angelika Kirkhmaier & Dmitri Lagutin URS	Liudmila Berezova & Vladimir Fedorov URS	Marina Morel & Gwendal Peizerat FRA

Year	Location	Gold	Silver	Bronze
1990	Colorado Springs USA	Marina Anissina & Ilia Averbukh URS	Elena Kustarova & Sergei Romashkin URS	Marie-France Dubreuil & Bruno Yvars CAN
1991	Budapest HUN	Aliki Stergiadu & Yuri Razguliaiev URS	Marina Morel & Gwendal Peizerat FRA	Jelena Kousstarova & Sergei Romashkin URS
1992	Hull CAN	Marina Anissina & Ilia Averbukh CIS	Yaroslava Necaeva & Yuri Chesnichenko CIS	Amelie Dion & Alexandre Alain CAN
1993	Seoul KOR	Ekaterina Svirina & Sergey Sakhnovsky RUS	Sylwia Nowak & Sebastian Kolasinski POL	Berangere Nau & Luc Moneger FRA
1994	Colorado Springs USA	Sylvia Nowak & Sebastian Kolasinski POL	Ekaterina Svirina & Sergey Sakhnovsky RUS	Agnes Jacquemard & Alexis Gayet FRA
1995	Budapest HUN	Olga Sharutenko & Dimitri Naumkin RUS	Stephanie Guardia & Franck Laporte FRA	Iwona Filipowicz & Michal Szumski POL
1996	Brisbane AUS	Ekaterina Davydova & Roman Kostomarov RUS	Isabelle Delobel & Olivier Schoenfelder FRA	Natalia Gudina & Vitaly Kurkudym UKR
1997	Seoul KOR	Nina Ulanova & Mikhail Stifunin RUS	Oksana Potdykova & Denis Petukhov RUS	Agata Blazowska & Marcin Kozubek POL
1998	Saint John CAN	Jessica Joseph & Charles Butler USA	Federica Faiella & Luciano Milo ITA	Oksana Potdykova & Denis Petukhov RUS
1999	Zagreb CRO	Jamie Silverstein & Justin Pekarek USA	Federica Faiella & Luciano Milo ITA	Natalia Romaniuta & Danil Barantsev RUS
2000	Oberstdorf GER	Natalia Romaniuta & Danil Barantsev RUS	Emilie Nussear & Brandon Forsyth USA	Tanith Belbin & Benjamin Agosto USA
2001	Sofia BUL	Natalia Romaniuta & Danil Barantsev RUS	Tanith Belbin & Benjamin Agosto USA	Elena Khaliavina & Maxim Shabalin RUS

Year	Location	Gold	Silver	Bronze
2002	Hamar NOR	Tanith Belbin & Benjamin Agosto USA	Elena Khaliavina & Maxim Shabalin RUS	Elena Romanovskaya & Alexandr Grachev RUS
2003	Ostrava CZE	Oksana Domnina & Maxim Shabalin RUS	Nora Hoffmann & Attila Elek HUN	Elena Romanovskaya & Alexandr Grachev RUS
2004	The Hague NED	Elena Romanovskaya & Alexandr Grachev RUS	Nora Hoffmann & Attila Elek HUN	Morgan Matthews & Maxim Zavozin USA
2005	Kitchener CAN	Morgan Matthews & Maxim Zavozin USA	Tessa Virtue & Scott Moir CAN	Anastasia Gorshkova & Ilia Tkachenko RUS
2006	Ljubljana SLO	Tessa Virtue & Scott Moir CAN	Natalia Mikhailova & Arkadi Sergeev RUS	Meryl Davis & Charlie White USA
2007	Oberstdorf GER	Ekaterina Bobrova & Dmitri Soloviev RUS	Grethe Gruenberg & Kristian Rand EST	Kaitlyn Weaver & Andrew Poje CAN
2008	Sofia BUL	Emily Samuelson & Evan Bates USA	Vanessa Crone & Paul Poirier CAN	Kristina Gorshkova & Vitali Butikov RUS
2009	Sofia BUL	Madison Chock & Greg Zuerlein USA	Maia Shibutani & Alex Shibutani USA	Ekaterina Riazanova & Jonathan Guerreiro RUS
2010	The Hague NED	Elena Ilinykh & Nikita Katsalapov RUS	Alexandra Paul & Mitchell Islam CAN	Ksenia Monko & Kirill Khaliavin RUS

Appendix K
Medalists at the Junior Grand Prix Finals in Figure Skating

Ladies

Year	Location	Gold	Silver	Bronze
1999	Detroit USA	Viktoria Volchkova RUS	Sarah Hughes USA	Daria Timoshenko RUS
2000	Gdansk POL	Deanna Stellato USA	Jennifer Kirk USA	Svetlana Bukareva RUS
2001	Ayr SCO	Ann Patrice McDonough USA	Kristina Oblasova RUS	Yukari Nakano JPN
2002	Bled SLO	Miki Ando JPN	Liudmila Nelidina RUS	Akiko Suzuki JPN
2003	The Hague NED	Yukina Ota JPN	Carolina Kostner ITA	Miki Ando JPN
2004	Malmö SWE	Miki Ando JPN	Lina Johansson SWE	Viktoria Pavuk HUN
2005	Helsinki FIN	Mao Asada JPN	Yu Na Kim KOR	Kimmie Meissner USA
2006	Ostrava CZE	Yu Na Kim KOR	Aki Sawada JPN	Binshu Xu CHN
2007	Sofia BUL	Caroline Zhang USA	Ashley Wagner USA	Megan Oster USA
2008	Gdansk POL	Mirai Nagasu USA	Rachel Flatt USA	Yuki Nishino JPN
2009	Goyang City KOR	Becky Bereswill USA	Yukiko Fujisawa JPN	Alexe Gilles USA
2010	Tokyo JPN	Kanako Murakami JPN	Polina Shelpen RUS	Christina Gao USA

Men

Year	Location	Gold	Silver	Bronze
1999	Detroit USA	Vincent Restencourt FRA	Ilia Klimkin RUS	Alexei Vasilevsky RUS
2000	Gdansk POL	Song Gao CHN	Stefan Lindemann GER	Fedor Andreev CAN
2001	Ayr SCO	Xiaodong Ma CHN	Sergei Dobrin RUS	Stanislav Timchenko RUS
2002	Bled SLO	Stanislav Timchenko RUS	Xiaodong Ma CHN	Kevin van der Perren BEL
2003	The Hague NED	Alexandr Shubin RUS	Sergei Dobrin RUS	Parker Pennington USA
2004	Malmö SWE	Evan Lysacek USA	Andrei Griazev RUS	Christopher Mabee CAN
2005	Helsinki FIN	Dennis Phan USA	Yasuharu Nanri JPN	Alexandr Uspenski RUS
2006	Ostrava CZE	Takahiko Kozuka JPN	Austin Kanallakan USA	Geoffry Varner USA
2007	Sofia BUL	Stephen Carriere USA	Brandon Mroz USA	Kevin Reynolds CAN
2008	Gdansk POL	Adam Rippon USA	Brandon Mroz USA	Armin Mahbanoozadeh USA
2009	Goyang City KOR	Florent Amodio FRA	Armin Mahbanoozadeh USA	Richard Dornbush USA
2010	Tokyo JPN	Yuzuru Hanyu JPN	Nan Song CHN	Ross Miner USA

Pairs

Year	Location	Gold	Silver	Bronze
1999	Detroit USA	Yulia Obertas & Dmitry Palamarchuk UKR	Laura Handy & Paul Binnebose USA	Viktoria Maksiuta & Vladislav Zhovnirsky RUS
2000	Gdansk POL	Aljana Savchenko & Stanislav Morozov UKR	Julia Shapiro & Alexei Sokolov RUS	Viktoria Shliakhova & Giorgy Petrovsky RUS
2001	Ayr SCO	Dan Zhang & Hao Zhang CHN	Kristen Roth & Michael McPherson USA	Yuko Kawaguchi & Alexandr Markuntsov JPN
2002	Bled SLO	Dan Zhang & Hao Zhang CHN	Julia Karbovskaya & Sergei Slavnov RUS	Yang Ding & Zongfei Ren CHN
2003	The Hague NED	Yang Ding & Zongfei Ren CHN	Jessica Dubé & Samuel Tetrault CAN	Jennifer Don & Jonathan Hunt USA
2004	Malmö SWE	Jessica Dubé & Bryce Davison CAN	Natalia Shestakova & Pavel Lebedev RUS	Maria Mukhortova & Maxim Trankov RUS
2005	Helsinki FIN	Maria Mukhortova & Maxim Trankov RUS	Brittany Vis & Nicholas Kole USA	Mariel Miller & Rockne Brubaker USA
2006	Ostrava CZE	Valeria Simakova & Anton Tokarev RUS	Julia Vlassov & Drew Meekins USA	Mariel Miller & Rockne Brubaker USA
2007	Sofia BUL	Keuna McLaughlin & Rockne Brubaker USA	Ksenia Krasilnikova & Konstantin Bezmaternikh RUS	Jessica Rose Paetsch & Jon Nuss USA
2008	Gdansk POL	Vera Bazarova & Yuri Larionov RUS	Ksenia Krasilnikova & Konstantin Bezmaternikh RUS	Ekaterina Sheremetieva & Mikhail Kuznetsov RUS
2009	Goyang City KOR	Lubov Iliushechkina & Nodari Maisuradze RUS	Yue Zhang & Lei Wang CHN	Ksenia Krasilnikova & Konstantin Bezmaternikh RUS
2010	Tokyo JPN	Wenjing Sui & Cong Han CHN	Narumi Takahashi & Mervin Tran JPN	Yue Zhang & Lei Wang CHN

Ice Dancing

Year	Location	Gold	Silver	Bronze
1999	Detroit USA	Jamie Silverstein & Justin Pekarek USA	Federica Faiella & Luciano Milo ITA	Natalia Romaniuta & Daniel Barantsev RUS
2000	Gdansk POL	Natalia Romaniuta & Daniel Barantsev RUS	Emilie Nussear & Brandon Forsyth USA	Kristina Kobaladze & Oleg Voiko UKR
2001	Ayr SCO	Tanith Belbin & Benjamin Agosto USA	Elena Khaliavina & Maxim Shabalin RUS	Miriam Steinel & Vladimir Tsvetkov GER
2002	Bled SLO	Elena Khaliavina & Maxim Shabalin RUS	Elena Romanovskaya & Alexandr Grachev RUS	Miriam Steinel & Vladimir Tsvetkov GER
2003	The Hague NED	Oksana Domnina & Maxim Shabalin RUS	Nora Hoffmann & Attila Elek HUN	Elena Romanovskaya & Alexandr Grachev RUS
2004	Malmö SWE	Nora Hoffmann & Attila Elek HUN	Elena Romanovskaya & Alexandr Grachev RUS	Morgan Matthews & Maxim Zavozin USA
2005	Helsinki FIN	Morgan Matthews & Maxim Zavozin USA	Tessa Virtue & Scott Moir CAN	Anna Cappellini & Matteo Zanni ITA
2006	Ostrava CZE	Tessa Virtue & Scott Moir CAN	Meryl Davis & Charlie White USA	Anna Cappellini & Luca Lanotte ITA
2007	Sofia BUL	Madison Hubbell & Keiffer Hubbell USA	Emily Samuelson & Evan Bates USA	Ekaterina Bobrova & Dmitri Soloviev RUS
2008	Gdansk POL	Maria Monko & Ilia Tkachenko RUS	Emily Samuelson & Evan Bates USA	Kristina Gorshkova & Vitali Butikov RUS
2009	Goyang City KOR	Madison Chock & Greg Zuerlein USA	Madison Hubbell & Keiffer Hubbell USA	Ekaterina Riazanova & Jonathan Guerreiro RUS
2010	Tokyo JPN	Ksenia Monko & Kirill Khaliavin RUS	Elena Ilinykh & Nikita Katsalapov RUS	Maia Shibutani & Alex Shibutani USA

Bibliography

CONTENTS

INTRODUCTION

The first book about figure skating, Robert Jones's *A Treatise on Skating* published in London in 1772, provides our only source for skating technique in the 18th century. The sport is much older, dating from the years after the Restoration in England in 1660, although it is not until a century after Jones's book that the term figure skating first appears. Because Jones provides our first description of skating specific figures, it serves as the point of departure for understanding the evolution of the sport into the disciplines, styles, and techniques employed today.

Skating in the 19th century varied from country to country as national styles evolved. In France, emphasis was placed on artistry, reflecting the French love of ballet, and was first described by Jean Garcin in his *Le vrai patineur* (The True Skater) published in Paris in 1813. The French adopted the term "patinage artistique" (artistic skating) for their sport. In Austria, primarily Vienna, a more flamboyant style evolved after Jackson Haines's two trips there in the 1860s. One of the most exhaustive books on skating technique in any language, *Spuren auf dem Eise* (Tracings on the Ice), was first published in 1881 by three members of the Vienna Skating Club. In Canada and the United States, a uniquely American style developed, first described by Edward Gill in *The Skater's Manual* in 1867 and expanded on by Frank Swift and Marvin Clarke a year later in *The Skaters Textbook.* By the 1880s, three distinct styles dominated: the English style, the American style, and the international style, which was originally called the Viennese style. The International Skating Union (ISU) formed in 1892, the governing body for figure skating, adopted the international style. The American style disappeared quickly, but British skaters, albeit a small number of them since World War I, have continued the English style into the 21st century as a separate branch of figure skating with its own test structures and competitions. The international style is employed for all ISU sanctioned competitions.

Many technical books on skating have been written. They are divided here into three categories, one for singles skating, another for pair skating, ice dancing, and synchronized skating, and a third for English style skating. Because figure skating has evolved continually over more than two centuries, elements employed, demands placed on the skaters, and styles described in the earlier books are significantly different from those employed today. Thus, dates of publication are important in researching styles and techniques. Among the most recent books, Carole Shulman's *The Complete Book of Figure Skating* provides an excellent and detailed overview of the technique employed today for disciplines other than synchronized skating. No comprehensive book on synchronized skating exists. A brief introduction to the discipline is provided by James R. Hines in *Figure Skating: A History*. Technical aspects and judging criteria are included in the ISU's *Judges' Handbook V, Synchronized Skating*.

The first general history of the sport, *Ice Skating: A History*, written by Nigel Brown, was published in 1959 and is remarkably good for its date, but more than 50 years have passed since its publication. The most recent is Hines's *Figure Skating: A History*, published in 2006. Three valuable and extensive historical studies include *Our Skating Heritage, A Centenary History of the National Skating Association of Great Britain, 1879–1979*, written by Dennis L. Bird for the 100th anniversary of the oldest national governing organization for figure skating. The other two, *Skating Around the World: The One Hundredth Anniversary History of the International Skating Union*, and *Skating in America: The 75th Anniversary History of the United States Figure Skating Association,* written by Benjamin T. Wright, provide detailed historical information on those respective organizations. Other books included in the General History section of the bibliography are also recommended. Histories of various skating clubs are included as a separate category. They provide useful information on elite skaters who represented those specific clubs, and for the older clubs, there are often excellent descriptions of skating practices, in some cases more than a century ago.

Appendixes in this book include medal winners for all of the major ISU championships. For skaters who placed fourth and below, the books in the category of Competition Results provide complete lists of competitors at the European and World Championships through 1991 and at the Olympic Winter Games through 1994. Results from more recent years and for all years in other ISU championships can be found in various issues of *Skating* magazine, *ISU World*, and *The Professional Skater*.

Following the judging scandal in the pairs competition at the Olympic Winter Games in 2002, the ISU adopted a new and dramatically different judging system. During its development and testing, many articles appeared in a variety of sources, including magazines and newspapers. Since its adoption in 2004, discussion has continued on websites and in blogs. A few of the early articles and two books, both written by opponents of the new judging system, are included in the section Judging Controversy of 2002 and the New Judging System. Information on the new judging system is available on the ISU and other websites. Articles by David Kirby, an ISU technical specialist, are published regularly in *The Professional Skater*.

Social issues, including ethnicity and sexuality, have received some recent attention. Three books are included under the heading Sociological Issues. They often discuss specific skaters for whom further information is available in biographies and autobiographies. Books included in other categories sometimes address sociological issues, a notable example being Jon Jackson's *On Edge*. Its subject is the ISU and its new judging system, but it deals extensively with homosexuality in skating.

Prior to World War II, books devoted to individual skaters, biographies and autobiographies, include only ones for Sonja Henie, *Wings on My Feet*, and pair skaters Maxi Herber and Ernst Baier, *Maxi und Ernst Baier erzählen*. Since the war, biographies and autobiographies have appeared more frequently, and with the heightened popularity enjoyed by figure skating in the 1990s, the number increased significantly. For convenience, the section Biographies and Autobiographies includes the entries under the names of individual skaters. Juvenile literature, which is relatively extensive, includes primarily biographies. They have not been included here, although it is noted that such literature sometimes includes valuable information such as birthdays, information on families and siblings, and early competition results.

Professional skating shows became tremendously popular beginning in the late 1930s and a few continue to tour today. For a survey of their history over time, see Hines's *Figure Skating: A History*. Books have been written on most of the major touring shows in the United States, and they include excellent pictures. Although there is no book for the first of them, the Ice Follies, L. E. Leipold's biography on Eddie Shipstad, one of the founders, includes much information on the show. The linage of Disney on Ice, which still tours today, reaches back to the Ice Follies.

Numerous books on figure skating do not fit conveniently in the specified categories. They are included in Miscellaneous Topics. Many are quite useful and, like most books on figure skating, include pictures.

Skating magazines have been published at various times, usually by governing bodies but also as commercial ventures. Most of them survived for relatively short periods of time. *Skating* magazine, the official publication of U.S. Figure Skating, is the most important over an extended period. Its first issue is dated December 1923, and it has been published continuously to the present, including the World War II years. It includes articles on skaters, skating technique, competition results both national and international, tests passed by U.S. skaters, and association news. Current Skating Periodicals include ones in various languages written for and marketed primarily to skating fans. *International Figure Skating* is the most important in English.

Numerous websites covering various aspects of figure skating are easily located through Google or other searches, but they are of uneven value and often disappear after short periods of time. The Useful Websites included here are primarily those of established governing bodies such as the International Skating Union and U.S. Figure Skating. They include up-to-date information relative to competitions, information on current skaters, rule changes, activities within various disciplines, and results for current and past competitions.

GENERAL HISTORY

Bang, Gunnar. *Konståkingens 100-åriga historia*. Malmö, Sweden: Absalons Forlag, 1966.

Bird, Dennis L. *Our Skating Heritage: A Centenary History of the National Skating Association of Great Britain, 1879–1979*. London: National Skating Association of Great Britain, 1979.

Brown, Nigel. *Ice Skating: A History*. New York: A. S. Barnes, 1959.

Chaikovsky, Anatoly. *Figures on Ice*. Moscow: Progress Publishers, 1978.

Copley-Graves, Lynn. *Figure Skating History: The Evolution of Dance on Ice*. Columbus, Ohio: Platoro Press, 1992.

Goodfellow, Arthur. *Wonderful World of Skates*. Mountainburg, Ark., 1972.

Hines, James R. "The Birth of Winter Olympic Sports: London 1908." *Journal of Olympic History* (August 2006).
———. *The English Style: Figure Skating's Oldest Tradition*. Westwood, Mass.: Neponset River Press, 2008.
———. *Figure Skating: A History*. Champaign: University of Illinois Press, 2005.
A History of the National Skating Association of Great Britain, 1879–1901 with a Catalogue of the Exhibition of Skates and Skating Matters in 1902. London: The National Skating Association, 1902.
Lambert, Luna. *The American Skating Mania: Ice Skating in the Nineteenth Century*. Washington, D.C.: Smithsonian Institution, 1979.
Lindsay, Peter Leslie. "A History of Sport in Canada, 1807–1867," PhD diss., University of Alberta, Edmonton, 1969.
Malone, John. *The Encyclopedia of Figure Skating*. New York: Facts on File, 1998.
Meisel, Alexander. *60 Jahre Sportplatz Engelmann im auftrage des Vereines Kunsteisbahn Engelmann*. Vienna: Paul Gerein, 1932.
Merriam, Robert L. *The Ancient Art of Skating*. Deerfield, Mass.: Deerfield Academy, 1957.
Moore, Teresa. *Reflections on the CFSA, 1987–1990*. Gloucester, Ontario: Canadian Figure Skating Association, 1993.
Wade, A. C. A. *The Skater's Cavalcade: Fifty Years of Skating*. London: Olympic Publications, 1939.
Wright, Benjamin T. *Reader's Guide to Figure Skating's Hall of Fame*. Boston: United States Figure Skating Association, 1981.
———. *Skating Around the World, 1892–1992: The One Hundredth Anniversary History of the International Skating Union*. Davos, Switzerland: International Skating Union, 1992.
———. *Skating in America: The 75th Anniversary History of the United States Figure Skating Association*. Colorado Springs: United States Figure Skating Association, 1996.
Young, David. *The Golden Age of Canadian Figure Skating*. Toronto: Summerhill Press, 1984.

HISTORIES OF SKATING CLUBS

100 Jahre Wiener Eislauf-Verein. Vienna, 1967.
Biberhofer, Franz. *Chronit des Wiener Eislaufvereines*. Vienna, 1906.
Cambridge Skating Club 1898–1948. n.p., n.d.
Charter and By-laws of the Philadelphia Skating Club and Humane Society. Philadelphia: J. B. Chandler, 1864.
The Edinburgh Skating Club with Diagrams of Figures and a List of Members. Edinburgh, 1865.
Ellis, W. D., P. G. Fanslow, and N. A. Schneider. *The Home Club—The Cleveland Skating Club Story*. n.p., 1986.
Fillmore, Stanley. *The Pleasure of the Game: The Story of the Toronto Cricket, Skating and Curling Club: 1827–1977*. Toronto: Charter House, 1977.

LaMond, Annette. *A History of the Cambridge Skating Club, 1897—2001*. Cambridge, Mass.: Cambridge Skating Club, 2002.

Lewis, John F. *Skating and the Philadelphia Skating Club*. Philadelphia, 1895.

One Hundred Years of the Philadelphia Skating Club and Humane Society. Philadelphia: n.p., 1949.

COMPETITION RESULTS

75 Years of European and World's Championships in Figure Skating. Davos, Switzerland: International Skating Union, 1967.

Results: Figure Skating Championships, 1968–1991. Davos, Switzerland: International Skating Union, 1992.

Skating in the Olympic Games, 1908–1994. Davos, Switzerland: International Skating Union, 1994.

JUDGING CONTROVERSY OF 2002 AND THE NEW JUDGING SYSTEM

Elfman, Lois. "Imperialist Union, Blind Judgements of the ISU Put into Crisis." *International Figure Skating* 9 (May–June 2003): 40–44.

———. "Judging Faces the Jury." *International Figure Skating* 8 (January–February 2003): 24–25.

———. "To the Point: The Skating World Tries Out a New Judging System." *International Figure Skating* 10 (March–April 2004): 40–44.

Elfman, Lois, and Mark Lund. "The Beef Goes On." *International Figure Skating* 8 (July–August 2002): 39–41.

Garbetto, Sonia Bianchetti. *Cracked Ice: Figure Skating's Inner World*. Milano, Italy: Libreria dello Sport, 2004.

Jackson, Jon, and James Perrira. *On Edge: Backroom Dealing, Cocktail Screwing, Triple Axels, and How Top Skaters Get Screwed*. New York: Thunder's Mouth Press, 2005.

SOCIOLOGICAL ISSUES

Kestnbaum, Ellyn. *Culture on Ice*. Middletown, Conn.: Wesleyan University Press, 2003.

Lund, Mark A., Lois Elfman, and Rebecca Patrick. *Frozen Assets: The New Order of Figure Skating*. Worcester, Mass.: Ashton International Media, 2002.

Ryan, Joan. *Little Girls in Pretty Boxes*. New York: Doubleday, 1995.

PROFESSIONAL SKATING SHOWS

Brennan, Christine. *Champions on Ice*. Plattsburgh, N.Y.: McClelland & Stewart, 2002.

Langdon, Claude. *Earls Court*. London: Stanley Paul, 1953.

Leipold, L. E. *Eddie Shipstad: Ice Follies Star*. Minneapolis, Minn.: T. S. Denison, 1971.
Shuffle, Ted. *Holiday on Ice: The First Fifty Years*. Amsterdam: Arena International Bookings, 1994.
Wilner, Barry. *Stars on Ice: An Intimate Look at Skating's Greatest Tour*. Kansas City, Mo.: Andrews McMeel, 1998.

SINGLES SKATING TECHNIQUE

Anderson, George. *The Art of Skating: Containing Many Figures Never Previously Described*. Ann Arbor, Mich.: UMI Books on Demand, 2001. Reprint of 2nd ed., 1868.
Bass, Howard. *Let's Go Skating*. New York: St. Martin's Press, 1974.
———. *Skating: Elegance on Ice*. London: Chartwell Books, 1980.
———. *Winter Sports*. New York: A. S. Barnes, 1966.
Benson, Claude E. *Skating and Bandy*. London: George Routledge & Sons, 1921.
Boeckl, Wilhelm Richard. *Willy Boeckl on Figure Skating*. n.p., 1937.
Brokaw, Irving. *The Art of Skating*. New York: Scribner, 1910.
———. *The Art of Skating*. New York: American Sports Publishing, 1915.
———. *The Art of Skating*. New York: American Sports Publishing, 1917.
———. *The Art of Skating*. New York: Scribner, 1926.
Browne, George H. *Figure Skating with Seventy-four Illustrations and Diagrams*. Boston: Perry Mason, 1892.
———. *A Handbook of Figure Skating*. Springfield, Mass.: Barney & Berry, 1900. Additional and expanded editions in 1910 and 1913.
———. *The New Skating*. Cambridge, Mass. Reprinted for the author in 1910.
———. *A Skating Primer*. Springfield, Mass.: Barney & Berry, 1912.
Crawley, A. E. *Skating, International, Speed*. London: Methuen, 1920.
Cruikshank, James A. *Figure Skating for Women*. New York: American Sports Publishing, 1922.
Cyclos. *The Art of Skating: With Plain Directions for the Acquirement of the Most Difficult and Elegant Moves*. Glasgow: Thomas Murray, 1852.
Dědič, Josef. *Single Figure Skating for Beginners and Champions*. Prague: Olympia, 1974.
Diamantidi, Demeter, C. V. Korper, M. Wirth. *Spuren auf dem Eise*. Vienna: Alfred Hölder, 1881, 1882.
Dobe, Walter. *The Skater's Monitor, Instructor, and Evening Companion*. Edinburgh: John Menzies, 1846.
Fassi, Carlo. *Figure Skating with Carlo Fassi*. New York: Scribner, 1980.
Fuchs, Gilbert. *Theorie und Praxis des Kunstlaufes am Eise*. Laibach: Selbstverlag, 1926.
Garcin, Jean. *Le vrai patineur*. Paris: J. Gillé Fils, 1813.
Gassner, Paul von. *Figure and Dance Skating*. New York: A & S Publishing Co., 1949.

Gill, Edward L. *The Skater's Manual: A Complete Guide to the Art of Skating*. New York: Andrew Peck, 1867.
Heathcote, J. M., and C. G. Tebbutt. *Skating*. London: Longmans, Green, 1892.
Hedges, Sid G. *Ice-Rink Skating*. London: C. Arthur Pearson, 1932.
Helfrich, George. *Der Eislauf in Kunsthistorischer Darstellung*. St. Petersburg, Russia: Verlag des Petersburger Eislaufvereins, 1903.
———. *Die Dame auf Schlittschuhen*. Munich: Bergverlag Rudolf Rother, 1926.
———. *Kunst des Eislaufs*. Munich: Bergverlag Rother, n.d.
Heller, Mark, ed. *The Illustrated Encyclopedia of Ice Skating*. New York: Paddington Press, 1979.
Holletschek, Robert. *Kunstfertigkeit im Eislaufen*. Troppau: Verlag von Buchholz & Diebel, 1904.
Horne, Peri. *Ice Skating*. London: Museum Press, 1968.
How to Become a Figure Skater: Containing Full Instructions for Excelling at Figure and Speed Skating; Spalding's Athletic Library. New York: American Sports Publishing, 1904.
Hügin, Otto, and Jack Gerschwiler. *The Technique of Skating*. London: Castle, 1977.
Huxhagen, Ernst. *Uebungs-Schule des Eis-Kunstlaufens*. Braunschweig: Commissions—Verlag von F. Wagner's Hof Buchhandlung, 1888.
Jomland, Einar, Ron Priestly, James Waldo, and Michael Kirby. *Skating on Ice*. New York: Sterling Publishing, 1963.
Jones, Ernest. *The Elements of Figure Skating*. London: George Allen, 1952.
Jones, Robert. *A Treatise on Skating*. London, 1772.
Judges' Handbook I, Compulsory Figures. Davos, Switzerland: International Skating Union, 1984.
Judges' Handbook II, Single Free Skating and the Technical Program. Davos, Switzerland: International Skating Union, 1993.
Kirby, Michael. *The Young Sportsman's Guide to Ice Skating*. New York: Thomas Nelson & Sons, 1962.
Lewis, Frederic. *Modern Skating*. Chicago: Reilly & Lee, 1938.
Lindsay, Sally. *Figure Skating*. Chicago: Rand McNally, 1963.
Lussi, Gustave, and Maurice Richards. *Championship Figure Skating*. New York: A. S. Barnes, 1951.
Magnus, Louis. *Le patinage artistique*. Paris: Bibliothèque Larousse, 1914.
Meagher, George A. *Lessons in Skating*. New York: Dodd, Mead, 1900.
———. *A Guide to Artistic Skating*. London: T. C. & E. C. Jack, 1919.
Mettez, G. *Traité pratique de patinage sur glace*. Paris: n.p., n.d.
Meyer, Bror. *Skating with Bror Meyer*. New York: Doubleday, 1921.
Milton, Steve. *Skate: 100 Years of Figure Skating*. North Pomfret, Vt.: Trafalgar Square Publishing, 1996.
Ogilvie, Robert S. *Basic Ice Skating Skills*. Philadelphia: J. B. Lippincott, 1968.
———. *Handbook of New Era Figures*. Rochester, Minn.: Professional Skaters Guild of America, 1993.
Owen, Maribel Vinson. *The Fun of Figure Skating*. New York: Harper & Row, 1960.

Petkevich, John Misha. *Sports Illustrated Figure Skating Championship Techniques*. New York: Winner's Circle Books, 1989.
Putnam, Harold, and Dwight Parkinson. *Skating*. New York: A. S. Barnes, 1939.
Richardson, T. D. *The Art of Figure Skating*. New York: A. S. Barnes, 1962.
———. *The Complete Figure Skater*. London: Methuen, 1948.
———. *The Girl's Book of Skating*. New York: Roy Publishers, 1959.
———. *Ice-Rink Skating*. London: C. Arthur Pearson, 1949.
———. *Modern Figure Skating*. London: Methuen, 1930.
———. *Modern Figure Skating*, Revised Edition. London: Methuen, 1938.
Salchow, Ulrich. *Kunstlaufen auf dem Eise*. Leipzig: Grethlein, 1920.
Salvesen, Charles E. *The Foundation of Skating*. Edinburgh: Moray Press, 1938.
Schäfer, Karl. *Living Pictures of My Figure Skating*. Vienna: Carl Kravani, 1937.
Shulman, Carole. *The Complete Book of Figure Skating*. Champaign, Ill.: Human Kinetics, 2002.
Swift, Frank, and Marvin R. Clark. *The Skaters Textbook*. New York: John A. Gray & Green, 1868.
Syers, Edgar, and Madge Syers. *The Art of Skating (International Style)*. London: Horace Cox, 1913.
Taylor, Duff. *Skating*. London: Seeley, Service, 1930.
Turner, Roger F. *Edges*. Toronto: Mansfield Press, 1973.
Vandervell, H. E., and T. Maxwell Witham. *A System of Figure Skating, Being the Theory and Practice of the Art as Developed in England, with a Glance at Its Origin and History*. London: Macmillan, 1869.
Vinson, Maribel Y. *Advanced Figure Skating*. New York: McGraw-Hill, 1940.
———. *Primer of Figure Skating*. New York: McGraw-Hill, 1938.
White, Harold D. J. *Figure Skating Technique*. London: Routledge & Sons, 1933.
Witham, T. Maxwell. *A System of Figure Skating, Being the Theory and Practice of the Art as Developed in England, with a Glance at Its Origin and History*. London: Horace Cox, 1897.
Wood, Rev. J. G., et al. *Skating and Sliding*. London: Routledge and Sons, 1872.
Yamaguchi, Kristi, Christie Ness, and Judy Meacham. *Figure Skating for Dummies*. Foster City, Calif.: IDG Books Worldwide, 1997.
Yglesias, Herbert Ramon. *Figure Skating*. London: Routledge and Sons, n.d.

PAIR SKATING, ICE DANCING, AND SYNCHRONIZED SKATING TECHNIQUE

Arnold, Richard. *Dancing on Skates*. New York: St. Martin's Press, 1985.
Bestimmungen über das Eistanzen. Davos, Switzerland: Internationale Eislauf-Vereingung, 1961.
Dench, Robert, and Rosemarie Stewart. *Pair Skating and Dancing on Ice*. New York: Prentice Hall, 1943.
Feix, Gustav. *Das Kunstlaufen und der Tanz auf dem Eis*. Vienna: Saturn Verlag, 1935.
Ice Dances, Volume I. Boston: United States Figure Skating Association, 1936.

Ice Dances, Volume II. Boston: United States Figure Skating Association, 1940.
Ice Dances. London: National Skating Association of Great Britain, 1974.
Judges' Handbook III, Pair Skating. Davos, Switzerland: International Skating Union, 1993.
Judges' Handbook IV, Ice Dancing. Davos, Switzerland: International Skating Union, 1988.
Judges' Handbook V, Synchronized Skating. Lausanne, Switzerland: International Skating Union, 1999.
Kay, Muriel. *The Key to Rhythmic Ice Dancing*. Columbus, Ohio: Platoro Press, 1992.
———. *Origins of Ice Dance Music*. Columbus, Ohio: Plataro Press, 1992.
Kent, Herbert Vaughan. *Combined Figures and Ice-Valsing*. London: Hutchinson & Co., 1930.
Law, Ernest. *Dancing on Ice Described and Analysed with Hints on How to Do It*. London: G. Bell and Sons, 1925.
———. *Valsing on Ice Described and Analysed with Hints for Attaining Proficiency in the Art*. London: Hugh Rees, 1908.
Moskvina, Tamara, and Igor Moskvin. *Pair Skating as Sport and Art*. Davos, Switzerland: International Skating Union, 1993.
Radspinner, William Ambrose. *Skating and Skate Dancing*. New York: n.p., 1950.
Readhead, Monty. *Ice Dancing*. London: Pelham Books, 1968.
Thompson, Norcliffe G., and F. Laura Cannan. *Hand-in-Hand Figure-Skating*. London: Longmans, Green, 1896.
Weyden, Erik Van Der. *Dancing on Ice*. London: C. Arthur Pearson, 1951.

ENGLISH STYLE SKATING TECHNIQUE

Adams, Douglas. *Skating*. London: George Bell and Sons, 1890.
Benson, E. F. *English Figure Skating: A Guide to the Theory and Practice of Skating in the English Style*. London: George Bell and Sons, 1908.
Cobb, Humphrey H. *Figure Skating in the English Style*. London: Eveleigh Nash, 1913.
Heathcote, J. M., and C. G. Tebbutt. *Skating*. London: Longmans, Green, 1892.
Lowther, Henry Cecil. *Combined Figure Skating*. London: Horace Cox, 1902.
Monier-Williams, Montagu, Winter Randall Pidgeon, and Arthur Dryden. *Figure Skating Simple and Combined*. New York: Macmillan, 1892.
Thompson, Norcliffe. *Combined Hand-in-hand Figure Skating*. Breinigsville, Penn., n.d.
Wood, George. *Combined Figure Skating*. London: F. E. Robinson, 1899.

MISCELLANEOUS TOPICS

Boo, Michael. *The Story of Figure Skating*. New York: William Morrow, 1998.
Brennan, Christine. *Edge of Glory: The Inside Story of the Quest for Figure Skating's Gold Medals*. New York: Scribner, 1998.
———. *Inside Edge*. New York: Scribner, 1996.

Constitution and General Regulations, 1998–2000. Lausanne, Switzerland: International Skating Union, 1998.
Goodfellow, Arthur R. *The Skating Scene: The Fact Book of Skating Champions & Championships*. Tucson, Ariz.: n.p., 1981.
Gutman, Dan. *Ice Skating: From Axels to Zambonis*. New York: Viking, 1995.
Hagnauer, Jeanine. *Le patinage sur glace*. Paris: Editions Mondiales, 1968.
Jomland, Einar, and Jim Fitzgerald. *Inside Ice Skating*. Chicago: Contemporary Books, 1978.
Milton, Steve. *Skate Talk: Figure Skating in the Words of the Stars*. Buffalo, N.Y.: Firefly Books, 1997.
———. *Super Skaters: World Figure Skating Stars*. New York: Crescent Books, 1997.
Nichols, Nikki. *Frozen in Time: The Enduring Legacy of the 1961 U.S. Figure Skating Team*. Cincinnati, Ohio: Emmis Books, 2006.
Richardson, T. D. *Champions All: Camera Studies by E. R. Hall*. London: Frederick Muller, 1938.
Sheffield, Robert, and Richard Woodward. *The Ice Skating Book*. New York: Universe Books, 1980.
Sivorinovsky, Alina. *Inside Figure Skating*. New York: Friedman/Fairfax Publishers, 1999.
Skating through the Years. Boston: United States Figure Skating Association, 1942.
Skating through the Years. Boston: United Skates Figure Skating Association, 1957.
Smith, Beverley. *Figure Skating: A Celebration*. Toronto: McClelland & Stewart, 1994.
———. *Talking Figure Skating: Behind the Scenes in the World's Most Glamorous Sport*. Toronto: McClelland & Stewart, 1998.
———. *A Year in Figure Skating*. Toronto: McClelland & Stewart, 1996.
Steenwyk, Elizabeth Van. *Stars on Ice*. New York: Dodd, Meade, 1980.
———. *Women in Sports: Figure Skating*. New York: Harvey House, 1976.
Stevenson, Sandra. *The BBC Book of Skating*. London: British Broadcasting Corporation, 1984.
Turner, Roger F. *Polished Steel*. Bryn Mawr, Pa.: Dorrance, 1984.
United States Figure Skating Association. *The Official Book of Figure Skating*. New York: Simon & Schuster, 1998.
Whedon, Julia. *The Fine Art of Ice Skating: An Illustrated History and Portfolio of Stars*. New York: Abrams, 1988.
Wilkes, Debbi, and Greg Cable. *Ice Time: A Portrait of Figure Skating*. Scarborough, Ontario: Prentice Hall Canada, 1994.
Zane, D. B. *The Great Zamboni*. Cypress, Calif.: Dizon Publishing, 1998.

BIOGRAPHIES AND AUTOBIOGRAPHIES

Babilonia, Tai, and Randy Gardner

Babilonia, Tai, and Randy Gardner, with Martha Lowder Kimball. *Forever Two As One*, Jamestown, N.Y.: Millpond Press, 2002.

Baiul, Oksana

Baiul, Oksana. *Oksana Baiul: Secrets of Skating*. New York: Universe Publishing, 1997.
Baiul, Oksana, and Heather Alexander. *Oksana: My Own Story*. New York: Random House, 1997.

Barber, Karen, and Nicky Slater

Barber, Karen, and Nicky Slater, with Sandra Stevenson. *Spice on Ice: The Story of Britain's Ice Dance Champions*, London: Sidgwick & Jackson, 1985.

Belousova, Liudmila, and Oleg Protopopov

Shelukhin, Anatoly A. *Symphony on Ice: The Protopopovs*. Columbus, Ohio: Platoro Press, 1993.

Boitano, Brian

Boitano, Brian, with Suzanne Harper. *Boitano's Edge: Inside the Real World of Figure Skating*. New York: Simon & Schuster, 1997.

Bonaly, Surya

Bonaly, Surya, with Isabelle Rivère. *Surya Bonaly, L'enfant du soleil*. Paris: TFI Editions, 1995.

Brasseur, Isabelle, and Lloyd Eisler

Prouse, Lynda D. *Brasseur & Eisler: To Catch a Dream*. Toronto: Macmillan Canada, 1996.

Browning, Kurt

Browning, Kurt, with Neil Stevens. *Kurt: Forcing the Edge*. Toronto: HarperCollins, 1991.

Button, Dick

Button, Dick. *Dick Button on Skates*. Englewood Cliffs, N.J.: Prentice Hall, 1955.

Cousins, Robin

Cousins, Robin, with Howard Bass. *Robin Cousins: Skating for Gold*. London: Stanley Paul, 1980.

Kimball, Martha Lowder. *Robin Cousins*. Baltimore: Gateway Press, 1998.

Cranston, Toller

Oglanby, Elva Clairmont. *Toller*. Toronto: Cage Publishing, 1975.

Curry, John

Money, Keith. *John Curry*. New York: Knopf, 1978.
Oglanby, Elva. *Black Ice: The Life and Death of John Curry*. London: Victor Gollancz, 1995.

Dijkstra, Sjoukje

Maegerlein, Heinz. *Triumph auf dem Eis: Sjoukje Dijkstra, Marika Kilius, Hansjürgen Bäumler, Manfred Schnelldorfer*. Berlin: Verlag Bartels & Wernitz, 1964.

Du Bief, Jacqueline

Du Bief, Jacqueline. *Thin Ice*. London: Cassell and Company, 1956.

Duchesnay, Isabelle and Paul

Duchesnay, Isabelle, and Paul Duchesnay. *Isabelle et Paul Duchesnay: Notre passion*. Paris: Robert Laffont, 1992.

Fleming, Peggy

Fleming, Peggy, and Peter Kaminsky. *The Long Program: Skating toward Life's Victories*. New York: Pocket Books, 1999.
Steenwyk, Elizabeth Van. *Peggy Fleming: Cameo of a Champion*. New York: McGraw-Hill, 1978.
Young, Stephanie, and Bruce Curtis. *Peggy Fleming: Portrait of an Ice Skater*. New York: Avon Books, 1984.

Galindo, Rudy

Galindo, Rudy, with Eric Marcus. *Icebreaker: The Autobiography of Rudy Galindo*. New York: Pocket Books, 1997.

Gordeeva, Ekaterina

Gordeeva, Ekaterina, with E. M. Swift. *My Sergei: A Love Story*. New York: Warner Books, 1996.

Hamill, Dorothy

Dolan, Edward F., and Richard B. Lyttle. *Dorothy Hamill: Olympic Skating Champion*. Garden City, N.Y.: Doubleday, 1979.

Hamill, Dorothy, with Elva Clairmont. *On and Off the Ice*. New York: Knopf, 1983.

———. *A Skating Life: My Story*. With Deborah Amelon. New York: Hyperion, 2007.

Steenwyk, Elizabeth Van. *Dorothy Hamill Olympic Champion*. New York: Harvey House, 1976.

Hamilton, Scott

Brennan, Kristine. *Scott Hamilton*. Philadelphia: Chelsea House Publishers, 1999.

Hamilton, Scott, with Lorenzo Benet. *Landing It: My Life on and off the Ice*. New York: Kensington Books, 1999.

Steere, Michael. *Scott Hamilton: A Behind the Scenes Look at the Life and Competitive Times of America's Favorite Figure Skater*. New York: St. Martin's Press, 1985.

Harding, Tonya

Coffey, Frank, and Joe Layden. *Thin Ice: The Complete Uncensored Story of Tonya Harding, America's Bad Girl of Ice Skating*. New York: Pinnacle Books, 1994.

Haight, Abby, and J. E. Vader. *Fire on Ice: The Exclusive Inside Story of Tonya Harding*. New York: Times Books, 1994.

Prouse, Lynda D. *The Tonya Tapes*. New York: World Audience, 2008.

Heiss, Carol

Bolstad, Helen Cambria. *Golden Skates: The Story of Carol Heiss—Teen-Age Champion*. New York: Scholastic, 1958.

Parker, Robert. *Carol Heiss: Olympic Queen*. New York: Doubleday, 1961.

Henie, Sonja

Henie, Sonja. *Wings on My Feet*. New York: Prentice Hall, 1940.

Kirby, Michael. *Figure Skating to Fancy Skating: Memories of the Life of Sonja Henie*. Raleigh, N.C.: Pentland Press, 2000.

Strait, Raymond, and Leif Henie. *Queen of Ice, Queen of Shadows. The Unsuspected Life of Sonja Henie*. Lanham, Md.: Scarborough House, 1985.

Herber, Maxi, and Ernst Baier

Wellmann, Benno, ed. *Maxi und Ernst Baier erzählen*. Dusseldorf: Droste Verlag u. Druckerei, 1951.

Hughes, Sarah

Sivorinovsky, Alina. *Sarah Hughes: Skating to the Stars*. New York: Berkley Books, 2001.

Jackson, Donald

Gross, George. *Donald Jackson: King of Blades*. Toronto: Queen City Publishing, 1977.

Kerrigan, Nancy

Caffey, Wayne, and Filip Bondy. *Dreams of Gold: The Nancy Kerrigan Story*. New York: St. Martin's Press, 1994.

Reisfeld, Randi. *The Kerrigan Courage, Nancy's Story*. New York: Ballantine Books, 1994.

Kilius, Marika, and Hans-Jürgen Bäumler

Maegerlein, Heinz. *Triumph auf dem Eis: Sjoukje Dijkstra, Marika Kilius, Hansjürgen Bäumler, Manfred Schnelldorfer*. Berlin: Verlag Bartels & Wernitz, 1964.

Menzel, Roderich. *Weltmeister auf dem Eis: Kilius / Bäumler*. Munich: Franz Schneider Verlag, 1963.

Kwan, Michelle

Epstein, Edward Z. *Born to Skate: The Michelle Kwan Story*. New York: Ballantine Books, 1997.

Kwan, Michelle. *Michelle Kwan, My Story, Heart of a Champion*. New York: Scholastic, 1998.

Lovitt, Chip. *Skating for the Gold: Michelle Kwan and Tara Lipinski*. New York: Pocket Books, 1997.

Lipinski, Tara

Lipinski, Tara. *Triumph on Ice: An Autobiography*. New York: Bantam Books, 1997.

Lovitt, Chip. *Skating for the Gold: Michelle Kwan and Tara Lipinski*. New York: Pocket Books, 1997.

Lynn, Janet

Lynn, Janet, with Dean Merrill. *Peace and Love*. Carol Stream, Ill.: Creation House, 1973.

Magnussen, Karen

Magnussen, Karen, and Jeff Cross. *Karen: The Karen Magnussen Story*. New York: Macmillan, 1973.

Manley, Elizabeth

Oglanby, Elva Clairmont. *Thumbs Up! The Elizabeth Manley Story*. Toronto: Macmillan Canada, 1990.

Prouse, Lynda D. *Elizabeth Manley, As I Am, My Life After the Olympics*. Toronto: Macmillan Canada, n.d.

Orser, Brian

Orser, Brian, with Steve Milton. *Orser: A Skater's Life*. Toronto: Key Porter Books, 1988.

Sabovčík, Jozef

Prouse, Lynda D. *Jumpin' Joe: The Jozef Sabovčík Story*. Toronto: Macmillan Canada, 1998.

Salé, Jamie, and David Pelletier

Smith, Beverley. *Gold on Ice: The Salé and Pelletier Story*. Toronto: Key Porter Books, 2002.

Schnelldorfer, Manfred

Maegerlein, Heinz. *Triumph auf dem Eis: Sjoukje Dijkstra, Marika Kilius, Hansjürgen Bäumler, Manfred Schnelldorfer*. Berlin: Verlag Bartels & Wernitz, 1964.

Scott, Barbara Ann

Moore, Cay. *She Skated into Our Hearts*. Toronto: McClelland & Stewart, 1948.

Scott, Barbara Ann. *Skate with Me*. New York: Doubleday, 1950.

Shipstad, Eddie

Leipold, L. E. *Eddie Shipstad: Ice Follies Star*. Minneapolis, Minn.: T. S. Denison, 1971.

Stojko, Elvis

Stojko, Elvis. *Heart and Soul*. Toronto: Rocketeer Publishing, 1997.

Torvill, Jayne, and Christopher Dean

Hennessy, John. *Torvill & Dean*. London: David & Charles, 1983.

Hilton, Christopher. *Torvill and Dean: The Full Story*. London: Oxford Illustrated Press, 1994.

Torvill, Jayne, and Christopher Dean. *Torvill and Dean, Fire on Ice*. London: Weidenfeld and Nicolson, 1994.
Torvill, Jayne, and Christopher Dean, with John Man. *Torvill and Dean: The Autobiography of Ice Dancing's Greatest Stars*. Secaucus, N.J.: Birch Lane Press, 1996.

Trenary, Jill

Trenary, Jill, with Dale Mitch. *Jill Trenary: The Day I Skated for Gold*. New York: Simon and Schuster, 1989.

Witt, Katarina

Heimo, Bernard, and Félix Clément. *Katarina Witt*. Altstätten, Germany: Panorama Verlag, 1988.
Witt, Katarina, with E. M. Smith. *Only with Passion*. New York: Public Affairs, 2005.

CURRENT SKATING PERIODICALS

Blades on Ice. Tucson, Ariz. Published bimonthly, 1990–.
Ice Skating International Online. Manhattan Beach, California: www.crl.com/~iceskate/ 1996–.
International Figure Skating. Quincy, Mass.: Madavor Media, published bimonthly, 1996– .
ISI Newsletter. Buffalo Grove, Illinois: Ice Skating Institute, published six times annually, 1959–.
Patinage Magazine. Rouen, France: 1986–.
Pirouette. Stuttgart, Germany: published monthly, 1958–.
The Professional Skater. Rochester, Minnesota: The Professional Skaters Association, published bimonthly, 1970–.
Skating. Colorado Springs, Colorado: U.S. Figure Skating, published 10 times annually, 1923–.
ISU World. Lausanne, Switzerland: International Skating Union, published three times annually, 1997–.

USEFUL WEBSITES

www.isu.org	International Skating Union
www.usfsa.org	U.S. Figure Skating
www.skatecanada.ca	Skate Canada
www.iceskating.org.uk	National Skating Association of the United Kingdom
www.skatepsa.com	Professional Skaters Association
www.ifsmagazine.com	International Figure Skating magazine

www.sk8stuff.com	Figure skater's website
www.figureskating.about.com	General information
www.goldenskate.com	General information
www.icenetwork.com	General information

About the Author

James R. Hines, a musicologist, is a professor emeritus from Christopher Newport University in Newport News, Virginia, where he taught for 35 years. Hines, a dance skater on rollers as a teenager, has maintained a decades-old interest in skating, especially its history from ancient times to the present. Only one badly out of date and no longer available history of figure skating had previously been written. Seeing a need and to fill that void, Hines wrote the comprehensive *Figure Skating: A History*, which was published in 2006. It is widely recognized as the definitive history of the sport. His ongoing research has resulted in a monograph, *The English Style: Figure Skating's Oldest Tradition*, articles in the *Journal of Olympic History* and other publications, and lectures on skating history. He is currently studying the early evolution of ice dancing and pair skating in preparation for another monograph. Hines serves also as an elector to the World Figure Skating Hall of Fame.